MW01691295

Grade 4 | Unit 5

Geology

Teacher Guide

Amplify Core Knowledge Language Arts

Core Knowledge®

ISBN 978-1-68161-259-1

Printed in the USA
06 LSCKV 2021

Grade 4 | Unit 5

Contents

GEOLOGY

Introduction 1

Lesson 1 Geology 6

Core Connections (45 min.)
- Review Prior Knowledge

Reading (45 min.)
- Read-Aloud: Chapter 1
- Word Work: *Dense*

Lesson 2 Earth's Layers and Plate Tectonics 36

Reading (45 min.)
- Review
- Introduce the Chapter
- Read Chapter 2
- Lesson Wrap-Up
- Word Work: *Crust*

Language (30 min.)
- Grammar: Introduce Commas
- Introduce Suffix *-ly*

Writing (15 min.)
- Examine Similes

Lesson 3 Close Reading: Earth's Layers and Moving Plates 62

Reading (45 min.)
- Review
- Close Reading
- Lesson Wrap-Up
- Word Work: *Exert*

Writing (45 min.)
- Review Similes
- Model an Explanation of a Simile
- Draft a Detailed Explanation of a Simile

Lesson 4 Earthquakes and Tsunamis 80

Reading (45 min.)
- Review
- Introduce the Chapter
- Read "Earth's Shakes and Quakes"
- Lesson Wrap-Up
- Word Work: *Fault*

Language (30 min.)
- Grammar: Practice Commas
- Morphology: Practice Suffix *-ly*

Writing (15 min.)
- Introduce an Informational Pamphlet

Lesson 5 Close Reading: Earthquakes and Tsunamis 106

Reading (45 min.)
- Review
- Review the Chapter
- Read "Earth's Shakes and Quakes"
- Lesson Wrap-Up
- Word Work: *Trigger*

Writing (45 min.)
- Take Notes
- Draft an Informational Pamphlet

Lesson 6 Volcanoes, Geysers, and Hot Springs 124

Reading (45 min.)
- Introduce the Chapter
- Read "Earth's Fiery Volcanoes"
- Lesson Wrap-Up
- Word Work: *Fine*

Language (45 min.)
- Grammar: Introduce Commas and Quotation Marks
- Morphology: Introduce Root *rupt*
- Spelling: Introduce Spelling Words

Lesson 7 Myths and Volcanoes 154

Reading (45 min.)
- Introduce the Chapter
- Read "Mythic Volcano Spirits"
- Lesson Wrap-Up
- Word Work: *Lofty*

Writing (45 min.)
- Introduce a Wiki Entry
- Model Taking Notes for a Wiki Entry

Lesson 8 Three Types of Rocks and the Rock Cycle 184

Reading (45 min.)
- Review
- Introduce the Chapter
- Read "Earth's Building Blocks"
- Lesson Wrap-Up
- Word Work: *Class*

Writing (45 min.)
- Take Notes for a Wiki Entry
- Draft a Wiki Entry

Lesson 9 Close Reading: Rocks and the Rock Cycle 206

Reading (45 min.)
- Review Chapter 6
- Close Reading: Read "Earth's Building Blocks"
- Discuss Chapter and Lesson Wrap-Up
- Word Work: *Compact*

Language (45 min.)
- Grammar: Practice Commas and Quotation Marks
- Morphology: Practice Root *rupt*
- Spelling: Practice Spelling Words

Lesson 10 Weathering and Erosion, Part 1 228

Spelling (15 min.)
- Assessment

Reading (45 min.)
- Review
- Introduce the Chapter
- Read "Earth's Powerful Forces of Change"
- Discuss Chapter and Lesson Wrap-Up
- Word Work: *State*

Writing (30 min.)
- Revise and Edit a Wiki Entry
- Lesson Wrap-Up

Lesson 11 Weathering and Erosion, Part 2 256

Reading (45 min.)
- Review
- Close Reading
- Discuss Chapter and Lesson Wrap-Up
- Word Work: *Deposit*

Language (45 min.)
- Grammar: Sequencing Adjectives
- Morphology: Suffixes and Roots
- Spelling: Introduce Spelling Words

Lesson 12 Mountains 286

Reading (45 min.)
- Introduce the Chapter
- Read "Earth's Mighty Mountains"
- Discuss Chapter and Lesson Wrap-Up
- Word Work: *Sheer*

Writing (45 min.)
- Introduce a Descriptive Paragraph
- Plan a Descriptive Paragraph

Lesson 13 Under the Sea, Part 1 316

Reading (45 min.)
- Review
- Introduce the Chapter
- Read "Earth's Undersea World"
- Lesson Wrap-Up
- Word Work: *Expedition*

Writing (45 min.)
- Descriptive Paragraph Planning
- Draft a Descriptive Paragraph

Lesson 14 Under the Sea, Part 2 342

Reading (45 min.)
- Review
- Read "Earth's Undersea World"
- Discuss Chapter and Lesson Wrap-Up
- Word Work: *Firsthand*

Language (45 min.)
- Grammar: Practice Sequencing Adjectives
- Morphology: Suffixes and Roots
- Spelling

Lesson 15 Unit Assessment 352

Spelling (15 min.)	Unit Assessment (75 min.)
• Spelling Assessment	• Unit Assessment

Middle-of-Year Assessment 371

Pausing Point 392

Teacher Resources 396

Grade 4 | Unit 5

Introduction

GEOLOGY

Introduction

This introduction includes the necessary background information to teach the Geology unit. This unit contains 15 daily lessons, plus four Pausing Point days that may be used for differentiated instruction. You may choose to use all four days at the end of the unit, or you may use one day immediately after Lesson 7 and three days at the end of the unit. If you use one Pausing Point day after Lesson 7, you may administer Activity Page PP.1 to assess students' understanding of the content at this midpoint, or you may use the day to focus on writing, spelling, grammar, or morphology skills covered in Lessons 1–7. Each entire lesson will require a total of 90 minutes. Lesson 15 is devoted to a unit assessment. It is recommended that you spend no more than 19 days total on this unit.

WHY THE GEOLOGY UNIT IS IMPORTANT

Note: To prepare for this unit, read this entire introduction, preview the unit and content assessments, and preview the Teacher Resources section of this Teacher Guide. You may wish to collect assessment Activity Pages 15.2, PP.1, and PP.2 from students before beginning the unit.

The Big Idea of this unit is that the earth is composed of layers that, through heat and pressure, cause movements that result in geological features above and below the earth's surface. Tectonic plate theory explains how mountains, volcanoes, and trenches are created on land and under the sea. Information about the rock cycle, weathering, and erosion also explains how the earth is continually changing. This unit explores the relationships between these different geological processes and how they affect the landscape and related environments of the earth.

Prior Knowledge in CKLA™

Students who have received Core Knowledge Language Arts (CKLA) instruction in Grades K–3 will already have pertinent background knowledge for this unit. These students may have gained relevant background knowledge during the following domains:

Taking Care of the Earth (Grade K)

Astronomy (Grade 1)

The History of the Earth (Grade 1)

- Identify geographical features of the earth's surface: oceans and continents.

  Note: Students who received instruction in The History of the Earth in Grade 1 will build upon this knowledge in this unit.

- Explain that much of our knowledge of the earth and its history is the result of the work of many scientists.
- Identify and describe the layers of the earth: crust, mantle, and core (outer and inner).
- Describe volcanoes and geysers.
- Describe how heat, pressure, and time cause many changes inside the earth.
- Identify the three types of rocks: igneous, sedimentary, and metamorphic.
- Describe how heat, pressure, and time cause the formation of igneous, sedimentary, and metamorphic rocks.
- Define the terms *geology* and *geologist*.

Cycles in Nature (Grade 2)

READER

The Reader for this unit, *The Changing Earth*, includes complex text and prepares students in Grade 4 for the increased vocabulary and syntax demands aligned texts will present in later grades. *The Changing Earth* focuses on the composition of the earth and the forces that change Earth's surface. Students will learn about the theory of plate tectonics and how it explains the presence of volcanoes, mountains, underwater trenches, ridges, and other geological features. Students will also study geological processes like rock formation, weathering, and erosion in order to understand how the earth changes over time and why it looks the way it does.

The Reader also includes three selections that may be used for enrichment. Although the Teacher Guide does not include lessons for these enrichment selections, the Activity Book includes activity pages students may complete independently. Please use these selections at your discretion, considering students' needs and the time available in your school day.

There are some bolded words in the glossary that are not addressed in the reading lessons. These words are still important for students to reference as they read this Reader. These words have an asterisk (*) next to them in the glossary.

WRITING

In the writing lessons, students will review the stages of the writing process and engage in several short writing projects. In this unit, students will examine and explain similes; draft an informational pamphlet about tsunamis; write a wiki entry about a specific volcano; and create a descriptive paragraph about a type of rock or item in the rock cycle, incorporating literary devices they have encountered in previous Grade 4 units, such as alliteration, personification, and simile.

MIDDLE-OF-YEAR ASSESSMENT

In this unit a Middle-of-Year (MOY) Assessment is provided and should be administered at the end of the unit. You should spend no more than two days total on the MOY Assessment. There are three main group components of the assessment: a written assessment of silent reading comprehension, a written assessment of grammar, and a written assessment of morphology. Two other components, the oral reading of words in isolation and the fluency assessments, are administered one-on-one with students.

The written assessment of silent reading comprehension is meant to be completed in one 90-minute block of time and will be administered on MOY Assessment Day 1. The grammar and morphology assessments are meant to be completed during one 50-minute block and one 40-minute block of time on MOY Assessment Day 2.

In addition you will pull students aside, one at a time, and administer the Word Reading in Isolation Assessment to students who scored 10 or fewer on the Reading Comprehension Assessment. As time allows you may also administer the Word Reading in Isolation Assessment to students who scored between 11 and 13 on the Reading Comprehension Assessment. Administer the Fluency Assessment to all students.

After administering the MOY Assessment, you will complete an analysis summary of individual student performance using the Grade 4 MOY Assessment Summary Sheet, found in each individual student's Activity Book (Activity Page A.2).

GEOLOGY AND DIVERSITY

Before teaching this unit, we suggest that you read the article "Race and Racism in Geosciences" by Kuheli Dutt, Diversity Officer for Lamont-Doherty Earth Observatory of Columbia University. In the article, Dutt attempts to confront shortcomings in diversity, inclusion, and racial bias training in the geosciences, offering a new perspective to the way in which sciences are taught.

While reading "Race and Racism in Geosciences," we recommend that you reflect on how our individual privileges may affect the way in which geosciences and other sciences are taught. Educators can provide a more inclusive curriculum if we acknowledge our privileges and ensure that our biases do not interfere with students' experience with the *Geology* unit.

FLUENCY SUPPLEMENT

A separate component, the Fluency Supplement, is available for download on the Amplify website. This component was created to accompany Core Knowledge Language Arts (CKLA) materials for Grades 4 and 5. It consists of selections from a variety of genres, including poetry, folklore, fables, and other selections. These selections provide additional opportunities for students to practice reading with fluency and expression (prosody). There are sufficient selections so you may, if desired, use one selection per week. For more information on implementation, please consult the supplement.

TEACHER RESOURCES

At the back of this Teacher Guide, you will find a section titled "Teacher Resources." In this section, you will find the following:

- Core Connections Area of Study Cards
- Core Connections Earth Image Card
- Core Connections Geology Image Cards
- Glossary for The Changing Earth
- Pronunciation Guide for The Changing Earth
- Wiki Entry Rubric
- Wiki Entry Editing Checklist
- Resources for the Enrichment Selections in The Changing Earth
- Activity Book Answer Key

DIGITAL COMPONENTS

In the Advance Preparation section of each lesson, you will be instructed to create various posters, charts, or graphic organizers for use during the lesson. Many of these items, along with other images such as maps or diagrams, are also available as digital components at CoreKnowledge.org/CKLA-files and at CKLA.Amplify.com.

LESSON

1

Geology

PRIMARY FOCUS OF LESSON

Core Connections

Students will be able to identify different areas of study about the earth and ask the types of questions geologists ask about the earth. **[RI.4.1]**

Reading

Students will be able to describe how people's knowledge of what happens on Earth's surface has changed over time, including explaining the continental drift hypothesis and the existence of Pangaea.
[RI.4.1, RI.4.3, RI.4.7, RI.4.8]

FORMATIVE ASSESSMENT

Activity Page 1.1	**Areas of Study about the Earth** Students determine which questions would be asked and answered by an archaeologist, a geographer, and an ecologist, respectively. **[RI.4.1]**
Activity Page 1.3	**Evidence Collector's Chart** Students look in the text for evidence supporting geological events. **[RI.4.1]**
Activity Page 1.4	**Evidence of Changes on Earth** Students look in the text for evidence supporting geological events. **[RI.4.1]**

LESSON AT A GLANCE

	Grouping	Time	Materials
Core Connections (45 min.)			
Review Prior Knowledge	Small Groups/ Whole Group	45 min.	❏ Area of Study Cards ❏ Activity Page 1.1 ❏ Earth Image Card ❏ Web graphic organizer ❏ Geology Image Cards
Reading (45 min.)			
Read-Aloud: Chapter 1	Whole Group	40 min.	❏ *The Changing Earth* ❏ Activity Pages 1.2–1.5 ❏ Evidence Collector's Chart ❏ Scissors ❏ Glue
Word Work: *Dense*	Whole Group	5 min.	
Take-Home			
Reading	Independent		❏ Activity Pages 1.5, 1.6 ❏ Fluency Supplement selection (optional)

ADVANCE PREPARATION

Core Connections

- Prepare or project one copy of each of the four Area of Study Cards found in Teacher Resources or in the digital components for this unit.
- Prepare or project one copy of the Earth Image Card found in Teacher Resources or in the digital components for the unit.
- Prepare and display a web graphic organizer on the board/chart paper. It should have a central circle large enough to hold the Earth Image Card. Draw four lines out from this circle. One Area of Study Card will be placed at the end of each line.
- Prepare or project one copy of each of the four Geology Image Cards found in Teacher Resources or in the digital components for this unit.
- Prepare to group students into three groups.

Reading

- This lesson contains a Think-Pair-Share activity.
  - You may access a digital version of The Big Question in the digital components for this unit.
- Prepare and display an Evidence Collector's Chart on the board/chart paper. Alternatively, access a digital version in the digital components for this unit. This chart will be on display throughout the unit. Students will use Activity Page 1.3, which matches this chart.

Chart for Activity Page 1.3

Chapter 1	What is the cause?	What evidence is there?	Letter
	At some point, Pangaea broke up and the pieces slowly moved apart over a long period.		
	Tectonic plates move very slowly due to the heat and pressure in Earth's mantle.		
	Material in the mantle moves beneath stuck rocks at a fault, causing pressure to build over time and then suddenly release as the rocks break and slip past each other, shaking the ground.		

	Tremendous pressure and heat in the mantle force magma in a chamber below Earth's crust to move upward through a crack in Earth's surface.		
	Rocks are created, destroyed, and recreated in a continuous cycle.		
	Over time, weathering breaks rocks into smaller pieces and erosion moves these pieces to new locations.		
	Tectonic plates subduct underneath one another and move up and down against each other, and magma pushes up into the crust.		
	Tectonic plates interact to create seafloor spreading and underwater subduction zones.		

Fluency (optional)

- Choose and make sufficient copies of a text selection from the online Fluency Supplement to distribute and review with students for additional fluency practice. If you choose to do a fluency assessment, you will assess students in Lesson 5. See the Unit 1 Teacher Guide introduction for more information on using the Fluency Supplement.

ACADEMIC VOCABULARY AND SPANISH COGNATES

analyze, v. to closely study and think about information or ideas in order to better understand and explain them

apply, v. 1. to put to use; 2. to relate to

cause, n. 1. something that produces a result or effect; 2. **v.** to make something happen

distinguish, v. to recognize or identify a difference between two or more things

effect, n. a result; a change produced by a cause or something that happens

evidence, n. proof; information and facts that are helpful in forming a conclusion or supporting an idea

observe, v. to watch something with careful attention

process, n. a series of actions or steps that happen in a particular order

review, v. to look over something carefully or look over something again

SPANISH COGNATES FOR ACADEMIC VOCABULARY IN GEOLOGY

- analizar
- causa
- distinguir
- efecto
- evidencia
- observar

Start Lesson

Lesson 1: Geology

Core Connections

45M

Primary Focus: Students will be able to identify different areas of study about the earth and ask the types of questions geologists ask about the earth. **[RI.4.1]**

REVIEW PRIOR KNOWLEDGE (45 MIN.)

Introduce Areas of Study about Earth

- Tell students they will begin a unit called Geology, and that the Reader for this unit is called *The Changing Earth*. Point out that the Reader title provides a hint as to what they will be studying in this unit. Ask, "Judging from the title of the Reader, what do you predict the Reader will be about?" (how the earth changes).
- Explain that, before reading the first chapter of the Reader, you will discuss what students may already know about the earth. Tell students that this discussion will help them understand the topics in this unit.
- Think-Pair-Share. Share two things with a neighbor that you know or think you know about the earth.

- Tell students there are many ways to study and learn about the earth. Explain that the following examples are areas of study about the earth that students likely have encountered in other CKLA units:
    - Geography: the study of the characteristics of the earth's surface
    - Ecology: the study of relationships between living things and their environments
    - Archaeology: the study of past human life and activities by examining bones, tools, and other objects left behind

Check for Understanding

Ask students whether studying the Great Pyramids of Egypt qualifies as geography, ecology, or archaeology (archaeology). Repeat with mapping the coast of Mexico (geography) and investigating why lions live where they do (ecology).

Examine Questions about Areas of Study

Activity Page 1.1

- Have students turn to Activity Page 1.1. Explain that the list contains questions related to the different areas of study you just introduced. These are questions that someone studying topics in a particular area might ask. Some of the questions relate to geography, some relate to archaeology, and some relate to ecology. Ask a student to read the first question, "What are Earth's seven continents?" Explain that this is a question someone studying geography might ask.
    - You may wish to provide students with the answer to the question: Asia, North America, South America, Africa, Europe, Australia, and Antarctica.
- Ask a student to read the second question, "What clues do the ruins of ancient buildings provide about the ancient Roman civilization?"
- Guide students in discussing what area a person asking this question might study, pointing out that ruins of ancient buildings are the remains of buildings built by humans long ago. Explain that this is a question that someone studying archaeology might ask.
    - You may wish to provide students with an answer to the question: answers may include that ruins might suggest the purpose of a building or how it was used—as a dwelling, as a place of worship, for protection, etc.

- Ask a student to read the next question, "What is the name for the place where an animal or plant normally lives and grows?"
- Ask students to discuss what area a person asking this question might study. Guide students to understand that this question relates to ecology; it is about where an animal or plant lives. A *habitat* is the place where an animal or plant normally lives and grows.
- Explain that some information in the questions may be familiar and some information may be new. Explain that all students will be able to use the information provided to participate in the activity.
- Tell students they will work in groups to determine which questions from the list on Activity Page 1.1 relate to a particular area of study about the earth. Each group will receive a card with an area of study listed, its definition, and a related image. Group members will write on the card the questions they decide are related to their area of study. Then, as a class, students will discuss each area of study and related questions, offering explanations and justifications for their question choices.
- Divide students into three groups. Provide each group with an Area of Study Card. Select one student in each group to be the recorder.
- Direct each group to examine its Area of Study Card and discuss the questions from the list on Activity Page 1.1 to determine which apply to the area of study on the card. Have the recorder for each group write the questions chosen by the group on the card.
- Circulate among groups and offer guidance as needed in helping students discuss questions and make decisions. For example, ask guiding questions to help them reach a conclusion, or ask them to explain why they chose a particular question.
- When students have finished recording questions on their cards, have each group share its conclusions with the class, providing explanations and justifications for the questions chosen. Use the following chart as a reference when each group discusses information about its area of study, ensuring all students understand the questions. You may wish to ask students to answer the questions as well, providing support when needed.

Support

Before students begin working in small groups, read through the remaining questions on Activity Page 1.1.

Area of Study	Questions	Answers
geography	• What are Earth's seven continents? • What are the names of the oceans of the world? • What are the four main directions on a map? • What are names of important rivers of the world?	• Asia, North America, South America, Africa, Europe, Australia, and Antarctica • Atlantic, Pacific, Indian, and Arctic • north, south, east, and west • the Nile, Indus, Tigris, and Yangtze Rivers
ecology	• What is the name of the place where an animal or plant normally lives and grows? • What can cause changes in an ecosystem? • How would you describe the tropical rain forest of the Amazon River? • What features make up the environment?	• a habitat • natural events like volcanoes, and humans • home to a variety of plants and animals • the air, water, minerals, organisms, and all other living and nonliving factors that surround and affect an organism
archaeology	• What clues do the ruins of ancient buildings provide about the ancient Roman civilization? • What was the city of London like in the Middle Ages? • What features were common characteristics of ancient Islamic mosques? • What do the pictures embroidered on the Bayeux Tapestry illustrate?	• the purpose of the building or how it was used—as a dwelling, as a place of worship, for protection, etc. • more and more people moved into the city; it became overcrowded and dirty • domes, turrets, tile decoration • the Battle of Hastings, the conquest of England by William the Conqueror, what soldiers wore for battle

- After each group shares, place its Area of Study Card on the web graphic organizer.

Introduce Geology as an Area of Study

- Tell students that in this unit, they will learn about another area of study about the earth called geology. Show students the Area of Study Card for geology. Read the definition of geology from the card: geology is the study of the earth's characteristics, what it is made of, and the processes that shape and change it.
- Explain that you have chosen four images related to geology. Place all images where students can see them.
- Have students take a few minutes to examine the first image, an erupting volcano. Then ask students what questions people studying geology might ask

Speaking and Listening
Presenting

Entering/Emerging
Work with students to understand *wh–* questions. Model by pointing to a familiar object and asking, "What is this?" or by indicating another student and asking, "Who is that?" Then point to the liquid in the picture and ask, "What do you see?" Have students repeat the question. Help them construct a simple answer.

Transitioning/Expanding
Help students generate *wh–* and *how* questions, using the sentence starters *What is ____, Why is ____,* and *How is ____.* Start by having them create questions about familiar classroom objects, then guide them to ask similar questions about the picture.

Bridging
Have students work with a partner to practice asking and answering *wh–* questions and questions beginning with *how.* Ask students to take turns asking and answering questions about the picture that begin with *what, why, how,* and *where.*

about what they see in the image. Record student answers on the board/chart paper. The following are examples of questions students may ask related to the image:

- Why is the liquid coming out of the volcano bright orange and red, as if it's on fire?
- How does the liquid coming out of the volcano shoot up high in the air like that?
- Where does the liquid come from?

- Follow the same procedures for the other three images. The following are examples of questions students may come up with related to the images.
- Grand Canyon:
  - How did the rocks get different-colored layers on them?
  - What shaped the rocks to look like this?
  - Why are some rocks higher up than other rocks?
- Fossils:
  - What shaped the things in this image?
  - Where can you find things that look like this?
  - What are these things made of?
- Cappadocia houses:
  - What are these made of?
  - How did the rocks get carved out like this?
  - What are these rocks used for?
- Then, as a class, choose one question about each image to record on the Area of Study Card for geology.
- Place the Area of Study Card for geology on the web graphic organizer.

Check for Understanding

Ask, "What do all these images have in common?"

» They all show something about geology.

- Summarize for students that all four of the areas of study on the web examine the earth in different ways. Remind students that they will be focusing on geology in this unit and that they may find the answers to the questions on the Area of Study Card for geology as they progress through the unit.

Wrap-Up

- Ask students to describe what they learned about in this lesson.
    - Answers may vary but should include that different areas of study about the earth focus on different things.
- Ask students to describe what questions they asked related to geology.

Lesson 1: Geology

Reading

45M

Primary Focus: Students will be able to describe how people's knowledge of what happens on Earth's surface has changed over time, including explaining the continental drift hypothesis and the existence of Pangaea.
[RI.4.1, RI.4.3, RI.4.7, RI.4.8]

READ-ALOUD: CHAPTER 1 (40 MIN.)

Introduce the Reader

- Ensure each student has a copy of the Reader, *The Changing Earth*.
- Read the title of the Reader with students and explain that this Reader is a nonfiction, informational book about geology. A nonfiction, informational book is explanatory, providing facts and other information about real topics. Point out that the book does include one literary chapter, which includes retellings of myths, or stories told by early people to explain unpredictable events.
- Have students turn to the table of contents. Either read several chapter titles from the table of contents aloud or have students read them. Explain that reading chapter titles in a book can be very informative.

Student Reader:
The Changing Earth

Challenge

Ask students to identify which chapter might be the literary chapter. ("Mythic Volcano Spirits")

Check for Understanding

Ask students to describe the information they gather by reading the chapter titles in this table of contents.

» Answers will vary but may include information about volcanoes, mountains, and the world below the surface of the ocean.

- Give students a few moments to flip through the Reader and comment on the images they see. Students may comment, for example, on pictures of rocks, images of natural forces such as volcanoes and earthquakes, or maps.
- Ask students to share any comments they have about the Reader. Point out that all of these ideas should refer in some way to geology.

Introduce the Chapter

- Tell students that you will read aloud Chapter 1, "Earth's Changing Surface." They should follow along in their Reader as you read.
- Have students turn to the table of contents, locate the chapter, and then turn to the first page of the chapter.
- Preview the core vocabulary words before reading the chapter.
- Begin by telling students the first vocabulary word they will encounter in this chapter is *catastrophe*.
- Have them find the word on page 2 of the Reader. Explain that each vocabulary word is bolded the first time it appears in the chapter.
- Explain that the glossary contains definitions of all the vocabulary words in this Reader. Have students refer to the glossary at the back of the Reader and locate *catastrophe*, and then have a student read the definition.
- Explain the following:
    - the part of speech
    - alternate forms of the word

Check for Understanding

Have students give examples of a catastrophe.

» Possible answers: a damaging hurricane, earthquake, or tornado.

Activity Page 1.2

- Have students reference Activity Page 1.2 while you read each word and its meaning.

  Note: We have chosen the following words as core vocabulary words to be learned and used as scientists would use them in the context of studying geology: *observation*, *evidence*, *conclude*, and *hypothesis*.

catastrophe, n. a terrible, sudden event (catastrophes) (2)

erupt, v. to send out rock, lava, and ash in a sudden explosion (erupted, n. eruption) (2)

observation, n. 1. the act of paying careful attention in order to gather information; 2. a statement based on paying careful attention to something (observations) (4)

evidence, n. proof; information and facts that are helpful in forming a conclusion or supporting an idea (4)

fossil, n. the preserved remains of something that lived long ago (fossils) (4)

geologist, n. a scientist who studies the makeup of the earth and the forces and processes that shape and change it (geologists) (6)

climate, n. the average weather conditions of a particular area (7)

conclude, v. to decide something or form an opinion based on information you have (concluded, n. conclusion) (7)

dense, adj. thick or heavy (denser) (8)

hypothesis, n. an idea that has been suggested and may be true but has not yet been proven (9)

continental drift, n. a process in which continents slowly move over time on the surface of the earth (9)

Vocabulary Chart for Chapter 1 "Earth's Changing Surface"		
Vocabulary Type	**Tier 3 Domain-Specific Words**	**Tier 2 General Academic Words**
Core Vocabulary	erupt fossil geologist hypothesis continental drift	catastrophe observation evidence climate conclude dense
Spanish Cognates for Core Vocabulary	fósil geólogo hipótesis	catástrofe observación evidencia clima denso
Multiple-Meaning Core Vocabulary Words	erupt	dense
Sayings and Phrases		

- Have one student read The Big Question at the beginning of the chapter. Ensure students understand the meaning of The Big Question before reading the chapter.
    - How did people's understanding of what was happening on Earth's surface change over time?

Read "Earth's Changing Surface"

- Read the chapter aloud as students follow along in their Readers. Ask students to snap their fingers when they encounter the word *geology* in any of its forms (such as *geologist*).

Chapter 1

Earth's Changing Surface

THE BIG QUESTION
How did people's understanding of what was happening on Earth's surface change over time?

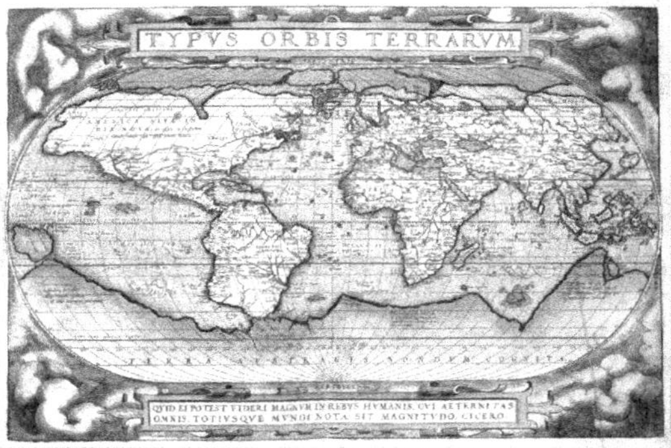

1570 CE world map

If you had lived in Europe during the Middle Ages, the idea that the earth changes would have seemed crazy. At that time, people believed that mountains, valleys, and other landscape features had always been there. True, rare natural **catastrophes** sometimes occurred. Earthquakes, for example, shook the ground and triggered landslides. In some places, volcanoes **erupted** and sent up fountains of lava, or red-hot melted rock. However, people viewed these catastrophes as punishments from God, not as the earth changing.

2

- Read pages 2 and 3 aloud as students read along silently.

Literal. People living in Europe during the Middle Ages described the idea that the earth changes as crazy. Why might they have described this idea as crazy?

» At that time, they believed that features of the landscape had always been there. Even though they could see the changes caused by natural catastrophes like earthquakes and volcanoes, they believed these events were punishments from God, not the earth changing.

Support

What evidence of Earth's changes did people living during the Middle Ages observe?

» Natural catastrophes such as earthquakes, landslides, and volcanoes sometimes occurred.

Support

What did people believe was the cause of natural catastrophes?

» They believed God made the catastrophes happen as punishment for things people did.

During the 1400s, 1500s, and 1600s, European explorers set sail on voyages of discovery. They found new continents and islands. Mapmakers created the first relatively accurate maps of the entire world. When people studied these maps, they noticed something interesting. Several continents looked as if they might fit together like pieces of a jigsaw puzzle. Take a look at a world map or globe. See how the eastern edge of South America looks as if it fits into the western edge of Africa? If you could somehow push these two continents together across the Atlantic Ocean, their edges would match up.

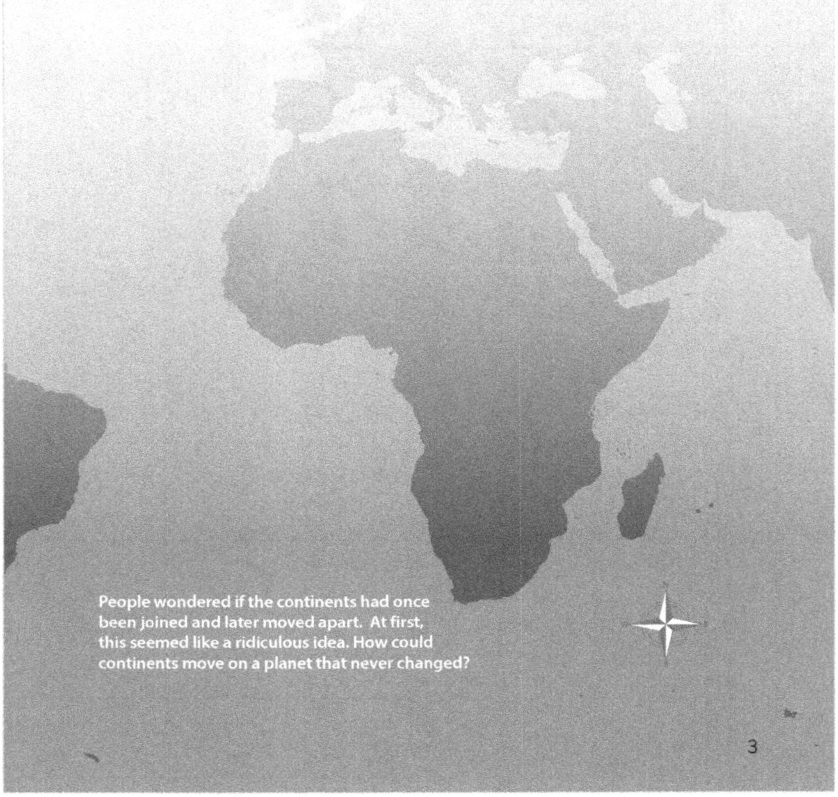

People wondered if the continents had once been joined and later moved apart. At first, this seemed like a ridiculous idea. How could continents move on a planet that never changed?

3

- You may wish to remind students about early European explorers they studied in the Grade 3 European Exploration of North America domain and unit. Prior to this period in the history of European exploration, most Europeans were not aware that the continents of North and South America even existed. Students may remember learning about Christopher Columbus's journey in search of the Spice Islands or the Indies, and his subsequent exploration of the Americas. Students may remember hearing about the journeys of the conquistadors Juan Ponce de León, Hernando de Soto, and Francisco Vasquez de Coronado. They may also remember hearing about the explorers John Cabot, Henry Hudson, and Samuel de Champlain, who explored North America.

- Ask students to look at the old map on page 2 and the modern map in the background of pages 2 and 3. Help students find the eastern part of South America and the western part of Africa. Encourage students to notice the way the eastern edge of South America and the western edge of Africa appear to fit together. Have students trace the coasts of these two continents with their fingers.

  Inferential. What do you think early mapmakers thought about why those coastlines looked as if they fit together?

  » Possible answers: it was a coincidence; God had made them that way.

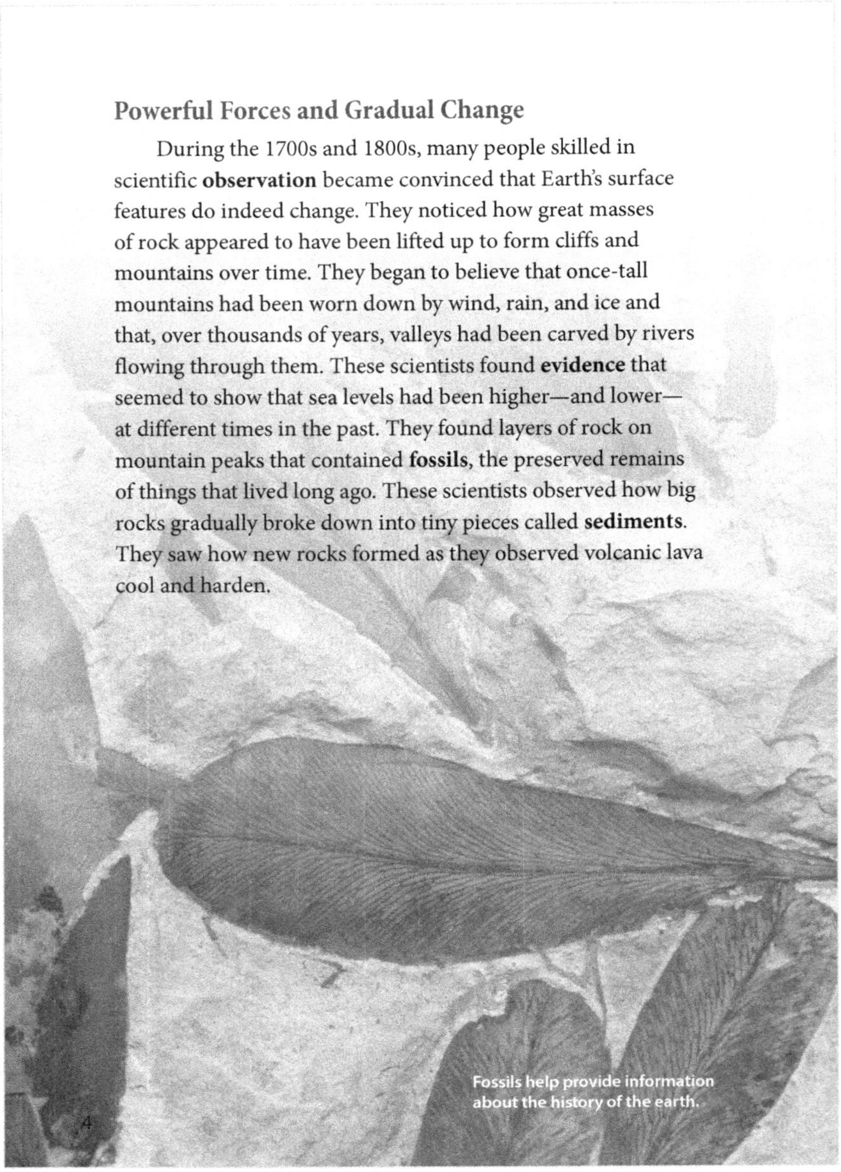

Powerful Forces and Gradual Change

During the 1700s and 1800s, many people skilled in scientific **observation** became convinced that Earth's surface features do indeed change. They noticed how great masses of rock appeared to have been lifted up to form cliffs and mountains over time. They began to believe that once-tall mountains had been worn down by wind, rain, and ice and that, over thousands of years, valleys had been carved by rivers flowing through them. These scientists found **evidence** that seemed to show that sea levels had been higher—and lower—at different times in the past. They found layers of rock on mountain peaks that contained **fossils**, the preserved remains of things that lived long ago. These scientists observed how big rocks gradually broke down into tiny pieces called **sediments**. They saw how new rocks formed as they observed volcanic lava cool and harden.

Fossils help provide information about the history of the earth.

4

Pronunciation Table	
Word	**CK Code**
Shen Kua	/shen/ /kwə/

- Read pages 4 and 5 aloud as students read along silently.

All these observations led many scientists to believe that powerful natural **forces** were at work changing Earth's surface. Most of these changes were thought to have taken place very slowly. Over long periods of time, slow, gradual changes added up to produce dramatic results. These scientists were convinced that Earth's rocky surface had changed continuously throughout the planet's long history. It had changed in the past, and Earth was changing in the present, too.

These ideas laid the foundation for the modern science of geology. Geology is the study of the makeup of the earth and the forces and processes that shape and change it. Rocks are very important in geology. That's because rocks hold clues to how Earth's surface has changed over time. Together with fossils, rocks provide information about the history of the earth.

Shen Kua's Observations

Shen Kua was a Chinese scientist and mathematician who lived from 1031–1095 CE. He studied rocks and fossils and made many observations of Earth's surface features. Shen Kua realized that Earth's surface is shaped very slowly by powerful forces. Some forces wear rocks down. Others make new rocks and push them up to become mountains. Shen Kua reached these conclusions hundreds of years before European scientists did.

5

Literal. What conclusions did scientists make about the history of the earth based on the evidence they observed? How were these conclusions different from the ideas of earlier Europeans?

» They believed that powerful natural forces were at work changing Earth's surface; that most of these results or effects took place very slowly; and that slow gradual changes over long periods added up to produce dramatic results. These ideas were different because earlier Europeans had been convinced that continents could not move and the earth could not change.

Evaluative. One meaning of the word *dramatic* is "very noticeable." How might the things observed by European scientists be considered dramatic results?

» Answers may vary but should include that scientists compared observations and records made over long periods and noticed extreme differences. Once-tall mountains getting smaller over time is a noticeable difference. The creation of valleys by rivers where valleys did not previously exist is a noticeable difference. Changes in sea levels are noticeable differences, given how much of Earth is covered by water. Fossils found at the tops of mountains, a place where living things likely can't survive, indicate a noticeable difference.

Discoveries of rock layers, as well as coal and salt, indicated that the continents had once been joined.

Search for Clues

So what about the jigsaw-puzzle fit of the continents? During the 1800s and early 1900s, **geologists** studied rock layers on the continents. They made many intriguing discoveries. For example, rock layers along the northern and eastern coasts of South America match rock layers along Africa's western coast. Also, deposits of **coal** and salt in eastern North America are similar to those in southern Europe.

Geologists found fossils of an ancient fern called *Glossopteris* in similar rock layers in Africa, India, Australia, and South America. They found fossils of an ancient reptile, *Lystrosaurus*, in both southern Africa and India. In South America and Africa, fossils of another ancient reptile, *Cynognathus*, turned up directly across the Atlantic Ocean from each other.

These discoveries seemed to indicate that the continents had once been joined—but how? Furthermore, how had they become separated? Several scientists proposed explanations, but they were quite far-fetched. One involved a gigantic eruption from the center of the earth that ripped all the land apart. Another suggested that part of Earth's land broke away to become the moon and what was left became the

6

- Read pages 6 and 7 aloud as students read along silently.
- Allow students time to look at the map and notice where areas of similar rock layers are noted along the coasts of South America and Africa. Help students identify the four modern continents depicted: clockwise from bottom left, they are South America, North America, Europe, and Africa. Guide students to identify areas on different continents showing similar deposits of coal and salt and similar fossil layers.

Literal. Have students explain what the map shows, using information from the legend to support their thinking.

continents. Few people paid much attention to these ideas. A better explanation was needed, one with evidence to support it. In the early 1900s, Alfred Wegener provided just that.

Enter Alfred Wegener

Born and educated in Germany, Alfred Wegener was interested in many scientific subjects, including weather, astronomy, and cold, polar regions. Around 1910, Wegener read a scientific paper about similar fossils and rock formations found on different continents. He was intrigued by the mystery of the matching continents and he wanted to solve this mystery.

Alfred Wegener

Wegener gathered evidence. He pulled together discoveries made by many other scientists about rock formations, fossils, and mountain ranges. Polar explorers had recently unearthed fossils of *Glossopteris* in Antarctica. Similar fossils had previously been found in other parts of the world. This seemed to indicate that ice-covered Antarctica might once have been joined to South America, Africa, India, and Australia. It also meant that Antarctica had once had a **climate** warm enough for ferns to grow.

From this evidence, Wegener **concluded** that all the present-day continents had been joined as one huge landmass long ago. He understood, as with any new discovery, that his conclusions might be altered or challenged in the future by more evidence. Nonetheless, he believed that the existing evidence supported his conclusions.

7

Evaluative. Why was it intriguing to Wegener and other geologists that different continents have similar fossils and rock formations?

» Similar fossils and rock formations were found on different continents that are now separated by great distances across large oceans. Fossils of an ancient fern were found in ice-covered Antarctica; the discovery of fossils of this ancient plant in Antarctica seemed odd since this type of fern did not grow in the cold, ice-covered climate of Antarctica during Wegener's time. Similarities across continents and evidence of living things from the past might mean the continents were once joined and/or in different locations from where they were in Wegener's time. If the continents had once been joined and/or had moved, scientists wanted to figure out how such drastic changes could have happened.

Literal. What similarities did geologists observe as they examined fossils on different continents?

» Fossils of the ancient reptile Lystrosaurus were found in southern Africa and India; fossils of the ancient reptile Cynognathus were found in South America and Africa; fossils of the ancient fern Glossopteris were found in Africa, India, Australia, and South America.

Literal. What similarities did geologists observe as they examined rock formations on different continents?

» Rock formations along the northern and eastern coasts of South America match those along Africa's western coast. Deposits of coal and salt in eastern North America are very similar to those in southern Europe.

Pronunciation Table	
Word	**CK Code**
Pangaea	/pan*jee*ə/

Support

Why was it surprising to find fossils of ferns on the continent of Antarctica?

» Antarctica is ice-covered today and was also ice-covered in Wegener's time; it must have once been warm enough for ferns to grow there.

Continents that Drift

If Wegener's conclusions were correct, then how had the continents moved apart? An important clue came from the ocean. The ocean was still largely unexplored in Wegener's day. In the 1870s, however, scientists discovered that much of the ocean bottom was made of basalt, a heavy, **dense** rock that is formed when lava cools and hardens. Lava is magma that has erupted up above Earth's crust from deep underground. Most rocks that make up the continents are lighter and less dense than basalt.

Seafloor Discoveries

In 1872, the research ship HMS *Challenger* set out on a four-year mission to gather information about the ocean floor. The ship visited every ocean except the Arctic Ocean. Scientists on board dredged up mud, rocks, and ocean creatures from the seafloor.

Journal of HMS *Challenger*

Challenger scientists also took soundings, or measures of water depth, by lowering weighted lines into the water. They measured out the line until the weight landed on the bottom. The scientists used the soundings to make rough maps of the seafloor in different places. They discovered that the seafloor has vast plains, tall mountain ranges, and deep valleys.

HMS *Challenger*

8

- Read pages 8 and 9 aloud as students read along silently.

Literal. You have learned that a simile is a literary device that compares things using *like* or *as*. The author uses a simile on page 9 to compare the movement of continents to the movement of pieces of ice in a drink. How did Wegener think these two things were similar?

» Ice is less dense than water so ice floats in a drink, which is made with water. Rocks that make up the continents are less dense than rocks on the ocean bottom, so Wegener thought continents might float above the denser rocks of the ocean bottom and move around like ice floating in a drink.

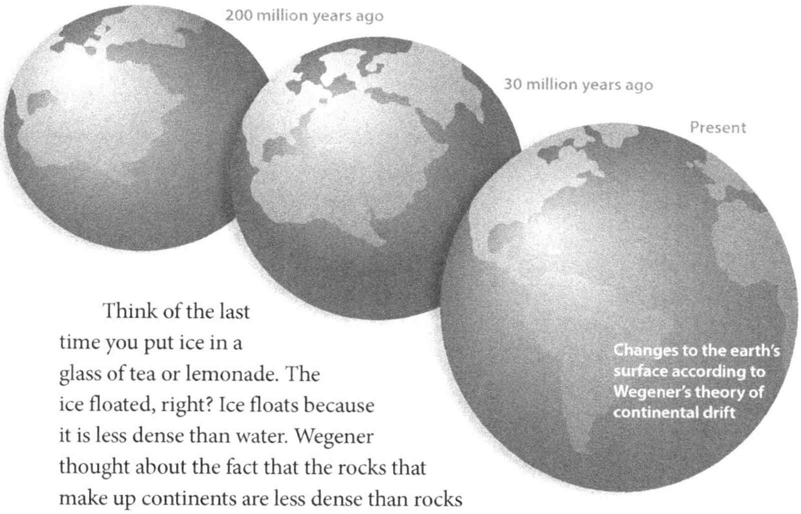

Changes to the earth's surface according to Wegener's theory of continental drift

Think of the last time you put ice in a glass of tea or lemonade. The ice floated, right? Ice floats because it is less dense than water. Wegener thought about the fact that the rocks that make up continents are less dense than rocks on the seafloor. "What if continents were like enormous pieces of ice?" he wondered. "Could they float over the denser rocks of the ocean bottom and move around?"

In 1915, Wegener published a book titled *The Origins of Continents and Oceans*. In it, he presented his **hypothesis** about how the earth's continents had moved over time. He called the process **continental drift**.

Wegener proposed that millions of years ago, Earth had one huge landmass. He described it as a supercontinent and named it Pangaea, from the Greek word *pangaia*, meaning "all the Earth." At some point, Pangaea broke up, and the pieces—the continents—very slowly **drifted** away from each other. As the continents moved, mountain ranges pulled apart. Rock formations split. New oceans filled in the widening gaps between the landmasses. Groups of plants and animals that had once lived together were separated. As continents drifted, their climates changed. Antarctica's climate, for example, grew so cold that the continent's plants and animals died. Only their fossils remained, buried under snow and ice.

9

Literal. What was Wegener's hypothesis about continental drift?

» Wegener proposed that millions of years ago, Earth was one huge landmass called Pangaea. Over time Pangaea broke up and the pieces slowly drifted apart, separating rock formations and plant and animal groups. New oceans filled the gaps among the landmasses and climates changed as continents drifted.

Evaluative. What do you think other scientists and scholars thought about Wegener's ideas at first? Why?

» Answers will vary but may include: they liked his ideas, because they made sense; they rejected his ideas, because they were very different from what people before him had believed.

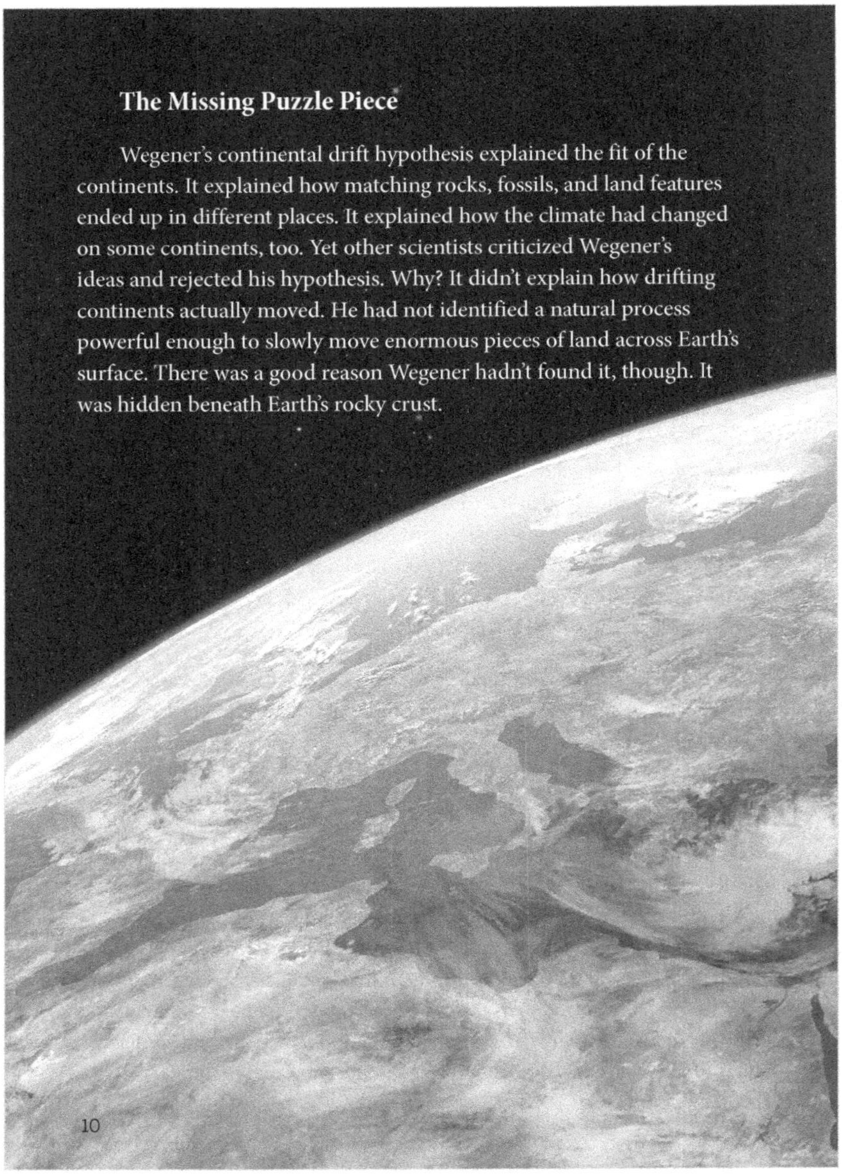

The Missing Puzzle Piece

Wegener's continental drift hypothesis explained the fit of the continents. It explained how matching rocks, fossils, and land features ended up in different places. It explained how the climate had changed on some continents, too. Yet other scientists criticized Wegener's ideas and rejected his hypothesis. Why? It didn't explain how drifting continents actually moved. He had not identified a natural process powerful enough to slowly move enormous pieces of land across Earth's surface. There was a good reason Wegener hadn't found it, though. It was hidden beneath Earth's rocky crust.

10

- Read page 10 aloud as students read along silently.

  Literal. How did other scientists in the early 1900s respond to Wegener's hypothesis?

  » They criticized Wegener's ideas and rejected his hypothesis.

Check for Understanding

Literal. Why did scientists respond this way?

» Wegener had not identified how continents moved.

Challenge

Do you think Wegener was wise to publish his theories even without all the evidence he needed, or would it have made more sense not to publish them? Explain your answer.

» Answers will vary.

LESSON WRAP-UP (15 MIN.)

Discuss Chapter Questions

Note: Questions 1 and 2 and Activity Pages 1.3 and 1.5 relate to The Big Question of the chapter.

- Use the following questions to discuss the chapter.

1. **Literal.** During the 1700-1800s, which observations were made from evidence gathered over long periods that indicated Earth's surface features do change?

    » Answers may vary but should include: evidence gathered over long periods showed once-tall mountains had been worn down by wind, rain, and ice; valleys had been carved by rivers flowing through them; there was evidence of sea levels being higher and lower at different times in the past; fossils were found in layers of rock on mountain peaks; big rocks gradually broke down into sediments; lava cooled and hardened.

2. **Evaluative.** How did evidence of change on the earth's surface over time help Wegener develop his continental drift hypothesis?

    » He examined patterns in the evidence, which led him to conclude that Pangaea had broken apart and the continents had slowly drifted away from each other. Evidence, such as rock layers along the northern and eastern coasts of South America matching rock layers along Africa's west coast, indicated those two continents had once been joined; deposits of coal and salt in North America were very similar to deposits in southern Europe, indicating those two continents had once been joined; fossils of the same kinds of animals and plants were found on different continents, indicating the continents had once been joined.

- Have students turn to Activity Pages 1.3 and 1.4 and refer to the displayed Evidence Collector's Chart.
- Tell students that after reading each chapter in *The Changing Earth*, they will examine a cause of change on the earth from the chapter, listed in the chart on Activity Page 1.3 (and in the chart on display). Remind students a cause is something that produces a result or effect. Tell them a cause is also a reason or explanation that geologists have hypothesized based on observations. (Students will not add information to the chart for Chapter 5, "Mythic Volcano Spirits," a literary chapter.)
- Tell students that, after examining the cause statement, they will review information in the chapter to determine what effect the cause produced. Tell students evidence represents the effect of a cause.

Reading
Reading Closely

Entering/Emerging
This section of the reading relies heavily on the concepts of cause and effect. Help students use and understand words such as *why* and *because*. Ask questions such as "Why didn't scientists believe Wegener?" Help them answer using words like *because*.

Transitioning/Expanding
Have students generate simple sentences with *why* and *because*. Point out a place in the text where cause and effect is used. Help students ask *why* questions about the information. Have them answer using the word *because*.

Bridging
Help students create compound sentences of the type, "Wegener studied science *because* ____." Have students complete the sentences so they give a reason. Point out that these sentences give examples of cause and effect.

Activity Pages 1.3 and 1.4

- After determining what evidence presented in the chapter shows a result of the cause, the students will examine a collection of images on Activity Page 1.4. The images represent evidence of a variety of causes discussed in *The Changing Earth*. These images are examples of the kind of evidence geologists examine to determine how powerful forces above and below Earth's surface work to change the earth. Students must determine which image represents evidence of the cause statement for that specific chapter. Students will cut that image out and glue it to the chart in the "What evidence is there?" column. Then students will write a few key words about the image.
- Note for students that each image has a small letter in the corner. Tell students they will gather a letter from each image as they add images to the chart. At the end of the unit, students will examine a geology riddle and unscramble the collected letters to answer the riddle.
- Tell students they will record the chapter number in the far left column to indicate which chapter the information in each row relates to.
- Call on a student to read aloud the information under "What is the cause?" in the first row.
- Explain that students must determine what evidence about Pangaea breaking apart is in the chapter. Have students look back through the chapter to find information about Pangaea breaking apart (last paragraph on page 9).
- Have students examine the images on Activity Page 1.4. Engage students in a discussion about the images, talking about what is represented in the images and which image best represents evidence of the breaking apart of Pangaea and the movement of its pieces (image showing similar patterns of fossil and rock formations on different continents).
- Ensure students understand why the correct image is the one showing evidence of similar fossil and rock patterns on different continents (The image shows the continents closer together, somewhat as they would have been as Pangaea, and how the similar patterns are spread across different continents, showing evidence of how the pieces slowly moved apart over time.).
- Have students cut out the correct image and glue it to the chart in the correct row in the "What evidence is there?" column. Have students write the following information for chapter number, key words, and letter in the chart on Activity Page 1.3:

Partial Chart for Activity Page 1.3			
Chapter #	**What is the cause?**	**What evidence is there?**	**Letter**
1	*Movement of tectonic plates caused Pangaea to break up and the pieces to slowly move apart over a long period.*	*image:* *similar fossil and rock patterns on different continents* *key words:* similar rocks, fossils on different continents	N

- Tell students that there will be many examples of evidence and causes in each chapter, but that they will focus on information most closely related to The Big Question in each chapter.
- Have students turn to Activity Page 1.5. Ensure students understand the directions and tell them they will complete Activity Page 1.5 for homework.

Activity Page 1.5

WORD WORK: *DENSE* (5 MIN.)

1. In the chapter you heard and read, "Basalt is a heavy, dense rock formed from cooled, hardened lava."
2. Say the word *dense* with me.
3. *Dense* means "thick or heavy."
4. The dense fog blocked our view of the mountaintop.
5. What are some other examples of *dense*? Be sure to use the word *dense* in your response.
   - Ask two or three students to use the target word in a sentence. If necessary, guide and/or rephrase students' responses to make complete sentences: "____ is dense because ____."
6. What part of speech is the word *dense*?
   - » adjective

- Use a Making Choices activity for follow-up. I am going to read several sentences. If the sentence I read is about something that is dense, say, "That is dense." If the sentence I read is not about something that is dense, say, "That is not dense."

1. The fox took cover in the bushes, where he was hidden from view.
    » That is dense.
2. The bread was sliced very thin.
    » That is not dense.
3. In the jungle, the tree coverage was so thick, we couldn't see the sky.
    » That is dense.
4. When we flew on a plane, we could not see the ground below because of the clouds.
    » That is dense.
5. On a clear day, you can see for miles.
    » That is not dense.

End Lesson

Lesson 1: Geology

Take-Home Material

READING

Activity Pages 1.5 and 1.6

- Have students take home Activity Page 1.5 to read and complete for homework and Activity Page 1.6 to use as a reference throughout the unit.
- Have students take home a text selection from the Fluency Supplement if you are choosing to provide additional fluency practice.

LESSON

2

Earth's Layers and Plate Tectonics

PRIMARY FOCUS OF LESSON

Reading

Students will identify and describe Earth's layers, describe the movement of tectonic plates, and identify evidence of how Earth's layers and tectonic plates interact to change the Earth's surface. **[RI.4.1, RI.4.3, RI.4.8]**

Grammar

Students will identify the correct location of commas in dates, addresses, city and state, and items in a series. **[L.4.2]**

Morphology

Students will distinguish between root words and words with the suffix –*ly* and use those words correctly in sentences. **[L.4.4]**

Writing

Students will explain similes related to geology concepts. **[L.4.5]**

FORMATIVE ASSESSMENT

Activity Page 1.3	**Evidence Collector's Chart** Students look in the text for evidence supporting geological events. **[RI.4.1]**
Activity Page 1.4	**Evidence of Changes on Earth** Students look in the text for evidence supporting geological events. **[RI.4.1]**
Activity Page 2.2	**Practice Commas** Students determine where to insert commas in sentences. **[L.4.2]**
Activity Page 2.3	**–*ly*: Suffix Meaning "in a ___ Way"** Students choose the appropriate adjectives or adverbs to complete sentences. **[L.4.4]**
Activity Page 2.4	**Similes About Earth's Changes** Students analyze similes used to describe geological processes. **[L.4.5]**

LESSON AT A GLANCE

	Grouping	Time	Materials
Reading (45 min.)			
Review	Whole Group	5 min.	❏ *The Changing Earth* ❏ Activity Pages 1.3–1.5, 2.1 ❏ Evidence Collector's Chart ❏ scissors ❏ glue
Introduce the Chapter	Whole Group	5 min.	
Read Chapter 2	Whole Group	20 min.	
Lesson Wrap-Up	Whole Group	10 min.	
Word Work: *Crust*	Whole Group	5 min.	
Language (30 min.)			
Grammar: Introduce Commas	Whole Group/ Independent	15 min.	❏ Commas Poster ❏ Activity Page 2.2
Morphology: Introduce Suffix *–ly*	Whole Group/ Independent	15 min.	❏ Suffixes Poster ❏ Activity Page 2.3
Writing (15 min.)			
Examine Similes	Whole Group/ Independent	15 min.	❏ Activity Page 2.4 ❏ *The Changing Earth*
Take-Home Material			
Grammar; Morphology			❏ Activity Pages 2.2, 2.3

ADVANCE PREPARATION

Reading

- You may access a digital version of The Big Question in the digital components for this unit.
- Display the Evidence Collector's Chart from Lesson 1.

Language

Grammar

- Prepare and display a Commas Poster with the following information for use during the grammar lesson, or access a digital version in the digital components for this unit. Display this poster throughout the unit.

  Commas

  A comma is a punctuation mark used to separate words or numbers in dates and addresses, as well as a series of words in a sentence.

- Write the following examples on the board/chart paper:
  - His little sister was born on January 2 1992.
  - The Declaration of Independence is dated July 4 1776.
  - I visited my relatives in Birmingham Alabama.
    - The White House
    - 1600 Pennsylvania Avenue NW
    - Washington DC 20500
  - Tectonic plates can move apart collide or slide sideways past one another.
  - We went to a museum a park a theater and a restaurant on our trip.

Morphology

- If you did not do so in previous units, prepare and display a Suffixes Poster with the following information for use during the morphology lesson. Leave enough space at the bottom to list suffixes and their meanings throughout the year. Select a convenient place in the classroom to display the poster, as it will be used and displayed throughout the school year in the same way you are using the Prefixes and Roots posters. Alternatively, you may access a digital version in the digital components for this unit.

  Suffixes

  A suffix is a syllable or syllables placed at the end of a root word to change the word's meaning and/or to form a different word.

- Select a place in the classroom to display the poster for the rest of the year.

Start Lesson

Lesson 2: Earth's Layers and Plate Tectonics

Reading

45M

Primary Focus: Students will identify and describe Earth's layers, describe the movement of tectonic plates, and identify evidence of how Earth's layers and tectonic plates interact to change the Earth's surface.
[RI.4.1, RI.4.3, RI.4.8]

REVIEW (5 MIN.)

Activity Page 1.5

- As a class, review Activity Page 1.5 that students completed for homework. Discuss the examples of evidence students wrote. Encourage students to use content and academic vocabulary as they talk about their examples of evidence observed by scientists.

1. Which is the best evidence you were able to find?
   » Answers may vary but may include: many examples of similar fossils and rock layers were found on different continents that are now separated by great distances across large oceans; fossils of the ancient fern Glossopteris were found in ice-covered Antarctica, which today does not have a climate warm enough for this fern to grow; fossils of the ancient reptile Lystrosaurus were found in southern Africa and India; fossils of the ancient reptile Cynognathus were found in South America and Africa; fossils of the ancient fern Glossopteris were found in Africa, India, Australia, and South America; rock formations along the northern and eastern coasts of South America match those along Africa's western coast; and deposits of coal and salt in eastern North America are very similar to those in southern Europe.

INTRODUCE THE CHAPTER (5 MIN.)

- Tell students they will read Chapter 2, "Earth's Layers and Moving Plates."
- Have students turn to the table of contents, locate the chapter, and then turn to the first page of the chapter.
- Preview the core vocabulary words before reading the chapter.
- Begin by telling students that one of the first vocabulary words they will encounter in this chapter is *seismic wave*.
- Have them find *seismic wave* on page 13 of the Reader. Remind them that each vocabulary word is bolded the first time it appears in the chapter.

- Have students refer to the glossary at the back of the Reader and locate seismic wave. Then have a student read the definition.

Check for Understanding

What causes a seismic wave?

» an earthquake

- Explain the following:
  - The part of speech
  - Alternate forms of the word

Activity Page 2.1

- Have students reference Activity Page 2.1 while you read each word and its meaning.

  Note: Magma, lava, and basalt are related to each other. Magma is completely melted rock. Lava is magma that comes out onto Earth's surface. Basalt is rock formed when lava cools and solidifies.

Academic Vocabulary and Spanish Cognates

seismic wave, n. a surge of energy traveling out from an earthquake's source through the earth (seismic waves) (13)

pressure, n. the weight or force produced when something presses or pushes against something else (15)

basalt, n. heavy, dense rock formed from cooled, hardened lava (16)

magma, n. melted rock in Earth's mantle (17)

lava, n. red-hot melted rock that has erupted above Earth's crust from deep underground (17)

basin, n. a large area in the earth that is lower than the area around it (basins) (17)

ocean trench, n. a narrow, extremely deep valley formed when the seafloor dips down as one tectonic plate slides under another (ocean trenches) (17)

theory, n. an explanation for why something happens based on evidence (17)

plate tectonics, n. a theory that Earth's crust and the solid top part of the mantle are broken up into sections that fit together but move against each other (17)

exert, v. to cause a force to be felt or have an effect (exerts) (19)

Vocabulary Chart for Chapter 2, "Earth's Layers and Moving Parts"		
Vocabulary Type	**Tier 3** **Domain-Specific Words**	**Tier 2** **General Academic Words**
Core Vocabulary	seismic wave basalt magma lava basin ocean trench plate tectonics	pressure theory exert
Spanish Cognates for Core Vocabulary	basalto lava tectónica de placas	
Multiple-Meaning Core Vocabulary Words	basin	pressure
Sayings and Phrases	on the right track driving force	

- Have one student read The Big Question at the beginning of the chapter. Ensure students understand the meaning of The Big Question before reading the chapter.
    - How do tectonic plates and Earth's layers interact to change the surface of the earth?

Chapter 2

Earth's Layers and Moving Plates

THE BIG QUESTION
How do tectonic plates and Earth's layers interact to change the surface of the earth?

Alfred Wegener's continental drift hypothesis explained many of the "why" questions. It explained why the edges of some continents fit together like puzzle pieces. It explained why continents separated by vast oceans have similar types of rock formations and fossils. What the hypothesis couldn't explain was "how." How could a mass of solid rock as large as Asia or North America move thousands of miles across Earth's surface? It would take an enormously powerful force to do that. Geologists in Wegener's day didn't know of any force on Earth's surface powerful enough to move continents.

12

READ CHAPTER 2 (20 MIN.)

- Have students read pages 12 and 13 silently.

As a result, most geologists rejected the idea of continental drift. For decades, Wegener's hypothesis was harshly criticized. Still, a few geologists thought Wegener was on the right track. What if the driving force behind continental drift was below Earth's surface? How can you discover what lies beneath Earth's crust? Oddly enough, earthquakes helped scientists answer these questions.

What Waves Reveal

Have you ever tossed a small rock into a pond? Little waves travel out from the spot where the rock hits the water's surface. Although you can't see them, waves travel through the water below the surface, too.

An earthquake is a bit like a rock plunking into water. During an earthquake, the ground shakes. The shaking is caused by waves of energy traveling out from the earthquake's source through the earth. Scientists call these **seismic waves.** Powerful seismic waves can travel very long distances. They can travel through Earth's crust and deep into its interior.

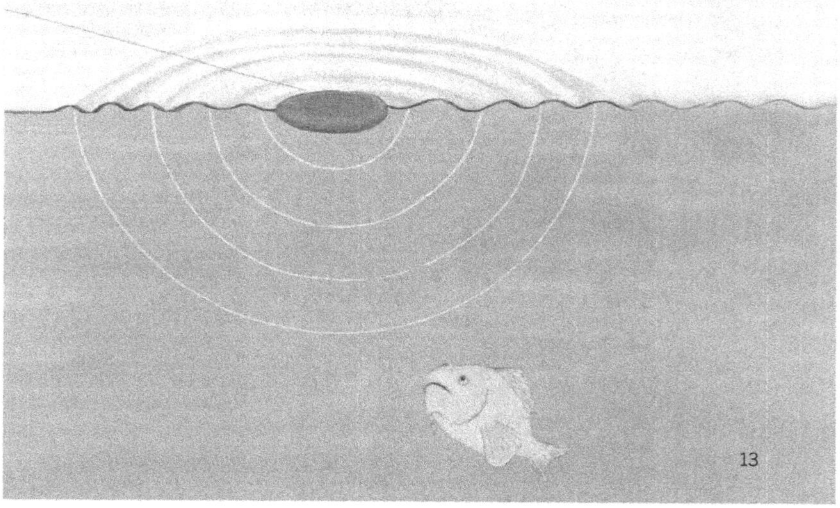

13

Inferential. How is a small rock thrown into water like seismic waves?

» Seismic waves travel out through the earth from the source of an earthquake. A small rock thrown into water makes waves that travel out from the spot where the rock hit the water. Both seismic waves and waves created when a small rock hits water travel out from a source.

Check for Understanding

Ask: Where can seismic waves travel?

» into the crust and into the Earth's interior

Support

What happens when a small rock hits water?

» Little waves travel out from the spot where the rock hits the water's surface. Waves also travel below the surface, but you can't see them.

Support

What happens during an earthquake?

» Waves of energy travel out from the earthquake's source through the earth and cause the ground to shake.

Around the time Alfred Wegener was thinking about continental drift, scientists were studying Earth's interior using seismic waves. How? Using instruments called seismographs, they tracked seismic waves traveling through the planet. Seismic waves move in slightly different ways as they move through different materials. For instance, they travel faster through solids than liquids. Studying seismic waves helped scientists identify Earth's four main layers.

Earth's deepest layer is a solid inner core of very hot metal. This metal may be nearly as hot as the sun's surface. The next layer, the outer core, is also made of hot metal, but it's liquid, not solid. The mantle surrounds the outer core. The mantle is Earth's largest and thickest layer and consists of very hot, very dense rock. The rock is solid in the lower and upper parts of the mantle. In between, however, is a region where the rock is neither liquid nor solid.

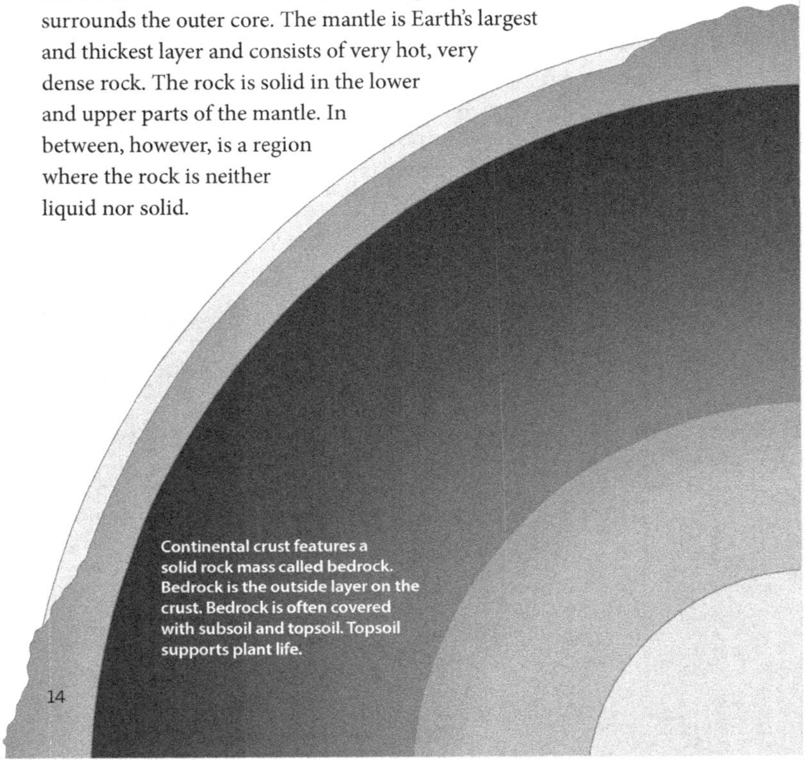

Continental crust features a solid rock mass called bedrock. Bedrock is the outside layer on the crust. Bedrock is often covered with subsoil and topsoil. Topsoil supports plant life.

14

- Have students read pages 14 and 15 silently.

Literal. What did scientists learn from studying seismic waves?

» By studying seismic waves, scientists were able to identify Earth's four main layers: the inner core, the outer core, the mantle, and the crust.

Evaluative. Suppose seismic waves enter a 100-mile long lake and a 100-mile long mountain made of rocks at the same moment. What would happen?

» The waves would go through the rock more quickly than through the lake.

Literal. Name and describe characteristics of each layer, while referring to the image that spans pages 14 and 15.

- Explicitly call students' attention to the fact that the text provides very clear definitions of the inner core, outer core, mantle, and crust. Point out that by carefully reviewing both the text and the image, students should be able to easily answer this question.
    - » The inner core is solid and made of very hot metal; the outer core is made of hot liquid metal; the mantle is the earth's largest and thickest layer, made of very hot, very dense rock; the top and bottom parts of the mantle are solid, but the region in the middle is neither liquid nor solid; this material does slowly move; the crust is the thin, rocky outer layer of the earth; there are two types of crust: oceanic crust and continental crust; the oceanic crust is covered by ocean water; most of the continental crust is dry land, but some of the crust around the edges is covered by water; oceanic crust is thinner but heavier than continental crust.

Check for Understanding

What lies between the solid rock that forms the lower and upper parts of the Earth's mantle?

- » a region that is neither solid nor liquid

The slow movement and behavior of this material, caused by heat and **pressure**, have an impact on Earth's surface. Above the mantle is Earth's outermost layer, the thin, rocky crust. There are two types of crust: oceanic crust and continental crust. Oceanic crust is covered by ocean water. Most of the continental crust is dry land, but some of the crust around the edges is covered by water. Oceanic crust is thinner but heavier than continental crust.

For scientists interested in continental drift, it was the slowly moving material in the middle of the mantle that caught their attention. Did material movement in the mantle contribute to crust movement, too? Could this be part of the reason why continents drift? Some scientists thought so. Before they could be sure, however, they needed evidence that Earth's crust was actually moving.

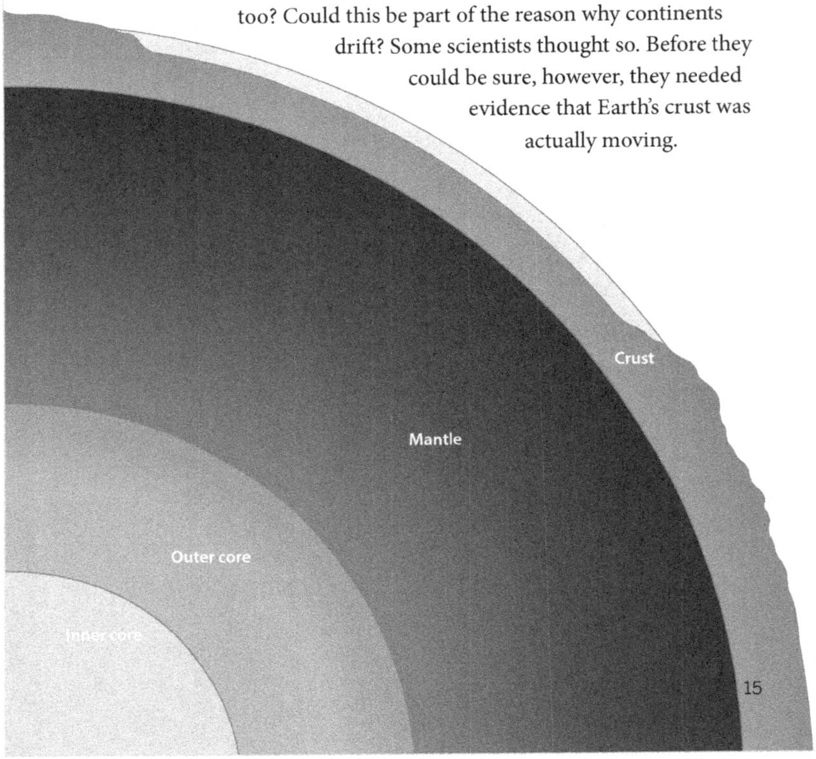

15

Evaluative. Why was this new knowledge about Earth's layers important for scientists?

» Answers may vary, but may include: learning about Earth's layers and their characteristics led scientists to new questions; they thought the new information about the mantle and the crust might hold answers to the mystery of continental drift; they were inspired to learn more about how the mantle and the crust interacted with each other; and they were inspired to look for evidence that the earth's crust was actually moving.

Clues from the Seafloor

During the 1940s and 1950s, new technology enabled scientists to make detailed maps of the seafloor. The maps revealed long chains of underwater mountains, called mid-ocean ridges, in all of Earth's oceans. There was a split, or rift, that ran down the center of these ridges. The rift was like a seam in a pants leg, where two pieces of fabric come together.

Scientists dredged up rock samples from mid-ocean ridges. All the rocks were **basalt**. Mid-ocean ridges seemed to be like long, skinny strings of volcanoes running along the seafloor.

Scientists collected rocks at various distances from the rift along a mid-ocean ridge. They discovered that rocks from the edge of the rift had formed very recently. Rocks farther away from the rift were older. The farther scientists got from the rift, on either side, the older the rocks were.

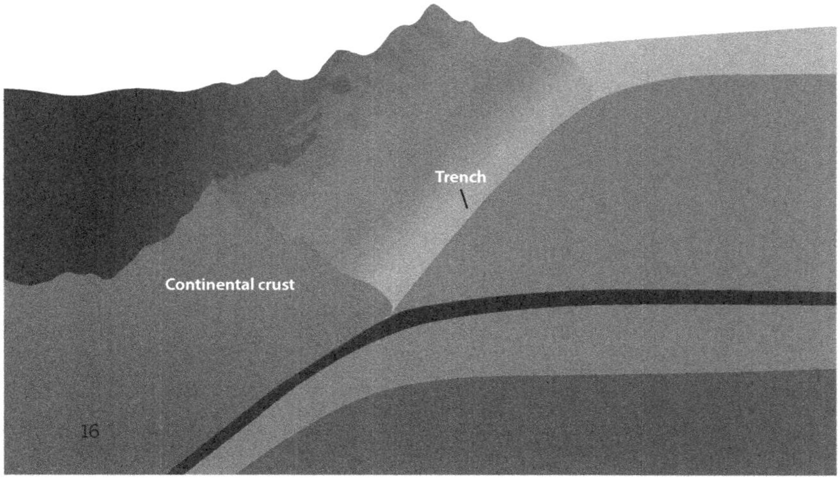

- Have students read pages 16 and 17 silently.

The scientists concluded that mid-ocean ridges form along huge cracks in Earth's crust. **Magma** beneath the crust erupts through these cracks as **lava**. The lava cools into basalt, creating new oceanic crust on either side of the rift.

As new crust is added, older crust gets pushed outward, away from the rift. Inch by inch, year after year, oceanic crust spreads outward into ocean **basins** on either side of mid-ocean ridges. Scientists called this process seafloor spreading. They theorized that as the seafloor slowly spreads, continents bordering the ocean slowly move apart. Here was one explanation of how continents could drift!

Scientists knew the earth wasn't getting bigger. If new crust forms along mid-ocean ridges, then old crust must be destroyed somewhere else. Scientists guessed that deep **ocean trenches** are places where crust is sinking down into the mantle.

In the 1960s, scientists formed a new **theory** about how Earth's surface changes. They called the theory **plate tectonics**.

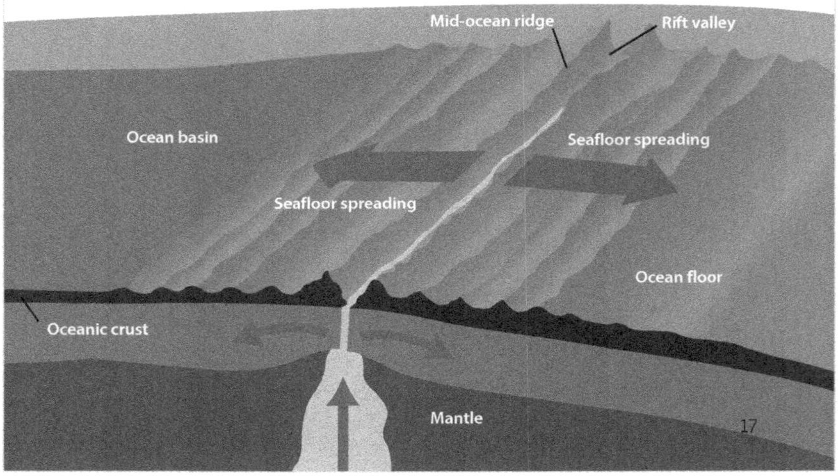

17

Literal. Why did scientists suspect that ocean trenches were part of the answer to the puzzle of continental drift?

» Scientists knew the earth wasn't getting any bigger; they guessed that if new crust was being created along mid-ocean ridges, then old crust must be destroyed somewhere else; new maps of the seafloor revealed incredibly deep valleys along the edges of several ocean basins; scientists guessed that deep ocean trenches are places where crust is sinking down into the mantle.

Evaluative. Call students' attention to the illustration that covers the bottom of both pages. Have them tell a partner what the illustration shows and what the information it provides might mean.

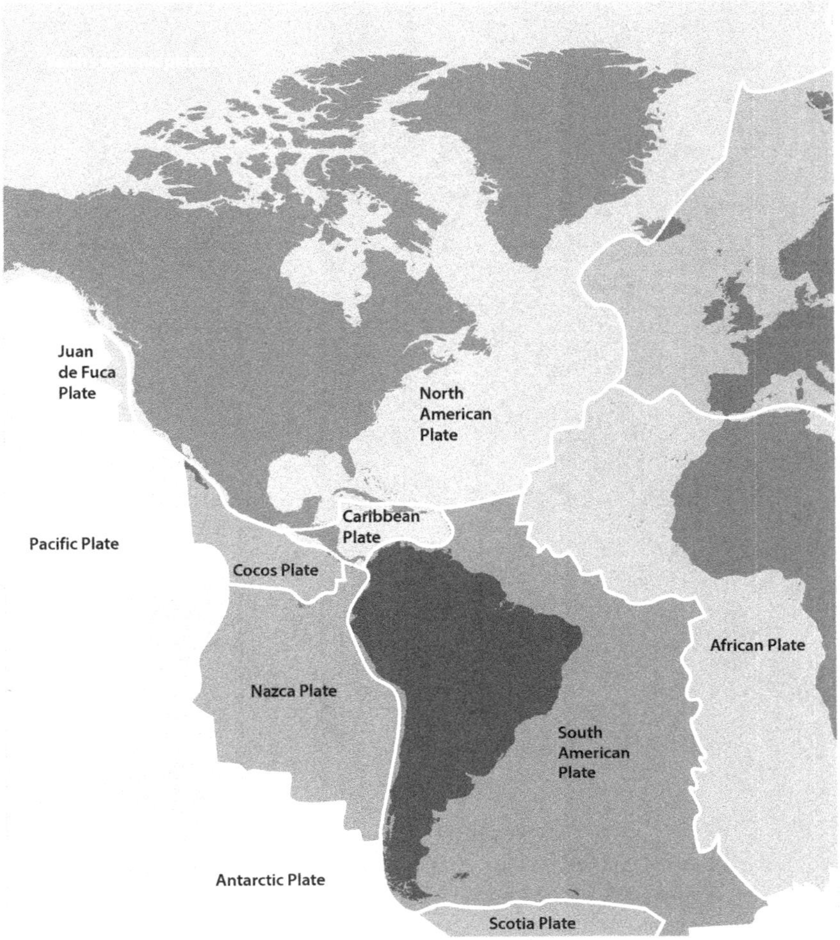

Moving Plates

Scientists are still learning about plate tectonics. The theory of plate tectonics states that Earth's crust, together with the solid top of the mantle, is broken up into sections. These huge, rocky slabs are called

18

- Have students read pages 18 and 19 silently.

  Literal. How does the theory of plate tectonics provide an explanation for how continents can move?

  » According to the theory of plate tectonics, the earth's crust and the solid top part of the mantle are broken up into huge rocky slabs called tectonic plates that fit tightly together. As the material in the mantle beneath the tectonic plates slowly moves due to heat and pressure, it exerts enormous pressure on the plates above. The pressure is great enough to cause the plates, which include continents, to move very, very slowly.

  Literal. Have students find South America on the map. Ask them to identify the plate that lies directly to the west of most of the continent.

  » the Nazca Plate

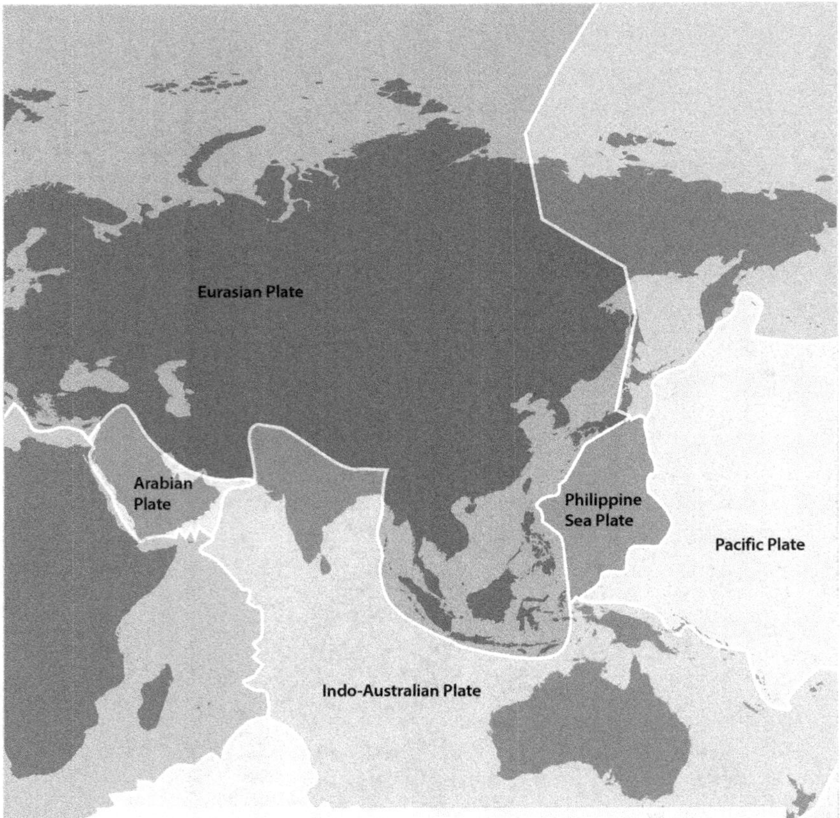

tectonic plates. Tectonic plates fit tightly together. They aren't fixed in place though; they can move. They move because of heat and pressure in the mantle. As the material in the mantle slowly moves, it **exerts** enormous pressure on the overlying plates. All that pressure forces the plates to move as well—very, very slowly.

Earth's tectonic plates have been slowly moving and interacting for billions of years. They interact mostly along their edges, or boundaries. Plate boundaries are where two or more tectonic plates meet.

Challenge

On the map, find an island on a plate boundary and identify the two plates that make up the island.

» Possible answer: Iceland rests on both the Eurasian and North American Plates.

A Matter of Time

At some boundaries, tectonic plates are moving apart. As the plates separate, molten rock flows up from the mantle into the space between them, creating new crust. Mid-ocean ridges are an example of this type of plate interaction. Tectonic plates along the mid-ocean ridge in the Atlantic Ocean are moving apart at a rate of about 0.8 to 2 inches per year. That may not seem like much, but it adds up. Two hundred million years ago, the landmasses of North America and Europe were joined. So were South America and Africa. Thanks to separating plates, these continents now lie on opposite sides of a vast ocean.

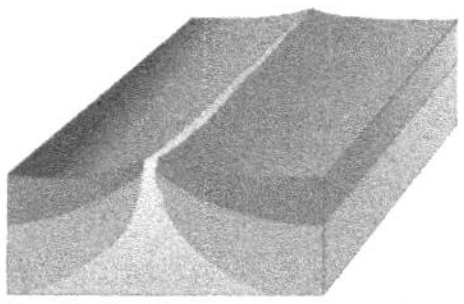
Tectonic plates move apart.

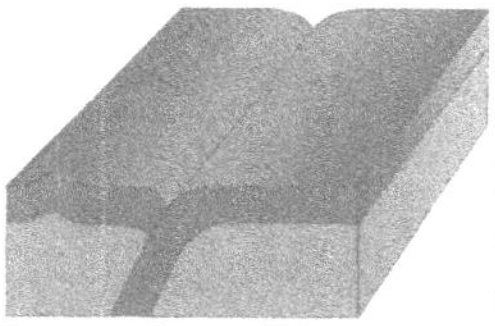
Tectonic plates collide.

At other plate boundaries, tectonic plates are **colliding**, or crashing together. In some places, colliding plates slowly crash into each other. The crust at their edges gradually crumples and is pushed higher and higher, creating mountains. In other places, one of the colliding plates slides under the other. Two plates are colliding this way along the western coast of South America. A heavier oceanic plate is sliding under a lighter continental plate. Scientists call this process **subduction**. Subduction has created a deep ocean trench off the coast of Chile and Peru. It has also had a role in creating the towering Andes Mountains along the western edge of South America. Similar plate interactions have formed mountain ranges throughout Earth's long history.

Finally, tectonic plates slide sideways past one another. It's never a smooth process. Plate edges press together hard. They often get stuck while the

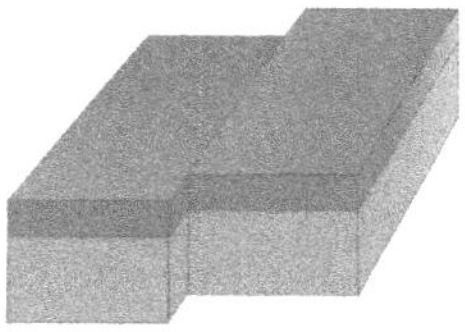
Tectonic plates slide sideways past one another.

20

- Have students read pages 20 and 21 silently.

  Literal. What is subduction?

  » Subduction is the name of the process when an oceanic plate slides under a continental plate.

Support

Review with students how subduction creates both high mountains and deep ocean trenches.

pressure keeps building. Eventually the pressure gets too great. The stuck edges break free, causing the plates to jerk past each other.

Providing the Answers

The theory of plate tectonics answered many questions in geology. It explained how Wegener's Pangaea broke apart. It explained how the continents have been slowly rearranged over millions of years. The movement of the plates also explained mid-ocean ridges, deep ocean trenches, patterns in the locations of mountains, and many other features on Earth's surface. The theory has become the cornerstone of modern geology.

As plates move, interesting things happen. Most of the time, they happen incredibly slowly. Sometimes, though, the effects of plate movements are sudden and dramatic. Think earthquakes and volcanoes!

Core Conclusions

You may never have heard of the Danish scientist Inge Lehmann. Among seismologists, however, she is famous. Around 1900, scientists thought the earth had just three layers: an outer crust, a solid mantle, and a liquid core. Lehmann studied seismograph records of earthquakes. She analyzed how seismic waves changed as they traveled through Earth's interior. Lehmann collected thousands of records organized in boxes—there were no computers back then! She saw patterns in how seismic waves behaved as they moved through Earth. Lehmann concluded that Earth's core has two parts: a liquid outer core and a solid inner core. In 1936, she announced her findings and changed our view of Earth!

21

Challenge

Why did Inge Lehmann need thousands of records, or pieces of data, to come to her conclusion?

» She needed lots of data to see patterns in how seismic waves traveled in and through the Earth.

Pronunciation Table

Word	CK Code
Inge Lehmann	/ing*gə/ /lee*mon/

LESSON WRAP-UP (10 MIN.)

Note: Question 2 and Activity Page 1.3 relate to The Big Question of the chapter.

- Use the following question to discuss the chapter.

2. **Evaluative.** What evidence did scientists use to figure out the theory of plate tectonics? Why did scientists have to rely on this evidence?

   » Answers may vary but should include: some of the evidence scientists studied that could provide clues about changes to the earth was left a very long time ago. For example, the older rock farther away from mid-ocean ridges was deposited a long time ago, and scientists would have to use some kind of tool or test to figure out how old the rock was. Mountains existed and scientists had to examine them as they were to look for clues about changes to the earth. Some of the evidence scientists studied that could provide clues about changes to the earth came from inside the earth or deep beneath the ocean. For example, scientists analyzed seismic waves to learn about the layers and materials inside the earth. Scientists saw deep ocean trenches that were the result of a process creating them deep beneath the ocean.

Activity Pages 1.3 and 1.4

- Have students turn to Activity Pages 1.3 and 1.4 and refer to the displayed Evidence Collector's Chart.
- Remind students that this chart is being used throughout the unit to collect evidence of changes to the earth related to specific causes of geologic change. The evidence represents what geologists examine to determine how powerful forces above and below Earth's surface work to change the earth.
- Have a student read aloud the information under "What is the cause?" in the second row.

3. Which pages in the text provide evidence about why tectonic plates move very slowly?

   » pages 18 and 19

- Have students refer to the remaining images on Activity Page 1.4. Engage students in a discussion about the images, talking about which image represents evidence of tectonic plate movement as presented in the chapter.

4. Which image represents this evidence? How do you know?

   » the map showing continents as they are today; it shows where the continents exist now, which is evidence of tectonic plate movement because the continents are no longer together as Pangaea.

- Have students cut out the correct image, glue it to the chart in the "What evidence is there?" column, and write the following information for chapter number, key words, and letter in the chart:

Partial Chart for Activity Page 1.3			
Chapter #	**What is the cause?**	**What evidence is there?**	**Letter**
2	*Tectonic plates move very slowly due to heat and pressure in Earth's mantle.*	*image: map of continents as they look today* *key words:* continents rearranged over time	E

WORD WORK: *CRUST* (5 MIN.)

1. In the chapter you read, "How can you discover what lies beneath Earth's crust?"
2. Say the word *crust* with me.
3. *Crust* means Earth's outermost layer, featuring a rocky surface.
4. Earth's crust is made up of continental crust on land and oceanic crust under water.
5. What are some other examples of a statement you could make about Earth's crust? Be sure to use the word *crust* in your response.
6. What part of speech is the word *crust*?

    » noun

- Use a Multiple-Meaning Word activity for follow-up. Tell students the word *crust* is a word with multiple meanings. Share the following with students:
    - **Meaning 1:** crust—Earth's outermost layer, featuring a rocky surface
    - **Meaning 2:** crust—the hard outer layer that covers something

Support

If necessary, guide and/or rephrase students' responses to make complete sentences: "Earth's crust ____."

- I am going to read several sentences. Listen to the context, or the text surrounding *crust* in the sentence, for clues as to which meaning is being used. When you think a sentence is an example of Meaning #1, hold up one finger. When you think a sentence is an example of Meaning #2, hold up two fingers.

1. The rocky surface of the mountain is part of the crust.
   » 1
2. Some people throw away the crust from their sandwich but it is my favorite part.
   » 2
3. Oceanic crust is thinner but heavier than continental crust.
   » 1
4. The freezing rain left a crust on the snow already on the ground.
   » 2
5. The pie's crust was lightly browned and crisp.
   » 2

Lesson 2: Earth's Layers and Tectonic Plates

Language

30M

GRAMMAR: INTRODUCE COMMAS (15 MIN.)

Primary Focus: Students will identify the correct location of commas in dates, addresses, city and state, and items in a series. **[L.4.2]**

- Tell students that today they will focus on commas.
- Refer to and read the Commas Poster you prepared in advance.
- Tell students that commas are used in sentences for many reasons. Explain that you will focus on three common uses of the comma: in a date, an address or city and state, and items in a series.
- Tell students that, first, you will focus on the usage of the comma within a date.
- Explain that when a date is written out with the month, day, and year, a comma is used to set apart the day and the year.

Reading for Information
Reading Closely

Entering/Emerging
Work on multiple-meaning words with students. Provide simple sentence frames for them to complete using the word *feet*, *light*, and *can* in both their meanings.

Transitioning/Expanding
Help students construct simple sentences using both meanings of *feet*, *light*, and *can*.

Bridging
Have students explain the two meanings of *feet*, *light*, and *can*. Then have students work in pairs to create sentences using each of these words in both of their meanings.

- Refer to the first example on the board/chart paper.
  - His little sister was born on January 2 1992.
- Explain that the comma should be placed between the day (2) and the year (1992) in the date. Then insert the comma in the correct location (January 2, 1992).
- Refer to the second example on the board/chart paper.
  - The Declaration of Independence is dated July 4 1776.

Check for Understanding

Ask students where the comma should be placed in the date in this sentence.

» between the day, 4, and the year, 1776

- Next, tell students that a comma goes in a particular place within an address or when writing out the name of a city and state.
- Explain that when an address or city and state (or in the case of Washington, DC, the city and district) is written out, a comma is used to set apart the city and the state. Refer to the third example on the board/chart paper.
  - I visited my relatives in Birmingham Alabama.
- Explain that the comma should be placed between the city (Birmingham) and the state (Alabama). Then insert the comma in the correct location (Birmingham, Alabama). Note for students that if the state abbreviation AL had been used instead of the full state name, the comma would still go between the city and the state.
- Refer to the fourth example on the board/chart paper.
  - The White House 1600 Pennsylvania Avenue NW Washington DC 20500
- Explain that a comma should be placed between the city (Washington) and the state or district (DC). Then insert the comma in the correct location (Washington, DC).
- Tell students that, lastly, you will focus on using a comma within items in a series.
- Explain that when multiple items are listed in a series in a sentence, a comma is used to set apart each item in the series.

- Refer to the fifth example on the board/chart paper.
    - Tectonic plates can move apart collide or slide sideways past one another.
- Explain that a comma should be placed after each item in the series except for the last item. A comma goes after *apart* and after *collide* but not after *another*. Then insert the commas in the correct locations (Tectonic plates can move apart, collide, or slide sideways past one another.).
- Refer to the sixth sentence on the board/chart paper.
    - We went to a museum a park a theater and a restaurant on our trip.

Check for Understanding

Ask: Should there be a comma after *museum*? (yes) Should there be a comma after *we*? (no)

- Ask students where the commas should be placed in this sentence. (after *museum*, *park*, and *theater*) Then insert the commas in the correct locations (We went to a museum, a park, a theater, and a restaurant on our trip.).
- Have students turn to Activity Page 2.2 and guide them through the first two sentences, making sure they add commas in the appropriate locations. Have students complete Activity Page 2.2 for homework, or if you feel they need more assistance, complete the activity page as a teacher-guided activity.

MORPHOLOGY: INTRODUCE SUFFIX –*LY* (15 MIN.)

Primary Focus: Students will distinguish between root words and words with the suffix –*ly* and use those words correctly in sentences. **[L.4.4]**

- Refer to the Suffixes Poster you displayed in the classroom and read it with students.
- Tell students that the suffix they will study this week is –*ly*. Explain that –*ly* is of Latin origin. Write the suffix –*ly* on the poster and point out that it is pronounced /lee/.
- Tell students that the suffix –*ly* means "in a ____ way" with the blank being the word to which –*ly* is added. Write the meaning of the suffix on the poster.
- Tell students that when –*ly* is added to the end of an adjective, the word becomes an adverb.

Language
Productive

Entering/Emerging
Write *I like to eat ____* on the board. Have children name foods they like. Add commas. Read the sentence together.

Transitioning/Expanding
Have student pairs use the sentence starter *Our favorite things to eat are ____* and list three foods they like. Help them add commas.

Bridging
Have individuals create sentences that name three foods they like. They should add commas and share their sentences with others.

Activity Page 2.2

Language Interpreting

Entering/Emerging
Introduce the words *quickly* and *slowly*. Demonstrate writing slowly. Have students complete the sentence *You are writing* ____. Repeat with *quickly*.

Transitioning/Expanding
Use words and gestures to model *quickly* and *slowly*. Write slowly. Have students say a sentence with *slowly* to tell what you are doing. Repeat with *quickly*.

Bridging
Use words and gestures to model *quickly/slowly*. Have students write *quickly*, then *slowly*. Have them explain what they did using *First* ____/*Then* ____ and *quickly/slowly*.

- Tell students that adverbs describe verbs. The adverbs created with the suffix –*ly* describe how a verb happens.
- Write *careful* on the board/chart paper.

5. What is the meaning of the word *careful*? Use it in a sentence.
   » *Careful* means paying attention to avoid risks, mistakes, or accidents. Possible sentence: His parents always tell him to be careful and look both ways before he crosses the street.

- Add the suffix –*ly* to *careful* and have students read the new word; then discuss the meaning of the new word. (*Carefully* means in a careful way or in a way that involves paying attention to avoid risks, mistakes, or accidents.)
- Share the following example of *carefully* used in a sentence:
  - The floor was wet and slippery, so I walked carefully to avoid falling.

6. What sentences use the word *carefully*?
   » Answers may vary.

Check for Understanding

Ask students for synonyms of *carefully*.

» Possible answers: *wisely*, *cautiously*, *safely*

- Write *speedy* on the board/chart paper. Briefly discuss the meaning of the word and then use it in a sentence. (*Speedy* means moving fast. "I was surprised by how speedy the cars actually were as they raced around the track.")
- Explain that when you add the suffix –*ly* to an adjective ending in –*y*, you must first change the –*y* to an –*i*, and then add –*ly*.
- Change the –*y* in *speedy* to an –*i* and add the suffix –*ly*. Have students read the new word; then discuss the meaning of the new word. (*Speedily* means in a speedy way or in a way that is moving fast.)
- Share the following example of *speedily* used in a sentence:
  - I was late for my dentist appointment, so I walked speedily to the office.

7. What other sentences use the word *speedily*?
   » Answers may vary.

8. What are some synonyms of *speedily*?

    » possible answers: *quickly*, *swiftly*, *rapidly*

- Continue in this manner for the remaining *–ly* words, using the following chart as a guide.

-*ly* Words				
English Root Word	**Meaning**	**Affixed Word**	**Meaning**	**Sentence**
accidental	(adjective) happening unexpectedly, not on purpose	accidentally	(adverb) in an accidental way; in a way that is unexpected or not on purpose	I accidentally dropped my new flower vase and broke it.
loud	(adjective) noisy	loudly	(adverb) in a loud or noisy way	He was singing so loudly that I could hear him three houses away.
easy	(adjective) not hard to do or get	easily	(adverb) in an easy way; in a way that is not hard to do or get	We were able to complete the 100-piece puzzle easily so we tried working on a 200-piece puzzle next.
temporary	(adjective) lasting for a short or limited time, not permanent	temporarily	(adverb) in a temporary way; in a way that lasts for a short or limited time	The children are staying at their grandparents' house temporarily while their parents travel for work.

Activity Page 2.3

- Have students turn to Activity Page 2.3. Read the title with students. Have students read the words in the box aloud.
- Go through the first two examples with students. Invite students to explain how they knew which word fit in each blank.
- Explain that students will complete the remainder of the page for homework.

Lesson 2: Earth's Layers and Plate Tectonics

Writing

15M

Primary Focus: Students will explain similes related to geology concepts. [L.4.5]

EXAMINE SIMILES (15 MIN.)

- Tell students that today they will examine similes.
- Remind students that they have already learned what a simile is.

1. Ask students to define a simile.

   » a literary device that compares things using *like* or *as*

- Encourage students to provide examples of similes they have read, heard, or used.

Check for Understanding

The basketball player was as graceful as a dancer when he went up to dunk the ball. Is that an example of a simile?

» yes

- Have students turn to Activity Page 2.4. Direct students' attention to the column headers in the chart on Activity Page 2.4. Explain that the first column includes similes from the Reader, the second column asks students to determine what things are being compared using a simile, and the third column asks students to explain what the simile means.
- Direct students' attention to the simile from the text in the first row. (What if continents were like enormous pieces of ice?)
- Ask students what the simile listed in the chart is comparing. Guide them to understand that the simile is comparing continents to pieces of ice floating in a drink. Guide students to write this information in the chart on Activity Page 2.4 under the "What is the simile comparing?" column.

2. What does the simile mean?

   » The rocks that make up the continents are less dense than the rocks on the ocean bottom, so Wegener wondered if continents could float above the rocks on the

Language
Selecting and applying

Entering/Emerging
Help students work as a group to complete the similes *The Earth is round like* ____ and *I am as strong as* ____.

Transitioning/Expanding
Have students work in pairs to complete the similes *The Earth is round like* ____ and *I am as strong as* ____.

Bridging
Have students work on their own to complete the similes *The Earth is round like* ____ and *I am as strong as* ____.

Activity Page 2.4

Support

Have students turn to page 9 in the Reader and silently read the first paragraph, which contains this information.

ocean bottom just like ice floats in a drink, which is made with water, because ice is less dense than water.

- Guide students to record the meaning of the simile in the chart on Activity Page 2.4 under the "What does the simile mean?" column.
- Using the following chart, guide students to analyze the remaining similes and fill in the appropriate information. Have students complete the last simile on their own or with a partner before discussing the answer.

  Note: You may also choose to use the third simile as an exit ticket.

Similes Chart

Page	Simile from Text	What is the simile comparing?	What does the simile mean?
13	*An earthquake is a bit like a rock plunking into water.*	an earthquake and a rock in water	Seismic waves travel out through the earth from the source of an earthquake just as a rock is a source of waves traveling out from the spot where it hit the water.
16	*The rift was like a seam in a pants leg, where two pieces of fabric come together.*	a rift in mid-ocean ridges and a seam in a pants leg	The seam in a pants leg dips down where the two pieces of fabric come together so the seam lies a little bit lower than the pieces of fabric. The rift down the center of the mid-ocean ridges, where tectonic plates are moving apart, dips down between the ridges; the rift lies a little bit lower than the ridges themselves.

Wrap-Up

Ask a student to explain what a simile is.

» A simile is a literary device that compares things using *like* or *as*.

End Lesson

Lesson 2: Earth's Layers and Tectonic Plates

Take-Home Material

GRAMMAR; MORPHOLOGY

- Have students complete Activity Pages 2.2 and 2.3 for homework.

Support

Remind students that *dense* means thick or heavy. Ice floats in water because it is not as thick or heavy as water.

Support

If students need help putting the simile meaning into words, provide the sentence frame "____ helps me understand ____ because ____."

Support

You may wish to point out the familiar idea or item in each simile: a rock plunking into water and a seam in a pants leg.

Activity Pages 2.2 and 2.3

LESSON

3

Close Reading: Earth's Layers and Moving Plates

PRIMARY FOCUS OF LESSON

Reading

Students will explain characteristics of Earth's layers, describe how tectonic plates move, and explain how these forces interact to change Earth's surface, including the seafloor. **[RI.4.1, RI.4.2, RI.4.8]**

Writing

Students will write a detailed explanation of a simile. **[L.4.5, W.4.2]**

FORMATIVE ASSESSMENT

Activity Page 2.4	**Similes About Earth's Changes** Students analyze similes used to describe geological processes. **[L.4.5]**
Activity Page 3.1	**Excerpt from "Earth's Layers and Moving Plates"** Students use vocabulary from the text to complete a short passage. **[RI.4.1]**

LESSON AT A GLANCE

	Grouping	Time	Materials
Reading (45 min.)			
Review	Whole Group	10 min.	❏ *The Changing Earth* ❏ Activity Page 3.1 ❏ Paper, plastic or ceramic cup
Close Reading	Whole Group	25 min.	
Lesson Wrap-Up	Whole Group	5 min.	
Word Work: *Exert*	Whole Group/ Pairs	5 min.	
Writing (45 min.)			
Review Similes	Whole Group	5 min.	❏ Activity Page 2.4 ❏ Board/chart paper ❏ Writing Journal
Model an Explanation of a Simile	Whole Group	20 min.	
Draft a Detailed Explanation of a Simile	Whole Group/ Pairs	20 min.	
Take-Home Material			
Reading			❏ Activity Page 3.1

ADVANCE PREPARATION

Reading

Note: You may access a digital version of The Big Question in the digital components for this unit.

- Have a paper, plastic, or ceramic cup ready for the Access activity.

Language

Grammar; Morphology

- Collect Activity Pages 2.2 and 2.3 to review and grade as there are no grammar or morphology lessons today.

Start Lesson

Lesson 3: Close Reading

Reading

45M

Primary Focus: Students will explain characteristics of Earth's layers, describe how tectonic plates move, and explain how these forces interact to change Earth's surface, including the seafloor. **[RI.4.1, RI.4.2, RI.4.8]**

REVIEW (10 MIN.)

- Give students a few moments to look back at the headings, images, and captions in Chapter 2, "Earth's Layers and Moving Plates." Allow students to look at the Reader as you discuss the following questions. Have students share their ideas with a partner before explaining their thinking with the whole class.

1. What are tectonic plates?

   » Tectonic plates are huge rocky slabs, or sections, that are made up of Earth's crust together with the solid top part of the mantle; they are not fixed in place and can move due to heat and pressure in the mantle beneath them.

2. Describe the different ways tectonic plates can move.

   » Tectonic plates can move apart at mid-ocean ridges due to a process called *seafloor spreading*; they can collide and create mountains as the crust crumples and is pushed higher and higher; an oceanic plate can slide beneath a continental plate in a process called *subduction*; and tectonic plates can slide past one another after the pressure builds up and the stuck edges break free.

- Encourage students to use their hands to show how tectonic plates might move and how they act when they come together.
- Tell students they will reread Chapter 2, "Earth's Layers and Moving Plates."
- Have students turn to the table of contents, locate the chapter, and then turn to the first page of the chapter.
- Have one student read The Big Question at the beginning of the chapter. Ensure students understand the meaning of The Big Question before reading the chapter.
    - How do tectonic plates and Earth's layers interact to change the surface of the earth?

As a result, most geologists rejected the idea of continental drift. For decades, Wegener's hypothesis was harshly criticized. Still, a few geologists thought Wegener was on the right track. What if the driving force behind continental drift was below Earth's surface? How can you discover what lies beneath Earth's crust? Oddly enough, earthquakes helped scientists answer these questions.

What Waves Reveal

Have you ever tossed a small rock into a pond? Little waves travel out from the spot where the rock hits the water's surface. Although you can't see them, waves travel through the water below the surface, too.

An earthquake is a bit like a rock plunking into water. During an earthquake, the ground shakes. The shaking is caused by waves of energy traveling out from the earthquake's source through the earth. Scientists call these **seismic waves**. Powerful seismic waves can travel very long distances. They can travel through Earth's crust and deep into its interior.

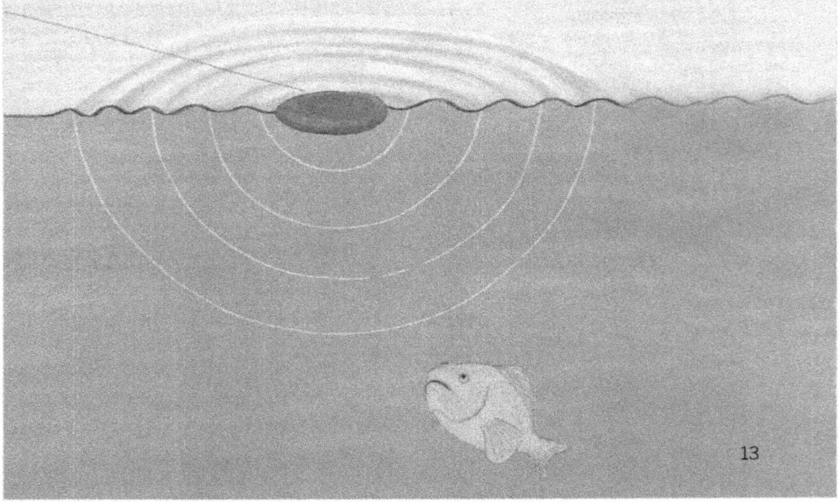

13

CLOSE READING (25 MIN.)

- Reread the title of the chapter as a class, "Earth's Layers and Moving Plates." As you read portions of the chapter, pause to explain or clarify the text at each point indicated.
- Have students silently read the first paragraph on page 13.

Inferential. How does the author's choice of wording help explain what many geologists believed about Wegener's hypothesis of continental drift?

» The author uses the word *rejected* to indicate how most geologists responded to Wegener's hypothesis. *Rejected* means refused to believe or accept something. In addition, the author uses the words *harshly criticized* to describe how most geologists felt about Wegener's hypothesis. *Criticized* means expressed disapproval or talked about the problems something has. *Harshly* means in a severe or unkind way. If most geologists rejected Wegener's hypothesis and also harshly criticized it, they refused to believe it was true and they also expressed disapproval or talked about the problems it had in a severe, unkind way.

Inferential. You have learned an *idiom* is a phrase that does not make sense using the meaning of the individual words, but that has a meaning of its own. The author uses an idiom in this paragraph, *on the right track*. *On the right track* means doing something right or doing something that is likely to lead to success. What does the author mean by "a few geologists thought Wegener was on the right track"?

» A few geologists thought Wegener's idea about continental drift was accurate, if not exactly correct.

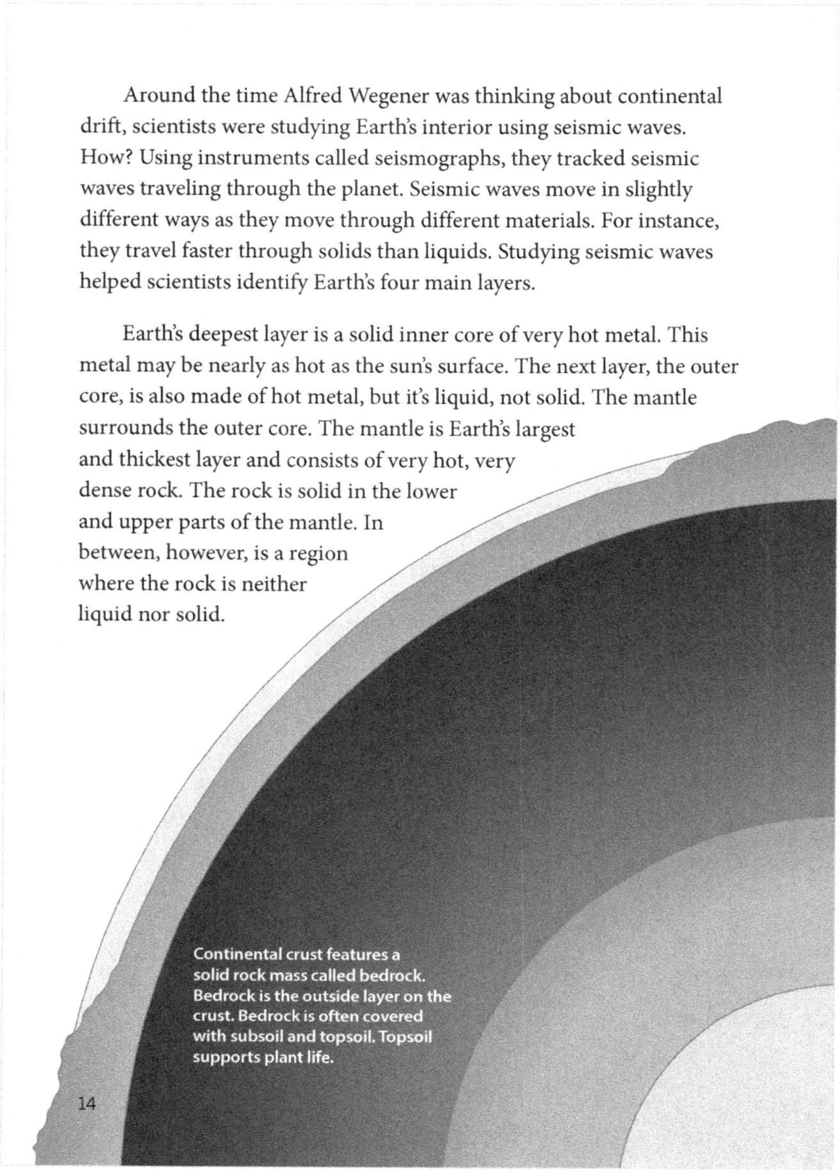

Around the time Alfred Wegener was thinking about continental drift, scientists were studying Earth's interior using seismic waves. How? Using instruments called seismographs, they tracked seismic waves traveling through the planet. Seismic waves move in slightly different ways as they move through different materials. For instance, they travel faster through solids than liquids. Studying seismic waves helped scientists identify Earth's four main layers.

Earth's deepest layer is a solid inner core of very hot metal. This metal may be nearly as hot as the sun's surface. The next layer, the outer core, is also made of hot metal, but it's liquid, not solid. The mantle surrounds the outer core. The mantle is Earth's largest and thickest layer and consists of very hot, very dense rock. The rock is solid in the lower and upper parts of the mantle. In between, however, is a region where the rock is neither liquid nor solid.

Continental crust features a solid rock mass called bedrock. Bedrock is the outside layer on the crust. Bedrock is often covered with subsoil and topsoil. Topsoil supports plant life.

14

- Have students silently read the paragraph that begins "Earth's deepest layer . . . ."

  Literal. Which parts of Earth's layers are described as solid and which parts are described as liquid?

  » The inner core is solid; both the lower part and the top part of the mantle are solid; the crust is solid; the material in between the lower and upper parts of the mantle is neither liquid nor solid; the outer core is liquid.

Check for Understanding

How are the inner core and the outer core different from each other?

» The inner core is solid and the outer core is liquid.

Inferential. What information in the text helps you determine whether Earth's crust is liquid or solid?

» The words *rocky crust* imply the crust is solid, since we know rocks are solid.

Reading for Information

Reading Closely

Entering/Emerging
Touch and name the inner, outer, lower, and upper parts of a cup. Then touch a part and have students give the word to describe it.

Transitioning/Expanding
Touch and name the inner, outer, lower, and upper parts of a cup. Then touch a part. Have students say a sentence to describe it.

Bridging
Have students challenge each other to identify parts of the cup, using sentences like *Touch the upper part of the cup.*

Support

Solids take up a definite amount of space and have a definite shape. A brick is an example. Liquids take up a definite amount of space but can change shape. Syrup is an example.

The slow movement and behavior of this material, caused by heat and **pressure**, have an impact on Earth's surface. Above the mantle is Earth's outermost layer, the thin, rocky crust. There are two types of crust: oceanic crust and continental crust. Oceanic crust is covered by ocean water. Most of the continental crust is dry land, but some of the crust around the edges is covered by water. Oceanic crust is thinner but heavier than continental crust.

For scientists interested in continental drift, it was the slowly moving material in the middle of the mantle that caught their attention. Did material movement in the mantle contribute to crust movement, too? Could this be part of the reason why continents drift? Some scientists thought so. Before they could be sure, however, they needed evidence that Earth's crust was actually moving.

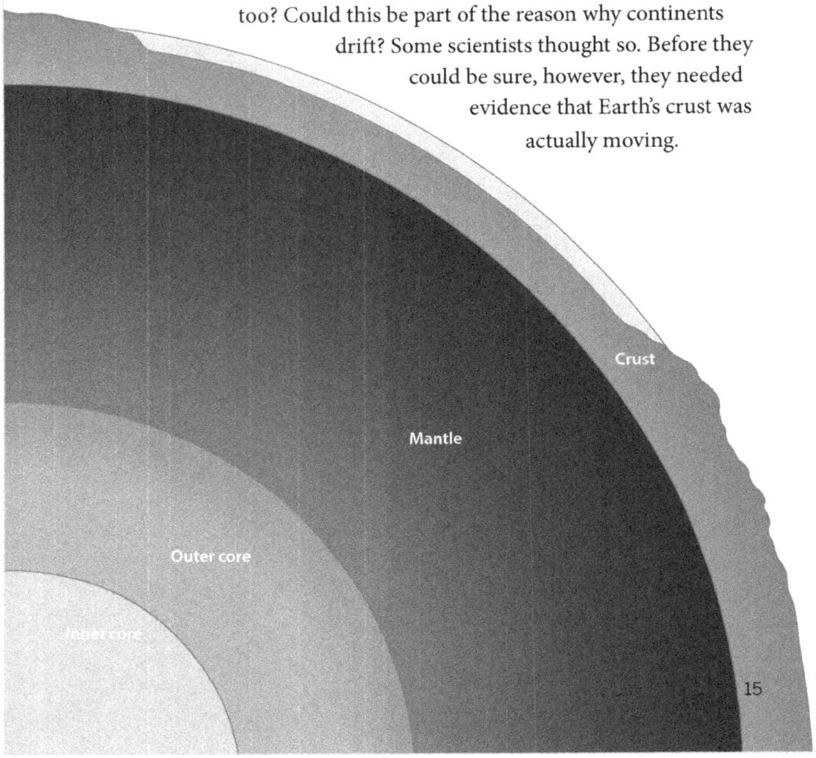

15

- Silently read the second paragraph on page 15.

Evaluative. *Caught their attention* is an idiom meaning attracted the interest of. Why do you think the author uses *caught their attention* in the last paragraph?

» Answers may vary but may include the idea that the only thing scientists noticed as moving was material in the mantle. The movement attracted their interest, making them wonder if the mantle's very slowly moving material led to movement in the crust.

Clues from the Seafloor

During the 1940s and 1950s, new technology enabled scientists to make detailed maps of the seafloor. The maps revealed long chains of underwater mountains, called mid-ocean ridges, in all of Earth's oceans. There was a split, or rift, that ran down the center of these ridges. The rift was like a seam in a pants leg, where two pieces of fabric come together.

Scientists dredged up rock samples from mid-ocean ridges. All the rocks were **basalt**. Mid-ocean ridges seemed to be like long, skinny strings of volcanoes running along the seafloor.

Scientists collected rocks at various distances from the rift along a mid-ocean ridge. They discovered that rocks from the edge of the rift had formed very recently. Rocks farther away from the rift were older. The farther scientists got from the rift, on either side, the older the rocks were.

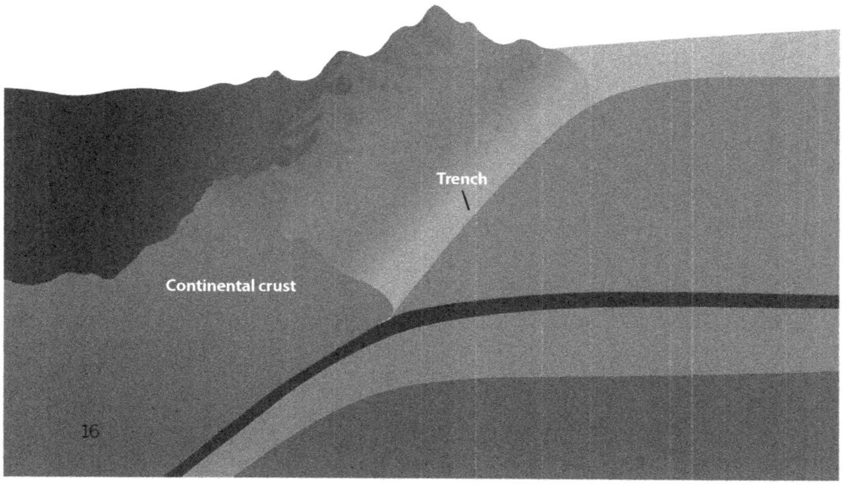

- Have students silently read page 16 and the first paragraph at the top of page 17.

Inferential. The word *revealed* means made known or brought something into view. Why do you think the author chose to use the word *revealed* when stating maps revealed long chains of underwater mountains?

» Because the seafloor is covered with water and because of the water depth, scientists could not see the seafloor without the help of technology. The maps created with the help of technology showed long chains of underwater mountains, which scientists did not previously know were there. The maps made these underwater chains known to scientists.

The scientists concluded that mid-ocean ridges form along huge cracks in Earth's crust. **Magma** beneath the crust erupts through these cracks as **lava**. The lava cools into basalt, creating new oceanic crust on either side of the rift.

As new crust is added, older crust gets pushed outward, away from the rift. Inch by inch, year after year, oceanic crust spreads outward into ocean **basins** on either side of mid-ocean ridges. Scientists called this process seafloor spreading. They theorized that as the seafloor slowly spreads, continents bordering the ocean slowly move apart. Here was one explanation of how continents could drift!

Scientists knew the earth wasn't getting bigger. If new crust forms along mid-ocean ridges, then old crust must be destroyed somewhere else. Scientists guessed that deep **ocean trenches** are places where crust is sinking down into the mantle.

In the 1960s, scientists formed a new **theory** about how Earth's surface changes. They called the theory **plate tectonics**.

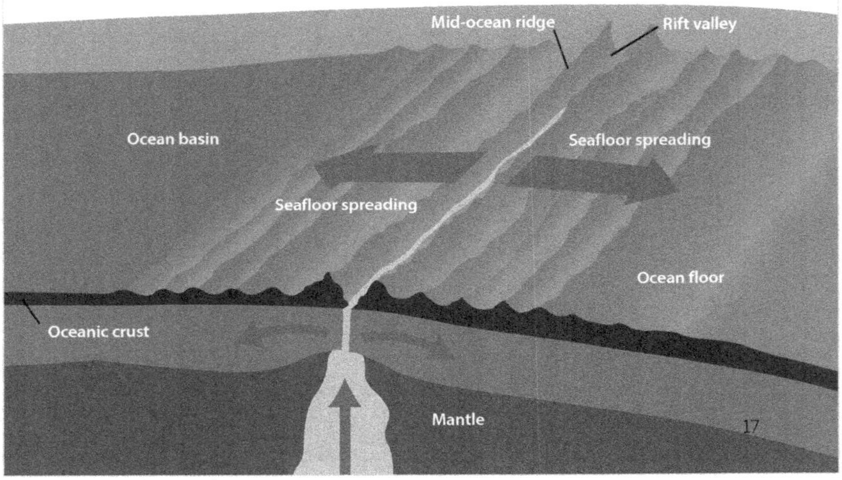

- Have students use the word *revealed* in a sentence.
  - » Answers will vary. Possible answers: The magician opened her fist and revealed a quarter; The dog sniffed at the door and revealed that food was hidden inside the room.
- Have students use their hands to demonstrate how a rift in the seafloor might look. Ask them to explain how their hands show the characteristics of the rift.

Literal. You have learned that *conclude* means to decide something or form an opinion based on information you have. What did scientists conclude about mid-ocean ridges?

- » Mid-ocean ridges form along huge cracks in Earth's crust.

Evaluative. What information on page 16 provides evidence for the scientists' conclusion?

» Maps revealed long chains of underwater mountains or mid-ocean ridges; these ridges have a rift or split that runs down their centers; rock samples taken from various distances from the rift show that the rocks farther away from the rift are older.

Check for Understanding

Some rocks on the seafloor are newer then others. Where are the newest rocks likely to be found?

» near rifts

pressure keeps building. Eventually the pressure gets too great. The stuck edges break free, causing the plates to jerk past each other.

Providing the Answers

The theory of plate tectonics answered many questions in geology. It explained how Wegener's Pangaea broke apart. It explained how the continents have been slowly rearranged over millions of years. The movement of the plates also explained mid-ocean ridges, deep ocean trenches, patterns in the locations of mountains, and many other features on Earth's surface. The theory has become the cornerstone of modern geology.

As plates move, interesting things happen. Most of the time, they happen incredibly slowly. Sometimes, though, the effects of plate movements are sudden and dramatic. Think earthquakes and volcanoes!

Core Conclusions

You may never have heard of the Danish scientist Inge Lehmann. Among seismologists, however, she is famous. Around 1900, scientists thought the earth had just three layers: an outer crust, a solid mantle, and a liquid core. Lehmann studied seismograph records of earthquakes. She analyzed how seismic waves changed as they traveled through Earth's interior. Lehmann collected thousands of records organized in boxes—there were no computers back then! She saw patterns in how seismic waves behaved as they moved through Earth. Lehmann concluded that Earth's core has two parts: a liquid outer core and a solid inner core. In 1936, she announced her findings and changed our view of Earth!

21

- Have students silently read the first paragraph under the heading "Providing the Answers."

  Evaluative. *Cornerstone* means foundation or an idea of basic importance that supports something. What does the author mean by the statement, "The theory has become the cornerstone of modern geology"?

  » Answers may vary but could include: plate tectonics is now considered a theory of basic importance to the area of study called geology; plate tectonics is the foundation that supports the study of geology, and the theory occupies an important place in the study of geology; the theory of plate tectonics is the basic idea that explains how and why the earth changes.

LESSON WRAP-UP (5 MIN.)

Note: Question 3 and Activity Page 3.1 relate to The Big Question of the chapter.

- Use the following question to discuss the chapter.

3. **Evaluative.** Why might the earth's mantle be the most important layer for scientists to study for understanding changes on the earth's surface?

   » Answers may vary but should include: the earth's mantle has three layers, the middle of which contains a slowly moving material. This material is what causes tectonic plates to slowly move over time, changing the earth's surface. Magma erupts from the mantle through cracks in the earth's crust, creating new crust around rifts along mid-ocean ridges. The new crust pushes old crust outward, resulting in seafloor spreading. In addition, the material in the mantle exerts enormous pressure on tectonic plates, slowly forcing them to move. Sometimes tectonic plates collide, crumpling their edges and pushing crust higher. Other times, one plate slides under another plate, which is called subduction. The mantle contains the slowly moving material that causes tectonic plates to move, which is an important feature of the earth, so studying the mantle is an important thing for scientists to do.

- Tell students they will take home Activity Page 3.1 to read and complete.

WORD WORK: *EXERT* (5 MIN.)

1. In the chapter you read, "As the material in the mantle slowly moves, it exerts enormous pressure on the overlying plates."
2. Say the word *exert* with me.
3. *Exert* means to cause a force to be felt or have an effect.
4. The backhoe had to exert a lot of force to lift and move the large boulder to a new location.
5. What are some other examples of exerting a lot of effort or force? Be sure to use the word *exert* in your response.

   » Answers will vary.

- If necessary, guide and/or rephrase students' responses to make complete sentences: "____ exerted a lot of effort to ____."

6. What part of speech is the word *exert*?

   » verb

Check for Understanding

Which sentence uses *exert* correctly: *She exerted plenty of effort to swim across the river* or *She did not have much exert when she walked to school this morning?*

» the first

- Use a Discussion activity for follow-up. Talk with your partner about a time when you, or someone you know, exerted a lot of force or effort to create an effect. Be sure to use the word *exert* in complete sentences as you discuss this with your partner.

Lesson 3: Close Reading

Writing

45M

Primary Focus: Students will write a detailed explanation of a simile. [L.4.5; W.4.2]

REVIEW SIMILES (5 MIN.)

4. Have students explain what a *simile* is.

» A simile is a literary device that compares things using *like* or *as*.

Activity Page 2.4

- Have students turn to Activity Page 2.4 and explain the similes they analyzed during the previous lesson, either to a partner or to the class as a whole. You may wish to have students read an explanation aloud without revealing the simile and have other students use the explanation to identify the original simile.

MODEL AN EXPLANATION OF A SIMILE (20 MIN.)

- Tell students you will model writing a more detailed explanation of a simile analyzed during the previous lesson. The explanation will expand upon the meaning of the simile.
- Explain that you will refer to Activity Page 2.4 to write a detailed explanation of the simile comparing continents to pieces of ice. The explanation will be in complete sentences.

5. Besides expressing a complete thought, what features do all sentences need to have?

    » a subject, predicate, capitalization, and punctuation

- Tell students you will begin your explanation by stating what the Reader says. Direct students to look at the "Simile from Text" column (What if continents were like enormous pieces of ice?).
- Write the first sentence of your explanation of the simile on the board/chart paper:
    - In the Reader, the author says Wegener wondered, "What if continents were like enormous pieces of ice?"
- Tell students the next sentence in your explanation should tell what two things the simile compares.

Check for Understanding

Direct students to look at the "What is the simile comparing?" column. Ask what two things are being compared.

» continents and pieces of ice in a drink

- Write the second sentence of your explanation on the board/chart paper:
    - This is a simile comparing continents to pieces of ice in a drink.
- Have students sketch a quick picture showing ice in a drink on one side and continents on the earth's surface on the other. Ask students to tell each other about their pictures.
- Tell students the third sentence in your explanation should provide information about the familiar idea or item that the geology concept is being compared to in the Reader. Direct students to look at the "What does the simile mean?" column (Ice floats in a drink, which is made with water, because ice is less dense than water.).
- Write the third sentence of your explanation on the board/chart paper:
    - We know that ice floats in a drink, which is made with water, because ice is less dense than water.
- Have students label their sketches so the ice is labeled "more dense" and the water is labeled "less dense." Ask students to do the same with the sketch of the continents, labeling the continents "less dense" and the earth below it "more dense."

Writing
Text Structure

Entering/Emerging
Work individually with students to help them identify the parts of a complete sentence. Have them name each part.

Transitioning/Expanding
Have students work in pairs to identify the parts of a complete sentence. Have them use a sentence to name each part.

Bridging
Have students work independently to identify the parts of a complete sentence. Have them use compound sentences to name the parts.

Support

Remind students that *dense* means thick or heavy. Ice floats in a drink that is made with water because ice is not as thick or heavy as water.

- Tell students the next part of your explanation should connect the familiar idea or item to the geology concept in the Reader. It should tell how the familiar idea or item has helped you better understand the concept in the Reader.
- Direct students to again look at the "What does the simile mean?" column. (The rocks that make up continents are less dense than the rocks on the ocean bottom, so Wegener wondered if continents could float over the rocks on the ocean bottom.)
- Write the next part of your explanation on the board/chart paper:
    - Thinking about ice floating in a drink helps us understand continents because the rocks that make up the continents are less dense than the rocks on the ocean bottom. Wegener wondered if continents could float above the ocean bottom like pieces of ice float in a drink.
- Tell students that the last sentence in your explanation should explain what we now know about the concept in the Reader.
- Write the last sentence of your explanation on the board/chart paper:
    - We now know that this was part of Wegener's hypothesis about continental drift.
- Once you have completed your explanation of the simile, it should appear on the board/chart paper as follows:
    - In the Reader, the author says Wegener wondered, "What if continents were like enormous pieces of ice?" This is a simile comparing continents to pieces of ice in a drink. We know that ice floats in a drink, which is made with water, because ice is less dense than water. Thinking about ice floating in a drink helps us understand continents because the rocks that make up the continents are less dense than the rocks on the ocean bottom. Wegener wondered if continents could float above the ocean bottom like pieces of ice float in a drink. We now know that this was part of Wegener's hypothesis about continental drift.

6. Ask students to explain the simile with reference to the sketches they drew.
    » Check students' answers.

Challenge

You may give students the option of elaborating on this explanation by using details to create a clear picture for readers.

DRAFT A DETAILED EXPLANATION OF A SIMILE (20 MIN.)

- Tell students that now they will draft their own detailed explanation of one of the other similes with a partner. Remind students that the explanation should expand upon the meaning of the simile.

- Assign partners and have students open their writing journals. Using your modeled explanation of a simile as a guide and Activity Page 2.4 as a reference, have students complete their own detailed explanation of a simile with a partner, focusing on one of the other similes analyzed during the previous lesson: an earthquake and a rock in water or a rift in mid-ocean ridges and a seam in a pants leg.
- Circulate and check in with students as they use Activity Page 2.4 to write complete sentences, providing support and guidance as needed.
- As time allows, encourage students to share their completed explanation of a simile aloud.

Check for Understanding

What two things are being compared?

» Answers will vary.

- **Feedback—**Provide reinforcing or corrective feedback about starting the explanation with the statement from the Reader, clearly naming the two things compared in the simile, and explaining how the simile helps them understand the geology concept from the Reader.
- Collect the drafted explanations of a simile to review and monitor student progress. Written feedback may include comments such as:
    - This clearly explains the purpose of the simile.
    - This identifies the two concepts compared in the simile. Is there more information you could add about how the two concepts are compared?

End Lesson

Support

You may wish to write sentence starters on the board/chart paper for each of the five sentences of the explanation, such as:
In the Reader ____, or, This is a simile comparing ____.

Challenge

Give students who are ready and able the opportunity to draft a detailed explanation individually instead of with a partner.

Challenge

Offer students the option of creating a simile related to a concept not discussed in the previous lesson, such as plate tectonics or subduction. Students should also draft a detailed explanation of the simile.

Lesson 3: Close Reading: Earth's Layers and Tectonic Plates

Take-Home Material

READING

- Have students take home Activity Page 3.1 to read to a family member to build fluency. Students should then complete the activity on the page.

Activity Page 3.1

LESSON

4

Earthquakes and Tsunamis

PRIMARY FOCUS OF LESSON

Reading
Students will explain what causes earthquakes, how scientists measure the intensity of earthquakes, and how faults and tsunamis relate to earthquakes. **[RI.4.1, RI.4.3, RI.4.8]**

Grammar
Students will practice using commas for dates, addresses, city and state, and items in a series. **[L.4.2]**

Morphology
Students will practice distinguishing between root words and words with the suffix *–ly*, and using those words correctly in sentences. **[L.4.4]**

Writing
Students will describe an informational pamphlet and identify a specific pamphlet's purpose and intended audience. **[W.4.8, W.4.9]**

FORMATIVE ASSESSMENT

Activity Page 3.1	**Excerpt from "Earth's Layers and Moving Plates"** Students use vocabulary from the text to complete a short passage. **[RI.4.1]**
Activity Page 4.1	**Vocabulary for "Earth's Shakes and Quakes"** Students learn essential vocabulary for the lesson. **[RI.4.1]**
Activity Page 4.2	**Excerpt from "Earth's Shakes and Quakes"** Students answer questions about a passage describing plate tectonics and its connection to earthquakes. **[RI.4.1]**
Activity Page 4.3	**Practice Commas** Students insert commas in sentences. **[L.4.2]**
Activity Page 4.4	***–ly* Suffix Meaning "in a ____ way"** Students identify the adverb or adjective that completes various sentences. **[L.4.4]**

LESSON AT A GLANCE

	Grouping	Time	Materials
Reading (45 min.)			
Review	Whole Group	5 min.	❑ Answer Key for Activity Page 3.1 ❑ Activity Pages 3.1, 4.1, 4.2 ❑ *The Changing Earth*
Introduce the Chapter	Whole Group	10 min.	
Read "Earth's Shakes and Quakes"	Whole Group	20 min.	
Lesson Wrap-Up	Whole Group	5 min.	
Word Work: *Fault*	Whole Group	5 min.	
Language (30 min.)			
Grammar: Practice Commas	Whole Group/ Partners	15 min.	❑ Commas Poster ❑ Activity Page 4.3
Morphology: Practice Suffix *-ly*	Whole Group/ Partners	15 min.	❑ Suffixes Poster ❑ Activity Page 4.4
Writing (15 min.)			
Introduce an Informational Pamphlet	Whole Group	15 min.	❑ Earthquake Pamphlet ❑ *The Changing Earth*
Take-Home Material			
Reading; Grammar; Morphology			❑ Activity Pages 4.2–4.4

ADVANCE PREPARATION

Reading

Note: You may access a digital version of The Big Question in the digital components for this unit.

- Prepare a word card for each of the following words: *seismograph, autograph, photograph, seismometer, thermometer, speedometer*.

Grammar

- Write the following examples on the board/chart paper.

1. My favorite summer activities are swimming in the pool picking peaches and going to the beach.
2. Alfred Wegener was born on November 1, 1880.
3. 60 E. Broadway
   Bloomington MN 55425

- Determine student pairs for completing the first portion of Activity Page 4.3.

Morphology

- Prepare word cards with the following word pairs: *sure/unsure, science/scientist, agree/disagree, possible/impossible, play/player, easy/easily*

Writing

- Create an Earthquake Pamphlet to display during the writing lesson, or access a digital version in the digital components for this unit.

Start Lesson

Lesson 4: Earthquakes and Tsunamis

Reading

45M

Primary Focus: Students will explain what causes earthquakes, how scientists measure the intensity of earthquakes, and how faults and tsunamis relate to earthquakes. **[RI.4.1, RI.4.3, RI.4.8]**

REVIEW (5 MIN.)

- Using the Answer Key at the back of this Teacher Guide, review student responses to Activity Page 3.1, which was assigned for homework in the previous reading lesson.

- Remind students that they read about tectonic plates in the previous lesson and for homework.

4. What does the theory of plate tectonics state?

    » The theory of plate tectonics states that huge, rocky slabs of Earth's crust and the top of the mantle are broken up into sections called plates. Tectonic plates fit tightly together and slowly move across Earth's surface.

- Remind students that at the end of Activity Page 3.1, Sam said:

    ◦ "Hmmm . . . I wonder if earthquakes have anything to do with moving tectonic plates?"

5. Ask students what they think about what Sam said.

    » Answers may vary. Students are not expected to know the correct answer. This question is meant to get students thinking about whether earthquakes and moving tectonic plates are related, and if so, how. Explain that students will find out the answer in this reading lesson.

INTRODUCE THE CHAPTER (10 MIN.)

- Tell students they will read Chapter 3, "Earth's Shakes and Quakes."
- Have students turn to the table of contents, locate the chapter, and turn to the first page of the chapter.
- Preview the core vocabulary words before reading the chapter.

6. Which vocabulary word will you encounter first in this chapter?

    » *Eyewitness*

- Have students find *eyewitness* on page 22 of the Reader. Remind students that each vocabulary word is bolded the first time it appears in the chapter.
- Review that the glossary contains definitions of all the vocabulary words in this Reader. Have students refer to the glossary at the back of the Reader and locate *eyewitness*. Have a student read the definition.
- Explain the following:
    ◦ the part of speech
    ◦ alternate forms of the word
- Have students reference Activity Page 4.1 while you read each word and its meaning.

Activity Page 4.1

eyewitness, n. a person who has seen something happen and is able to describe it (22)

experiment, n. a scientific test to try out something in order to learn about it (24)

fault, n. a crack in Earth's crust (faults) (24)

heave, v. 1. to move up and down over and over; 2. to lift, pull, push, or throw with a lot of effort (24)

trigger, v. to cause something to start or happen (triggered) (25)

pinpoint, v. to figure out the exact location of something (27)

magnitude, n. an earthquake's strength (28)

aftershock, n. a smaller, weaker earthquake that often follows a main earthquake event (aftershocks) (29)

tsunami, n. a gigantic wave of seawater caused by an earthquake in oceanic crust (tsunamis) (30)

surge, v. to move forward quickly, suddenly, and with force (surges) (30)

Vocabulary Chart for Chapter 3 "Earth's Shakes and Quakes"		
Vocabulary Type	**Tier 3 Domain-Specific Words**	**Tier 2 General Academic Words**
Core Vocabulary	fault magnitude aftershock tsunami	eyewitness experiment heave trigger pinpoint surge
Spanish Cognates for Core Vocabulary	magnitud tsunami	experimento
Multiple-Meaning Core Vocabulary Words	fault magnitude	heave
Sayings and Phrases	lost their lives	

- Have one student read The Big Question at the beginning of the chapter. Ensure students understand the meaning of The Big Question before reading the chapter.
    - What happens beneath Earth's surface to cause earthquakes?

Chapter 3

Earth's Shakes and Quakes

THE BIG QUESTION
What happens beneath Earth's surface to cause earthquakes?

Italian writer Francesco Petrarch penned the following **eyewitness** account in the Middle Ages. Can you guess what he was writing about?

"The floor trembled under my feet; when the books crashed into each other and fell down I was frightened and hurried to leave the room. Outside I saw the servants and many other people running anxiously to and fro. All faces were pale."

Francesco Petrarch

If you said an earthquake, you're correct! People in northern Italy had good reason to be pale and frightened on a winter's day in 1348 CE. On that day, a large earthquake struck. Thousands of people lost their lives.

Earthquakes are violent natural disasters that strike without warning. Suddenly, the ground begins to shake. Furniture topples,

22

READ "EARTH'S SHAKES AND QUAKES" (20 MIN.)

Pronunciation Table	
Word	**CK Code**
Francesco Petrarch	/fran*ches*koe/ /pe*trark/

- Have students read pages 22 and 23 silently.

  Inferential. What is a synonym for the word *penned* in the first sentence?

  » *Wrote*

Literal. How does the author describe earthquakes here?

» The author describes earthquakes as violent natural disasters that strike without warning.

objects tumble from shelves, and buildings may even collapse. In 1348 CE, people had no idea what caused earthquakes. Today we know that earthquakes are the result of powerful natural forces at work in Earth's crust and mantle.

As you read in Chapter 2, scientists developed the theory of plate tectonics in the 1960s. The theory explains how Earth's surface and interior change over very long periods of time. Some plates are pulling apart at their boundaries, other plates are colliding, and still others are sliding past each other. A lot happens at plate boundaries, including most earthquakes. In fact, one of the easiest ways to locate plate boundaries is to determine where earthquakes are occurring!

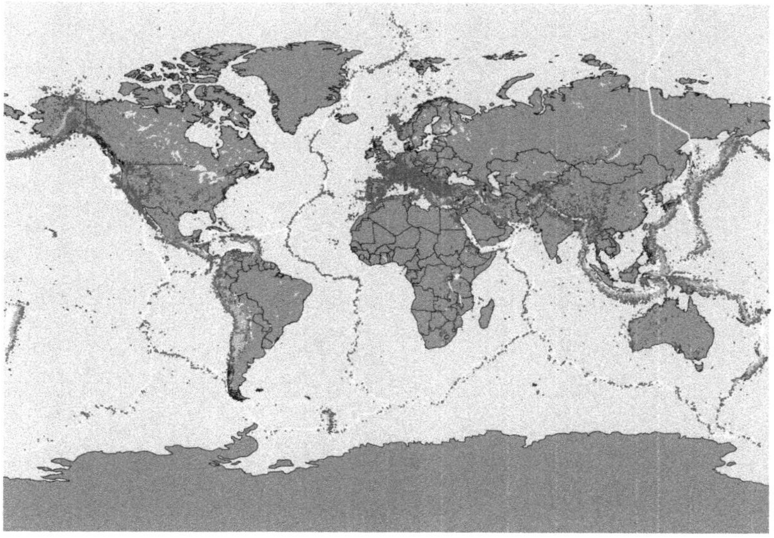

Locations of plate boundaries and past earthquake epicenters

23

Inferential. Why are plate boundaries important?

» Plate boundaries are important because of all the movement happening at them. At plate boundaries, some plates are pulling apart, some are colliding, and some are sliding past each other; most earthquakes happen at these boundaries.

- Have students use their hands to model the various ways plates act at their boundaries.

Support

Remind students that the *crust* is the outside layer of the earth, and the *mantle*, which is made up of very hot rock, is underneath it.

Check for Understanding

How can scientists determine where plate boundaries are located?

» They can look for places where earthquakes are common.

Forces and Faults

Try a little **experiment**. Extend your arms out in front of you parallel to the floor and put your hands together. Keep your palms and fingers flat against each other. Now start pressing your hands together. Gradually increase the pressure. When you can't press any harder, let your right hand quickly slide forward. That sudden slipping is what happens at a **fault**.

A fault is a fracture, or crack, in Earth's crust. Most faults occur along the boundaries of tectonic plates. As plates move, huge rough blocks of rock along either side of a fault get stuck against each other. Beneath the plates, however, material in the mantle keeps moving. This material exerts more and more pressure on the plates to also keep moving. Pressure builds along the stuck edges of the fault. Think of your hands as these edges, pressing harder and harder together. The pressure builds until the stuck blocks of rock suddenly break and slip past one another. As they do, a tremendous burst of energy is released. How much energy? Well, all the energy that accumulated in the rocks during the time they were stuck and couldn't move.

A fault in Iceland

The Pacific Plate is Earth's largest tectonic plate. It lies beneath the Pacific Ocean. Imagine how much energy it takes to move that gigantic rocky plate plus all the water on top of it. Then imagine all that energy being released at a fault in just a moment. Such a colossal burst of energy travels outward from the fault in all directions as seismic waves. Seismic waves make the ground **heave** and shake. This violent shaking is what we call an earthquake.

24

- Read the first paragraph aloud.
- Lead students through the experiment, demonstrating it for them as necessary. Have students describe in their own words what they notice and feel, and have them relate it to what might happen at a fault.
- Have students read the rest of page 24 and page 25 silently.

Inferential. What role do faults play in earthquakes?

» Faults are the places where earthquakes originate, or start from. When blocks of rock move against each other at a fault, a huge amount of built-up pressure is released as energy, traveling in all directions as seismic waves. Seismic waves shake the ground, and this event is called an earthquake.

Support

What are faults and where do they occur?

» Faults are cracks in Earth's crust. Most faults occur along the boundaries of tectonic plates.

Support

What is an earthquake?

» An earthquake is the shaking of the ground caused by seismic waves.

San Andreas Fault

In the United States, one of the most famous faults is the San Andreas Fault in California. It lies along the boundary between two tectonic plates that are slowly moving past each other. The movement, however, is far from steady. For years at a time, blocks of rock bordering the San Andreas Fault stay stuck. Pressure slowly builds. Then—wham!—they slip and **trigger** an earthquake. The 1906 San Francisco earthquake was one of the worst in American history. The sudden slip that triggered it was huge. It caused rocks on either side of the fault to move more than 20 feet in just seconds!

Effects of the 1906 San Francisco earthquake

25

Literal. What effects of the 1906 San Francisco earthquake do you see in the image on page 25?

» The image on page 25 shows that a fence that had once been joined in a line was split apart, the pieces becoming separated by several feet. The image supports the statement from the text, "It caused rocks on either side of the fault to move more than 20 feet in just seconds!"

Check for Understanding

Have students demonstrate with their hands what happened along the San Andreas Fault in the years before 1906, and what happened in 1906.

» before 1906: no movement; in 1906: sudden forceful movement

Shake, Heave, Sway, and Lurch

All earthquakes begin with huge blocks of rock moving along faults. The place in Earth's crust where this happens is an earthquake's **focus**. Think of it as the earthquake's heart, the source of seismic waves. The focus may be deep in the crust or close to the surface.

The **epicenter** is the point on Earth's surface directly above an earthquake's focus. Some kinds of seismic waves produced by earthquakes travel deep into Earth's interior. Surface waves, however, are seismic waves that are first noticeable at the epicenter. During an earthquake, surface waves are what make the ground shake, heave, sway, and lurch. They are the cause of most earthquake damage.

In Chapter 2, you read about seismographs, which scientists use to record the shaking of Earth's surface caused by seismic waves. The time it takes for seismic waves to reach a seismograph is important in determining where the earthquake occurred. The longer that seismic waves take to reach a seismograph, the farther away the earthquake is from the seismograph.

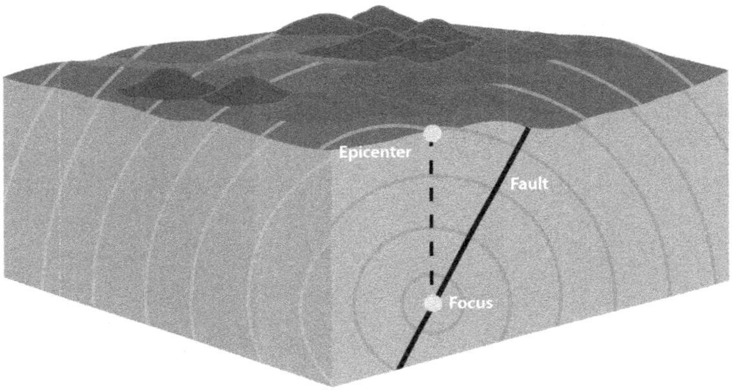

The place in Earth's crust where an earthquake begins is its focus. Its epicenter is the point on Earth's surface directly above the focus.

26

Support

What is an earthquake's focus?

» An earthquake's focus is the place in Earth's crust where blocks of rock move along a fault. It is also the place from which seismic waves move outward.

- Have students read pages 26 and 27 silently.

Inferential. Why do you think the author compares an earthquake's focus to a heart?

» The author compares the earthquake's focus to a heart as a way of showing that the focus is an important part of the earthquake. The focus is the source of the earthquake, where it begins. The author is showing that, in the same way a heart can be considered the source of life in the body, the earthquake's focus is the source of the earthquake in the earth.

- Ask students to explain the diagram on the bottom of page 26 to a partner.

Check for Understanding

How are the focus and the epicenter of an earthquake related?

» The epicenter is the point directly above the focus on the earth's surface.

Reading for information
Reading Closely

Entering/Emerging
Display the word cards for *seismograph*, *autograph*, and *photograph*. Explain the meanings of the words and review that *graph* means "write." Repeat with *seismometer*, *thermometer*, and *speedometer*, explaining that *meter* means "measure."

Transitioning/Expanding
Read and define the six words above, pointing out and explaining the roots *graph* and *meter*. Ask students to name the words with the root meaning "write" and the words with the root meaning "measure."

Bridging
Read and define the six words above, pointing out and explaining the roots. Have students use each word in a sentence.

Seismographs: Now and Then

A modern seismograph, also called a seismometer, records the shaking of Earth's surface caused by seismic waves. A **seismogram** is the record a seismograph makes. A seismogram shows seismic waves as jagged up-and-down lines. Scientists compare multiple seismograms in order to **pinpoint** an earthquake's epicenter.

Modern seismograph

Zhang Heng, a Chinese scientist, invented the first-known seismograph around 132 CE. It didn't look anything like a modern seismograph. It was shaped like a large vase. The vase had eight dragons around the outside, each looking downward and holding a ball loosely in its mouth. Below the eight dragons were open-mouthed frogs. When an earthquake struck, the balls fell into the frogs' mouths below. Depending on which balls fell, it was possible to estimate the distance and direction to the earthquake's source.

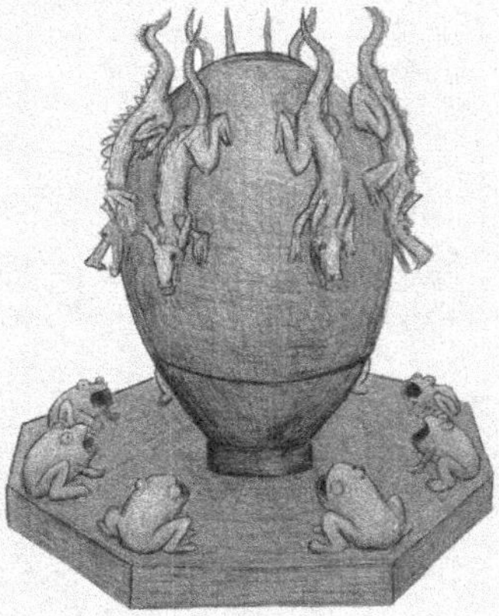
First-known seismograph

27

Evaluative. Why do scientists compare multiple seismograms to determine an earthquake's epicenter?

» Scientists compare multiple seismograms to look for patterns that help them determine how far the earthquake is from each seismograph. Multiple seismograms can provide information about an earthquake from seismographs at different distances from the potential epicenter. Scientists can look at patterns across seismograms to help them pinpoint an earthquake's epicenter, or the point on Earth's surface directly above the earthquake's focus or source.

Inferential. How are the first seismograph and the modern seismograph similar? You may wish to have students create a chart or Venn diagram to show the similarities, in addition to describing them orally.

» The two are similar in that they both were created to help people determine where earthquakes occur. The first seismograph was used to help estimate the distance and direction to an earthquake's source. The modern seismograph is used to help pinpoint an earthquake's epicenter.

Measuring an Earthquake's Strength

Scientists also use seismographs to measure an earthquake's strength, or **magnitude**. During a small earthquake, Earth's surface may shake only a little. The seismogram shows these relatively low-energy seismic waves as little wiggles. During a big earthquake, Earth's surface shakes a lot harder. The seismogram shows these high-energy waves as big zigzags.

The Richter scale is another way scientists measure an earthquake's magnitude. The Richter scale assigns a number to an earthquake based on the largest seismic wave recorded for that earthquake. The higher the Richter scale number, the stronger the earthquake. For example, a magnitude 5.0 earthquake on the Richter scale causes 10 times as much ground shaking as a magnitude 4.0 earthquake. A magnitude 6.0 earthquake causes 10 times more shaking than a 5.0, and so on.

Damage caused by earthquakes

28

Pronunciation Table	
Word	**CK Code**
Richter	/rik*ter/

- Have students read pages 28 and 29 silently.

Literal. What tool do scientists use to measure the intensity of earthquakes? What scale do they use to report the measurement?

» Scientists measure the intensity of earthquakes using seismographs and report the results using the Richter scale.

The Modified Mercalli Intensity Scale also uses numbers to measure earthquake strength. The numbers are based on survivors' descriptions and the amount of earthquake damage. The higher the number, the stronger the earthquake. The Mercalli scale is less scientific than the Richter scale, as few people describe events in the same way.

Pressure along faults can build up for years, even centuries. When blocks of rock along a fault finally move, the resulting earthquake happens very quickly. Most earthquakes last just a few seconds. Still, the trouble may not be over after the ground stops shaking. Large earthquakes are often followed by **aftershocks**. Aftershocks are like mini-earthquakes. They are usually smaller and weaker than the main earthquake event. Aftershocks happen as blocks of rock along the newly slipped fault settle into place.

Modified Mercalli Scale		Richter Scale	
I	Felt by almost no one	2.5	Generally not felt but recorded on seismometers
II	Felt by very few people		
III	Noticed by many, but they often do not realize it is an earthquake.	3.5	Felt by many people
IV	Felt indoors by many; feels like a truck has struck the building.		
V	Felt by nearly everyone; many people awakened. Swaying trees and poles may be observed.		
VI	Felt by all; many people run outdoors. Furniture moved; slight damage occurs.	4.5	Some local damage may occur.
VII	Everyone runs outdoors. Poorly built structures considerably damaged; slight damage elsewhere.		
VIII	Specially designed structures damaged slightly; others collapse.	6.0	A destructive earthquake
IX	All buildings considerably damaged; many shift off foundations. Noticeable cracks in ground.		
X	Many structures destroyed. Ground is badly cracked.	7.0	A major earthquake
XI	Almost all structures fall. Very wide cracks in ground.		
XII	Total destruction. Waves seen on ground surfaces; objects are tumbled and tossed.	8.0 and up	Great earthquakes

The Mercalli scale is less scientific than the Richter scale.

29

Literal. What is the difference between an earthquake and an aftershock?

» An earthquake is what happens when blocks of rock at a fault finally give way and a great amount of pressure is released. An aftershock is what happens when blocks of rock along the newly slipped fault settle into place. An aftershock is usually smaller and weaker than the main earthquake.

Challenge

Discuss with students the similarities and differences between the Modified Mercalli scale and the Richter scale, as explained in the chart on page 29.

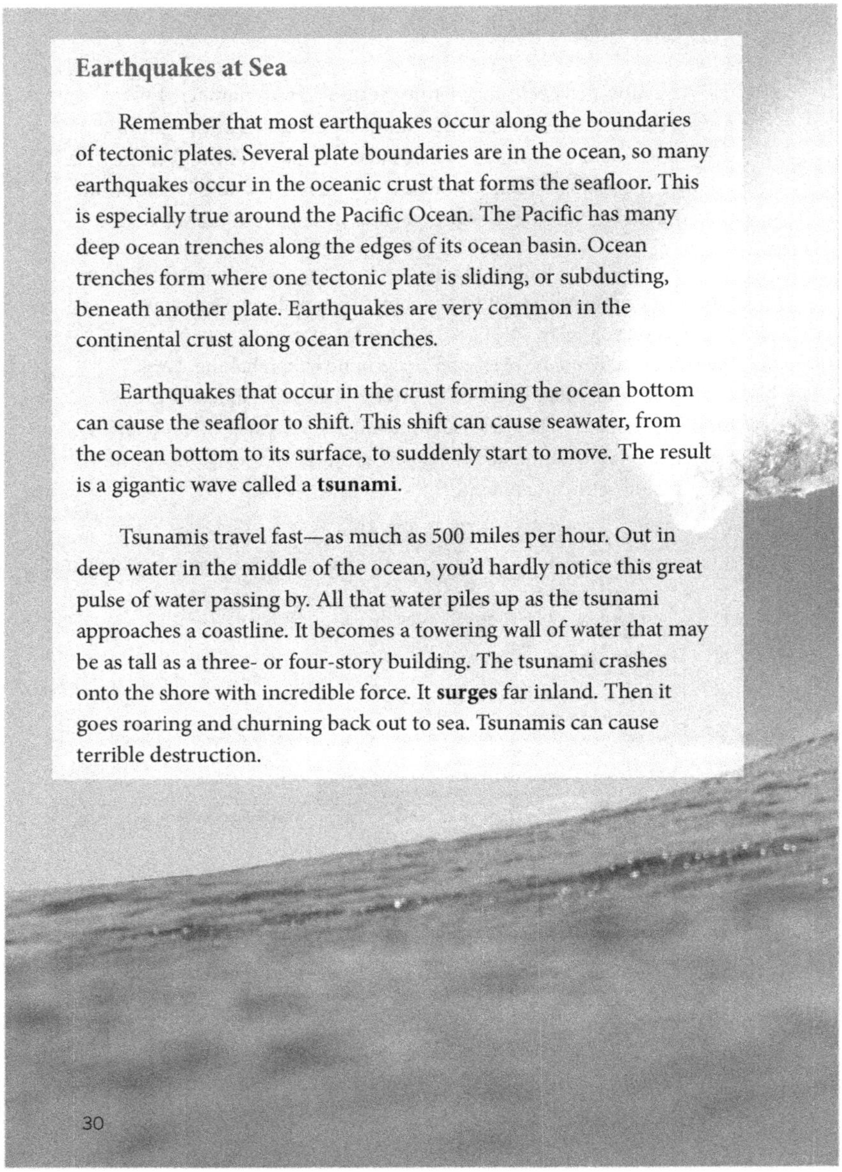

Earthquakes at Sea

Remember that most earthquakes occur along the boundaries of tectonic plates. Several plate boundaries are in the ocean, so many earthquakes occur in the oceanic crust that forms the seafloor. This is especially true around the Pacific Ocean. The Pacific has many deep ocean trenches along the edges of its ocean basin. Ocean trenches form where one tectonic plate is sliding, or subducting, beneath another plate. Earthquakes are very common in the continental crust along ocean trenches.

Earthquakes that occur in the crust forming the ocean bottom can cause the seafloor to shift. This shift can cause seawater, from the ocean bottom to its surface, to suddenly start to move. The result is a gigantic wave called a **tsunami**.

Tsunamis travel fast—as much as 500 miles per hour. Out in deep water in the middle of the ocean, you'd hardly notice this great pulse of water passing by. All that water piles up as the tsunami approaches a coastline. It becomes a towering wall of water that may be as tall as a three- or four-story building. The tsunami crashes onto the shore with incredible force. It **surges** far inland. Then it goes roaring and churning back out to sea. Tsunamis can cause terrible destruction.

30

Pronunciation Table	
Word	**CK Code**
tsunami	/soo*no*mee/

Support

Review with students that a tsunami is a gigantic wave of seawater. It forms as a result of an earthquake in the oceanic crust that forms the seafloor, which causes the seafloor to shift.

- Have students read page 30 silently.

Inferential. How are earthquakes and tsunamis connected?

» An earthquake in the ocean triggers a tsunami. A tsunami forms as a result of the seafloor shifting after an earthquake in the oceanic crust that forms the seafloor.

LESSON WRAP-UP (5 MIN.)

Note: Question 7 relates to The Big Question of the chapter.

- Use the following questions to discuss the chapter.

7. **Literal.** What happens beneath Earth's surface to cause earthquakes?

    » At faults, huge blocks of rock get stuck against each other. Beneath Earth's surface, material in the mantle moves beneath the stuck rocks. This causes pressure to build. When the pressure builds to the point that the rocks break and slip past one another, energy is suddenly released. The energy travels through the earth as seismic waves. These waves cause an earthquake, which is evident when the ground shakes.

8. **Evaluative.** On Activity Page 3.1, Sam asked the question, "Hmmm . . . I wonder if earthquakes have anything to do with moving tectonic plates?" How would you respond to Sam's question?"

    » Answers may vary but should note that earthquakes do have something to do with moving tectonic plates. As plates move, huge blocks of rock along the sides of a fault get stuck against each other. Material in the mantle keeps moving beneath the plates and exerts more and more pressure on the plates to also keep moving. Pressure builds along the stuck edges of the fault until the stuck blocks of rocks suddenly break and slip past one another. As they slip past one another, they release a tremendous amount of energy. This energy travels out as seismic waves, which make the ground heave and shake. This is an earthquake.

- Have students take home Activity Page 4.2 to read and complete for homework.

WORD WORK: *FAULT* (5 MIN.)

1. In the chapter you read, "That sudden slipping is what happens at a fault."
2. Say the word *fault* with me.
3. *Fault* means "a crack in Earth's crust."
4. An earthquake occurs when a huge block of rock moves along a fault.
5. What are some words the author uses that help you understand the meaning of the word *fault* in this context? Be sure to use the word *fault* in your response.
    - » Answers will vary. If necessary, guide and/or rephrase students' responses to make complete sentences: "When the author uses the word *fault* together with the word *slipping*, it makes me think that something is happening at a crack in Earth's crust" or "When the author uses the phrase *happens at a fault*, it makes me think that something is occurring at a particular place."
6. What part of speech is the word *fault*?
    - » noun

- Use a Multiple-Meaning Word activity for follow-up. Tell students the word *fault* has multiple meanings. Share the following with students.
    - Meaning 1: a crack in Earth's crust
    - Meaning 2: responsibility for wrongdoing
- I am going to read several sentences. Listen to the context, or the text surrounding *fault* in the sentence, for clues as to which meaning is being used. When you think a sentence is an example of Meaning 1, hold up one finger. When you think a sentence is an example of Meaning 2, hold up two fingers.

1. It was my fault that we missed the train because I overslept.
    - » 2
2. One of the most famous faults in America is the San Andreas Fault in California.
    - » 1
3. She blamed herself for the dog running away, but it really wasn't anyone's fault.
    - » 2

4. His mother punished him for breaking a glass even though he said it was his brother's fault.

   » 2

5. Most faults occur along the boundaries of tectonic plates.

   » 1

6. When energy is released at a fault, it triggers an earthquake.

   » 1

Lesson 4: Earthquakes and Tsunamis

Language

30M

GRAMMAR: PRACTICE COMMAS (15 MIN.)

Primary Focus: Students will practice using commas for dates, addresses, city and state, and items in a series. **[L.4.2]**

Practice Commas

- Refer to the Commas Poster and read it with students.
- Refer to the three examples you prepared in advance.
    - My favorite summer activities are swimming in the pool picking peaches and going to the beach.
    - Alfred Wegener was born on November 1, 1880.
    - 60 E. Broadway
Bloomington MN 55425
- Read each example aloud while students follow along. Use Think-Pair-Share. Have students decide where the comma or commas should be placed in each example. Then insert the commas in the correct locations.
    - My favorite summer activities are swimming in the pool, picking peaches, and going to the beach.
    - Alfred Wegener was born on November 1, 1880.
    - 60 E. Broadway
Bloomington, MN 55425

Language
Reading closely

Entering/Emerging
Help students associate pauses in lists with commas. Read the second sentence on Activity Page 4.3 with students, emphasizing the pauses. Have them repeat. Read it again, having students draw commas in the air when you pause.

Transitioning/Expanding
Have students read the second sentence on Activity Page 4.3 aloud chorally, drawing commas in the air to emphasize the pauses.

Bridging
Have students read the second sentence on Activity Page 4.3 aloud individually, drawing commas in the air to emphasize the pauses.

Check for Understanding

Ask students why there should be a comma after *Bloomington*.

» The comma separates the city (*Bloomington*) from the state (*Minnesota*).

Activity Page 4.3

- Have students turn to Activity Page 4.3.
- Pair students to work together to complete the first portion of Activity Page 4.3.
- Once students have completed the first portion of Activity Page 4.3, review the correct answers as a whole group.
- Still working in pairs, have students come up with one sentence that contains a date, an address, a city and state, or items in a series. Be sure the sentences include commas in the appropriate places.
- Select a few pairs to share their sentences. As time allows, have them write their sentences on the board/chart paper. Alternatively, have them dictate their sentences as you write them on the board/chart paper.
- Have students complete the second portion of Activity Page 4.3 for homework.

Language
Prefixes and suffixes

Entering/Emerging
Read the word cards you prepared earlier. Help students understand the meaning of each word, including the prefix or suffix. Have students identify words with prefixes and words with suffixes.

Transitioning/Expanding
Help students identify the meanings of the word pairs on the word cards. Ask them which have prefixes and which have suffixes.

Bridging
Help students identify the meanings of the base words on the word cards. Help them determine the meanings with prefixes and suffixes attached.

MORPHOLOGY: PRACTICE SUFFIX *-LY* (15 MIN.)

Primary Focus: Students will have additional practice distinguishing between root words and words with the suffix *–ly*, and using those words correctly in sentences. **[L.4.4]**

Practice Suffix *–ly*

- Refer to the Suffixes Poster from the previous lesson and review the definition of *suffix*.
- Remind students that the suffix *–ly* means "in a ____ way," with the blank being the word to which *–ly* is added. When *–ly* is added to the end of an adjective, the word becomes an adverb.
- Remind students that adverbs with *–ly* describe verbs, specifically how a verb happens.
- Tell students you will give them two word choices. Then you will read a sentence with a blank and they must decide which word choice is most appropriate in the blank.

- Practice with the following example:
    - *Easy* or *easily?* The crowd at the party was so large that I could ____ leave early without anyone noticing.

9. Ask students if *easy* or *easily* would be most appropriate in the blank.

    » *Easily*, because it describes how the verb *leave* happens.

- Continue in this manner with the following examples:
    - *Speedy* or *speedily?* My grandmother's farm animals move ____ to the barn when they know it's feeding time. (*speedily*)
    - *Careful* or *carefully?* My hands were full, so I was ____ to avoid dropping everything. (*careful*)

Check for Understanding

Loud or *loudly?* When my sister screamed ____, my mom sent her to her room.

» loudly

- *Accidental* or *accidentally?* He tripped me, but it was ____, so I wasn't upset with him. (*accidental*)
- *Temporary* or *temporarily?* After we found out our house had mold, we had to stay in a hotel ____, until the house could be cleaned. (*temporarily*)

- In the time remaining, have students think of and share sentences that correctly use one of the root words or affixed words. (Answers will vary.)
- Have students turn to Activity Page 4.4. Briefly review the directions and complete the first question as a class. Tell students to complete the rest of the activity page for homework.

Activity Page 4.4

Lesson 4: Earthquakes and Tsunamis

Writing

15M

Primary Focus: Students will describe an informational pamphlet and identify a specific pamphlet's purpose and intended audience. **[W.4.8, W.4.9]**

INTRODUCE AN INFORMATIONAL PAMPHLET (15 MIN.)

- Tell students that today they will learn about writing in a particular format and for a particular audience.
- Explain that *format* is the design and arrangement of something. *Audience* means "the person or group of people who read a particular piece of writing." The *intended audience* is the person or group of people you hope will read your finished piece of writing. When writing, it is important to keep the audience in mind.
- In this lesson the format will be an informational pamphlet.

1. Ask students if they know what a pamphlet is and to tell where they have seen one before.

    » A pamphlet is a small, thin booklet, flier, or handout; pamphlets can be found in places like museums, doctors' offices, and some kinds of stores.

- Explain or elicit that a pamphlet often provides information on a particular topic. A pamphlet sometimes answers frequently asked questions, or questions that different people commonly ask about a topic.
- Explain that the audience of a pamphlet is generally people who do not know very much about the particular topic presented in the pamphlet. The purpose of the pamphlet is to inform the audience about the topic presented.
- Display the Earthquake Pamphlet you prepared in advance.
- Explain that this pamphlet was created to provide more information about earthquakes. It is meant to answer common questions that people might have about them.
- Ask a different student to read each question and answer aloud.

2. Who might be the audience for this particular pamphlet?

    » Answers may vary but could include people who recently experienced an earthquake; people who moved to an area where earthquakes happen often; people who want to know more about earthquakes in general.

- Explain that the facts included in the pamphlet can be found in *The Changing Earth*. For example, the question, "How does tectonic plate movement cause an earthquake?" is answered with information on page 24. The text says, "As plates move, huge rough blocks of rock along either side of a fault get stuck against each other. Beneath the plates, however, material in the mantle keeps moving. Pressure builds along the stuck edges of the fault . . . The pressure builds until the stuck blocks of rock suddenly break and slip past one another. As they do, a tremendous burst of energy is released. How much?—all the energy that accumulated in the rocks during the time they were stuck and couldn't move." In the pamphlet, the facts from the text are rephrased to appeal to, or be interesting to, the intended audience.

Wrap-Up

- Call on students to summarize what *format* and *audience* mean. Call on a student to summarize what a pamphlet is.
- Explain that in the next writing lesson, students will write their own pamphlet about tsunamis.

End Lesson

Lesson 4: Earthquakes and Tsunamis

Take-Home Material

READING; GRAMMAR; MORPHOLOGY

Activity Pages 4.2–4.4

- Have students take home Activity Pages 4.2–4.4 to read and complete for homework.

LESSON

5

Close Reading: Earthquakes and Tsunamis

PRIMARY FOCUS OF LESSON

Reading

Students will describe key causes and effects of earthquakes, including the role faults play in earthquakes and the relationship between tsunamis and earthquakes. **[RI.4.1, RI.4.2, RI.4.3]**

Writing

Students will use their paraphrased notes to draft an informational pamphlet about tsunamis. **[W.4.8, W.4.9]**

FORMATIVE ASSESSMENT

Activity Page 1.3	**Evidence Collector's Chart** Students look in the text for evidence of geological events. **[RI.4.1]**
Activity Page 1.4	**Evidence of Changes on Earth** Students look in the text for evidence of geological events. **[RI.4.1]**
Activity Page 4.2	**Excerpt from "Earth's Shakes and Quakes"** Students answer questions about a passage describing plate tectonics and its connection to earthquakes. **[RI.4.1]**
Activity Page 5.1	**"Earth's Shakes and Quakes"** Students answer questions from the text and identify the source page for each piece of information. **[RI.4.1]**
Activity Page 5.2	**Take Notes on Tsunamis** Students paraphrase information in the text regarding tsunamis. **[W.4.8]**
Activity Page 5.3	**Tsunami Pamphlet** Students compose answers to questions about tsunamis. **[W.4.9]**

LESSON AT A GLANCE

	Grouping	Time	Materials
Reading (45 min.)			
Review	Whole Group	5 min.	❏ Answer Key for Activity Page 4.2 ❏ Activity Pages 1.3, 1.4, 4.2, 5.1 ❏ *The Changing Earth* ❏ Evidence Collector's Chart ❏ Scissors ❏ Glue
Review the Chapter	Whole Group	5 min.	
Read "Earth's Shakes and Quakes"	Small Groups	20 min.	
Lesson Wrap-Up	Whole Group	10 min.	
Word Work: *Trigger*	Whole Group	5 min.	
Writing (45 min.)			
Take Notes	Whole Group	25 min.	❏ *The Changing Earth* ❏ Activity Pages 5.2, 5.3 ❏ Earthquake Pamphlet
Draft an Informational Pamphlet	Independent	20 min.	

ADVANCE PREPARATION

Reading

Note: You may access a digital version of The Big Question in the digital components for this unit.

- Display the Evidence Collector's Chart from Lesson 1.

Writing

- You may want to display the Earthquake Pamphlet from Lesson 4 for students to use as a guide while writing their own pamphlet about tsunamis.

Fluency (optional)

- If students were assigned a selection from the Fluency Supplement, determine which students will read the selection aloud and when.

Language

Grammar; Morphology

- Collect Activity Pages 4.3 and 4.4 to review and grade, as there are no grammar or morphology lessons today.

Start Lesson

Lesson 5: Close Reading: Earthquakes and Tsunamis

Reading

45M

Primary Focus: Reading: Students will describe key causes and effects of earthquakes, including the role faults play in earthquakes and the relationship between tsunamis and earthquakes. **[RI.4.1, RI.4.2, RI.4.3]**

REVIEW (5 MIN.)

- Using the Answer Key at the back of this Teacher Guide, review student responses to Activity Page 4.2, which was assigned for homework. You may wish to have students work in pairs to check and compare each other's answers.

REVIEW THE CHAPTER (5 MIN.)

- Tell students they will reread Chapter 3, "Earth's Shakes and Quakes."
- Have students turn to the table of contents, locate the chapter, and then turn to the first page of the chapter.
- You may wish to review the following vocabulary words before you reread the chapter. Consider having one student name a word and then choose another student to give the definition; the student who successfully gives the definition then gets to select the next word and choose a classmate to give the definition.

eyewitness, n. a person who has seen something happen and is able to describe it (22)

experiment, n. a scientific test to try out something in order to learn about it (24)

fault, n. a crack in Earth's crust (faults) (24)

heave, v. 1. to move up and down over and over; 2. to lift, pull, push, or throw with a lot of effort (24)

trigger, v. to cause something to start or happen (triggered) (25)

pinpoint, v. to figure out the exact location of something (27)

magnitude, n. an earthquake's strength (28)

aftershock, n. a smaller, weaker earthquake that often follows a main earthquake event (aftershocks) (29)

tsunami, n. a gigantic wave of seawater caused by an earthquake in oceanic crust (tsunamis) (30)

surge, v. to move forward quickly, suddenly, and with force (surges) (30)

1. If you forget the meaning of a word in the chapter, what can you do?
    » Look it up in the glossary or a dictionary.

- Have one student read The Big Question at the beginning of the chapter. Ensure students understand the meaning of The Big Question before reading the chapter.
    - What happens beneath Earth's surface to cause earthquakes?

Activity Page 5.1

- Before reading the chapter, divide students into two groups using the following guidelines:
  - Small Group 1: This group should include students who need extra scaffolding and support to read and comprehend the text. Use the guided reading supports to guide students through reading the text. This is an excellent time to make notes in your anecdotal records. Students may complete Activity Page 5.1 with your support during reading.
  - Small Group 2: This group should include students who are capable of reading and comprehending text without guided support. These students may work as a small group, in pairs, or independently to read the chapter, discuss it with others in Small Group 2, and then complete Activity Page 5.1. Make arrangements to check that students in Small Group 2 have answered the questions on Activity Page 5.1 correctly.

READ "EARTH'S SHAKES AND QUAKES" (20 MIN.)

- The following guided reading supports are intended for use with Small Group 1.

Pronunciation Table

Word	CK Code
Francesco Petrarch	/fran*ches*koe/ /pe*trark/

Chapter 3

Earth's Shakes and Quakes

THE BIG QUESTION
What happens beneath Earth's surface to cause earthquakes?

Italian writer Francesco Petrarch penned the following **eyewitness** account in the Middle Ages. Can you guess what he was writing about?

"The floor trembled under my feet; when the books crashed into each other and fell down I was frightened and hurried to leave the room. Outside I saw the servants and many other people running anxiously to and fro. All faces were pale."

Francesco Petrarch

If you said an earthquake, you're correct! People in northern Italy had good reason to be pale and frightened on a winter's day in 1348 CE. On that day, a large earthquake struck. Thousands of people lost their lives.

Earthquakes are violent natural disasters that strike without warning. Suddenly, the ground begins to shake. Furniture topples,

22

- Read pages 22 and 23 aloud, as students read along silently.

Literal. What words, including strong verbs, does Francesco Petrarch use to signal he is describing an earthquake?

» Answers may vary, but may include: "the floor <u>trembled</u> under my feet"; "the books <u>crashed</u> into each other and fell down"; "I was <u>frightened</u> and <u>hurried</u> to leave the room"; "people running <u>anxiously</u> to and fro"; and "all faces were pale."

objects tumble from shelves, and buildings may even collapse. In 1348 CE, people had no idea what caused earthquakes. Today we know that earthquakes are the result of powerful natural forces at work in Earth's crust and mantle.

As you read in Chapter 2, scientists developed the theory of plate tectonics in the 1960s. The theory explains how Earth's surface and interior change over very long periods of time. Some plates are pulling apart at their boundaries, other plates are colliding, and still others are sliding past each other. A lot happens at plate boundaries, including most earthquakes. In fact, one of the easiest ways to locate plate boundaries is to determine where earthquakes are occurring!

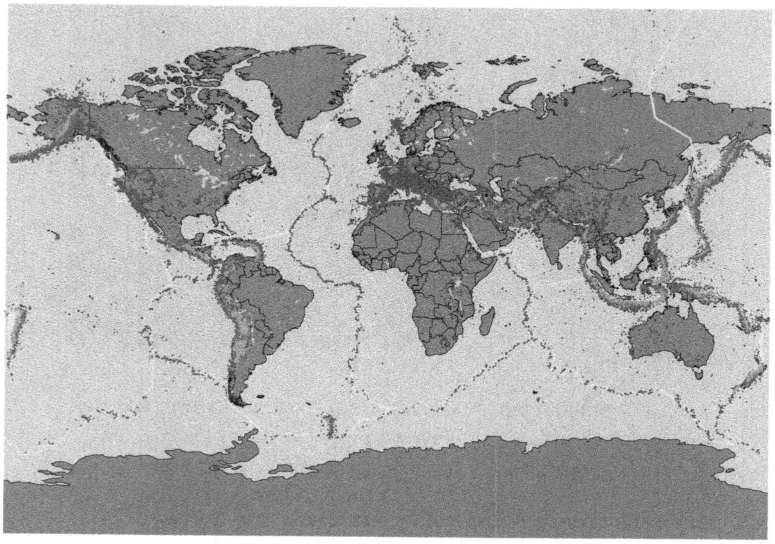

Locations of plate boundaries and past earthquake epicenters

23

Literal. What is the relationship between tectonic plates and earthquakes?

» Most earthquakes happen at tectonic plate boundaries.

- Have students record the answer to question 1 on Activity Page 5.1.

Check for Understanding

What might tectonic plates next to each other be doing at any given time?

» sliding past each other; pushing against each other; pulling apart from each other

Forces and Faults

Try a little **experiment**. Extend your arms out in front of you parallel to the floor and put your hands together. Keep your palms and fingers flat against each other. Now start pressing your hands together. Gradually increase the pressure. When you can't press any harder, let your right hand quickly slide forward. That sudden slipping is what happens at a **fault**.

A fault is a fracture, or crack, in Earth's crust. Most faults occur along the boundaries of tectonic plates. As plates move, huge rough blocks of rock along either side of a fault get stuck against each other. Beneath the plates, however, material in the mantle keeps moving. This material exerts more and more pressure on the plates to also keep moving. Pressure builds along the stuck edges of the fault. Think of your hands as these edges, pressing harder and harder together. The pressure builds until the stuck blocks of rock suddenly break and slip past one another. As they do, a tremendous burst of energy is released. How much energy? Well, all the energy that accumulated in the rocks during the time they were stuck and couldn't move.

A fault in Iceland

The Pacific Plate is Earth's largest tectonic plate. It lies beneath the Pacific Ocean. Imagine how much energy it takes to move that gigantic rocky plate plus all the water on top of it. Then imagine all that energy being released at a fault in just a moment. Such a colossal burst of energy travels outward from the fault in all directions as seismic waves. Seismic waves make the ground **heave** and shake. This violent shaking is what we call an earthquake.

24

- Have students read pages 24 and 25 silently.

Evaluative. How does the experiment help you understand what happens at a fault?

» Answers may vary but should include that as you press your hands together with a lot of force, you can feel the pressure of each hand against the other one. This helps you understand the pressure that builds when huge blocks of rock are stuck against each other at a fault. Then, when you can't press your hands together any harder and you let your right hand quickly slide forward, you feel how fast that happens and how the pressure and energy is released when your hand slides. This helps you understand what happens when the rocks stuck against each other at a fault slip past each other: a tremendous burst of energy is released.

Support

What is a fault? Why are faults important?

» A fault is a crack in Earth's crust. Earthquakes originate, or begin, along faults.

San Andreas Fault

In the United States, one of the most famous faults is the San Andreas Fault in California. It lies along the boundary between two tectonic plates that are slowly moving past each other. The movement, however, is far from steady. For years at a time, blocks of rock bordering the San Andreas Fault stay stuck. Pressure slowly builds. Then—wham!—they slip and **trigger** an earthquake. The 1906 San Francisco earthquake was one of the worst in American history. The sudden slip that triggered it was huge. It caused rocks on either side of the fault to move more than 20 feet in just seconds!

Effects of the 1906 San Francisco earthquake

25

Literal. How much energy is released when blocks of rock that were stuck break and slip past each other?

» All the energy that accumulated in the rocks during the time they were stuck and couldn't move is released.

- Have students record the answer to question 2 on Activity Page 5.1.

Shake, Heave, Sway, and Lurch

All earthquakes begin with huge blocks of rock moving along faults. The place in Earth's crust where this happens is an earthquake's **focus**. Think of it as the earthquake's heart, the source of seismic waves. The focus may be deep in the crust or close to the surface.

The **epicenter** is the point on Earth's surface directly above an earthquake's focus. Some kinds of seismic waves produced by earthquakes travel deep into Earth's interior. Surface waves, however, are seismic waves that are first noticeable at the epicenter. During an earthquake, surface waves are what make the ground shake, heave, sway, and lurch. They are the cause of most earthquake damage.

In Chapter 2, you read about seismographs, which scientists use to record the shaking of Earth's surface caused by seismic waves. The time it takes for seismic waves to reach a seismograph is important in determining where the earthquake occurred. The longer that seismic waves take to reach a seismograph, the farther away the earthquake is from the seismograph.

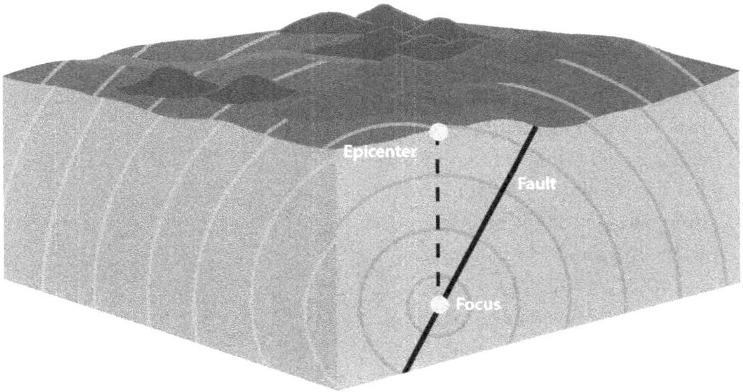

The place in Earth's crust where an earthquake begins is its focus. Its epicenter is the point on Earth's surface directly above the focus.

26

- Have students read pages 26 and 27 silently.

Literal. According to the text, what effects do surface waves have? Have students show a partner where in the text they found the information that supports their answer.

» The text says surface waves make the ground shake, heave, sway, and lurch during an earthquake. The text also says that surface waves cause most earthquake damage.

- Have students record the answer to question 3 on Activity Page 5.1.

Seismographs: Now and Then

A modern seismograph, also called a seismometer, records the shaking of Earth's surface caused by seismic waves. A **seismogram** is the record a seismograph makes. A seismogram shows seismic waves as jagged up-and-down lines. Scientists compare multiple seismograms in order to **pinpoint** an earthquake's epicenter.

Modern seismograph

Zhang Heng, a Chinese scientist, invented the first-known seismograph around 132 CE. It didn't look anything like a modern seismograph. It was shaped like a large vase. The vase had eight dragons around the outside, each looking downward and holding a ball loosely in its mouth. Below the eight dragons were open-mouthed frogs. When an earthquake struck, the balls fell into the frogs' mouths below. Depending on which balls fell, it was possible to estimate the distance and direction to the earthquake's source.

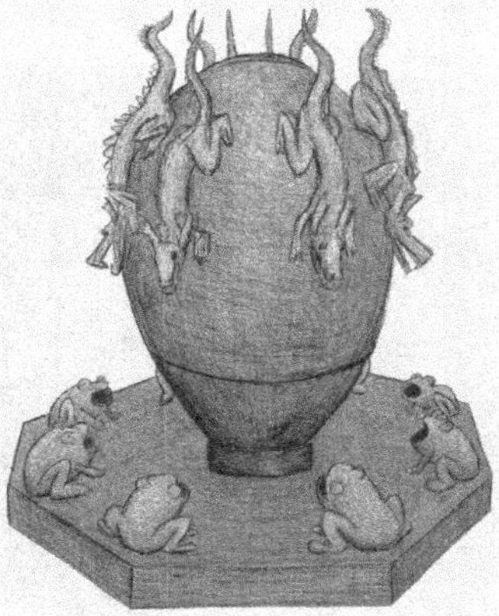

First-known seismograph

27

Support

What is an earthquake's epicenter?

» An earthquake's epicenter is the point on Earth's surface directly above an earthquake's focus.

Support

What is an earthquake's focus?

» An earthquake's focus is the place in Earth's crust where blocks of rock are moving along a fault, triggering an earthquake.

Evaluative. Why might it be important for scientists to pinpoint an earthquake's epicenter?

» Answers may vary but should include that pinpointing an earthquake's epicenter will help scientists determine where the earthquake's focus is. Knowing where the focus is can direct scientists to examine what might be happening below the earth's surface at that location. This will help them understand things like why the earthquake happened, whether this is the first earthquake in that location, and how to prepare for future earthquakes.

Pronunciation Table	
Word	**CK Code**
Richter	/rik*ter/

Measuring an Earthquake's Strength

Scientists also use seismographs to measure an earthquake's strength, or **magnitude**. During a small earthquake, Earth's surface may shake only a little. The seismogram shows these relatively low-energy seismic waves as little wiggles. During a big earthquake, Earth's surface shakes a lot harder. The seismogram shows these high-energy waves as big zigzags.

The Richter scale is another way scientists measure an earthquake's magnitude. The Richter scale assigns a number to an earthquake based on the largest seismic wave recorded for that earthquake. The higher the Richter scale number, the stronger the earthquake. For example, a magnitude 5.0 earthquake on the Richter scale causes 10 times as much ground shaking as a magnitude 4.0 earthquake. A magnitude 6.0 earthquake causes 10 times more shaking than a 5.0, and so on.

Damage caused by earthquakes

28

- Have students read pages 28 and 29 silently.

Check for Understanding

How are a seismograph and the Richter scale similar?

» Both a seismograph and the Richter scale are used by scientists to determine an earthquake's magnitude.

Reading for Information
Vocabulary

Entering/Emerging
Review the meanings of *similar* and *different*. Then point to two students and have the class tell you if their hair colors are *similar* or *different*.

Transitioning/Expanding
Ask the class to identify two students whose hair colors are *similar*, and two whose hair colors are *different*. Have them express their ideas in simple sentences.

Bridging
Ask the class to identify two students whose hair colors are *similar*, and two whose hair colors are *different*. Have them express their ideas using the word *because*.

Literal. How is a seismograph different from the Richter scale?

» A seismograph produces wiggly lines to show the energy of seismic waves. The Richter scale applies numbers to measure the magnitude of an earthquake based on the largest seismic wave recorded.

- Have students record the answers to question 4 on Activity Page 5.1.

Pronunciation Table	
Word	**CK Code**
tsunami	/soo*no*mee/

The Modified Mercalli Intensity Scale also uses numbers to measure earthquake strength. The numbers are based on survivors' descriptions and the amount of earthquake damage. The higher the number, the stronger the earthquake. The Mercalli scale is less scientific than the Richter scale, as few people describe events in the same way.

Pressure along faults can build up for years, even centuries. When blocks of rock along a fault finally move, the resulting earthquake happens very quickly. Most earthquakes last just a few seconds. Still, the trouble may not be over after the ground stops shaking. Large earthquakes are often followed by **aftershocks**. Aftershocks are like mini-earthquakes. They are usually smaller and weaker than the main earthquake event. Aftershocks happen as blocks of rock along the newly slipped fault settle into place.

Modified Mercalli Scale		Richter Scale	
I	Felt by almost no one	2.5	Generally not felt but recorded on seismometers
II	Felt by very few people		
III	Noticed by many, but they often do not realize it is an earthquake.	3.5	Felt by many people
IV	Felt indoors by many; feels like a truck has struck the building.		
V	Felt by nearly everyone; many people awakened. Swaying trees and poles may be observed.		
VI	Felt by all; many people run outdoors. Furniture moved; slight damage occurs.	4.5	Some local damage may occur.
VII	Everyone runs outdoors. Poorly built structures considerably damaged; slight damage elsewhere.		
VIII	Specially designed structures damaged slightly; others collapse.	6.0	A destructive earthquake
IX	All buildings considerably damaged; many shift off foundations. Noticeable cracks in ground.		
X	Many structures destroyed. Ground is badly cracked.	7.0	A major earthquake
XI	Almost all structures fall. Very wide cracks in ground.		
XII	Total destruction. Waves seen on ground surfaces; objects are tumbled and tossed.	8.0 and up	Great earthquakes

The Mercalli scale is less scientific than the Richter scale.

29

- Have students read pages 30 and 31 silently.

Inferential. Based on the author's descriptive language when explaining a tsunami, is a tsunami a positive or negative result of an earthquake? How do you know? Use Think-Pair-Share to have students answer this question.

» Negative: the author describes a tsunami as a gigantic wave, a great pulse of water, and a towering wall of water; the author uses violent words like *crashes, roaring, churning, terrible,* and *destruction* to describe a tsunami.

- Have students record the answer to question 5 on Activity Page 5.1.

LESSON WRAP-UP (10 MIN.)

Note: Activity Page 1.3 relates to The Big Question of the chapter.

Activity Pages 1.3 and 1.4

- Have students turn to Activity Pages 1.3 and 1.4 and refer to the displayed Evidence Collector's Chart.
- Remind students that they will use this chart throughout the unit to collect evidence of changes to the earth related to specific causes of geologic change. The evidence represents what geologists examine to determine how powerful forces above and below Earth's surface work to change the earth.
- Have a student read aloud the information under "What is the cause?" in the third row. Explain that students must determine what evidence is in the chapter about material moving in the mantle at a fault, building pressure, and then causing stuck rocks to suddenly slip past each other and shake the ground.

2. Where can this evidence be found?

    » page 24

- Have students refer to the remaining images on Activity Page 1.4.

3. Which image represents evidence of what happens at a fault that leads to the ground's shaking?

    » the image showing earthquake damage to a bridge

- Ensure students understand why the image showing how a bridge was damaged during an earthquake is the correct image. (The image shows how a large bridge broke into pieces and collapsed, which is evidence of the shaking of an earthquake causing damage to things on Earth's surface.)
- Have students cut out the correct image, glue it to the chart in the "What evidence is there?" column, and write the following information for chapter number, key words, and letter in the chart:

Partial Chart for Activity Page 1.3

Chapter #	What is the cause?	What evidence is there?	Letter
3	*Material in the mantle moves beneath stuck rocks at a fault, causing pressure to build over time and then suddenly release as the rocks break and slip past each other, shaking the ground.*	*image: bridge broken into pieces as result of an earthquake* *key words:* rocks moving at a fault	E

WORD WORK: *TRIGGER* (5 MIN.)

1. In the chapter you read, "Then—wham!—they slip and trigger an earthquake."
2. Say the word *trigger* with me.
3. *Trigger* means "to cause something to start or happen."
4. My alarm went off early this morning, triggering me to wake up before I was ready.
5. What are some other examples of something being a trigger for something else? Be sure to use the word *trigger* in your response.
   » Answers will vary.

- If necessary, guide and/or rephrase students' responses to make complete sentences: "____ triggers ____" or "____ triggered me to ____."

6. What part of speech is the word *trigger*?
   » verb

- Use a Synonyms and Antonyms activity for follow-up.

7. What does *trigger* mean? What are some synonyms of, or words that have a similar meaning to, *trigger*?
   » sample answers: *cause, start, prompt, activate*
8. What are some words or phrases that are antonyms, or words that have the opposite meaning, of trigger?
   » sample answers: *stop, shut off, end, discontinue*

- As students discuss synonyms and antonyms, guide them to use the word *trigger* in a complete sentence: "A synonym of *trigger* is *start*."

Lesson 5: Close Reading: Earthquakes and Tsunamis

Writing

45M

Primary Focus: Students will use their paraphrased notes to draft an informational pamphlet about tsunamis. **[W.4.8, W.4.9]**

TAKE NOTES (25 MIN.)

- Tell students that today they will paraphrase text in *The Changing Earth* to take notes on tsunamis. They will then use these notes to draft an informational pamphlet on tsunamis.

- Remind students that in the Middle Ages unit they took notes on different people who lived during the Middle Ages.

4. What does *taking notes* mean?

   » "Scanning the text and images for key words and specific information related to a chosen topic."

5. What does it mean to paraphrase information from a text?

   » to write the information in your own words

- Have students turn to pages 30 and 31 in the Reader and silently read the page.

Activity Page 5.2

- Once students have finished reading the pages, have them turn to Activity Page 5.2. Read through all the questions in the chart as a class so students are clear about what information they should scan the text for.
- Point out that tsunamis are the focus of their writing, so all their notes should relate to tsunamis. *To focus* is to select one specific moment, object, or idea, and use precise details to write about it. Remind students that they learned about focus when writing personal narratives.
- Remind students to take notes by paraphrasing the text they just read, or writing the information in their own words. Students should write key information in the shortest form possible.

Support

If students need help paraphrasing the text and taking notes, you may wish to guide the whole class in taking notes together or have students work in pairs to take notes.

Check for Understanding

Have students tell how they expressed the answer to the first question on Activity Page 5.2.

» Check that students have included all the important information; that they have used their own words; and that they have used a short form.

Support

Display the Earthquake Pamphlet from Lesson 4 for students who may need to use it as a guide.

- Consider providing students with information for notes relating to the last question on Activity Page 5.2, "How can we prepare and protect ourselves?" as that specific information is not in the Reader. See the sample Tsunami Pamphlet in this lesson for more information. You may wish to have students record the following notes for the last question:
  - Know the tsunami warning signal where you live, quickly evacuate if tsunami approaches.

DRAFT AN INFORMATIONAL PAMPHLET (20 MIN.)

- Explain that students will now write a pamphlet based on the notes they took on Activity Page 5.2.
- Have students turn to Activity Page 5.3. Explain that they will draft their pamphlets by composing answers to the questions.
- Tell students they should use the notes they took on Activity Page 5.2 to guide them as they write their answers.
- Remind students that they should write the answers in complete sentences. A complete sentence has a subject, a predicate, capitalization, and punctuation, and it expresses a complete idea.
- Guide students through the process of transforming their notes into sentences by completing the "Tsunamis are caused by . . ." statement as a whole group. Have students read the notes they took for the first question on Activity Page 5.2. Then have students read the statement on Activity Page 5.3. Have students think of different ways to complete the sentence, keeping the audience in mind. Call on multiple students to provide possible ways to phrase the sentence. Write one or two examples on the board/chart paper. (Tsunamis are caused by earthquakes in the oceanic crust; tsunamis are caused by the seafloor shifting after an earthquake.)
- Have students complete the rest of Activity Page 5.3 individually. Alternatively, have students complete the rest of the activity page in pairs or small groups.
- Circulate and check in with students, providing support and guidance as needed to assist them with the transformation of notes to sentences, or with the phrasing of sentences for a particular audience.
- To close, have students share some of their answers to the questions.
    - **Feedback:** Provide reinforcing or corrective feedback, showing effective ways for students to turn their notes from the text into sentences in their own words.
- Collect Activity Page 5.3 to review and monitor student progress. Written feedback may include comments such as:
    - This point is clear and written in your own words.
    - This makes me want to know more. What additional information could you add?
    - This sentence is a quote directly from the text. How can you rewrite the sentence in your own words?

End Lesson

Writing
Producing

Entering/Emerging
Work with individual students to ensure that they can turn notes into complete sentences.

Transitioning/Expanding
Have pairs help each other turn notes into complete sentences.

Bridging
Have students work independently to turn notes into complete sentences, then check with a partner to make sure they have done this process correctly.

Activity Page 5.3

Challenge

After composing answers to the questions, students may use their own lined paper to write additional questions and answers for an extension page of the pamphlet.

LESSON

6

Volcanoes, Geysers, and Hot Springs

PRIMARY FOCUS OF LESSON

Reading

Students will explain how and where volcanoes, geysers, and hot springs are formed and what the differences are between dormant, extinct, and active volcanoes. **[RI.4.1, RI.4.3, RI.4.4]**

Grammar

Students will determine where to insert quotation marks and commas in sentences containing direct quotes or dialogue. **[L.4.2]**

Morphology

Students will identify the meaning of the root *rupt* and use these words in sentences. **[L.4.4]**

Spelling

Students will practice spelling words based on familiar roots. **[L.4.2]**

FORMATIVE ASSESSMENT

Activity Page 1.3	**Evidence Collector's Chart** Students look in the text for evidence supporting geological events. **[RI.4.1]**
Activity Page 1.4	**Evidence of Changes on Earth** Students look in the text for evidence supporting geological events. **[RI.4.1]**
Activity Page 6.1	**Vocabulary for "Earth's Fiery Volcanoes"** Students learn and practice vocabulary words relating to the chapter. **[RI.4.4]**
Activity Page 6.2	**Commas and Quotation Marks** Students punctuate sentences with dialogue or quotes. **[L.4.2]**
Activity Page 6.3	**Root *rupt*** Students write and complete sentences using words with the root *rupt*. **[L.4.4]**
Activity Page 6.4	**Spelling Words** Students practice spelling words that use familiar roots. **[L.4.2]**
Activity Page 6.5	**Practice Spelling Words** Students practice spelling words that use familiar roots. **[L.4.2]**

LESSON AT A GLANCE

	Grouping	Time	Materials
Reading (45 min.)			
Introduce the Chapter	Whole Group	5 min.	❏ *The Changing Earth* ❏ Activity Pages 1.3, 1.4, 6.1 ❏ Evidence Collector's Chart ❏ scissors ❏ glue
Read "Earth's Fiery Volcanoes"	Whole Group	25 min.	
Lesson Wrap-Up	Whole Group	10 min.	
Word Work: *Fine*	Whole Group	5 min.	
Language (45 min.)			
Grammar: Introduce Commas and Quotation Marks	Whole Group	15 min.	❏ Commas Poster Addition ❏ Quotation Marks Poster ❏ Activity Page 6.2
Morphology: Introduce Root *rupt*	Whole Group	15 min.	❏ Roots Poster ❏ Activity Page 6.3
Spelling: Introduce Spelling Words	Whole Group	15 min.	❏ Activity Pages 6.4, 6.5, SR.1
Take-Home Material			
Grammar; Morphology; Spelling			❏ Activity Pages 6.2–6.5 ❏ Fluency Supplement selection (optional)

ADVANCE PREPARATION

Reading

- Display the Evidence Collector's Chart from Lesson 1.
- You may access a digital version of The Big Question in the digital components for this unit.

Language

Grammar

- Prepare an addition to the Commas Poster from Lesson 2 as indicated, and display it for use during the grammar lesson, or access Commas Poster Addition in the digital components for this unit. This poster will be on display throughout the unit.

  Commas

  A comma is a punctuation mark used to separate words or numbers in dates and addresses, as well as to separate a series of words in a sentence.

  A comma is also used to indicate that a pause is needed in a sentence. When used with quotation marks, a comma helps to set off a quotation from the rest of a sentence and indicates that a pause is needed.

- Prepare and display a Quotation Marks Poster with the following information for use during the grammar lesson, or access a digital version in the digital components for this unit. This poster will be on display throughout the unit.

  Quotation Marks

  Quotation marks are punctuation marks used to show exactly what a person says or has said (dialogue). They are also used when copying the exact words from a written text.

- Write the following sentences on the board/chart paper:
  - The text states, "Erupting volcanoes are dramatic natural events."
  - What I asked my friends is your favorite color?
  - Green Seth responded is my favorite color.
  - My favorite color Bonnie said is purple.

Morphology

- During this lesson, you will reference the Roots Poster you displayed in Unit 2.

Fluency (optional)

- Choose and make sufficient copies of a text selection from the online Fluency Supplement to distribute and review with students for additional fluency practice. If you choose to do a fluency assessment, you will assess students in Lesson 10.

Start Lesson

Lesson 6: Volcanoes, Geysers, and Hot Springs

Reading

45M

Primary Focus: Students will explain how and where volcanoes, geysers, and hot springs are formed and what the differences are between dormant, extinct, and active volcanoes. **[RI.4.1, RI.4.3, RI.4.4]**

INTRODUCE THE CHAPTER (5 MIN.)

- Tell students they will read Chapter 4, "Earth's Fiery Volcanoes."
- Have students turn to the table of contents, locate the chapter, and then turn to the first page of the chapter.
- Preview the core vocabulary words before reading the chapter.
- Begin by telling students the first vocabulary word they will encounter in this chapter is *volcano*.
- Have students find the word on page 32 of the Reader.

1. How is each vocabulary word printed the first time it appears in the chapter?
    » in bold

- Have students refer to the glossary at the back of the Reader and locate *volcano*. Then have a student read the definition.
- Explain the following:
    - the part of speech
    - alternate forms of the word
- Have students reference Activity Page 6.1 while you have volunteers read each word and its meaning. Have students act out each vocabulary word by using their fingers to sketch a picture in the air, using their hands to indicate the process described, and so on.

Activity Page 6.1

volcano, n. a hill or mountain that forms over a crack in Earth's crust from which lava erupts (volcanoes) (32)

crater, n. a bowl-shaped opening at the top of a volcano or geyser (32)

fine, adj. very small (33)

subduction zone, n. the place where one tectonic plate is sliding beneath another tectonic plate (subduction zones) (36)

descend, v. to move downward (descends) (36)

hotspot, n. a very hot region deep within Earth's mantle where a huge magma chamber forms (hotspots) (38)

plume, n. a column of magma that rises from the mantle into a chamber beneath Earth's crust (40)

hot spring, n. a naturally flowing source of hot water (hot springs) (40)

Vocabulary Chart for Chapter 4, "Earth's Fiery Volcanoes"

Vocabulary Type	Tier 3 Domain-Specific Words	Tier 2 General Academic Words
Core Vocabulary	volcano crater subduction zone hotspot plume hot spring	fine descend
Spanish Cognates for Core Vocabulary	volcán cráter zona de subducción	descender
Multiple-Meaning Core Vocabulary Words	crater plume	fine
Sayings and Phrases	recorded history chains of islands	

- Read to learn about volcanoes and how they relate to tectonic plate boundaries.
- Have one student read The Big Question at the beginning of the chapter. Ensure students understand the meaning of The Big Question before reading the chapter.
    - How do scientists determine where volcanoes might develop?

Chapter 4

Earth's Fiery Volcanoes

THE BIG QUESTION
How do scientists determine where volcanoes might develop?

Imagine seeing new land form right before your eyes. You can do just that on the island of Hawaii in the Hawaiian Island chain. There, the Kilauea **volcano** has been erupting continuously since 1983. At times, red-hot lava shoots out of the **crater** at the volcano's top. More often, lava oozes out of cracks on the volcano's sides. As the lava flows downhill, it cools and hardens into volcanic rock. When lava flows all the way to the ocean, it cools to form rock along the shore. This adds new land to the island, making it a little bigger than it was before.

Erupting volcanoes are dramatic natural events. They can be a creative force, adding new land—even whole islands—to our planet. They also bring minerals from deep inside the earth to the surface. However, volcanoes can be dangerous and destructive. Large volcanic eruptions can flatten entire forests. They can fill the air with poisonous gases and hot, choking ash. They can release rivers of lava that burn and bury everything in their path. Erupting volcanoes can also trigger earthquakes, tsunamis, and landslides. They can even change the weather all around the world.

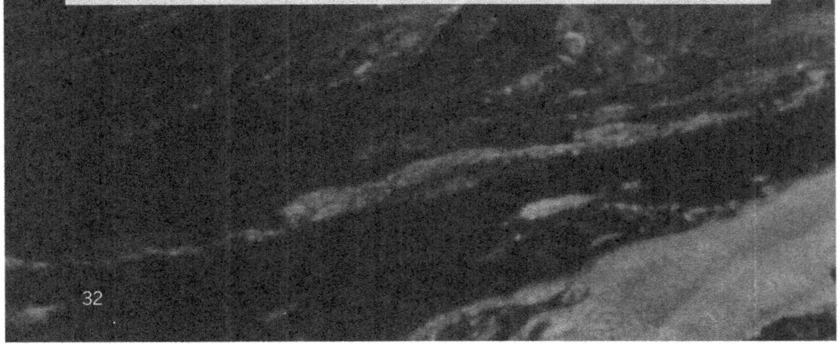

32

READ "EARTH'S FIERY VOLCANOES" (25 MIN.)

Pronunciation Table	
Word(s)	**CK Code**
Kilauea	/kee*lə*wae*ə/

- Have students read pages 32 and 33 silently.

Literal. According to the text, what are some ways in which erupting volcanoes can change Earth's surface? You may wish to have students answer this question in small groups. If you do, challenge each group to find as many ways as they can, and ask them to compare their answers with a second group's after a minute or two.

» Answers may vary but should include: add new land to Earth's surface; bring minerals from deep inside the earth to the surface; flatten entire forests; release rivers of lava that can burn and bury everything in their path; and trigger earthquakes, tsunamis, and landslides.

The Year without a Summer

In the spring of 1815, a volcano called Tambora erupted in Indonesia. It was the largest volcanic eruption in recorded history. Tambora's eruption blasted enormous amounts of ash high into the atmosphere. In the months that followed, winds distributed the ash around the globe. The **fine** ash particles in the air blocked some of the sunlight reaching Earth's surface. Less sunlight meant less warmth. Because of Tambora, the weather was much colder than normal in 1816. There were hard frosts in New England all summer long. A foot of snow fell in eastern Canada in June. Weeks of cold rain killed most of the crops in Europe. Many people called 1816 "the year without a summer."

33

Literal. Describe a specific example of how and why the eruption of a volcano affected the weather.

» In the spring of 1815, a volcano erupted in Indonesia, sending very small pieces of ash into the air all over the earth. The ash blocked the sunlight so the summer that followed was much colder than usual in many places around the world.

Inferential. Think, Pair, Share: discuss what problems the world might face today if there were another volcanic eruption such as the one that took place in 1815.

» Answers will vary, but might include that there could be significant food shortages, along with problems finding enough heating fuel.

Reading for Information Vocabulary

Entering/Emerging
Find the words *new, hot,* and *cold* on page 32. Use actions and simple language to convey the meaning of each word. Help students make simple phrases such as *a hot day, a cold drink, a new book.*

Transitioning/Expanding
Introduce *new, hot,* and *cold* as above. Have students use the words in simple sentences.

Bridging
Introduce *new, hot,* and *cold* as above. Have students create more complex sentences using the words.

What is a Volcano?

A volcano is a hill or mountain that forms over a crack in Earth's crust from which lava erupts. The crack leads down to a chamber, or huge space, filled with magma, which comes from the mantle. Tremendous pressure and heat in the mantle force magma in the chamber upward through the crack. If the pressure is great enough, magma erupts on the surface as lava.

- Have students read pages 34 and 35 silently.

  Literal. What goes on below Earth's surface to form a volcano? What happens above Earth's surface to form a volcano? You may wish to have different students answer this question, each describing a new step in the process. The first student describes the initial stage, the second student the second stage, and so on.

  » Below Earth's surface, tremendous pressure and heat in the mantle force magma in the chamber below Earth's crust to move upward through the crack in Earth's surface. If pressure is great enough, magma from below Earth's surface erupts as lava above Earth's surface. Each time lava erupts, a new layer of rock forms on Earth's surface, making the volcano bigger and bigger.

Some volcanic eruptions are relatively calm and quiet whereas others are sudden and violent. Each time lava erupts, a new layer of rock forms, making the volcano bigger and bigger. Many volcanoes gradually become high, cone-shaped mountains. Mount Vesuvius in Italy and Mount Fuji in Japan are good examples of volcanoes with this distinctive shape.

Vesuvius and Fuji have something else in common. They are active volcanoes. An active volcano is one that has erupted in the past 10,000 years and is likely to erupt again. When an active volcano hasn't erupted in a long time, it is considered a dormant volcano. Extinct volcanoes are those that have not erupted for at least 10,000 years.

Literal. What are the differences between active, dormant, and extinct volcanoes?

» Active volcanoes are ones that have erupted in the past 10,000 years and will likely erupt again. Dormant volcanoes are active volcanoes that haven't erupted in a long time. Extinct volcanoes are volcanoes that have not erupted for at least 10,000 years.

Check for Understanding

What term would be used to describe a volcano that last erupted in 15,000 BCE?

» extinct

- If students cannot answer the question, review with them the information about volcanoes in the last paragraph of page 35.

Inferential. The text states that active volcanoes are "likely to erupt again." Using this information about active volcanoes, what can you conclude about dormant and extinct volcanoes to further distinguish between the three types of volcanoes? Have students use Think-Pair-Share to answer this question.

» Dormant volcanoes could erupt again but haven't done so in many years. Extinct volcanoes most likely will not erupt again.

Pronunciation Table	
Word(s)	**CK Code**
Mauna Loa	/mon*ə/ /loe*ə/
Paricutin	/par*ee*koo*teen/
Krakatoa	/krak*ə*toe*ə/

Action at the Edge

If you wanted to see a lot of volcanoes, where would you look? Volcanoes form where there are cracks and weak spots in Earth's crust. You'll find those mostly along the boundaries of tectonic plates that are moving apart. Volcanoes are also common where two plates are slowly colliding and one plate is subducting under the other.

The Pacific Plate is one of Earth's largest tectonic plates. It lies beneath the Pacific Ocean. Along its boundaries, the Pacific Plate is subducting under several other plates. Geologists call the places where this is happening **subduction zones**. Deep ocean trenches and many volcanoes have formed along subduction zones. This is because the edge of a subducting plate melts as it **descends** into Earth's hot mantle. Magma moves up through cracks in the crust and erupts to form volcanoes above the subduction zone.

World's Tallest Mountain

The largest active volcano is Mauna Loa, a volcano on the island of Hawaii. Mauna Loa's last big eruption was in 1984. The volcano's peak is 13,796 feet above sea level but its base sits on the seafloor. From top to bottom, this enormous volcano measures more than 33,000 feet. Mount Everest is considered the world's highest mountain at 29,029 feet above sea level, even though Mauna Loa is taller. This is because nearly 20,000 feet of Mauna Loa are hidden beneath the sea.

Mauna Loa

36

- Have students read pages 36 and 37 silently.

Check for Understanding

Where are volcanoes most likely to be found: the edge of a subducting plate or the middle of a tectonic plate?

» the edge of a subducting plate

- If students cannot answer, have them explain what they know about subducting plates. Then discuss why the edges of these plates are common locations for volcanoes, using page 36 for reference.

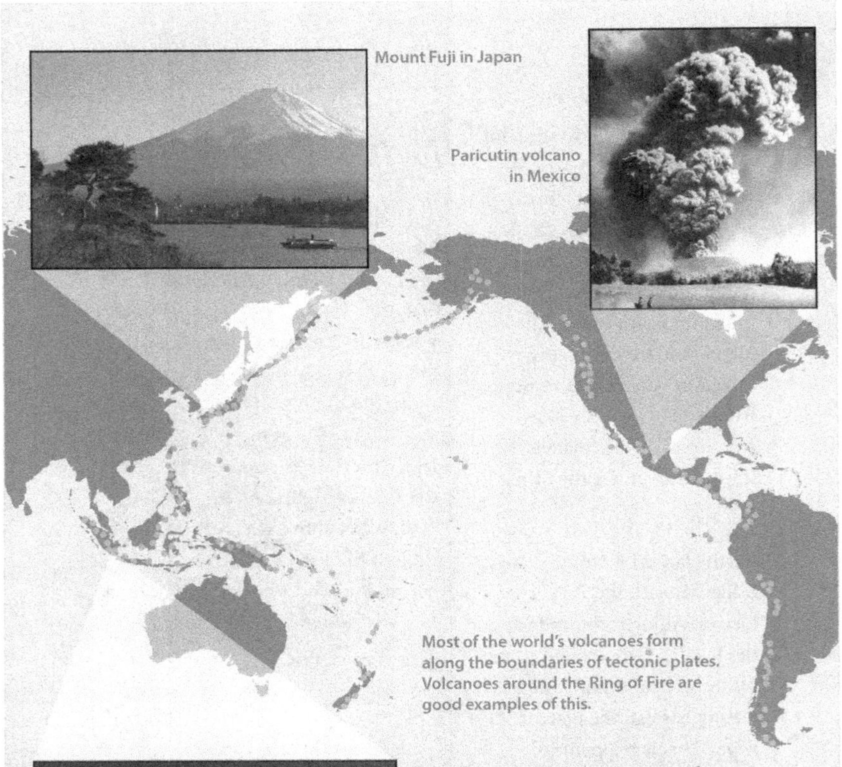

Mount Fuji in Japan

Paricutin volcano in Mexico

Most of the world's volcanoes form along the boundaries of tectonic plates. Volcanoes around the Ring of Fire are good examples of this.

Krakatoa volcano in Indonesia

More than 450 active volcanoes lie around the edges of the Pacific Plate. Those are just the ones on land! Many more rise up from the seafloor and are hidden beneath the ocean's surface. Together, all these volcanoes form what is called the Ring of Fire around much of the Pacific Ocean. It is one of the most volcanically active regions on Earth.

37

Inferential. Using information on these pages and in the image on page 37, why do you think the Ring of Fire was given its name?

» Answers may vary but should include: the text states that the Ring of Fire is one of the most volcanically active regions on the earth; the image shows that active volcanoes lie around the edges of the Pacific Plate, forming a ring around much of the Pacific Ocean.

Hotspots

Not all volcanoes form along plate boundaries. Some occur in places that geologists call **hotspots**. A hotspot is a very hot region deep within the mantle. A huge magma chamber forms beneath Earth's crust at a hotspot. Magma periodically erupts from the chamber through cracks in the crust.

Geologists have identified dozens of hotspots worldwide. Some are beneath continental crust. Others are beneath oceanic crust. Hotspots underneath oceanic crust have formed many islands. The process begins when magma erupting from a hotspot forms a volcano on the seafloor. With repeated eruptions, the volcano grows taller and taller over time. Eventually the top of the volcano may rise above the ocean's surface and form an island.

38

Pronunciation Table	
Word(s)	**CK Code**
Molokai	/mol*o*chee/
Maui	/mow*ee/
Kauai	/koo*wie/
Oahu	/oe*wo*hoo/
Loihi	/loo*ee*hee/

- Have students read pages 38 and 39 silently.

Literal. Have students explain to a partner what the illustration on page 38 shows.

Over a very long period of time, ocean hotspots may form chains of islands. This is because hotspots remain in the same place while tectonic plates slowly keep moving. The Hawaiian Islands, for example, were formed by a hotspot located beneath the middle of the Pacific Plate. The island of Kauai formed about 5 million years ago. It began as an undersea volcano that grew tall enough to rise above the water. As the Pacific Plate inched its way northwest, however, Kauai moved along with it. At some point, the island was no longer directly above the hotspot. A new underwater volcano began forming on the seafloor. This volcano grew to form the island of Oahu. Next came the island of Molokai, then Maui, and finally the island of Hawaii. Hawaii currently lies over the hotspot, which is why it has so many active volcanoes. Eventually, Hawaii will drift away from the hotspot and a new island will begin to form.

Island of Hawaii

Several miles to the southeast of Hawaii, there is an underwater volcano called Loihi. Scientists estimate its top will reach the sea surface in tens of thousands of years.

39

Literal. How does an undersea volcano become a chain of islands?

» Magma erupts from a hotspot underneath oceanic crust, forming a volcano on the seafloor. With repeated eruptions, the volcano grows over time until it rises above the ocean's surface, forming an island. Over time, tectonic plates move and the island moves with them. The hotspot stays in the same place, so the process begins again, resulting in multiple islands.

Literal. Ask students to work in pairs or small groups. Have them use props or their bodies to act out the process of a volcano forming on the seafloor.

Support

Review that a hotspot is a very hot region deep within the mantle where a huge magma chamber forms, and that magma periodically erupts from the chamber through cracks in the crust.

Support

Review that magma can erupt from a hotspot underneath oceanic crust, forming a volcano on the seafloor.

Evaluative. What observations suggest that hotspots don't move?

» Answers may vary but should include: the portions of Earth's layers that are closer to Earth's surface slowly move. The portions of Earth's layers closer to Earth's core do not move. Tectonic plates are made up of the crust and the solid top part of the mantle. Tectonic plates are close to Earth's surface and slowly move. Hotspots are very hot regions deep within the mantle. The mantle is a layer beneath the crust. Hotspots are not close to Earth's surface and are not part of tectonic plates, so they do not move.

A Garden of Geysers

Have you ever been to Yellowstone National Park? If so, you've stood over North America's largest hotspot. A great **plume** of magma rises from the mantle at this spot. It fills an enormous magma chamber beneath Earth's crust. In short, Yellowstone sits on top of one of the world's largest volcanoes. Geologists call it a supervolcano.

Heat from the magma beneath Yellowstone is what creates the park's **hot springs** and geysers. Geysers are hot springs that periodically erupt, like volcanoes of hot water. Geysers form when water drains down into openings in the ground above the magma chamber. Heat from the magma turns the water scalding hot. As the hot water rises back up through the openings, some of it turns to steam. This increases the pressure, forcing the mixture of steam and hot water to rush and bubble upward. When it reaches the surface, a hissing fountain of hot water and steam explodes out of the ground. Yellowstone's most famous geyser is called Old Faithful. It got its name because it erupts reliably more than a dozen times a day.

Magma itself hasn't erupted from the Yellowstone hotspot for hundreds of years. Could the Yellowstone supervolcano erupt again? It's possible, geologists say, but most doubt it will happen anytime soon.

Yellowstone National Park's geysers and hot springs are all created by the heat of the huge pool of magma below the ground.

40

- Ask students what they already know or think they know about geysers. Then have students read page 40 silently.

Literal. What happens both above and below Earth's surface to form geysers?

» Above Earth's surface, water drains down into openings in the ground above the magma chamber. Below Earth's surface, heat from the magma turns the water scalding hot. As the hot water rises back up through the openings below Earth's surface, it turns into steam, which increases the pressure, forcing the mixture of steam and hot water to rush and bubble upward. Then it explodes out of the ground and above Earth's surface as a hissing fountain of hot water and steam.

Evaluative. Ask students to compare and contrast geysers and volcanoes. Invite them to use words or drawings to explain the similarities and differences.

» Answers will vary but should explain that both geysers and volcanoes are created through heat from magma and that geysers are heated water while volcanoes are heated rock.

Challenge

Is the super volcano in Yellowstone National Park active, dormant, or extinct? How do you know?

» Active; it erupts more than a dozen times a day.

LESSON WRAP-UP (10 MIN.)

Note: Question 2 and Activity Page 1.3 relate to The Big Question of the chapter.

- Use the following questions to discuss the chapter:

2. **Inferential.** How do scientists determine where volcanoes might develop?

    » Scientists know that volcanoes develop where there is a crack in Earth's crust from which lava erupts. In order for lava to erupt, there must be a chamber of magma from the mantle underneath Earth's crust and there must be a great deal of pressure and heat in the mantle. Scientists have learned that these features necessary for a volcano to develop are commonly found along plate boundaries and above hotspots. Years of observation and research have shown that volcanoes do generally form along plate boundaries and above hotspots. In determining where plate boundaries and hotspots are located, scientists can also determine where volcanoes might develop.

3. **Inferential.** Why do you think volcanoes, geysers, and hot springs are common along plate boundaries and above hotspots?

    » Volcanoes, geysers, and hot springs are common along plate boundaries because they form where there are cracks, openings, and weak spots in Earth's crust. Cracks, openings, and weak spots often occur at tectonic plate boundaries, where tectonic plates are moving apart from one another or colliding with each other. Volcanoes are common above hotspots because magma erupts from a hotspot, which can form a volcano. Similar to volcanoes, geysers and hot springs can form above a hotspot because that is where a huge magma chamber forms. Water draining into the magma chamber causes geysers and hot springs to form above hotspots.

- Have students turn to Activity Pages 1.3 and 1.4 and refer to the displayed Evidence Collector's Chart.

Activity Pages 1.3 and 1.4

- Remind students that this chart is being used throughout the unit to collect evidence of changes to the earth related to specific causes of geologic change. The evidence represents what geologists examine to determine how powerful forces above and below Earth's surface work to change the earth.
- Have a student read aloud the information under "What is the cause?" in the fourth row. Explain that students must determine what evidence is in the chapter about pressure and heat in the mantle forcing magma upward through a crack in Earth's surface.

4. On which page is this information presented?

    » page 34

- Have students refer to the remaining images on Activity Page 1.4. Engage students in a discussion about the images.

5. Which image represents evidence of pressure and heat moving magma upward through a crack in Earth's surface?

    » the image showing lava erupting out of a volcano

- Ensure that students understand why the image showing lava erupting out of a volcano is the correct image. (The image shows the result, or evidence, of pressure and heat in the mantle forcing magma upward through a crack in Earth's surface as lava spewing out of a volcano; lava is magma that has erupted on Earth's surface.)
- Have students cut out the correct image, glue it to the chart in the "What evidence is there?" column, and write the following information for chapter number, key words, and letter in the chart:

Partial Chart for Activity Page 1.4			
Chapter 1	**What is the cause?**	**What evidence is there?**	**Letter**
4	*Tremendous pressure and heat in the mantle force magma in a chamber below Earth's crust to move upward through a crack in Earth's surface.*	*image:* *lava erupting out of a volcano* *key words:* magma erupts as lava	D

WORD WORK: FINE (5 MIN.)

1. In the chapter you read, "The fine ash particles in the air blocked some of the sunlight reaching Earth's surface."
2. Say the word *fine* with me.
3. *Fine* in this sentence means very small.
4. We shredded the cheese into very fine pieces and then sprinkled them on top of our tacos.
5. What are some other examples of things that are fine? Be sure to use the word fine in your response.

    » answers will vary

6. What part of speech is the word *fine*?

    » adjective

- Use a Multiple-Meaning Word activity for follow-up. Tell students the word *fine* is a word with multiple meanings. Share the following with students:
    - Meaning 1: fine—very small
    - Meaning 2: fine—very well or pleasant
- I am going to read several sentences. Listen to the context, or the text surrounding *fine* in the sentence, for clues as to which meaning is being used. When you think a sentence is an example of Meaning 1, hold up one finger. When you think a sentence is an example of Meaning 2, hold up two fingers.

1. Her mother says she was born on a fine spring day.

    » 2

2. In my opinion, the afternoon is a fine time to have a snack.

    » 2

3. A very fine rain was falling this morning.

    » 1

4. On special occasions, we set the table with my grandparents' fine china.

    » 2

5. Sand is made up of fine pieces of rock.

    » 1

Lesson 6: Volcanoes, Geysers, and Hot Springs

Language

45M

GRAMMAR: INTRODUCE COMMAS AND QUOTATION MARKS (15 MIN.)

Primary Focus: Students will determine where to insert quotation marks and commas in sentences containing direct quotes or dialogue. **[L.4.2]**

- Tell students that today they will focus on commas and quotation marks.
- Refer to the Commas Poster Addition. Read it aloud or have a student read it, noting the addition that addresses the use of commas with quotations.
- Remind students that commas are used in sentences to indicate where a pause is needed.
- Refer to the Quotation Marks Poster you prepared in advance and have a student read it aloud.

- Tell students that one way quotation marks are used in writing is to show that a statement has been taken directly from another text and is being quoted, or written exactly as it is in the original text. You may wish to remind students that the phrase "The Year Without a Summer" appears as a quote on page 33 of the Reader.
- Refer to the first sentence you prepared in advance. Read it aloud and explain that this sentence includes information being quoted from page 32 of *The Changing Earth*.
    - The text states, "Erupting volcanoes are dramatic natural events."
- Draw attention to the first part of the sentence, *The text states*,. Emphasize the comma after *states*. Explain that the comma separates the first part of the sentence from the second part of the sentence. Explain that the first part of the sentence shows what the text does (*The text states*).
- Note that the comma between the first part of the sentence and the second part of the sentence is a signal to pause before reading the second part of the sentence. Have students read the sentence including the appropriate pause. Point out that the comma comes before the quotation marks.

  Note: This lesson only briefly reviews the expected forms of commas and quotation marks. It instead focuses mainly on the split quotation form. However, if you feel your students need more instruction on the expected forms rather than the split quotation form, focus on the expected forms in this lesson instead. Additional resources can be found in earlier CKLA materials, specifically Grade 2, Unit 2, Lessons 4, 9, and 11, and Grade 3, Unit 4, Lessons 17 and 19.

- Point to the quotation marks in the second part of the sentence and explain that these show what is being quoted, or exactly what is written in the text ("*Erupting volcanoes are dramatic natural events.*"). Note that the quotation marks set off what is being quoted from what the text does.
- Point out that the end punctuation of what is being quoted is inside the quotation marks. Also, point out that both the first word of the sentence and the first word in quotation marks are capitalized.
- Explain that the sentence could also be organized differently so that the quotation is split up within the sentence. Tell students when a quotation is split up within a sentence, it is called a split or interrupted quotation. Rewrite the sentence on the board/chart paper as follows:
    - "Erupting volcanoes," the text states, "are dramatic natural events."

Language
Writing

Entering/Emerging
Have students say simple words and phrases. Copy them on the board with quotation marks, such as *Maria says, "Hi."* Have students read the sentences with you.

Transitioning/Expanding
Use the activity described above, but ask students to say more complex phrases or sentences rather than simple phrases or individual words.

Bridging
Use the activity described above, asking students to say complete sentences rather than words and phrases.

- Explain that, just as in the previous sentence, the quotation marks set off what is being quoted from what the text does.
- Point out that the comma after *volcanoes* still separates what is being quoted from what the text does and indicates a pause is needed.
- Note that there is another comma after *states*, setting off what the text does from the second part of what is being quoted. This second comma indicates another pause.

Check for Understanding

Read the sentence with and without pauses. Ask students to identify which way is appropriate, given the way the sentence is punctuated.

» the way with the pauses

- If students cannot identify the correct way to read the sentence, remind them that a comma often indicates a pause. Model reading the sentence correctly. Then try again with a different sentence.

- Point out that the end punctuation for each part of what is being quoted is inside the quotation marks (a comma in the first part and a period in the second part).
- Note that the first word of the sentence is also the first word in quotation marks and it is capitalized. Explain that the word *are* in the second part of what is being quoted is not capitalized because it is a continuation of the statement at the beginning of the sentence and is not the beginning of a new statement.
- Ask students if they know another way that quotation marks are used in writing. Draw out or explain that this way is to show that a person is speaking. Quotation marks set off what is being said from who is speaking. Remind students that when people are speaking in a story, it is called dialogue.
- Point to the first example of dialogue that you prepared in advance. Insert commas and quotation marks in the appropriate places, reinforcing why the placement of each is correct using the following guidelines. Note that this is another example of a split quotation.
    - "What," I asked my friends, "is your favorite color?"
    - The words being said are *What* and *is your favorite color*?. Quotation marks should go around these parts of the sentence.

- The words about who is doing the speaking are *I asked my friends*. Commas should go after *What* inside the quotation marks and after *friends* before the quotation marks.

- Point to the second example of dialogue that you prepared in advance. Have students direct you as to where the commas and quotation marks should be inserted. Note that both the second and third examples of dialogue are also examples of split quotations.
    - "Green," Seth responded, "is my favorite color."

Support

Have students take on the roles of Seth and Bonnie in the example sentences and say the dialogue aloud. Have them cup their hands around their mouths as they speak the words in quotation marks.

Check for Understanding

Have students punctuate the third example of dialogue with both commas and quotation marks.

» "My favorite color," Bonnie said, "is purple."

- If students cannot punctuate the sentence correctly, have them review the previous example and discuss why it is punctuated the way it is.

Activity Page 6.2

- Have students turn to Activity Page 6.2. Guide them through the first sentence. Make sure they rewrite the sentence properly, adding commas and quotation marks in the appropriate locations. Have students complete the rest of Activity Page 6.2 for homework, or if you feel they need more assistance, complete the activity page as a teacher-guided activity.

MORPHOLOGY: INTRODUCE ROOT *RUPT* (15 MIN.)

Primary Focus: Students will identify the meaning of the root *rupt* and use these words in sentences. **[L.4.4]**

- Remind students that prefixes are added to the beginning of root words and suffixes are added to the end of root words to make new words. Ask students to give examples of prefixes and suffixes that they remember from earlier lessons.
- Tell students that today they will focus on a word part that is a Latin root and can appear at different places within a word.
- Remind students that a root is a main element of a word that forms the base of its meaning. A prefix or suffix added to the root can change the meaning.

- Write the Latin root *rupt* on the Roots Poster on display in the classroom from Unit 2 and explain that it is pronounced /rupt/.
- Explain that *rupt* means "to break or burst." Add the meaning to the poster as well.
- Tell students that adding prefixes and suffixes can change the part of speech of a root. Tell students that words with the root *rupt* can be nouns, verbs, or adjectives.
- Write *erupt* on the board. Ask students to identify the part of speech and the meaning of the word. Remind students that they read about volcanoes erupting in Chapter 4 of *The Changing Earth*. (*Erupt* is a verb. It means to send out rock, lava, and ash in a sudden explosion.)

6. Have students provide sentences using the word *erupt*.

    » Answers may vary.

- Write *eruption* on the board. Ask students to discuss the possible meaning of *eruption* with the meaning of *erupt* in mind. Have students provide a possible definition and then use a 1-to-10 scale to describe how certain they are that they are correct, with 1 representing not at all sure and 10 representing certainty. (*Eruption* is a noun. It means the process of sending out rock, lava, and ash in a sudden explosion.)
- Remind students they also read the word *eruption* in Chapter 4 of *The Changing Earth*. (Tambora's eruption blasted enormous amounts of ash high into the atmosphere.)

7. What sentences can you create that use the word *eruption*?

    » Answers may vary.

- Continue in this manner for the remaining *rupt* words, using the following chart as a guide.

Words with the Root *rupt*		
Affixed Word	**Meaning**	**Sentence**
abrupt	(adjective) sudden and unexpected; breaking through suddenly	The firefighter had to make an abrupt departure from the restaurant after learning there was a fire nearby.
disrupt	(verb) to disturb something; to cause disorder by breaking through something that is happening	While some could say that a safety drill might disrupt class time, it is still an important exercise to be prepared in case of emergency.
uninterrupted	(adjective) continuing without breaking or being stopped by something	With all of the noises outdoors, it just might be impossible to have an uninterrupted night of sleep while camping!
rupture	(noun) a break or burst	A rupture in the water pipes caused water to soak everything in their apartment.

Activity Page 6.3

- Have students turn to Activity Page 6.3. Briefly review the directions. Complete the first two sentences together as a class.

Language
Productive

Entering/Emerging
Have students work in pairs with you to complete the rest of Activity Page 6.3. Provide guidance as needed.

Transitioning/Expanding
Have students work in pairs to complete the rest of Activity Page 6.3. Check their work with them when they are finished.

Bridging
Have students complete the rest of Activity Page 6.3 on their own. Ask them to compare their answers with a classmate when they are finished and fix any possible errors.

Check for Understanding

Have students complete the third sentence on their own.

» The answer is "uninterrupted." If students cannot answer the question, ask them to identify the word on the list that should mean unbroken.

- Have students complete the rest of Activity Page 6.3 for homework, or if you feel they need more assistance, complete the entire activity page as a teacher-guided activity.

SPELLING: INTRODUCE SPELLING WORDS (15 MIN.)

Primary Focus: Students will practice spelling words based on familiar roots. [L.4.2]

- Explain that students will practice 12 words related to roots they have studied in morphology.

Note: Apart from the roots, these words do not follow one single spelling pattern. However, multiple words in the list do include two less frequently used spellings that may be worth calling to students' attention:

- the spelling 'ch' pronounced as /k/ in *hierarchy*, *matriarch*, and *anarchy* (but not in *archrival*)
- the spelling 'ph' pronounced as /f/ in *autograph, biographer, calligraphy*, and *paragraph*

- Tell students they will be assessed on these words and will write a dictated sentence related to one or more of these words in Lesson 10. Tell students that after they write the words for the assessment, you will say a sentence out loud and students will write the sentence. You will say the sentence several more times to be sure students have had a chance to write the entire sentence.
- Introduce the words by writing them on the board/chart paper. First say the word aloud, and then sound out each syllable, naming each letter aloud as you write it. Continue syllable by syllable until the word is spelled correctly. You may wish to use the pronunciation chart to guide students in saying the words. Encourage students who may already know the words to say them with you.

  Note: Remember to point out specific spelling patterns in each word and their relationship to the sounds and spellings on the Individual Code Chart.

1. hierarchy
2. matriarch
3. archrival
4. anarchy
5. autograph
6. biographer
7. calligraphy
8. paragraph
9. eruption
10. uninterrupted
11. rupture
12. abrupt

Pronunciation/Syllabication Chart

Activity Page SR.1

- As you introduce and write each word, it may be helpful if you point out particular spelling patterns within each word and show students where these spellings are reflected on the Individual Code Chart located in the Activity Book (Activity Page SR.1) and in the Teacher Resources section of the Unit 1 Teacher Guide. For example, you might note that the word *hierarchy* includes a /k/ sound spelled as 'ch' in the second syllable of the word and then point out the 'ch' spelling for /k/ that is included on the Individual Code Chart.

Individual Code Type		
Word	**CK Code**	**Syllable Type**
hierarchy	/hie*er*ar*kee/	open*r-controlled*r-controlled*open
matriarch	/mae*tree*ark/	open*open*r-controlled
archrival	/arch*rie*vəl/	r-controlled*open*ə
anarchy	/an*ar*kee/	closed*r-controlled*open
autograph	/aw*toe*graf/	digraph*open*closed
biographer	/bie*o*grə*fer/	open*open*ə*r-controlled
calligraphy	/kə*li*grə*fee/	ə*open*ə*open
paragraph	/paer*ə*graf/	r-controlled*ə*closed
eruption	/ee*rup*shən/	open*closed*ə
uninterrupted	/un*in*ter*rupt*ed/	closed*closed*r-controlled*closed*closed
rupture	/rup*cher/	closed*r-controlled
abrupt	/ə*brupt/	ə*closed

- After writing and pronouncing the words, use the following chart to define each word and provide an example of how to use it in a sentence.

Spelling Word Chart		
Spelling Word	**Definition**	**Example Sentence**
hierarchy	(noun) a system in which people are placed into social classes of different levels of power and importance	When the server was promoted to assistant manager, he moved up in the restaurant hierarchy.
matriarch	(noun) a woman who controls a family, group, or government	We consider our grandmother the matriarch of our family because she holds the family together.
archrival	(noun) a chief or main rival or opponent	When the racecar driver was traded from one race team to another, his archrival suddenly became his teammate instead of his competition.
anarchy	(noun) a situation not controlled by rules or laws and without a leader	The government was overthrown after a protest, leading to anarchy throughout the country.
autograph	(noun) a person's handwritten signature	We waited for the baseball player after the game to ask for his autograph on my baseball.
biographer	(noun) a person who writes the story of someone's life	The biographer did lots of research, conducted interviews, and followed the legendary guitarist for a year before writing the musician's life story.
calligraphy	(noun) the art of beautiful handwriting	They requested that their wedding invitations be written in calligraphy, as they wanted their invitations to look nice for such a special occasion.
paragraph	(noun) a piece of writing that includes a few sentences focused on a certain subject in an organized manner	He wrote a paragraph about spaghetti, his favorite food.
eruption	(noun) 1. the process of sending out rock, lava, and ash in a sudden explosion; 2. an event in which something breaks or bursts in a sudden and often violent way	There was an eruption of laughter in the otherwise silent auditorium during a funny scene in the play.
uninterrupted	(adjective) continuing without breaking or being stopped by something	I rarely get the chance to work in my garden uninterrupted, but when I do, I can make good progress in taking care of the plants.
rupture	(noun) a break or burst	The doctors explained that a rupture in the appendix is very serious and requires emergency surgery, so I was lucky that they discovered the problem before that happened.
abrupt	(adjective) sudden and unexpected; breaking through suddenly	We had to leave the park in an abrupt way because it started to rain very hard.

Language
Spelling

Entering/Emerging
Work with students as a group to identify the roots *rupt*, *graph*, and *arch* in each word. Help students say each word chorally

Transitioning/Expanding
Work with pairs of students to identify the roots *rupt*, *graph*, and *arch* in each word. Have students say each word together

Bridging
Ask individual students to read and name the words with *rupt*, the words with *graph*, and the words with *arch*.

- Tell students the word list will remain on display until the assessment so they can refer to it until then.

Check for Understanding

Ask students to use the chart to identify and spell two words that include the letter combination *ph* to stand for the sound /f/ and two words that use the root *rupt*.

» possible answers: *autograph* and *paragraph*; *rupture* and *abrupt*

- If students cannot locate the words, have them go through the words in order, first looking for *ph*, then *rupt*.

Activity Pages
6.4 and 6.5

- Have students turn to Activity Pages 6.4 and 6.5. Explain that they will take home Activity Page 6.4 to practice the spelling words and complete Activity Page 6.5 for homework.

End Lesson

Lesson 6: Volcanoes, Geysers, and Hot Springs

Take-Home Material

GRAMMAR; MORPHOLOGY; SPELLING

Activity Pages 6.2—6.5

- Have students take home Activity Pages 6.2, 6.3, and 6.5 to complete for homework and Activity Page 6.4 to practice spelling the words.
- Have students take home a text selection from the Fluency Supplement if you are choosing to provide additional fluency practice.

LESSON

7

Myths and Volcanoes

PRIMARY FOCUS OF LESSON

Reading

Students will describe how myths were used in early civilizations to explain unusual events in nature such as volcanic activity.
[RL.4.1, RL.4.2, RL.4.4, RL.4.9]

Students will consult print and digital reference materials to determine or clarify the precise meaning of words and to identify alternate word choices.
[L.4.4c]

Writing

Students will describe what a wiki entry is and plan for writing their own wiki entry. **[W.4.2, W.4.4, W.4.5]**

FORMATIVE ASSESSMENT

Activity Page 7.1	**Vocabulary for "Mythic Volcanic Spirits"** Students learn essential vocabulary for the lesson. **[RL.4.4]**
Activity Page 7.2	**Mythic Volcanic Spirits** Students choose vocabulary activities to practice vocabulary terms from the lesson. **[RL.4.4]**
Activity Page 7.3	**Excerpts from *The Changing Earth*** Students compare information and stories about volcanoes based on the text. **[RL.4.1, RL.4.9]**
Activity Page 7.4	**Wiki Entry Rubric** This rubric is used to help assess student work. **[W.4.2, W.4.4]**
Activity Page 7.5	**Wiki Entry Editing Checklist** Students use this checklist to help them create a strong wiki entry. **[W.4.2, W.4.4]**

Writing Studio

WRITING STUDIO

If you are using Writing Studio, you may begin Unit 4, Lesson 1 after completing this lesson. If you have not done so already, you may wish to review the Writing Studio materials and their connection to this unit.

LESSON AT A GLANCE

	Grouping	Time	Materials
Reading (45 min.)			
Introduce the Chapter	Whole Group	5 min.	❑ *The Changing Earth* ❑ Activity Pages 7.1–7.3
Read "Mythic Volcano Spirits"	Whole Group	15 min.	
Lesson Wrap-Up	Whole Group	10 min.	
Word Work: *Lofty*	Whole Group	15 min.	
Writing (45 min.)			
Introduce a Wiki Entry	Whole Group	30 min.	❑ Volcano Wiki Entry ❑ Wiki Entry Rubric ❑ Wiki Entry Editing Checklist ❑ Activity Pages 7.4, 7.5 ❑ *The Changing Earth* ❑ Volcano Graphic Organizer
Model Taking Notes for a Wiki Entry	Whole Group	15 min.	
Take-Home Material			
Reading			❑ Activity Page 7.3

ADVANCE PREPARATION

Reading

Note: You may access a digital version of The Big Question in the digital components for this unit.

As possible, prepare to provide students access to grade-appropriate print and online/digital thesauruses.

Writing

- Create a Volcano Wiki Entry to display during the writing lesson. You may access a digital version in the digital components for this unit.
- Prepare and display the Wiki Entry Rubric and the Wiki Entry Editing Checklist, or access the digital versions in the digital components for this unit.
- Using the table below, prepare a Volcano Graphic Organizer to display and complete in class, or access a digital version in the digital components for this unit.

Volcano Graphic Organizer	
Name of the Volcano	
Location of the Volcano	
Type of Volcano; Date of Last Eruption	
Description of Volcano or of Last Eruption	
Other Facts	

References for Volcano Wiki Entry		
Title	**Date**	**Source (Book or Web Address)**

Language

Grammar; Morphology; Spelling

- Collect Activity Pages 6.2, 6.3, and 6.5 to review and grade, as there are no grammar, morphology, or spelling lessons today.

Start Lesson

Lesson 7: Myths and Volcanoes

Reading

45M

Primary Focus: Students will describe how myths were used in early civilizations to explain unusual events in nature such as volcanic activity.
[RL.4.1, RL.4.2, RL.4.4, RL.4.9]

Students will consult print and digital reference materials to determine or clarify the precise meaning of words and to identify alternate word choices. **[L.4.4c]**

INTRODUCE THE CHAPTER (5 MIN.)

- Tell students you will read aloud Chapter 5, "Mythic Volcano Spirits." They should follow along in their Readers.
- Have students turn to the table of contents, locate the chapter, and then turn to the first page of the chapter.
- Preview the core vocabulary words before reading the chapter.
- Begin by telling students the first vocabulary word they will encounter in this chapter is *offerings*.
- Have them find the word on page 42 of the Reader. Remind students that each vocabulary word is bolded the first time it appears in the chapter.
- Remind students that the glossary contains definitions of all the vocabulary words in this Reader. Have students refer to the glossary at the back of the Reader and locate *offering*; then, have a student read the definition.
- Explain the following:
    - the part of speech
    - alternate forms of the word
- Have students reference Activity Page 7.1 while you read each word and its meaning.

Activity Page 7.1

offering, n. something that is presented as an act of worship (*offerings*) (42)

strong-willed, adj. determined to do what you want even if other people tell you not to (43)

bitter, adj. 1. resentful and angry because of unfair treatment; 2. very cold (43)

outsmart, v. to trick or defeat someone by being clever (44)

revenge, n. the act of getting even for a wrongdoing (46)

caldera, n. a crater caused by the collapse of the top of a volcano (46)

lofty, adj. high up (47)

eternal, adj. lasting forever, with no beginning and no end (49)

elder, n. a person who is older, respected, and often in a position of authority (*elders*) (50)

Vocabulary Chart for Chapter 5, "Mythic Volcano Spirits"		
Vocabulary Type	**Tier 3** **Domain-Specific Words**	**Tier 2** **General Academic Words**
Core Vocabulary	caldera	offering strong-willed bitter outsmart revenge lofty eternal elder
Spanish Cognates for Core Vocabulary	caldera	eterno
Multiple-Meaning Core Vocabulary Words		bitter lofty
Sayings and Phrases	fond of out of the reach of gained the upper hand	

- Have one student read The Big Question at the beginning of the chapter. Ensure students understand the meaning of The Big Question before reading the chapter.
    - How do volcano myths help explain volcanic activity?

READ "MYTHIC VOLCANO SPIRITS" (15 MIN.)

Pronunciation Table	
Word(s)	**CK Code**
Pele	/pae*lae/
Kilauea	/kee*lə*wae*ə/
Na-maka-o-kaha'i	/no*mo*kə*oe*kə*hie/
Hi'iaka	/hee*ie*ə*kə/
Kauai	/koo*wie/
Lohi'au	/loe*ee*o/

Chapter 5

Mythic Volcano Spirits

THE BIG QUESTION
How do volcano myths help explain volcanic activity?

An erupting volcano seems almost alive. It hisses, rumbles, and makes the ground shake. It's easy to understand why ancient cultures thought powerful spirits lived inside volcanoes. Belief in volcano gods helped people make sense of volcanic eruptions. Some believed that when volcanoes were quiet, it meant the volcano gods were content. Some people also believed that when volcanoes erupted, it meant the gods were angry. People tried to keep volcano gods happy with **offerings** of food, flowers, and animals.

People told stories to help explain why unpredictable events like volcanoes occurred. Many stories included volcano gods as part of the explanation. These stories, or myths, were retold again and again. Over time, volcano myths became an important part of a culture's history and tradition. The myths were creative explanations for natural processes and events.

Hawaii's Goddess of Fire

Pele is the ancient Hawaiian goddess of fire and volcanoes. She is known for creating volcanic mountains and islands. When she unleashes fiery lava, she also destroys land and everything on it. Belief in Pele began centuries ago. Native Hawaiians believe the goddess lives in Kilauea, an active volcano on the island of Hawaii in the Hawaiian Island chain. This Hawaiian volcano myth tells the story of how she came to make her home there.

42

- Read pages 42 and 43 aloud as students read along silently.
- Ask a student to reread the title of the chapter and the first two sentences aloud.

Inferential. What is a synonym for the word *spirits* as it is used in this context?

» gods; supernatural forces

Literal. According to the text, how did people make sense of volcanic eruptions?

» People believed volcano gods lived inside volcanoes; when the gods were angry, volcanoes erupted, and when they were content, volcanoes were quiet.

Long ago, Pele lived in the spirit world with her parents and many brothers and sisters. Pele was ***strong-willed*** *and had a short temper. When she got angry, she caused things to burn and lava to erupt from the ground. Pele got along with most of her siblings except for her sister, Na-maka-o-kaha'i, the goddess of the ocean and seawater. Over time, Pele and Na-maka-o-kaha'i became* ***bitter*** *enemies. Pele decided to find a new home, so she set off across Earth's ocean in a great canoe. Several of her brothers and her youngest sister, Hi'iaka, came with her.*

The canoe landed on Kauai, the northernmost island in the Hawaiian Island chain. There, Pele met and fell in love with Lohi'au, the island's king. She boldly asked him to marry her. After a moment's hesitation, Lohi'au agreed. Who could say no to a goddess? Before the wedding could take place, however, Pele insisted on creating a suitable place for the couple to live. Pele's idea of a good home was a huge hole in the ground, warmed by fires of hot lava.

43

Inferential. Why might Pele have decided to find a new home? Use Think-Pair-Share to have students answer this question.

» Pele and her sister, Na-maka-o-kaha'i, were bitter enemies, so they hated each other and had lots of negative feelings toward each other. Pele may have thought she would be happier and better off living somewhere her sister did not live.

Challenge

Have students compare the relationship between the two sisters in this story to the relationship between characters in other folk stories they may know, such as Cinderella or Snow White.

Pele had a magic digging stick. When she jabbed the stick into the ground, a crater would open up in which volcanic fires burned. Pele began digging along Kauai's rocky coast. Every time she made a crater, seawater mysteriously flooded in and put out the flames. Much to her dismay, Pele discovered that her sister, Na-maka-o-kaha'i, had followed Pele to Kauai. Na-maka-o-kaha'i was trying to ruin Pele's plans to build a home and get married.

*Hoping to **outsmart** her hateful sister, Pele fled to Oahu, the next island in the Hawaiian chain. She took her youngest sister, Hi'iaka, and her brothers with her. Na-maka-o-kaha'i followed them and, once again, she caused seawater to fill every crater Pele dug. So Pele kept moving, traveling to the islands of Molokai and then Maui. There, too, Na-maka-o-kaha'i worked her watery magic. Time and again, she turned Pele's craters into cold, wet holes in the ground.*

44

Pronunciation Table	
Word(s)	**CK Code**
Oahu	/oe*wo*hoo/
Molokai	/mol*o*chee/
Maui	/mow*ee/

- Read pages 44 and 45 aloud as students read along silently.

Inferential. What natural occurrence is being explained in this passage? Describe what is happening in the narrative.

» The creation of volcanoes on the Hawaiian Island chain is being explained in this passage. Each time Pele moves to a new island to get away from her sister, she creates a volcano to live in, which creates a new island.

How is the creation of volcanoes described in Chapter 4, "Earth's Fiery Volcanoes"?

» Magma erupts from a hotspot underneath oceanic crust, forming a volcano on the seafloor. With repeated eruptions, the volcano grows over time until it rises above the ocean's surface, forming an island. Over time, tectonic plates move, and the island moves with them. The hotspot stays in the same place, so the process begins again, resulting in multiple islands.

Finally, Pele reached Hawaii, the largest island in the chain. Pele climbed the mountain called Kilauea and dug a crater at its top. The bright orange flames of volcanic fire flared and did not go out. Pele's crater on Kilauea was far above the sea, out of the reach of the ocean goddess.

Pele was pleased with her new home. She sent Hi'iaka to fetch her husband-to-be from Kauai. She told her little sister to be back in less than 40 days. She also warned Hi'iaka not to fall in love with Lohi'au herself. In turn, Hi'iaka made Pele promise to protect a grove of beautiful trees that grew on Kilauea. Hi'iaka adored the trees. She was afraid that if Pele lost her temper, she would send out rivers of lava to burn them down.

45

Reading
Literature Interpretation

Entering/Emerging
Have students act out and draw pictures of the following idioms in the text: *get along with*, *out of the reach of*, and *lost her temper*.

Transitioning/Expanding
Have students use the idioms above to complete simple sentence frames such as *I get along with* and *I lose my temper when* ____.

Bridging
Have students express the idioms above in their own words and then use the idioms in sentences of their own creation.

Inferential. What events are being depicted in the images on these pages? How do you know?

» The first image depicts the struggle between Pele and Na-maka-o-kaha'i. You can tell they are fighting by the way they are using their arms and by the way they are standing. The color of their clothing helps you understand what is happening, as do the different elements beneath each of them—lava and water. The second image depicts Pele sending her sister, Hi'iaka, to fetch her husband-to-be from Kauai. Again, colors are used to show each person. Each sister in these images wears a different color. Pele wears red/orange, Na-maka-o-kaha'i wears blue, and Hi'iaka wears green.

The journey took much longer than Hi'iaka expected. By the time she reached Kauai and found Lohi'au, more than 40 days had passed. On the trip back to Hawaii, Hi'iaka grew increasingly fond of Lohi'au. She also grew increasingly afraid of how Pele would react to their being so late in returning.

When Hi'iaka finally reached Kilauea with Lohi'au, she looked in horror on her beautiful forest. It was gone, burned to the ground by Pele's volcanic fire. To punish her older sister, Hi'iaka kissed Lohi'au. Enraged, Pele sent a huge river of lava streaming down the side of Kilauea. Lohi'au was buried beneath it.

Driven by the need for ***revenge****, Hi'iaka dug into the rocky side of the volcano. Lava began draining out and flowing toward the sea. One of Pele's brothers stopped Hi'iaka before all of Pele's volcanic fire drained away. Because so much lava had already been lost, the top of Kilauea collapsed. A great* ***caldera****, or bowl-shaped depression, was left behind. It is still visible at the volcano's top.*

Two of Pele's brothers took pity on the dead king—and on Hi'iaka, who truly loved him. They dug Lohi'au out of the lava

46

- Read pages 46 and 47 aloud as students read along silently.

Inferential. What volcanic activity does this passage explain?

» This passage explains a volcanic eruption.

Literal. What clues from the text help you determine what volcanic activity is being explained? Discuss the clues with a partner and make a list, then compare your list with another pair to be sure you have them all.

» She looked in horror on her beautiful forest; it was gone, burned to the ground by Pele's volcanic fire; enraged, Pele sent a huge river of lava streaming down the side of Kilauea.

Literal. What volcanic feature does this passage explain? Give a student the opportunity to answer; then ask other students to indicate their agreement or disagreement by showing a thumbs-up or a thumbs-down.

» It explains how a caldera formed at the top of Kilauea.

and brought him back to life. Hi'iaka and Lohi'au were married and lived happily ever after, while Pele remained in her ***lofty*** *volcano home.*

Some people believe that Pele still lives in Kilauea. When the volcano erupts, they say it's a sign her fiery temper is flaring again.

Princess Power

In 1880, Mauna Loa erupted. A large lava flow crept down the mountainside toward the city of Hilo. The Hawaiian princess Ruth Keelikolani traveled to the scene as the lava neared the city. Princess Ruth stood directly in the path of the advancing lava. She recited ancient chants and made offerings to Pele. The next day the lava flow stopped. This helped keep belief in Pele alive.

47

Check for Understanding

Why was the story of Pele important to the people of Hawaii?

» It gave them an explanation of how volcanoes were formed and why they sometimes erupted.

- If students do not answer the question correctly, review the function of myths and legends in society, using the information on the first pages of the chapter as a reference.

Inferential. How are Princess Ruth and Pele's sister Na-maka-o-kaha'i similar? How are they different?

» Answers may vary but should include the following: They are similar because both Princess Ruth and Na-maka-o-kaha'i were able to stop Pele's lava; they are different because Princess Ruth and Na-maka-o-kaha'i stopped Pele's lava in different ways. Princess Ruth stopped the lava by reciting ancient chants and making offerings to Pele. Na-maka-o-kaha'i stopped the lava by filling each Pele's craters with seawater.

The Origin of Crater Lake

The Klamath Indians of the Pacific Northwest have a myth about the creation of Oregon's Crater Lake. This deep, nearly circular lake fills the large caldera of an ancient, dormant volcano called Mount Mazama. Mazama is part of a chain of volcanoes that makes up a portion of the Cascade Mountain Range. Scientists believe that Mazama's caldera formed during its last major eruption nearly 8,000 years ago. Rain and melted snow filled the caldera to create what came to be known as Crater Lake. The following Klamath myth about Mazama's eruption and the lake's formation has its roots in these geological events.

Crater Lake in Oregon

48

Pronunciation Table	
Word(s)	**CK Code**
Monadalkni	/mon*ə*dok*nie/
Sahale Tyee	/so*ho*lee/ /tie*ee/

- Read pages 48 and 49 aloud as students read along silently.

Inferential. Is the Klamath Indian myth about the eruption of Mazama a part of the Hawaiian myth about volcanos? How do you know?

» No, the Klamath Indians did not live in Hawaii; they lived in the Pacific Northwest near Mount Mazama, which is located in the state of Oregon.

Literal. How do scientists think Crater Lake was formed?

» Crater Lake is a deep, nearly circular lake that fills the large caldera of the dormant Mount Mazama. A caldera is a kind of crater. Over time, rain and melted snow filled the caldera, creating a lake.

Long ago, the world was home to two great Spirit Chiefs. The Chief of the Below World, Monadalkni, lived inside the earth and ruled below ground. The Chief of the Above World, Sahale Tyee, ruled above ground, from Earth's surface to the starry heavens overhead.

Sometimes, Monadalkni visited the Above World. He climbed up through the inside of a snow-covered mountain and emerged from a hole at the top. From there, he could see far and wide. He could see the forests, the rivers, the lakes—and the camps of the Klamath people.

One day Monadalkni spotted the Klamath chief's daughter, Loha. Monadalkni thought Loha was the most beautiful woman he had ever seen. Immediately he wanted her to be his wife. He came down from the mountaintop and proposed to Loha. He promised her **eternal** *life if she would agree to marry him. Loha refused.*

So Monadalkni sent one of his Below World servants to ask again. The servant brought many gifts. He laid them out before Loha and tried to persuade her to marry his master. He reminded her that if she did, she would have eternal life and live in the mountain forever. Loha refused.

49

Support

If students are having difficulty following the story, help them act it out in small groups with different students playing the roles of the story's characters.

Inferential. What evidence in the text supports the meaning of *eternal*?

» live in the mountain forever

She ran to her father and asked for help. The chief of the Klamath people called the tribal ***elders*** *together. They all agreed that Loha should try to hide from Monadalkni, so she did.*

Monadalkni was very angry when he found out that Loha had refused him yet again. He raged inside his mountain, making it shake and rumble. He threw lightning bolts and spewed fireballs from his mouth. The top of the mountain exploded, which sent hot lava and choking clouds of ash raining down on the land. The Klamath people waded into streams and lakes trying to escape Monadalkni's fiery revenge. They cried out to Sahale Tyee for help.

50

- Read pages 50 and 51 aloud as students read along silently.

Inferential. What volcanic activity is explained in this passage?

» A volcanic eruption is explained in this passage.

Literal. What clues from the text help you determine what volcanic activity is being explained?

» He raged inside his mountain, making it shake and rumble; he threw lightning bolts and spewed fireballs from his mouth; the top of the mountain exploded, which sent hot lava and choking clouds of ash raining down on the land.

The Chief of the Above World came to the aid of his people. He fought Monadalkni and the two spirits waged a violent, fiery battle. Sahale Tyee eventually gained the upper hand and forced Monadalkni back down into his mountain. Sahale Tyee caused the top of the mountain to collapse, forever shutting off this entrance to the Below World.

The Klamath elders prayed for rain. The rains came and put out the volcanic fires. Rainwater filled the caldera on the mountaintop, creating the high, deep body of water known today as Crater Lake.

51

Literal. Summarize the Klamath myth's explanation of how Crater Lake was formed.

» The spirit of the Above World, Sahale Tyee, and the spirit of the Below World, Monadalkni, fought. Sahale Tyee finally pushed Monadalkni back down inside the mountain and made the top of the mountain collapse to keep Monadalkni inside the mountain. When it rained, water filled the deep caldera that had been created on the top of the mountain, creating what is now known as Crater Lake.

Literal. What features of Mount Mazama and Crater Lake does this passage explain?

» This passage explains how the volcano's caldera formed. It also explains how the caldera came to be filled with water, forming Crater Lake.

Support

Have students create a flowchart to help them order the events of the Crater Lake legend.

LESSON WRAP-UP (10 MIN.)

Note: Question 1 and Activity Page 7.3 relate to The Big Question of the chapter.

- Use the following question to discuss the chapter.

1. **Inferential.** How do volcano myths help explain volcanic activity?

    » Volcano myths are creative explanations for natural processes and events. These volcano myths explain volcano-related occurrences—how volcanoes form, how island chains form from volcanoes, why volcanic eruptions occur, and more. Many volcano myths include volcano gods as part of the explanation. According to these myths, volcanic activity is caused by the gods. Volcano myths help explain volcanic activity by attributing the activity to higher powers rather than natural occurrences that go on above and below Earth's surface.

Check for Understanding

What is one way in which these two myths are alike? What is one way in which they are different?

» Possible answers: They each explain how volcanoes formed; one was told in Hawaii, the other in Oregon.

- If students are not sure of an answer, have them review the two stories, asking guiding questions to help them draw distinctions and find similarities.

Activity Page 7.2

- Have students turn to Activity Page 7.2 to complete in class individually or with a partner. After students complete the activity page, collect it to review at a later date.
- Have students take home Activity Page 7.3 to read and complete for homework.

WORD WORK: *LOFTY* (15 MIN.)

1. In the chapter you read, "Hi'iaka and Lohi'au were married and lived happily ever after, while Pele remained in her lofty volcano home."
2. Say the word *lofty* with me.
3. Lofty means "high up."
4. The eagle built a lofty nest on the side of a cliff.

5. What are some examples of things that could be described as lofty? Be sure to use the word *lofty* in your response.

    » Answers will vary.

- Support. Guide and/or rephrase students' responses to make complete sentences: "____ is lofty because ____."

6. What part of speech is the word *lofty?*

    » adjective

- Use a Multiple-Meaning Word Activity for follow-up. Tell students the word *lofty* is a word with multiple meanings. Share the following with students.
    - Meaning 1: lofty—at a great height
    - Meaning 2: lofty—deserving to be admired
    - Meaning 3: lofty—thinking you are better than others
- Ask students for synonyms for each of the meanings of *lofty.*

    » Answers will vary, but may include:
    Meaning 1: high up, tall
    Meaning 2: noble, admirable
    Meaning 3: conceited, arrogant, snobby

- Remind students that at the start of the lesson, they looked at definitions in their glossaries. Ask students what reference they would use to find synonyms for a word.

    » a thesaurus.

- If you have print thesauruses in your classroom, pass them out to small groups.
- Use a print thesaurus to model finding synonyms for Meaning 1 of *lofty.*
- Tell students that there are many great tools on the internet to help with vocabulary, including online thesauruses to help find synonyms.
- Access an online thesaurus and model finding synonyms for Meaning 1 of *lofty.*
- Have students work in pairs or small groups to find synonyms for Meaning 2 or 3 of *lofty.*
- As an exit slip, have students write a sentence using a synonym for Meaning 2 or Meaning 3 of *lofty.*

- For homework, have students use a print or online thesaurus to find synonyms for one of the following words from Chapter 5 of the Reader:
    - spirits
    - hesitate
    - enraged
    - depression

Lesson 7: Myths and Volcanoes

Writing

45M

Primary Focus: Students will describe what a wiki entry is and plan for writing their own wiki entry. **[W.4.2, W.4.4, W.4.5]**

INTRODUCE A WIKI ENTRY (30 MIN.)

- Tell students that today they will learn about writing a wiki entry.
- Explain that a wiki is an online resource. Wikis provide information on many different topics or subjects. A wiki can be written or edited by multiple people, and can be updated over time. A wiki entry provides information on one particular topic or subject.

  Note: Since most of this lesson has been concerned with volcanoes in Hawaii and Hawaiian mythology, students may be interested to know that the word wiki is derived from a native Hawaiian word meaning "quick" or "fast."
- Display the Volcano Wiki Entry you created in advance.
- Explain to students that the focus of this wiki entry is to provide information about volcanoes. Remind them that they used focus to write their informational pamphlet about tsunamis. Focus is when a specific moment, object, or idea is selected, and precise details are used to write about it.

Check for Understanding

Ask students to name two important features of a wiki.

» Possible answers: A wiki is an online resource; a wiki is written; a wiki is usually the product of several people; a wiki can be updated; a wiki provides information about a particular subject.

If students have difficulty answering the question, review the information in the opening of the lesson.

Activity Page 7.4

- Have students turn to the Wiki Entry Rubric on Activity Page 7.4 as you refer to the version you prepared in advance. Tell students they will use this rubric to help them write their own wiki entry about a specific volcano. Tell them another copy of the rubric is found in Student Resources as well.
- Tell students you will all study the example Volcano Wiki Entry and compare it to information in the Wiki Entry Rubric. Note that the example is about volcanoes in general, and that the rubric addresses a single volcano that students will write about.

1. What do you think begins a wiki entry?

   » a title

2. What do you think the title indicates?

   » the focus of the entry

- Have a student read the title of the Volcano Wiki Entry aloud.
- Have a student read aloud the information in the "Exemplary" column of the rubric for the "Introduction" row. Then, have a student read aloud the first two headings and related sections of the Volcano Wiki Entry as others refer to the "Introduction" row of the rubric.
- Explain that the Volcano Wiki Entry begins with topic information about that is more general and basic, as noted in the "Exemplary" column of the rubric for the "Introduction" row.
- Have a student read aloud the information in the "Exemplary" column of the rubric for the "Body" row. Then, have a student read aloud the heading "Types of Volcanoes" and the section that follows, and have another student read aloud the heading "Additional Information" and the section that follows, as others refer to the "Body" row of the rubric.

Writing
Connecting

Entering/Emerging
Work with the key words in the rubric: *some*, *more*, *no*, and *all*. Use gestures, objects, and drawings to convey the meaning of these words.

Transitioning/Expanding
Introduce the four words above. Have students use the words to complete sentences such as *All of us are* ____.

Bridging
Use the four words above. Have students create sentences of their own using the words and demonstrating their understanding of each term's meaning.

3. How do these two sections of the Volcano Wiki Entry address the information in the "Exemplary" column of the rubric for the "Body" row?
    » The sections provide increasingly specific information about the topic.

- Explain that wiki entries often end with a concluding statement. Have a student read aloud the "Exemplary" column of the rubric for the "Conclusion" row. Then, read the final sentence in the Volcano Wiki Entry aloud as students refer to the "Conclusion" row of the rubric.

4. How does the sentence you read aloud address the information in the "Exemplary" column of the rubric for the "Conclusion" row?
    » The final sentence in the wiki entry provides a thought-provoking closing reflection about the topic.

- Explain that a wiki entry follows a logical structure of sentences within sections. A logical structure refers to the organization of writing that strengthens and clarifies the piece.
- Have a student read aloud the information in the "Exemplary" column of the rubric for the "Structure of the Piece" row.

5. How does the Volcano Wiki Entry address the information in the "Structure of the Piece" row of the rubric?
    » Sections are presented logically, and information has been paraphrased from the reference source.

- Have students turn to the Wiki Entry Editing Checklist on Activity Page 7.5 as you refer to the version you prepared in advance. Tell students they will use this checklist to help them write their wiki entry. Tell them another copy of the editing checklist can be found in Student Resources as well.
- Have different students read each section of the editing checklist and refer to the Volcano Wiki Entry to identify how it demonstrates items in each section of the editing checklist.
- When discussing the "Format" row of the editing checklist, note the following:
    - A wiki entry has a title and headings to help organize information; in the example, headings are bolded to start a new section.
    - Indenting is not used because traditional paragraph structure is often not followed in a wiki entry.
    - Lists are bulleted or numbered.

Support

You may wish to have students think of a metaphor or simile that describes how the parts of the wiki fit together, such as a group of beads on a string.

Activity Page 7.5

- A reference list is included at the end. It has a particular format: The title is first, underlined or italicized when using word processing on a computer; then the date the item was published (book) or accessed online (website) appears with the URL included for online resources; then multiple references are listed alphabetically by title.

MODEL TAKING NOTES FOR A WIKI ENTRY (15 MIN.)

- Explain that you will model taking notes for a wiki entry.
- Have students turn to page 40 in *The Changing Earth*. Have different students read each paragraph aloud.
- Display the Volcano Graphic Organizer you prepared in advance. Explain to students that you will use the graphic organizer to take notes on the Yellowstone supervolcano. Model taking notes using the notes in the completed Volcano Graphic Organizer below.
- Explain that it is important to keep notes concise by writing in fragments instead of complete sentences. In addition, it is important to paraphrase by putting the notes in your own words. This is especially important to help you avoid plagiarizing, or using another author's ideas or words without giving proper credit.

Check for Understanding

Ask students whether they should use complete sentences or sentence fragments for note-taking. Have them explain why.

» sentence fragments, because they are more concise

- If students do not know the answer to the question, ask them which is easier to write—complete sentences or sentence fragments.

Take Notes on a Volcano	
Name of the Volcano	supervolcano at Yellowstone
Location of the Volcano	North America
Type of Volcano; Date of Last Eruption	dormant; has not erupted in a long time but could erupt again; last major eruption was 640,000 years ago
Description of Volcano or of Last Eruption	located above a hotspot one of the world's largest volcanoes; called a supervolcano
Other Facts	heat from magma creates geysers and hot springs
	Old Faithful erupts more than a dozen times a day.
	North America's largest hotspot

- Explain that, after taking notes, it is important to record the references that were used. Direct students' attention to the "References for Volcano Wiki Entry" section that follows the graphic organizer.
- Model writing the example for a book reference as follows:

References for Volcano Wiki Entry		
Title	**Date**	**Source (Book or Web Address)**
The Changing Earth	2014	Book

- Remind students that if an online reference had been consulted, then you would also have had to record the article title, the full date the article was accessed, and the web address in the "References for Volcano Wiki Entry" section that follows the graphic organizer.
- Model writing an example for an online reference as follows:

References for Volcano Wiki Entry		
Title	**Date**	**Source (Book or Web Address)**
Top 10 Famous Volcanoes	March 3, 2014	content.time.com/time/specials/packages/article/ 0,28804,2014572_2014574_2014626,00.html

- Call on a student to summarize what a wiki entry is. Call on another student to give a few important aspects of a wiki entry (headings; information presented from general to specific; underlined vocabulary words; bulleted or numbered lists; concluding statement; references.)

  Note: Guidance for Teacher Use of Rubrics

  Rubrics are provided for evaluation of the content and structure of student writing composed within each unit. The criteria within the descriptions correspond to what is taught in the writing lessons. "Exemplary" to "Beginning" performance columns provide graduated descriptions for each criterion. The columns for "Strong," "Developing," and "Beginning" performance are shaded to help students initially attend to the description for "Exemplary" performance. The rubrics allow teachers and students to identify graduated steps for improvement when aspects of the writing do not meet all the taught criteria. To do this, teachers (and students) may highlight the language from each row that best describes the student writing. Consider the following sample rubric with bolding. The rubric communicates a corresponding piece of writing was evaluated as:

  - strong for the introductory section(s)
  - developing for the body sections
  - strong for the concluding statement
  - between Strong and Exemplary for the structure of the piece
  - strong for the writing overall

Rubric Sample				
Exemplary		**Strong**	**Developing**	**Beginning**
Introduction	Initial section(s) provides accurate, general information related to location and type of volcano.	**Initial section(s) provides accurate information related to either location or type of volcano, but not both.**	Initial section(s) provides information loosely related to location and/or type of volcano.	Initial section(s) lacks information related to location and type of volcano.
Body	Additional sections provide increasingly specific information about the volcano.	Additional sections provide more information about the volcano.	**Additional sections provide some information about the volcano.**	Additional sections provide little to no information about the volcano.
Conclusion	A final statement provides a thought-provoking summative or closing reflection about the volcano.	**A final statement provides a summative or closing reflection about the volcano.**	The summative or closing nature of the final statement is unclear.	No final statement is provided.
Structure of the Piece	**All sentences in sections are presented logically.**	Most sentences in sections are presented logically.	Some sentences in sections are presented logically.	Connections between sentences in sections are confusing.
	All information has been paraphrased.	**Most information has been paraphrased.**	Some information has been paraphrased.	Little information has been paraphrased.

Note: Guidance for Teacher Use of Editing Checklists

Editing checklists allow students and teachers to evaluate students' command of language conventions and writing mechanics within unit writing projects. They serve a different purpose than rubrics; rubrics measure the extent to which students apply specific instructional criteria they have been building toward across the unit, whereas editing checklists measure the extent to which students apply English language conventions and general writing mechanics. With regard to expectations for accountability, we recommend using the editing checklist to measure students' command of language conventions and writing mechanics only when students have received the appropriate instructional support and specific opportunity to review their writing for that purpose.

Wiki Entry Editing Checklist	
Meaning	**Notes**
Is correct grammar used? • Sentences are complete with subject and predicate. • Sentences are appropriate length (no run-ons). • The student has been supported with corrections for parts of speech, verb tense, and more complex sentence structure.	
Format	
Does the student use appropriate formatting for the piece of writing? • The volcano name is the title at the top. • Each section of the entry has a heading. • Indenting is not used. • If lists are included, they are bulleted or numbered. • There is a reference list at the end in the appropriate format.	
Capitals	
Is capitalization appropriately applied? • All sentences begin with a capital letter. • All proper nouns are capitalized. • Titles and headings have appropriate capital letters.	
Spelling	
Are all words spelled correctly? • Words using Core Knowledge Code are spelled appropriately. • Words from spelling and morphology lessons are spelled accurately. • The student has been supported with identifying misspellings to be looked up in reference sources as needed.	
Punctuation	
Is punctuation appropriately applied? • All sentences have appropriate ending punctuation. • Commas and quotation marks are all used correctly for the ways in which they have been taught. • The titles in the reference list are underlined or in italics.	

End Lesson

Lesson 7: Myths and Volcanoes

Take-Home Material

READING

- Have students take home Activity Page 7.3 to read and complete for homework.

Activity Page 7.3

Lesson 7: Myths and Volcanoes

Mid-Unit Content Assessment

- You may wish to pause one day before proceeding to Lesson 8 so you can assess students' comprehension of the domain content presented in the Reader thus far. During your next ELA period, administer the Mid-Unit Content Assessment (Activity Page PP.1), which will take approximately 30–45 minutes for students to complete. You may choose to collect the assessments so a grade can be assigned and/or you may review the answers with students after they complete the assessment. You may use the remainder of the period for remediation and/or enrichment, including having students reread Reader chapters or read Fluency Supplement selections.

Activity Page PP.1

LESSON

8

Three Types of Rocks and the Rock Cycle

PRIMARY FOCUS OF LESSON

Reading

Students will identify rocks as solids made of minerals, describe the formation, characteristics of three types, explain how the rock cycle causes long-term changes. **[RI.4.2, RI.4.3, RI.4.4]**

Writing

Students will use a graphic organizer to take notes by paraphrasing text and will also draft a wiki entry. **[W.4.2, W.4.4, W.4.8]**

FORMATIVE ASSESSMENT

Activity Page 7.3	**Excerpts from *The Changing Earth*** Students compare information and stories about volcanoes based on the text. **[RI.4.2]**
Activity Page 8.2	**Earth's Building Blocks** Students answer questions based on the text, citing the source for each response. **[RI.4.2, RI.4.4]**
Activity Page 8.3	**Take Notes on a Volcano** Students take notes about a volcano and provide information about their sources. **[W.4.2, W.4.8]**
Activity Page 8.4	**Volcano Wiki Entry** Students fill in a form giving information about a volcano they are researching. **[W.4.8]**

LESSON AT A GLANCE

	Grouping	Time	Materials
Reading (45 min.)			
Review	Whole Group	5 min.	❑ Answer Key for Activity Page 7.3 ❑ Activity Pages 7.3, 8.1, 8.2 ❑ *The Changing Earth*
Introduce the Chapter	Whole Group	5 min.	
Read "Earth's Building Blocks"	Small Groups	25 min.	
Lesson Wrap-Up	Whole Group	5 min.	
Word Work: Class	Whole Group	5 min.	
Writing (45 min.)			
Take Notes for a Wiki Entry	Whole Group/ Independent	20 min.	❑ Activity Pages 8.3, 8.4 ❑ Volcano Graphic Organizer ❑ *The Changing Earth* ❑ Volcano Wiki Entry
Draft a Wiki Entry	Independent	25 min.	

ADVANCE PREPARATION

Reading

- You may access a digital version of The Big Question in the digital components for this unit.
- Select an object for students to describe the texture of during Word Work.

Writing

- Display the completed Volcano Graphic Organizer and the Volcano Wiki Entry from Lesson 7 for students to reference.

Start Lesson

Lesson 8: Three Types of Rocks and the Rock Cycle

Reading

45M

Primary Focus: Students will identify rocks as solids made of minerals, describe the formation, characteristics of three types, explain how the rock cycle causes long-term changes. **[RI.4.2, RI.4.3, RI.4.4]**

REVIEW (5 MIN.)

- Using the Answer Key at the back of this Teacher Guide, review student responses to Activity Page 7.3, which was assigned for homework.
- Briefly ask students to explain where in the text they found the information to support their answers.

INTRODUCE THE CHAPTER (5 MIN.)

- Tell students they will read Chapter 6, "Earth's Building Blocks."
- Have students turn to the table of contents, locate the chapter, and then turn to the first page of the chapter.
- Preview the core vocabulary words before reading the chapter.

1. What is the first vocabulary word you will encounter in this chapter? How do you know?
   - » mineral; it is listed first among the core vocabulary words.
2. On what page will you find the word *mineral* for the first time? How do you know?
   - » Page 53; the page number appears in parentheses after the word.

- Have students find the word on page 53 of the Reader. Review that each vocabulary word is bolded the first time it appears in the chapter.
- Review that the glossary contains definitions of all the vocabulary words in this Reader. Have students locate *mineral* in the glossary at the back of the Reader. Have a student read the definition.
- Point out or explain the following:
    - the part of speech
    - alternate forms of the word
- Have students reference Activity Page 8.1 while you or a volunteer reads each word and its meaning.

Activity Page 8.1

mineral, n. a solid, nonliving substance found in the earth that makes up rocks (minerals) (53)

texture, n. the size, shape, and sorting of mineral grains in rocks (53)

solidify, v. to make or become hard or solid (solidifies) (54)

obsidian, n. a dark rock or natural glass formed from lava that cooled very quickly (54)

granite, n. a common igneous rock that forms from magma that cooled within Earth's crust (54)

durable, adj. able to last a long time in good condition (55)

compact, v. to closely pack or press together (compacts, compacting) (56)

dissolved, adj. mixed with liquid so no solid pieces are visible anymore (56)

Vocabulary Chart for Chapter 6 "Earth's Building Blocks"

Vocabulary Type	**Tier 3** **Domain-Specific Words**	**Tier 2** **General Academic Words**
Core Vocabulary	mineral solidify obsidian granite dissolved	texture durable compact
Spanish Cognates for Core Vocabulary	mineral solidificar obsidiana granito	textura durable
Multiple-Meaning Core Vocabulary Words	solidify dissolved	compact
Sayings and Phrases	building blocks naked eye	

- Have one student read The Big Question at the beginning of the chapter. Ensure students understand the meaning of The Big Question before reading the chapter.
    - How can changes in rocks over time be explained by the rock cycle?

READ "EARTH'S BUILDING BLOCKS" (25 MIN.)

Establish Small Groups

- Before reading the chapter, divide students into two groups using the following guidelines:

Activity Page 8.2

    - Small Group 1: This group should include students who need extra scaffolding and support to read and comprehend the text. Use the guided reading supports to guide students through reading the text. This is an excellent time to make notes in your anecdotal records. Students will discuss and complete portions of Activity Page 8.2 with your support during reading. In the interest of time, students will only discuss questions 1–6 on Activity Page 8.2 during reading, but will not be asked to record written responses to these questions on the activity page.
    - Small Group 2: This group should include students who are capable of reading and comprehending text without guided support. These students may work as a small group, as partners, or independently to read the chapter, discuss it with others in Small Group 2, and then complete Activity Page 8.2. Make arrangements to check that students in Small Group 2 have answered the questions on Activity Page 8.2 correctly. You may choose to do one of the following to address this:
    - Collect the pages and correct them individually.
    - Provide an answer key to students to check their own or a partner's work after they have completed the activity page.

    Confer with students individually or as a group at a later time.
- Over the course of the year, students may change groups, depending on individual students' needs.

  Note: The following guided reading supports are intended for use with Small Group 1.

Chapter 6

Earth's Building Blocks

THE BIG QUESTION
How can changes in rocks over time be explained by the rock cycle?

You don't have to look hard to find rocks. They are all around you—and under you, too! Earth's crust is made almost entirely of rocks. Mountains, hills, and cliffs are huge masses of rock that form landscape features. Pebbles in a streambed are smooth, rounded rocks. Chunky bits of broken rock form the gravel on a country road. Rocks go into making sidewalks and streets. Slabs of rock cover the outside of many buildings. Indoors, pieces of rock often make up floors, walls, stairs, and countertops. Museums are good places to see rocks that artists have carved into sculptures. The polished stones in some types of jewelry are rocks that people wear.

Rocks are all around. Some are carved into sculptures, others are used for jewelry.

52

- Have students read pages 52 and 53 silently.

Literal. Give examples of how rocks are used by people.

» possible answers: building sidewalks and streets, making gravel, covering the outsides of buildings, making up important features of the insides of buildings, making art objects

Literal. Give examples of where rocks can be found in nature.

» possible answers: in the Earth's crust; in streambeds; in mountains, cliffs, and hills

All the varieties of rocks can be organized into three classes.

Rocks and Building Blocks

Just what are rocks, exactly? Rocks are naturally occurring materials made of solid, nonliving substances called **minerals**. Think of minerals as the building blocks of rocks. Some rocks are formed from just one mineral. Most rocks, however, are combinations of two or more minerals. Minerals appear as different-sized pieces, or grains, in rocks. Some rocks have very tiny mineral grains, giving the rocks a smooth, even **texture**. Other rocks have larger mineral grains and a rougher texture.

Imagine hiking up a mountain and picking up rocks along the way. When you reach the top, you'll probably have quite a collection. Your rocks may have different colors and textures. Some may have stripes or layers. Some might be hard and others crumbly. Some have tiny grains whereas others have large grains that glitter when they catch the light. All this variety might seem confusing. Yet geologists organize all rocks into just three classes, or basic types: igneous, sedimentary, and metamorphic.

53

Literal. What are rocks? Ask students to indicate to a partner where in the text they found the information that answers the question.

» Rocks are naturally occurring materials made of solid, nonliving substances called minerals. This information appears in the second sentence.

Evaluative. Why would rocks with larger mineral grains have a rougher texture?

» Answers may vary but should include that minerals appear in rocks as grains, or pieces. Rocks with very tiny mineral grains have very tiny pieces of minerals in them. Having very tiny pieces of minerals gives rocks a smooth, even texture; the pieces are so small that they don't change the texture of the rocks. When rocks have larger mineral grains, they have larger pieces of minerals. Having larger pieces of minerals means the rocks appear to have more uneven pieces because bigger pieces of minerals make up the rocks. Bigger pieces give the rocks a less smooth texture.

Note: In the interest of time, students in Small Group 1 will only discuss questions 1–6 on Activity Page 8.2. They will not be asked to record written responses to these questions on the activity page.

Literal. How might rocks differ from each other? As before, have students identify where in the text they found the answer to the question.

» They may have different colors and textures; some may have stripes or layers; some might be hard and others crumbly; some may have tiny grains while others have large grains; and some may have grains that glitter when they catch the light. This information can be found in the last paragraph of the page.

Support

Tell students that to *solidify* means to make or become hard or solid.

Support

Remind students that the material that cools and hardens into rock on Earth's surface is called *lava*.

Reading for Information

Explaining

Entering/Emerging
To help students share a fact they've learned, provide them with the sentence starter *I learned that* ____. Have them share with the group.

Transitioning/Expanding
Provide students with the sentence starter *One thing I learned is that* ___ and have students share a fact from the chapter with a partner.

Bridging
Give students the sentence frame *I learned that and that* ____ and have them use it to tell a partner two things they learned from the chapter.

Born from Magma: Igneous Rock

Let's start with **igneous rocks**, the most abundant class of rocks on the earth. Igneous rocks form when magma cools and **solidifies**. When you think of igneous rocks, think of volcanoes.

There are two basic types of igneous rock. One type forms from magma that erupts onto Earth's surface as lava. The lava cools and hardens into rock. The faster it cools, the smaller the mineral grains will be in the resulting rock. **Obsidian** is an igneous rock formed from lava that cooled very quickly, so quickly, there wasn't time for the minerals to form grains. As a result, obsidian is as smooth and shiny as glass. In fact, it is often called volcanic glass. Basalt is an igneous rock formed from lava that took longer to cool. Basalt is typically a dark-colored rock. It has fairly small mineral grains that give it a fine-grained texture.

The second type of igneous rock forms from magma that solidifies below Earth's surface. Magma cools very slowly when it's deep beneath the surface. Slow cooling leads to igneous rocks with relatively large mineral grains. The slower the cooling, the larger the grains. **Granite** is a common igneous rock that forms from magma that cooled within Earth's crust. Granite usually contains mineral grains that are large enough to see with the naked eye.

Igneous rocks

54

- Have students read page 54 silently.

Literal. How does igneous rock form?

» Igneous rock forms when magma cools and solidifies.

Inferential. How do geologists distinguish between the two types of igneous rocks?

» One type forms on Earth's surface and the other type forms below Earth's surface.

Ask students to share one or two interesting or important facts they have learned from this chapter so far.

The Art of Making Stone Tools

Many prehistoric cultures made tools out of rock. Scientists working in East Africa have found obsidian stone tools that are nearly two million years old. Obsidian was especially prized by ancient tool makers. Obsidian breaks into pieces with sharp edges that are good for cutting and piercing.

To make a very sharp cutting tool, ancient tool makers struck a block of obsidian with another, harder rock. This caused a long, thin blade of obsidian to flake off. Although the blade was fragile, it had incredibly sharp edges. In fact, the edges of obsidian blades are much sharper than metal scalpels used by surgeons today.

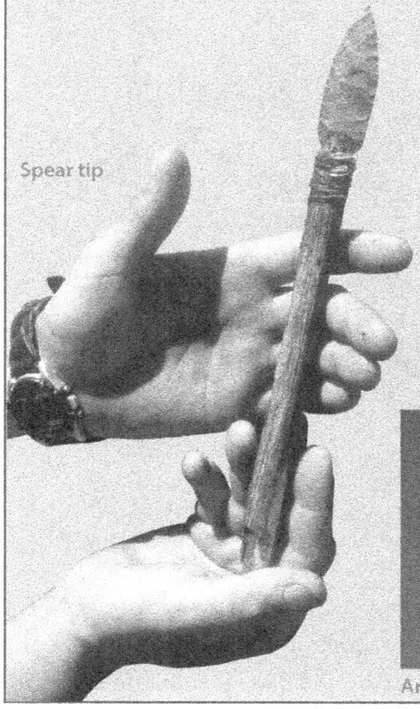

Spear tip

Making a spear tip or arrowhead was more time consuming. The tool makers started with a relatively flat piece of obsidian. They shaped it by striking off tiny flakes of rock, one after another, from the edges. They gradually shaped it into a sharp, **durable**—and often beautiful—pointed tool.

Arrowheads

55

- If time permits, have students read page 55 silently. If time is an issue, consider skipping ahead to page 56, where the main narrative continues.

Literal. Why was obsidian a prized material for ancient tool makers?

» Obsidian breaks into pieces with sharp edges that are good for cutting and piercing.

Layer after Layer: Sedimentary Rock

Sedimentary rock is the second major class of rocks. Sedimentary rocks are made of sediments. Sediments are tiny bits of rock and sand combined with fragments of once-living things. Sediments collect in low-lying areas both on land and in bodies of water. They form layers, one on top of another. Over long periods of time, the weight of overlying layers **compacts** the sediments in deeper layers, squeezing them closer together. Sediments also become cemented, or glued, together as **dissolved** minerals fill the spaces between the sediments. As the sediments dry, the dissolved minerals turn into solids, binding the sediments together. Over time, compacting and cementing processes transform sediments into sedimentary rock.

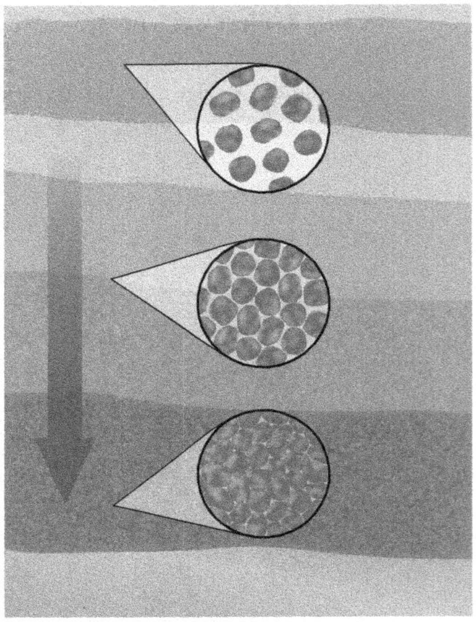

The weight of overlying layers compacts the sediments, squeezing them closer together.

Most sedimentary rocks are more easily broken than most igneous rocks. Hit a sedimentary rock with a hammer, and it will crumble or break apart. Some sedimentary rocks contain fossils. **Limestone** is a sedimentary rock often packed with the fossilized skeletons and shells of tiny ocean creatures. Some sedimentary rocks get their name from their sediments. Sandstone started as grains of sand, whereas mudstone formed from ancient mud.

56

- Have students read page 56 silently.

Literal. How does sedimentary rock form?

» Sedimentary rock forms over time. Sediments collect in layers, are bound together by solid minerals, and are compacted and cemented together.

Check for Understanding

Ask students to describe one way in which sedimentary rock forms differently from igneous rock.

» Possible answers: sedimentary rock forms in layers, and igneous rock does not; sedimentary rock is formed in streambeds, and igneous rock is formed inside the earth; igneous rock is created by volcanic activity, and sedimentary rock is not.

- If students cannot easily answer the question, review the processes by which both types of rocks are formed. You may wish to have students make and complete a Venn diagram or other graphic organizer to focus on the similarities and differences.

Literal. What happens when layers of sediments are compacted?

» The grains in the sediments are squeezed closer together.

Literal. What occurs when layers of sediments are cemented?

» Dissolved minerals fill the spaces between the sediments and glue the sediments together; the sediments dry and change into rock.

Challenge

Ask why most sedimentary rock breaks more easily than igneous rock. Guide students to understand that rock that has been compacted from various sources is not as solidly attached as molten, hardened igneous rock.

The eroded formations of these sedimentary rocks in Badlands National Park in South Dakota show their distinct layers. The oldest layers are at the bottom.

57

Changing Form: Metamorphic Rock

The third major class of rocks is **metamorphic rock**. Metamorphic rocks form when igneous or sedimentary rocks are exposed to extreme heat and pressure. They can even form from older metamorphic rocks. High temperatures and crushing pressure alter the minerals in the rocks. Mineral grains may be flattened or rearranged into layers, swirls, or stripes. They may also be changed into completely different minerals!

Remember granite, the igneous rock? When granite is subjected to intense heat and pressure, it becomes a metamorphic rock called gneiss. When the sedimentary rock limestone is squeezed and heated deep below ground, it becomes a metamorphic rock called marble.

Metamorphic rocks tend to form deep within Earth's crust. The pressure from countless tons of overlying rock is tremendous. Equally powerful is the heat rising from hot magma in the mantle beneath the crust. Metamorphic rocks often form where tectonic plates are slowly colliding. They can also form as magma travels up through cracks in Earth's crust and heats the rocks around the cracks. If the heat of the magma completely melts the rock again, then it becomes igneous rock. If the rock is heated just enough to be changed, however, it instead becomes metamorphic rock.

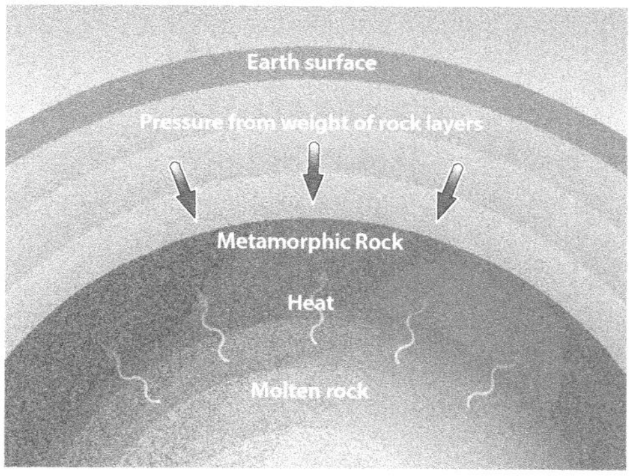

58

Pronunciation Table	
Word(s)	**CK Code**
gneiss	/nis/
Agnes Nyanhongo	/ag*nes/ /nie*an*hong*goe/
Zimbabwe	/zim*bob*wae/

- Have students read page 58 silently.

Literal. How does metamorphic rock form?

» Metamorphic rock forms when igneous, sedimentary, or older metamorphic rocks are exposed to extreme heat and pressure, which change the minerals in the rocks.

Inferential. What can you infer about when the first metamorphic rocks appeared on Earth, compared to igneous and sedimentary rocks? Why?

» Metamorphic rocks most likely came after igneous and sedimentary rocks, because they are made from these types of rocks.

Inferential. What role do tectonic plates play in metamorphic rock formation?

» Metamorphic rock often forms where tectonic plates are slowly colliding, so tectonic plate boundaries serve as an easy way to identify where metamorphic rock forms.

- Have students describe to a partner what the illustration at the bottom of page 58 signifies. Encourage pairs to share their thinking with the rest of the group.

Challenge

What else occurs or is created where tectonic plates are colliding?

» Mid-ocean ridges, mountains, ocean trenches, and faults are created and earthquakes occur where tectonic plates are colliding.

Check for Understanding

Ask students to name the three basic types of rock.

» igneous, sedimentary, metamorphic

- If students are uncertain of these answers, have them review the chapter thus far. Encourage them to look closely at headers and at the words that have been bolded.

Agnes Nyanhongo's Stone Sculptures

Zimbabwean sculptor Agnes Nyanhongo became interested in carving rock at an early age. Her father, Claud Nyanhongo, was a sculptor. She worked in his studio as a young girl and learned how to cut and polish rock. She is now one of Zimbabwe's most well-known artists. Agnes Nyanhongo carves many of her sculptures from a type of rock called serpentine. Serpentine is a metamorphic rock. The type of serpentine Agnes Nyanhongo uses for many of her sculptures is very dark in color. She usually polishes only some parts of her sculptures, leaving the rest simply raw stone.

Agnes Nyanhongo

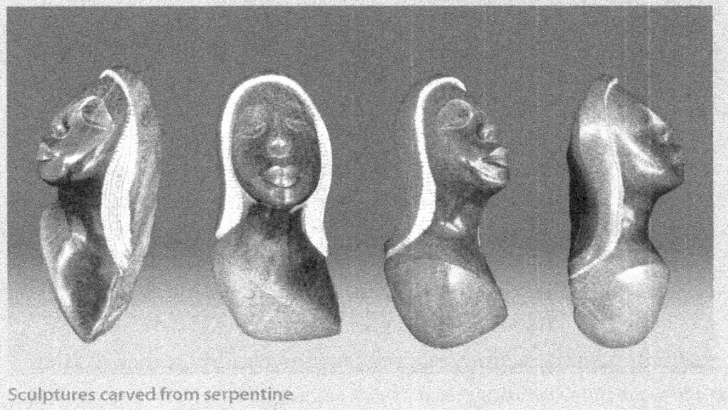

Sculptures carved from serpentine

59

- If time permits, have students read page 59 silently. As before, since page 59 is not part of the main text, you may also skip the page and go directly to page 60.
- Invite students to ask each other questions based on what they have read on this page. Explain that they can ask questions that require answers using information directly from the text, and that they can also ask questions that are more open-ended or speculative. You may wish to give an example of each.

The Rock Cycle

Rocks you see in the world around you might seem like permanent fixtures. Given enough time, however, all rocks change. They are created, destroyed, and recreated in a continuous cycle. Geologists call this ongoing process the **rock cycle**.

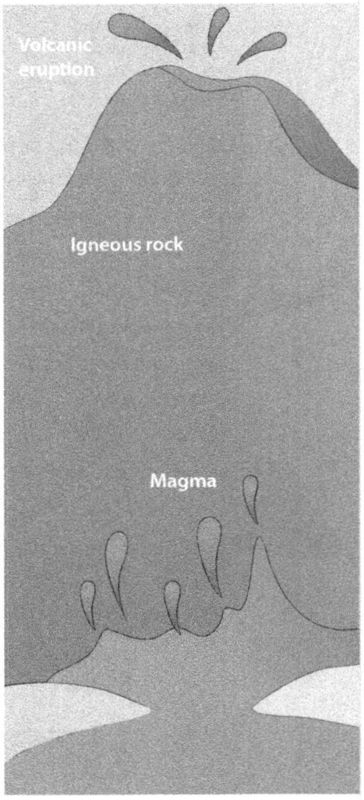

The rock cycle has no starting or ending point. You can jump in anywhere to see how it works. Let's begin with magma erupting from a towering volcano. The magma (now lava) cools and hardens into igneous rock. Over the course of thousands of years, sun, wind, rain, and freezing temperatures cause the rock to **weather**, or break down into smaller pieces. The pieces continue to weather, slowly breaking down into sediments. Howling winds, flowing water, and gravity gradually move the sediments down the sides of the volcano and beyond. Movement of sediments from place to place is called **erosion**.

Imagine that the sediments end up in a lake, where they settle to the bottom. Over long periods of time, more layers of sediments are deposited on top of them. Compacting and cementing processes eventually turn the deeply buried sediments into sedimentary rock.

Now imagine that the sedimentary rock is near the edge of a tectonic plate. The plate collides with another plate—very slowly, of course. Tremendous heat and pressure generated by the collision gradually turn the sedimentary rock into metamorphic rock. As the plates continue colliding, their rocky edges crumple. The metamorphic

60

- Have students read pages 60 and 61 silently.

  Literal. What is the rock cycle? Help students find where on this page the answer to the question can be found.

  » The rock cycle is an ongoing process of change in which rocks are created, destroyed, and recreated.

- Have students act out how erosion takes place over a period of many years, using the information on the page as a guide. They can use props or their own bodies. Encourage them to explain what is happening as they demonstrate it.

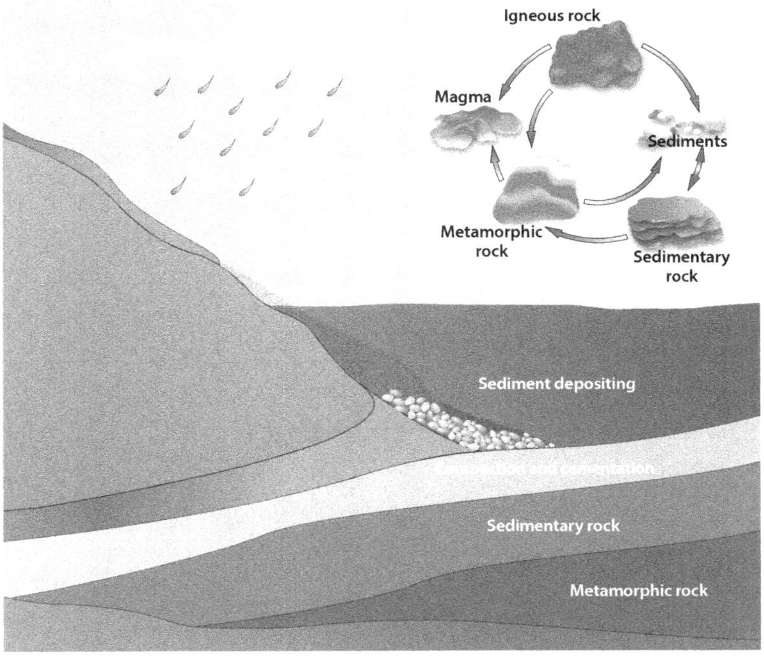

rock is slowly pushed up higher onto Earth's surface. Think mountains! Exposed to air, rain, and snow, the rock begins to weather and erode.

Alternatively, one tectonic plate might be sliding beneath another. The metamorphic rock along the edge of the descending plate gets hotter and hotter as it nears the mantle. At some point it melts into magma—magma that someday might erupt from a volcano again.

Understanding how rocks change helps geologists understand how Earth has changed over time.

61

- Have students describe what is happening in the illustration and relate it to what they have learned in the chapter so far.
- Have students respond to questions 7–15 on Activity Page 8.2. You may wish to have students compare their answers with a partner after they have completed the assignment and resolve any disagreements together.

LESSON WRAP-UP (5 MIN.)

Note: Question 3 relates to The Big Question of the chapter.

- Use the following question to discuss the chapter.

3. **Literal.** How can changes in rocks over time be explained by the rock cycle?

    » Answers may vary, but should include: Igneous rock forms from cooled lava. Over time, the rock weathers or breaks down into smaller pieces. These pieces continue to break down into sediments. Forces move the sediments to a place where they eventually settle. Over time, more sediment settles in the same place. Compacting and cementing processes turn the sediments, which started out as igneous rock, into sedimentary rock. Over time, the heat and pressure generated by tectonic plate collision turn the sedimentary rock into metamorphic rock. At some point the metamorphic rock melts into magma, which may someday erupt as lava and continue the rock cycle.

WORD WORK: CLASS (5 MIN.)

1. In the chapter you read, "Yet geologists organize all rocks into just three classes, or basic types: igneous, sedimentary, and metamorphic."
2. Say the word *class* with me.
3. *Class* means a group of people or things that are similar in some way.
4. You need a special license to drive vehicles in certain classes, such as a tractor trailer.
5. What are some other examples of classes of things? Be sure to use the word *class* in your response.

    » Answers will vary.

6. What part of speech is the word *class*?

    » noun

- Use a Synonyms activity for follow-up. What does the word *class* mean? What are some synonyms, or words with a similar meaning, of *class*? Prompt students to provide words such as *group*, *category*, and *type*. Turn to your partner and create sentences using the synonyms he or she provided.

Support

If necessary, guide and/or rephrase students' responses to make complete sentences: "A class of ____ might include ____."

Lesson 8: Three Types of Rocks and the Rock Cycle

Writing

45M

Primary Focus: Students will use a graphic organizer to take notes by paraphrasing text and will also draft a wiki entry. **[W.4.2, W.4.4, W.4.8]**

TAKE NOTES FOR A WIKI ENTRY (20 MIN.)

- Tell students that today they will take notes on a volcano and use the information to write a wiki entry.

1. What is a wiki?

- Provide prompts as needed to help students recall information about wikis from the previous lesson.
    - » A wiki is an online resource that provides information on many different topics or subjects. A wiki can be written or edited by multiple people, and can be updated over time. A wiki entry provides information on one particular topic or subject.

2. What are some of the advantages of a wiki?

- Use Think-Pair-Share to have students answer the question.
    - » Advantages may include having the ability to update quickly and easily as new information is found or learned, and the fact that multiple people are working on the wiki at the same time can increase the knowledge used to put the wiki together as well.
- Remind students that they have read about a number of different volcanoes in *The Changing Earth*. Tell students they can choose either Tambora or Mauna Loa to focus on in their wiki entry.
- Have students turn to Activity Page 8.3. Remind students that this graphic organizer is just like the Volcano Graphic Organizer you used to take notes in the previous lesson.
- Depending on which volcano students choose to write about, have them turn to the appropriate page in *The Changing Earth* (Tambora—page 33; Mauna Loa—page 36; Yellowstone—page 40).
- Have students read the page and identify the information in the text that relates to their specific volcano. Remind students to take notes by paraphrasing the text they just read, or writing information in their own words. Students should write key information in the shortest form possible.

Support

Students needing additional support may choose Yellowstone as the volcano to focus on for their entry and use the notes you took as a modeling exercise in Lesson 7 to fill in their graphic organizer.

Challenge

Explore an additional resource to take notes on one of the volcanoes, or have students take notes on a different volcano than those listed. See the Recommended Resources list in the unit digital components.

Activity Page 8.3

- Circulate around the room as students take notes, providing support and guidance as needed to assist students with paraphrasing.
- As students finish taking notes, ensure that their graphic organizers resemble the following.

Take Notes on a Volcano		
Name of the Volcano	**Tambora**	**Mauna Loa**
Location of the Volcano	Indonesia	Hawaii
Type of Volcano; Date of Last Eruption	active; spring of 1815	active; 1984
Description of Volcano or of Last Eruption	Eruption: blasted enormous amounts of ash high into the atmosphere	Volcano: peak is 13,796 feet above sea level, but base sits on the seafloor; from top to bottom, measures more than 33,000 feet
Other Facts	largest volcanic eruption in recorded history; ash from eruption distributed across the world, blocking sunlight reaching the earth, and leading to "the year without a summer"	largest active volcano; seafloor to top is taller than Mount Everest

Check for Understanding

Ask students whether the volcano they chose is active.

» for Tambura and Mauna Loa, yes; for Yellowstone, no

- If students do not provide the correct answer, help them review their notes or the text to find the accurate information.

Support

If students need help paraphrasing the text and taking notes, you may wish to have students work in pairs.

References for Volcano Wiki Entry		
Title	**Date**	**Source (Book or Web Address)**
The Changing Earth	2014	Book

DRAFT A WIKI ENTRY (25 MIN.)

- Have students turn to Activity Page 8.4 and begin drafting their wiki entry. Direct students to work on one heading at a time. Remind them to write complete sentences under the appropriate headings, using their notes.

3. In your notes, you used sentence fragments when writing about volcanoes. Why are you now using complete sentences?

    » Sentence fragments are a good way to take notes, because they are quick and easy, but for an actual finished product such as a wiki, complete sentences are easier to read and understand.

- Circulate as students write, providing support and guidance as needed.

Check for Understanding

As you circulate, check that students are using complete sentences. If students are not using complete sentences, review the four essential parts of full sentences: subject, predicate, initial capitalization, and final punctuation.

- **Feedback.** Provide reinforcing or corrective feedback as needed, using the following supports:
    - Have students ensure they have complete sentences.
    - Have students ensure that the information is presented beneath the appropriate headings.
- As you circulate, take note of which students could benefit from working in a small group during the next writing lesson.
- If students are ready to share some of their sentences, encourage them to do so.

End Lesson

Activity Page 8.4

Writing
Producing

Entering/Emerging
Guide students to convert the notes *big*, *active*, and *loud* into the sentences *The volcano is big*, *The volcano is active*, and *The eruption was loud*.

Transitioning/Expanding
Have students work in pairs to convert *active* and *loud* into sentences after you model converting *big* into *The volcano is big*.

Bridging
Have students independently convert all three words into sentences, then compare their sentences with a partner's.

Support

Display the Volcano Wiki Entry from the previous writing lesson for students who may need to use it as a guide.

LESSON

9

Close Reading: Rocks and the Rock Cycle

PRIMARY FOCUS OF LESSON

Reading

Students will describe what rocks are, explain the formation and characteristics of the three classes of rocks, and explain the features and importance of the rock cycle. **[RI.4.1, RI.4.2, RI.4.3]**

Grammar

Students will write dialogue that demonstrates the correct use of commas and quotation marks. **[L.4.2]**

Morphology

Students will practice creating and using sentences that include words with the root *rupt*. **[L.4.4]**

Spelling

Students will practice spelling targeted words with familiar roots. **[L.4.2]**

FORMATIVE ASSESSMENT

Activity Page 1.3	**Evidence Collector's Chart** Students look in the text for evidence supporting geological events. **[RI.4.1]**
Activity Page 1.4	**Evidence of Changes on Earth** Students look in the text for evidence supporting geological events. **[RI.4.1]**
Activity Page 9.1	**Excerpts from "Earth's Building Blocks"** Students answer questions about rock types and the rock cycle. **[RI.4.1, RI.4.2]**
Activity Page 9.2	**Commas and Quotation Marks** Students punctuate sentences, including excerpts from the text, that contain dialogue or quotes. **[L.4.2]**

Activity Page 9.3	**Root rupt** Students write and complete sentences using words with the root *rupt*. **[L.4.4]**
Activity Page 9.4	**Spelling Words** Students spell words that use familiar roots. **[L.4.2]**

LESSON AT A GLANCE

	Grouping	Time	Materials
Reading (45 min.)			
Review Chapter 6	Whole Group	5 min.	❑ *The Changing Earth* ❑ Activity Pages 1.3, 1.4, 9.1 ❑ Evidence Collector's Chart ❑ scissors ❑ glue
Close Reading: Read "Earth's Building Blocks"	Whole Group	25 min.	
Discuss the Chapter and Lesson Wrap-Up	Whole Group	10 min.	
Word Work: *Compact*	Whole Group	5 min.	
Language (45 min.)			
Grammar: Practice Commas and Quotation Marks	Whole Group/ Pairs	15 min.	❑ Commas Poster Addition ❑ Quotation Marks Poster ❑ Activity Page 9.2
Morphology: Practice Root *rupt*	Whole Group/ Pairs	15 min.	❑ Activity Page 9.3
Spelling: Practice Spelling Words	Whole Group	15 min.	❑ Activity Pages 9.4, SR.1
Take-Home Material			
Reading			❑ Activity Page 9.1

ADVANCE PREPARATION

Reading

- **Note:** You may access a digital version of The Big Question in the digital components for this unit.
- Display the Evidence Collector's Chart from Lesson 1.

Language

Grammar

- Write the following examples on the board/chart paper.
    - The text states Earth's crust is made almost entirely of rocks.
    - I wonder he said aloud if I will ever get to visit the Grand Canyon.
    - I have seen she exclaimed evidence of weathering and erosion.
- Determine student pairs for completing the first portion of Activity Page 9.2.

Morphology

- Determine student pairs for completing the first portion of Activity Page 9.3.

Start Lesson

Lesson 9: Close Reading: Rocks and the Rock Cycle

Reading

45M

Primary Focus: Students will describe what rocks are, explain the formation and characteristics of the three classes of rocks, and explain the features and importance of the rock cycle. **[RI.4.1, RI.4.2, RI.4.3]**

REVIEW CHAPTER 6 (5 MIN.)

- Tell students that they will reread Chapter 6, "Earth's Building Blocks."
- Ask students to tell a partner one thing that they remember from the chapter.
- Have students locate the chapter in the table of contents and then turn to the first page of the chapter.
- Have one student read The Big Question at the beginning of the chapter. Ensure students understand the meaning of The Big Question before reading the chapter.
    - How can changes in rocks over time be explained by the rock cycle?

All the varieties of rocks can be organized into three classes.

Rocks and Building Blocks

Just what are rocks, exactly? Rocks are naturally occurring materials made of solid, nonliving substances called **minerals**. Think of minerals as the building blocks of rocks. Some rocks are formed from just one mineral. Most rocks, however, are combinations of two or more minerals. Minerals appear as different-sized pieces, or grains, in rocks. Some rocks have very tiny mineral grains, giving the rocks a smooth, even **texture**. Other rocks have larger mineral grains and a rougher texture.

Imagine hiking up a mountain and picking up rocks along the way. When you reach the top, you'll probably have quite a collection. Your rocks may have different colors and textures. Some may have stripes or layers. Some might be hard and others crumbly. Some have tiny grains whereas others have large grains that glitter when they catch the light. All this variety might seem confusing. Yet geologists organize all rocks into just three classes, or basic types: igneous, sedimentary, and metamorphic.

53

CLOSE READING: READ "EARTH'S BUILDING BLOCKS" (25 MIN.)

- Read the title of the chapter as a class, "Earth's Building Blocks." Then read aloud portions of the chapter as indicated. Pause to explain or clarify the text or to ask questions when specified.
- Read page 53 aloud.

Inferential. You have learned that a metaphor is a literary device in which the words usually used to describe one thing are used to describe something different. The author states that minerals are the building blocks of rocks. What does this metaphor mean?

» Answers may vary but should include that building blocks serve as the foundation from which things are made. Buildings are actually made of blocks. If something is referred to as a building block for something else, it serves as the basis for the creation of the other thing. "Minerals are the building blocks of rocks" means that minerals serve as the foundation for the makeup of rocks; in other words, rocks are formed from minerals.

Support

What are minerals?

» Minerals are solid, nonliving substances found in the earth.

In small groups or pairs, have students complete the following sentences: Wood is the building block of ____; flour is the building block of ____; wool and cotton are the building blocks of ____.

» possible answers: wood—houses, tables, trees; flour—bread, cake; wool and cotton—clothing, sheets, towels

Born from Magma: Igneous Rock

Let's start with **igneous rocks**, the most abundant class of rocks on the earth. Igneous rocks form when magma cools and **solidifies**. When you think of igneous rocks, think of volcanoes.

There are two basic types of igneous rock. One type forms from magma that erupts onto Earth's surface as lava. The lava cools and hardens into rock. The faster it cools, the smaller the mineral grains will be in the resulting rock. **Obsidian** is an igneous rock formed from lava that cooled very quickly, so quickly, there wasn't time for the minerals to form grains. As a result, obsidian is as smooth and shiny as glass. In fact, it is often called volcanic glass. Basalt is an igneous rock formed from lava that took longer to cool. Basalt is typically a dark-colored rock. It has fairly small mineral grains that give it a fine-grained texture.

The second type of igneous rock forms from magma that solidifies below Earth's surface. Magma cools very slowly when it's deep beneath the surface. Slow cooling leads to igneous rocks with relatively large mineral grains. The slower the cooling, the larger the grains. **Granite** is a common igneous rock that forms from magma that cooled within Earth's crust. Granite usually contains mineral grains that are large enough to see with the naked eye.

Igneous rocks

54

- Read page 54 aloud.

Inferential. In the middle of the second paragraph, the author uses the phrase *in fact* in a sentence. The phrase *in fact* can be used to make an idea clearer by introducing specific or unexpected information. In what ways does the use of this phrase make the meaning of the information about obsidian clearer?

» The phrase *in fact* signals to the reader that the information following it is important and supports the point made in the previous sentence about obsidian. The information following *in fact* describes additional detail about the result of lava cooling so quickly. Grains are different-sized pieces of minerals visible in rocks. Obsidian is smooth and shiny because the lava that formed it cooled too quickly for grains to form. The statement with *in fact* provides additional information about the formation of obsidian.

Challenge

Why do you think the author wrote "relatively large mineral grains" instead of "large mineral grains"?

» Even though these mineral grains are larger than in other rocks, they are still very small. Using "large" would suggest that they were considerably bigger than they really are.

- Have students work with a partner to create a sentence using the phrase *in fact*. Ask pairs whether their sentences present a specific fact or an unexpected fact.

Inferential. Reread the sentence in the middle of the third paragraph that begins, "Slow cooling leads to . . . ." The word *relatively* means "when compared to others." How does the use of the word *relatively* in this sentence add to the reader's knowledge about igneous rocks?

» The word *relatively* signals that the mineral grains in igneous rocks formed from the slow cooling of lava are large compared to grains in other rocks.

Check for Understanding

Ask students what it means to say that a certain rock was formed "relatively recently."

» It was formed recently compared to other rocks.

If students do not understand the meaning of the word *relatively*, review the use of the word on page 54 of the Reader.

Inferential. The last sentence on the page contains the idiom *the naked eye*. *The naked eye* means "the human eye." If something can be seen with the naked eye, it can be seen without the help of a telescope, microscope, or other tool. If granite usually contains minerals that are large enough to see with the naked eye, what does that mean?

» A person can see the grains in granite just by looking at the rock. A person does not need any tools to help see the grains in granite because they are clearly visible in the rock.

The Art of Making Stone Tools

Many prehistoric cultures made tools out of rock. Scientists working in East Africa have found obsidian stone tools that are nearly two million years old. Obsidian was especially prized by ancient tool makers. Obsidian breaks into pieces with sharp edges that are good for cutting and piercing.

To make a very sharp cutting tool, ancient tool makers struck a block of obsidian with another, harder rock. This caused a long, thin blade of obsidian to flake off. Although the blade was fragile, it had incredibly sharp edges. In fact, the edges of obsidian blades are much sharper than metal scalpels used by surgeons today.

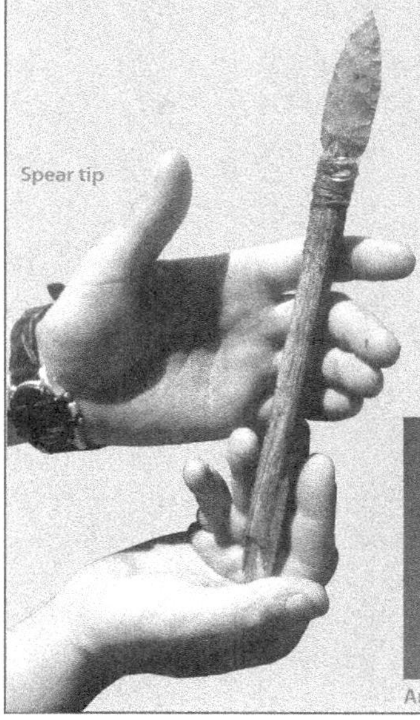

Spear tip

Making a spear tip or arrowhead was more time consuming. The tool makers started with a relatively flat piece of obsidian. They shaped it by striking off tiny flakes of rock, one after another, from the edges. They gradually shaped it into a sharp, **durable**—and often beautiful—pointed tool.

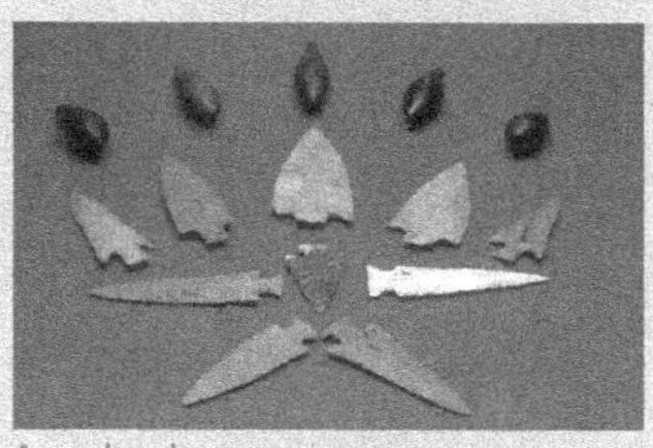

Arrowheads

55

- Read page 55 aloud.

  Evaluative. *Durable* means "able to last a long time in good condition." Why would it be important to people in prehistoric cultures that a rock for a tool be durable?

  » Some tools were time-consuming to make; if they were durable and lasted a long time, tool-makers may not have had to make new tools as often. In addition, if a tool was made of durable rock, the tool would last through many uses, whether it was part of a cutting tool, spear, or arrowhead.

Check for Understanding

Ask students to use the word *durable* in a sentence.

» Possible answers: Duct tape can be very durable because it lasts a long time; Some plastic toys break easily, so they are not very durable.

- If students cannot easily come up with a sentence, review the meaning of the word *durable*.

Layer after Layer: Sedimentary Rock

Sedimentary rock is the second major class of rocks. Sedimentary rocks are made of sediments. Sediments are tiny bits of rock and sand combined with fragments of once-living things. Sediments collect in low-lying areas both on land and in bodies of water. They form layers, one on top of another. Over long periods of time, the weight of overlying layers **compacts** the sediments in deeper layers, squeezing them closer together. Sediments also become cemented, or glued, together as **dissolved** minerals fill the spaces between the sediments. As the sediments dry, the dissolved minerals turn into solids, binding the sediments together. Over time, compacting and cementing processes transform sediments into sedimentary rock.

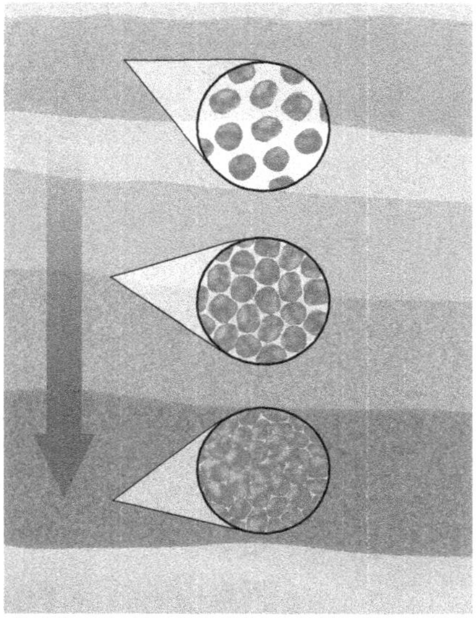

The weight of overlying layers compacts the sediments, squeezing them closer together.

Most sedimentary rocks are more easily broken than most igneous rocks. Hit a sedimentary rock with a hammer, and it will crumble or break apart. Some sedimentary rocks contain fossils. **Limestone** is a sedimentary rock often packed with the fossilized skeletons and shells of tiny ocean creatures. Some sedimentary rocks get their name from their sediments. Sandstone started as grains of sand, whereas mudstone formed from ancient mud.

56

The eroded formations of these sedimentary rocks in Badlands National Park in South Dakota show their distinct layers. The oldest layers are at the bottom.

57

Changing Form: Metamorphic Rock

The third major class of rocks is **metamorphic rock**. Metamorphic rocks form when igneous or sedimentary rocks are exposed to extreme heat and pressure. They can even form from older metamorphic rocks. High temperatures and crushing pressure alter the minerals in the rocks. Mineral grains may be flattened or rearranged into layers, swirls, or stripes. They may also be changed into completely different minerals!

Remember granite, the igneous rock? When granite is subjected to intense heat and pressure, it becomes a metamorphic rock called gneiss. When the sedimentary rock limestone is squeezed and heated deep below ground, it becomes a metamorphic rock called marble.

Metamorphic rocks tend to form deep within Earth's crust. The pressure from countless tons of overlying rock is tremendous. Equally powerful is the heat rising from hot magma in the mantle beneath the crust. Metamorphic rocks often form where tectonic plates are slowly colliding. They can also form as magma travels up through cracks in Earth's crust and heats the rocks around the cracks. If the heat of the magma completely melts the rock again, then it becomes igneous rock. If the rock is heated just enough to be changed, however, it instead becomes metamorphic rock.

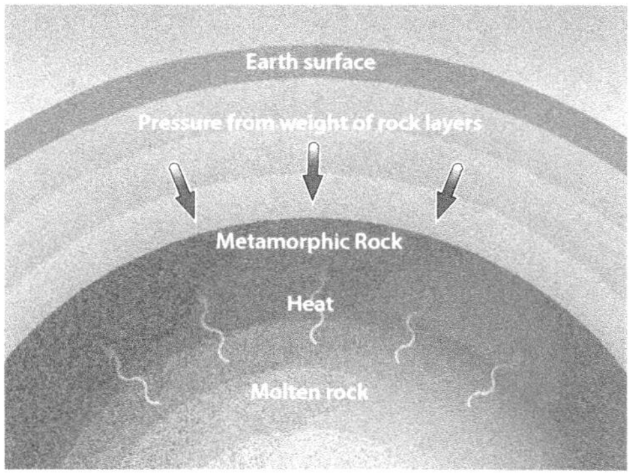

58

Pronunciation Table	
Word(s)	**CK Code**
gneiss	/nis/
Agnes Nyanhongo	/ag*nes/ /nie*an*hong*goe/
Zimbabwe	/zim*bob*wae/

- Read the last paragraph on page 58 aloud.

  Inferential. What role does heat from magma play in determining the class of rock formed?

  » Magma travels up through cracks in Earth's crust and heats the rocks around the cracks. If the heat of the magma completely melts the rock again, it becomes igneous rock. If the rock is heated just enough to be changed, it becomes metamorphic rock. The amount of heat determines what class of rock is formed.

Check for Understanding

What type of rock is formed when an existing rock is heated enough to be changed without actually melting?

» metamorphic

- If students cannot answer the question, have them review the information on the third paragraph of page 58.

Agnes Nyanhongo's Stone Sculptures

Agnes Nyanhongo

Zimbabwean sculptor Agnes Nyanhongo became interested in carving rock at an early age. Her father, Claud Nyanhongo, was a sculptor. She worked in his studio as a young girl and learned how to cut and polish rock. She is now one of Zimbabwe's most well-known artists. Agnes Nyanhongo carves many of her sculptures from a type of rock called serpentine. Serpentine is a metamorphic rock. The type of serpentine Agnes Nyanhongo uses for many of her sculptures is very dark in color. She usually polishes only some parts of her sculptures, leaving the rest simply raw stone.

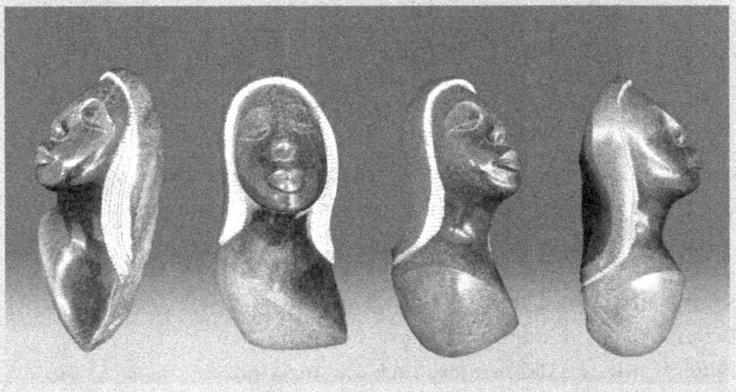

Sculptures carved from serpentine

59

- Read page 59 aloud.

Inferential. To polish means "to make something smooth and shiny." The author states that Agnes Nyanhongo polishes parts of her sculptures. Why might Agnes Nyanhongo have to polish her sculptures?

» Answers may vary, but should include that, because there are grains in metamorphic rock, Agnes Nyanhongo would need to polish her sculptures to make them smooth and shiny. She carves her sculptures out of serpentine, which is a type of metamorphic rock. Metamorphic rock has mineral grains, which give rock texture.

Challenge

Why might Agnes Nyanhongo choose to leave some parts of her sculptures unpolished?

» Answers may vary, but may include that having both polished and unpolished parts in a sculpture creates interesting color and texture contrasts.

The Rock Cycle

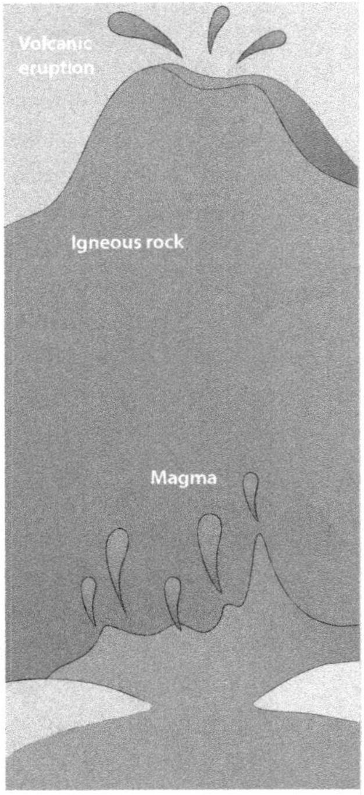

Rocks you see in the world around you might seem like permanent fixtures. Given enough time, however, all rocks change. They are created, destroyed, and recreated in a continuous cycle. Geologists call this ongoing process the **rock cycle**.

The rock cycle has no starting or ending point. You can jump in anywhere to see how it works. Let's begin with magma erupting from a towering volcano. The magma (now lava) cools and hardens into igneous rock. Over the course of thousands of years, sun, wind, rain, and freezing temperatures cause the rock to **weather**, or break down into smaller pieces. The pieces continue to weather, slowly breaking down into sediments. Howling winds, flowing water, and gravity gradually move the sediments down the sides of the volcano and beyond. Movement of sediments from place to place is called **erosion**.

Imagine that the sediments end up in a lake, where they settle to the bottom. Over long periods of time, more layers of sediments are deposited on top of them. Compacting and cementing processes eventually turn the deeply buried sediments into sedimentary rock.

Now imagine that the sedimentary rock is near the edge of a tectonic plate. The plate collides with another plate—very slowly, of course. Tremendous heat and pressure generated by the collision gradually turn the sedimentary rock into metamorphic rock. As the plates continue colliding, their rocky edges crumple. The metamorphic

60

- Read the first two paragraphs on page 60 aloud.

Inferential. Permanent fixtures are things that are part of something for a long time without changing. Why might rocks seem like permanent fixtures?

» Answers may vary, but should include that rocks may seem as if they have always been there and have always looked the way they do now. They are large and don't appear to move or change.

Inferential. Why aren't rocks permanent fixtures? What can happen to alter them over time?

» Answers may vary, but may include the power of wind and water to erode them over time, along with being broken, carved, or moved by humans.

Inferential. Why doesn't the rock cycle have a starting point or ending point?

» Answers may vary but should include that the rock cycle is an ongoing process that never stops. Rocks are created, destroyed, and recreated in a cycle that happens continuously. There is no place to mark the start and no place to mark the end because the cycle is ongoing.

DISCUSS THE CHAPTER AND LESSON WRAP-UP (10 MIN.)

Note: Activity Page 1.3 relates to The Big Question of the chapter.

- Have students turn to Activity Pages 1.3 and 1.4 and refer to the displayed Evidence Collector's Chart.

1. What is the purpose of this chart?

   » It describes evidence of changes to the Earth related to geology.

- Remind students that this evidence is what geologists examine to determine how powerful forces above and below Earth's surface work to change the planet.
- Have a student read aloud the information under "What is the cause?" in the fifth row. Explain that students must determine what evidence is in the chapter about rocks being created, destroyed, and recreated in a continuous cycle. (pages 60 and 61)

2. What do we call the process of rocks being created, destroyed, and recreated?

   » the rock cycle

- Have students refer to the remaining images on Activity Page 1.4. Engage students in a discussion about the images, talking about which image represents evidence of rocks being created, destroyed, and recreated in a continuous cycle. (Image showing the rock cycle and Earth's rock layers.)

3. Why is the correct image the one that shows the rock cycle and Earth's rock layers?

   » The image shows the cycle of how different types of rocks are created, destroyed, and recreated, and how these types of rocks are related in that cycle.

- Have students cut out the correct image, glue it to the chart in the "What evidence is there?" column, and write the following information for chapter number, key words, and letter:

Activity Pages
1.3 and 1.4

Reading for Information
Prefixes

Entering/Emerging
Help students understand that the prefix *re-* (as in *created* and *re-created*) means *again*. Write *do*, *write*, and *read* on the board. Add *re* in front of each. Read the words and explain their meanings with words and gestures.

Transitioning/Expanding
Model changing *do*, *write*, and *read* to *redo*, *rewrite*, and *reread* as above. Have students use these words in sentences.

Bridging
Have students use the words above in sentences and brainstorm other words with the prefix *re-*.

Chapter #	What is the cause?	What evidence is there?	Letter
6	*Rocks are created, destroyed, and recreated in a continuous cycle.*	*image: the rock cycle and Earth's rock layers* *key words:* igneous, sedimentary, and metamorphic rock	I

Activity Page 9.1

- Have students turn to Activity Page 9.1. Ensure students understand the directions. Tell them they will complete the activity page for homework.

WORD WORK: *COMPACT* (5 MIN.)

1. In the chapter you read, "Over long periods of time, the weight of overlying layers compacts the sediments in deeper layers, squeezing them closer together."
2. Say the word *compact* with me.
3. Compact means "to closely pack or press together."
4. The garbage truck compacts the trash after the workers place it in the truck.
5. What are some other examples of *compact?* Make up several sentences with the word *compact*.
   - » Answers will vary.
6. What part of speech is the word *compact?*
   - » verb

Support

If necessary, guide and/or rephrase students' responses to make complete sentences: "____ compacts ____ when it ____"

- Use an Antonyms activity for follow-up. An antonym, or word that has the opposite meaning, of the word *compact* is *spread*. I will read several sentences, and if the sentence describes something that is being compacted, say, "compact(s)." If the sentence describes something that is spreading out, say, "spread(s)."

1. Pressing snow together to create a good snowball (compacts/spreads) the snow so that it becomes firm and shaped.
   » compacts
2. My father tilted the wheelbarrow full of soil to (compact/spread) the soil where he wanted to plant vegetables.
   » spread
3. Applying pressure (compacts/spreads) the different bits of cookie dough into one solid piece.
   » compacts
4. Many people walking on the same trail over and over (compacts/spreads) the dirt of the trail so that it becomes very hard.
   » compacts
5. The wind (compacts/spreads) the dandelion seeds in the air.
   » spreads

Lesson 9: Close Reading: Rocks and the Rock Cycle

Language

45M

GRAMMAR : PRACTICE COMMAS AND QUOTATION MARKS (15 MIN.)

Primary Focus: Students will write dialogue that demonstrates correct use of commas and quotation marks. **[L.4.2]**

- Refer to the Commas Poster Addition and the Quotation Marks Poster and read them with students.
- Refer to the three examples you prepared in advance.

  The text states Earth's crust is made almost entirely of rocks.

  I wonder he said aloud if I will ever get to visit the Grand Canyon.

  I have seen she exclaimed evidence of weathering and erosion.

Support

Use guiding questions such as *What does the text state?* and *What did he say aloud?* to help students recognize what is being said or quoted in these sentences, and what simply indicates who said it.

Activity Page 9.2

Language
Punctuation

Entering/Emerging
Help students understand what is and isn't dialogue by having them read the dialogue orally while you speak the parts not in quotation marks. For example, you say, "The text states," and they say, "Earth's crust ____."

Transitioning/Expanding
Use the activity above, but have students work in pairs. One student speaks the dialogue while the other speaks the rest of the sentence.

Bridging
Have students work in pairs to write and read short dialogues as above.

- Read each sentence aloud and have students decide where the commas and quotation marks should be placed in each example. Then insert the commas and quotation marks in the correct locations.
  - The text states, "Earth's crust is made almost entirely of rocks."
  - "I wonder," he said aloud, "if I will ever get to visit the Grand Canyon."
  - "I have seen," she exclaimed, "evidence of weathering and erosion."
- Have students turn to Activity Page 9.2.

Check for Understanding

Have students complete the first question on Activity Page 9.2 independently.

» Just then, my dad asked, "What would you like to eat for dinner?"

- If students punctuate the sentence incorrectly, review the rules for punctuating sentences that contain direct quotations or dialogue.

- After students complete the first question on their own, pair them to work together to complete the next five items on Activity Page 9.2.
- Once students have completed this section of the activity page, review the correct answers as a whole group.
- Have students complete the second portion of Activity Page 9.2 independently.
- Collect completed Activity Page 9.2 to review and grade at a later time.

MORPHOLOGY: PRACTICE ROOT *RUPT* (15 MIN.)

Primary Focus: Students will practice creating and using sentences that include words with the root *rupt*. **[L.4.4]**

- Explain that you will give students two word choices, each of which features the root *rupt*. Then, you will read a statement. Students must decide which word the statement demonstrates. Have students use Think-Pair-Share to help them confirm their answers.

6. Disrupt or erupt? A noisy neighbor distracted me while I was trying to practice playing a new song on the piano.
   » disrupt
7. Abrupt or uninterrupted? During the marathon, he ran for two hours without stopping.
   » uninterrupted

Check for Understanding

Rupture or abrupt? A burst pipe underground closed the road all day.

» rupture

- If students do not choose the correct word, review the meanings of both *rupture* and *abrupt*.

- Have students turn to Activity Page 9.3. Read the directions and tell students to work in pairs to complete it. Invite students to use print or online dictionaries to help them if they are not certain of the meanings of these words. They may also find their work from Activity Page 6.3 useful, since it covered many of the same words.
- As time allows, ask a few partner pairs to share their sentences aloud.
- Collect completed Activity Page 9.3 to review and grade at a later time.

SPELLING: PRACTICE SPELLING WORDS (15 MIN.)

Primary Focus: Students will practice spelling targeted words with familiar roots. **[L.4.2]**

- Tell students they will practice writing the spelling words. Remind them to use the Individual Code Chart on Activity Page SR.1 as they practice.
- Have students turn to Activity Page 9.4, explaining that the spelling words are listed in the box on the activity page and on the board/chart paper from the first lesson.
- Have students read sentence 1 silently and fill in the blank. After students complete item 1, then call on one student to read the sentence aloud with the spelling word in the blank.

Language
Word Endings

Entering/Emerging
Point out the words on the activity page with the endings *–ed* and *–tion*. Have the group sort them into nouns and verbs according to the endings. Discuss the meaning of each word.

Transitioning/Expanding
Have pairs sort the words with the endings *–ed* and *–tion* into nouns and verbs. Discuss the meaning of each word.

Bridging
Have individual students sort the words with the endings *–ed* and *–tion* into nouns and verbs. Discuss the meaning of each word.

Activity Page 9.3

Activity Page 9.4

- Ask students if anyone had a different answer. Discuss the correct answer to ensure students understand why it is correct.
- Have students check their spelling against the spelling in the word bank on the activity page, make corrections if needed, and then turn the page over.
- Have students say, spell, and repeat the word with you. Make sure they are not looking at the activity page. Students may close their eyes, look up at the ceiling, or trace on the back of their paper with their finger to help them visualize the spelling as they work with you.

Check for Understanding

Repeat the process with the second word, checking to make sure students can spell the word correctly.

» autograph

- If students do not spell the word accurately, have them review the spelling by dividing the word into parts (*auto* and *graph*).

- Turn the page over and repeat the steps for the remaining items.
- As time allows, complete the say-spell-repeat steps for the unused words: *hierarchy*, *calligraphy*, *rupture*, and *anarchy*.
- As time allows, students can use the spelling words to write their own sentences on the back of their paper.
- Remind students to study the spelling words for the spelling assessment in the next lesson.

Language
Spelling

Entering/Emerging
Provide the correct word for students to spell so they do not need to identify it from the context of the sentence.

Transitioning/Expanding
For each item, give students a choice of two words from the list (one correct and one incorrect); then have students identify the correct word and spell it as above.

Bridging
For each item, tell students the line in which the correct word appears.

End Lesson

Lesson 9: Close Reading: Rocks and the Rock Cycle

Take-Home Material

READING

- Have students take home Activity Page 9.1 to read and complete for homework.

Activity Page 9.1

LESSON

10 Weathering and Erosion, Part 1

PRIMARY FOCUS OF LESSON

Spelling

Students will demonstrate their knowledge of the correct spelling of targeted words. **[L.4.2]**

Reading

Students will identify, define, and provide examples of weathering and erosion and how they reshape Earth's surface. **[RI.4.2, RI.4.3, RI.4.4]**

Writing

Students will revise and edit their writing using a writing rubric and editing checklist as guides. **[W.4.4, W.4.5]**

FORMATIVE ASSESSMENT

Flowchart	**Flowchart** Students create a flowchart to describe the process of chemical weathering. **[RI.4.2, RI.4.3]**
Activity Page 7.4	**Wiki Entry Rubric** This rubric is used to help assess student work. **[W.4.2, W.4.4]**
Activity Page 7.5	**Wiki Entry Editing Checklist** Students use this checklist to help them create a strong wiki entry. **[W.4.2, W.4.4]**
Activity Page 8.4	**Volcano Wiki Entry** Students fill in a form giving information about a volcano they are researching. **[W.4.8]**
Activity Page 9.1	**Excerpts from "Earth's Building Blocks"** Students answer questions about rock types and the rock cycle. **[RI.4.2, RI.4.4]**
Activity Page 10.1	**Spelling Assessment** Students spell words they have practiced over the course of several lessons. **[L.4.2]**
Activity Page 10.3	**"Earth's Powerful Forces of Change"** Students choose vocabulary activities to practice vocabulary terms from the lesson. **[RI.4.4]**

LESSON AT A GLANCE

	Grouping	Time	Materials
Spelling (15 min.)			
Assessment	Whole Group	15 min.	❏ Activity Page 10.1
Reading (45 min.)			
Review	Whole Group	5 min.	❏ Answer Key for Activity Page 9.1 ❏ Activity Pages 9.1, 10.2, 10.3 ❏ *The Changing Earth*
Introduce the Chapter	Whole Group	5 min.	
Read "Earth's Powerful Forces of Change"	Whole Group	20 min.	
Discuss Chapter and Wrap Up Lesson	Whole Group	10 min.	
Word Work: *State*	Whole Group	5 min.	
Writing (30 min.)			
Revise and Edit a Wiki Entry	Whole Group/ Independent	25 min.	❏ Activity Pages 7.4, 7.5, 8.4 ❏ Volcano Wiki Entry
Lesson Wrap-Up	Whole Group	5 min.	
Take-Home Material			
Reading			❏ Activity Page 10.3

ADVANCE PREPARATION

Spelling

- Erase or cover the list of spelling words prior to the assessment.

Reading

- Access a digital version of The Big Question in the digital components for this unit.
    - Read to learn how the powerful forces of weathering and erosion reshape Earth's surface.

Writing

- Prepare to display the Volcano Wiki Entry from Lesson 7.
- Prepare to assign students to small groups for additional support as needed.

Fluency (optional)

- If students were assigned a selection from the Fluency Supplement, determine which students will read the selection aloud and when. See the Unit 1 Teacher Guide introduction for more information on using the Fluency Supplement.

Start Lesson

Lesson 10: Weathering and Erosion

Spelling

15M

Primary Focus: Students will demonstrate their knowledge of the correct spelling of targeted words. **[L.4.2]**

ASSESSMENT

Activity Page 10.1

- Have students turn to Activity Page 10.1 for the spelling assessment.
- Using the following list, read the words one at a time in the following manner: Say the word, use it in a sentence, and then repeat the word.
- Tell students that at the end you will review the list once more.
- Remind students to pronounce and spell each word syllable by syllable.

Spelling Word	Example Sentence
1. archrival	The superhero outsmarted his archrival and saved the city.
2. paragraph	I read a very interesting paragraph about Yellowstone National Park.
3. rupture	Lava oozed onto Earth's surface from a rupture in the crust.
4. hierarchy	In the hierarchy of a basketball team, the coach is at the top.
5. biographer	The biographer won an award for her book about an undersea explorer.
6. abrupt	The movie's ending was abrupt and did not bring the story to an end.
7. matriarch	Mrs. Baker is the leader and matriarch of the local gardening club.
8. uninterrupted	They must have been tired because they slept uninterrupted for 10 hours.
9. anarchy	When anarchy broke out, the city was destroyed.
10. autograph	When she met her favorite musician, she asked for his autograph.
11. eruption	The people evacuated the island because of a major volcanic eruption.
12. calligraphy	They took a class to learn the art of calligraphy.

- After reading all of the words, review the list slowly, reading each word once more.
- Tell students that, starting with today's spelling assessment, you will also dictate a sentence for students to write. Explain that you will read the sentence several times.
- Have students write the following sentence as dictated:
    - Scientists examined evidence of the eruption near the volcano.
- Repeat the sentence slowly several times, reminding students to check their work for appropriate capitalization and punctuation.
- Collect all spelling assessments to grade later. Use of the template provided at the end of this lesson is highly recommended to identify and analyze students' errors.

Language
Spelling

Entering/Emerging
Use gestures and sketches to help students understand the meanings of the spelling words and sentences.

Transitioning/Expanding
Use gestures and simpler words and phrases to help students understand the meanings of the spelling words and sentences.

Bridging
Use words and phrases to help students understand the meanings of the spelling words and sentences.

Lesson 10: Weathering and Erosion

Reading

45M

Primary Focus: Students will identify, define, and provide examples of weathering and erosion and how they reshape Earth's surface. **[RI.4.2, RI.4.3, RI.4.4]**

REVIEW (5 MIN.)

- Using the Answer Key at the back of this Teacher Guide, review student responses to Activity Page 9.1, which was assigned for homework in the previous reading lesson.
- Invite students to explain briefly how they knew which word belonged in each blank. Encourage them to use words and terms such as *noun* and *adjective* in giving their explanations.

INTRODUCE THE CHAPTER (5 MIN.)

- Tell students they will read Chapter 7, "Earth's Powerful Forces of Change."
- Have students turn to the table of contents, locate the chapter, and then turn to the first page of the chapter.
- Preview the core vocabulary words before reading the chapter.
- Begin by telling students the first vocabulary words they will encounter in this chapter are *physical weathering* and *chemical weathering*. Tell students these words are explained later in the chapter and included in the glossary so they won't be previewed in this lesson.
- Tell students the next vocabulary word they will encounter in this chapter is *expand*.
- Have them find the word on page 63 of the Reader.

1. Why does this word appear in bold type?
   » Each vocabulary word is bolded the first time it appears in the chapter.
2. Where can you look in the text to find a definition of the word *expand*?
   » in the glossary, which contains definitions of all the vocabulary words in the Reader

- Have students refer to the glossary at the back of the Reader and locate *expand*. Have a student read the definition.
- Explain the following:
    - the part of speech
    - alternate forms of the word
- Have students reference Activity Page 10.2 while you read each word and its meaning. Review that words are listed in the order in which they appear in the chapter.
- Have students circle any unfamiliar words on Activity Page 10.2. Explain that, by circling words they do not know, students can see at a glance which words they need to study more closely.
- Explain that some of these words have multiple meanings; tell students that they should pay particular attention to the meaning or meanings given in the glossary, even if they may know other meanings.

Activity Page 10.2

expand, v. to get bigger (63)

contract, v. to shrink slightly or get smaller (63)

ultimately, adv. finally; at the end of a process (65)

pepper, v. to sprinkle or cover (67)

deposit, 1. **v.** to put or leave something in a particular place; 2. **n.** material laid down or left by a natural process (v. deposited, n. deposits) (67)

state, n. the condition of being a solid, liquid, or gas (69)

silt, n. very small sediments deposited by water (69)

canyon, n. a deep valley with steep sides and often a stream or river flowing through it (canyons) (70)

Vocabulary Chart for Chapter 7 "Earth's Powerful Forces of Change"		
Vocabulary Type	**Tier 3** **Domain-Specific Words**	**Tier 2** **General Academic Words**
Core Vocabulary	state silt canyon	expand contract ultimately pepper deposit
Spanish Cognates for Core Vocabulary	cañón	depósito
Multiple-Meaning Core Vocabulary Words	state	pepper
Sayings and Phrases	eats away at <an idea is almost> impossible to grasp	

- Have one student read The Big Question at the beginning of the chapter. Ensure students understand the meaning of The Big Question before reading the chapter.
    - How do weathering and erosion continually reshape Earth's surface?

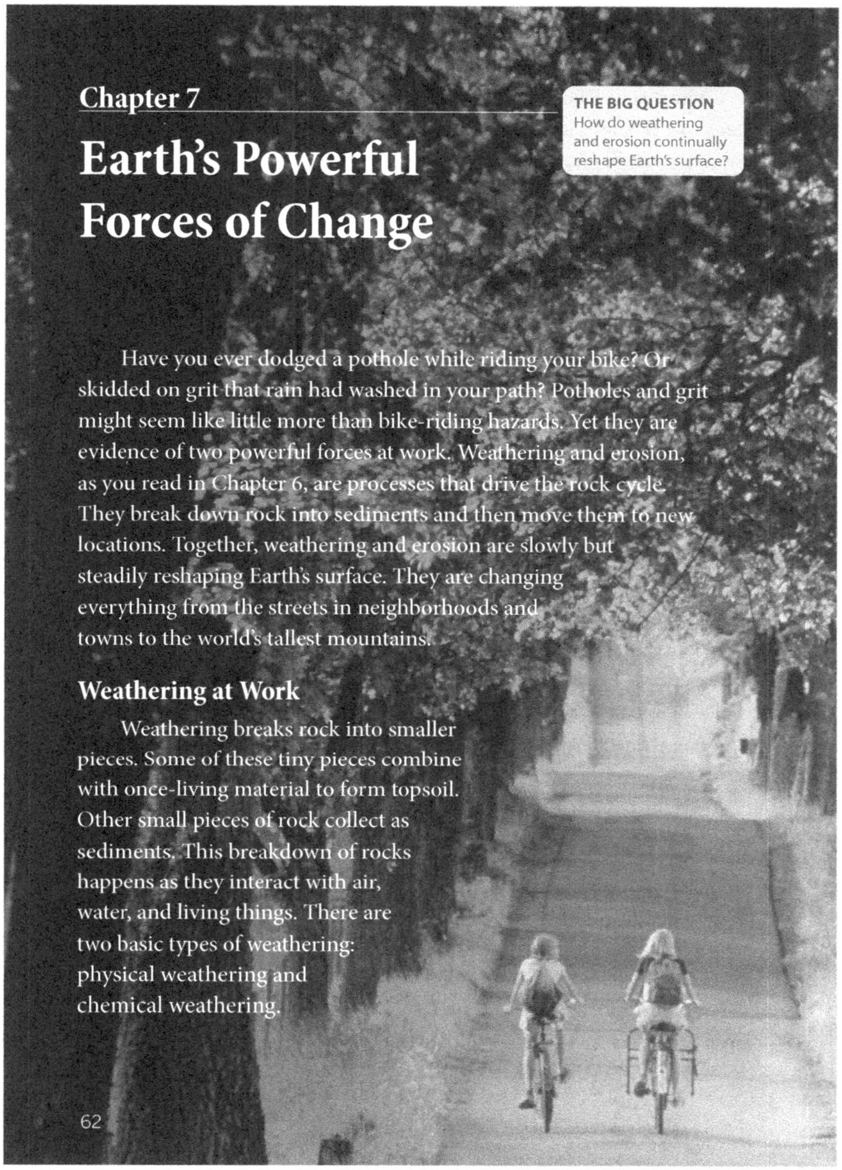

Chapter 7

Earth's Powerful Forces of Change

THE BIG QUESTION
How do weathering and erosion continually reshape Earth's surface?

Have you ever dodged a pothole while riding your bike? Or skidded on grit that rain had washed in your path? Potholes and grit might seem like little more than bike-riding hazards. Yet they are evidence of two powerful forces at work. Weathering and erosion, as you read in Chapter 6, are processes that drive the rock cycle. They break down rock into sediments and then move them to new locations. Together, weathering and erosion are slowly but steadily reshaping Earth's surface. They are changing everything from the streets in neighborhoods and towns to the world's tallest mountains.

Weathering at Work

Weathering breaks rock into smaller pieces. Some of these tiny pieces combine with once-living material to form topsoil. Other small pieces of rock collect as sediments. This breakdown of rocks happens as they interact with air, water, and living things. There are two basic types of weathering: physical weathering and chemical weathering.

62

READ "EARTH'S POWERFUL FORCES OF CHANGE" (20 MIN.)

- Have students read pages 62 and 63 silently.

Literal. How are topsoil and sediments alike?

» They both can be the result of weathering and erosion.

Physical weathering breaks big rocks into smaller ones without changing the minerals they contain. Widely swinging temperatures cause physical weathering. For example, rocks in a desert bake during the day beneath the sun's scorching heat. As rocks get hot, they **expand**. At night, temperatures in the desert fall. As rocks cool down, they **contract**, or shrink slightly. Expand, contract, expand, contract—this endless cycle gradually causes the rocks' outer layer to crumble or flake off.

Water also causes physical weathering. Water seeps into tiny cracks in rocks. If temperatures drop below freezing, the water turns to ice. Water expands as it freezes, pushing outward and enlarging the cracks. Geologists call this process ice wedging. Each time the water freezes, it opens cracks a little wider. Eventually, the rocks split apart. Ice wedging is what makes potholes in streets, too.

Plants and animals also cause rocks to weather. Tree roots squeeze into the cracks in rocks. As the roots grow, they act like wedges, forcing the cracks wider and wider. Eventually the rocks break apart. Badgers, chipmunks, and other animals burrow into cliffs and hillsides like tiny bulldozers. As they dig or tunnel into the ground, they push buried rocks to the surface where most weathering takes place.

Examples of physical weathering

Literal. Explain how physical weathering changes rocks and give some examples of physical weathering.

» Drastic changes in temperature, for example during day and night in the desert, cause rocks to expand and contract. The outer layer eventually crumbles or flakes off. Another example of physical weathering is if water seeps into the cracks of rocks; as the temperature changes from hot to cold, the water may freeze and melt repeatedly, eventually causing a rock to split. Also, roots of plants that squeeze into the cracks of rocks and animals burrowing can cause physical weathering.

Inferential. A *wedge* is a piece of wood or metal with one pointed end and one thicker end that is used to split something, to fit into a space, or to separate two things stuck together. Why is *ice wedging* an appropriate name for a physical weathering process?

» Answers may vary but should include that ice acts as a wedge, splitting rocks apart. Water seeps into cracks in rocks. It expands as it freezes, acting as a wedge as it pushes outward and enlarges the cracks. The cracks open a little wider each time the water freezes. Eventually the ice wedge forces rocks to split apart.

Check for Understanding

The temperature one afternoon in a certain place is nearly 100 degrees Fahrenheit. The temperature in the same place is below freezing later that night. What may happen to rocks in the area?

» They may begin to break apart or crumble.

- If students cannot answer the question, ask them to review the first paragraph on page 63 and discuss what they read with a partner.

Support

What else acts as wedges?

» Tree roots also act as wedges, forcing cracks in rocks to open wider and eventually splitting rocks apart.

Chemical weathering breaks down rocks by changing the minerals they contain. Rain is a powerful chemical weathering force. As rain falls, it mixes with the gas carbon dioxide in the air. The result is acid rain. Acid rain is strong enough to dissolve some minerals in rocks. Once dissolved, the minerals easily wash away, weakening the rock. Acid rain very slowly carves some rocks into different shapes. It gradually erases the lettering on old gravestones, and blurs the faces of stone statues. It eats away at the outside of ancient and even modern buildings. Where rain seeps into the ground, carbonic acid causes weathering of buried rocks as well. Over long periods of time, this often unobserved weathering creates caves deep underground.

64

Pronunciation Table	
Word(s)	**CK Code**
Yunnan	/yoo*nan/
Shilin	/shee*leen/

- Have students read pages 64 and 65 silently.

Literal. Explain how chemical weathering changes rocks and give some examples of chemical weathering.

» Chemical weathering changes rocks by changing the minerals the rocks contain. When rainwater mixes with chemicals in the air, like carbon dioxide or oxygen, it reacts with minerals in the rocks and changes their shape and color. Some plants, like moss, release chemicals that can change the surface of rocks.

Support

Review with students that acid rain can cause chemical weathering by dissolving some minerals in rocks.

Another gas in the air—oxygen—causes chemical weathering in rocks. With a little help from water, oxygen reacts with iron-containing minerals. The reaction changes the minerals, making the rocks brittle and crumbly, and turning them a rusty red color.

Some plants release rock-weathering substances. Take a peek under a patch of moss growing on a rock and you'll see little pits in the rock's surface. Acid from the moss plant caused the damage.

As a result of all weathering, rocks are broken down into smaller pieces and **ultimately** into sediments. Erosion is what gets those sediments moving.

Towering rock formations created by chemical weathering rise straight up out of the ground near Kunming, the capital of China's Yunnan Province. Some formations are as tall as a 10-story building. The Chinese call this place Shilin, or the Stone Forest.

65

Reading for Information
Interpret

Entering/Emerging
Have students use individual words and simple phrases to compare and contrast the two forms of weathering. Help them express their ideas in full sentences.

Transitioning/Expanding
Have students compare and contrast the forms of weathering using longer phrases and simple sentences. Guide them to express their ideas using more complex sentences.

Bridging
Have students work with partners to compare and contrast the forms of weathering using complete sentences. Have them share their ideas with another pair.

- When they finish reading this page, have students draw a flowchart to show the various stages in the process of chemical weathering. Encourage them to keep the flowchart close at hand to help them recall the details of the process.

Inferential. To *compare* means to examine similarities; to *contrast* means to examine differences. Compare and contrast physical weathering and chemical weathering.

» Both types of weathering break rocks down into smaller pieces and ultimately into sediments. Physical weathering breaks big rocks into smaller ones without changing the minerals in the rocks, whereas chemical weathering changes the minerals in the rocks. You may wish to have students complete a Venn diagram independently or with a partner to show these similarities or differences.

- Call attention to and discuss the image on pages 64 and 65. Invite students to share their impressions of the scene, focusing the discussion largely on how the forces of nature might have created the formations shown.

Sediments on the Move

Geologists describe erosion as any process or force that moves sediments to new locations. Wind, flowing water, moving ice, and gravity all transport sediments from place to place. These forces are the primary causes of erosion.

Have you ever stood on a sandy beach on a windy day? Did you notice that gusts of wind sent sand flying past? When air moves quickly across the ground, it picks up sediments and carries them away. Powerful winds can carry sediments for hundreds, even thousands, of miles.

On the windy beach, did your skin sting as it was struck by blowing sand? Wind carrying sediments can act like a sandblasting machine to wear away rocks in its path. When wind-driven sand

Delicate Arch, Arches National Park, Utah

66

Support

What is *erosion*?

» any process or force that moves sediments to new locations

- Have students read pages 66 and 67 silently.

Literal. How does wind cause weathering and erosion?

» Wind picks up sediments and carries them away, depositing them on land or in water.

hits rock, it chips off tiny pieces. The wind then whisks the pieces away. Over time, this form of weathering can polish rock surfaces or **pepper** them with tiny holes. It can shape huge blocks of rock into delicate stone arches and lofty towers. Weathering and wind erosion can also leave massive boulders balanced on slim supports. Have you seen wind-carved rocks like this?

As wind slows down, the sediments it carries fall back to Earth. They are **deposited** on land or in water. Where winds deposit sediments regularly, layers of sediment slowly build up. Over time, those layers may be transformed into sedimentary rock.

67

Inferential. How are sediments and sedimentary rock related?

» Sedimentary rock is made of sediments. Over time, sediments are compacted and cemented together, layer by layer, transforming them into sedimentary rock.

Inferential. The text explains that the effects of weathering and erosion usually take place "over time," such as the transformation of sediments into sedimentary rock. Do you think that "over time" most likely means over a period of several days, several weeks, several years, or more?

» more

Challenge

Have students speculate about why the text identifies the arch in the picture as having been created primarily by wind rather than by water.

Glaciers, like this one in Alaska, are powerful forces that can cause erosion.

- Have students read pages 68 and 69 silently.
- Ask students to tell a partner several things they see on the illustration on page 68. Ask them to predict how glaciers, such as the one shown in the image, might cause erosion.

Heading Downstream

Like wind, water also causes erosion. The tug of gravity pulls sediments out of wind and water. Flowing water picks up sediments and carries them downhill to new locations. A summer rain can wash fine sediments onto sidewalks and into gutters. A rushing mountain stream can sweep small stones into a valley. A flooded river can surge along with enough force to move large rocks many miles downstream.

As moving water slows, sediments sink to the bottom of the river or stream. The heaviest sediments are the first to be deposited. The finest sediments are the last. Layers of sediment accumulate at the mouths of rivers and on the bottoms of lakes. Vast layers of sediment are also deposited on the ocean floor over long periods of time. Like wind-deposited sediments, those laid down by water may someday be transformed into sedimentary rock.

Water doesn't have to be in its liquid **state** to erode sediments. Glaciers are enormous masses of ice found in polar regions and near the tops of tall mountains. Although ice is solid, glaciers do move. They flow—very, very slowly—downhill. As countless tons of ice creep over land or down mountainsides, they push, drag, and carry eroded sediments along. Moving glaciers also create sediments as they grind against rocks beside or below them. Glaciers are such powerful forces that they can carve huge U-shaped valleys through mountain ranges.

When glaciers melt, they deposit the sediments they have been carrying. About 20,000 years ago, glaciers covered large parts of North America, Europe, and Asia. As the climate warmed, the glaciers melted and retreated northward. They left behind massive deposits of sand, gravel, and **silt**, along with collections of rocks and boulders. You can still see these deposits as hills, mounds, and ridges on the landscape.

Check for Understanding

How does water cause erosion?

» Flowing water picks up sediments and carries them downhill to new locations.

- If students cannot answer the question accurately, review with them the information on this page of the Reader.

Evaluative. Based on the information in the text, how does the amount of flowing water affect the type of sediments that are eroded?

» The more moving water there is, the larger the sediments and rocks that are moved. A summer rain does not include much water so the sediments it moves are small. A rushing mountain stream has more water than a summer rain and moves faster so it can move small stones into a valley at the bottom of the mountain. A flooded river is overflowing with fast-moving water that is strong enough to move large rocks farther down the river.

Literal. In what ways do glaciers cause weathering and erosion?

» Glaciers cause weathering when they create sediments as they grind against rocks beside or below them as they move; as glaciers slowly move downhill, they push, drag, and carry eroded sediments along.

- Have students compare the information given in the text about how glaciers cause changes to the surface of the earth with the predictions they made after looking at the illustration on the previous page.

Weathering, Erosion, and Time

Weathering and erosion work slowly. It takes a long time to see their effects. Given time, these processes reshape Earth's surface on a scale so large it's almost impossible to grasp. For example, the Grand **Canyon** in the southwestern United States did not exist when dinosaurs roamed North America. Wind, rain, and the Colorado River slowly created it. These forces cut and shaped the landscape into what it is today—one of the world's largest canyons.

The Grand Canyon

70

- Have students read pages 70 and 71 silently.

  Inferential. What is one example or piece of evidence provided on these pages that weathering, erosion, and time work together to change Earth's surface?

  » Answers may vary but should include: Over time, the Grand Canyon was created by wind, rain, and the Colorado River working together to cut and shape the landscape. Over time, weathering and erosion wore down the Appalachian Mountains, which are not as tall as they once were.

Millions of years ago, the Appalachian Mountains in eastern North America were a towering mountain range. The highest peaks may have been more than 20,000 feet above sea level. Weathering and erosion gradually wore the Appalachians down. Their highest point today is just 6,684 feet high. As permanent as mountains seem, weathering and erosion inevitably change them. Even Earth's tallest peaks—Everest in Asia, Aconcagua in South America, Africa's Kilimanjaro, and Europe's Mont Blanc—won't last. They will eventually be worn down by these endless geological processes. But don't worry. Other geological processes are creating new mountains to take their place.

Check for Understanding

Fifty million years ago, a mountain stood 27,000 feet above sea level. What has probably happened to that mountain since then?

» It probably stands less than 27,000 feet above sea level.

- If students cannot answer the question accurately, ask them to describe what has happened over time to the Appalachian Mountains and why.

DISCUSS CHAPTER AND WRAP UP LESSON (10 MIN.)

Note: Question 3 and Activity Page 10.3 relate to The Big Question of the chapter.

- Use the following question to discuss the chapter.

3. **Evaluative.** How do weathering and erosion continually reshape Earth's surface?

   » Weathering breaks rocks down into smaller pieces. Physical weathering does not change the minerals in rocks. Expanding and contracting, ice wedging, the movement of plant roots and animals, and wind and glaciers all cause physical weathering. Chemical weathering changes the minerals in rocks. Acid rain, the reaction from oxygen, with the help of water, and iron-containing minerals, plants, and lichens all cause chemical weathering. Erosion is any process or force that moves sediments to new locations. Wind, flowing water, moving ice, and gravity all cause erosion. Sediments are moved to new locations, creating new layers of sediments that may be transformed into sedimentary rock.

- Have students turn to Activity Page 10.3. Review the directions and have students complete the activity page for homework.

Activity Page 10.3

WORD WORK: *STATE* (5 MIN.)

1. In the chapter you read, "Water doesn't have to be in its liquid state to erode sediments."
2. Say the word *state* with me.
3. *State* means the condition of being a solid, liquid, or gas.
4. Water flowing from the faucet is in a liquid state, but water frozen in an ice cube tray is in a solid state.
5. What are some other examples of *state*? Be sure to use the word *state* in your response.

   » Answers will vary. Be sure students use the meaning of state as used in this chapter rather than some other one of the word's meanings.

- Guide and/or rephrase students' responses to make complete sentences: "____ is in a ____ state when it ____."

6. What part of speech is the word *state*?

   » noun

- Use a Multiple-Meaning Word activity for follow-up. Remind students the word *state* has multiple meanings. Share the following with students.
    - Meaning 1: state (noun)—the condition of being a solid, liquid, or gas
    - Meaning 2: state (noun)—one of many smaller units of government that make up a country
    - Meaning 3: state (verb)—to express something in speech or writing
- We have been talking about Meaning 1 for *state*, the condition of being a solid, liquid, or gas. You also read, "In the United States, one of the most famous faults is the San Andreas Fault in California." This sentence is an example of Meaning 2 for *state*, one of many smaller units of government that make up a country. You also read, "The theory of plate tectonics states that Earth's crust, together with the solid top of the mantle, is broken up into sections." This sentence is an example of Meaning 3 for *state*, to express something in speech or writing.
- I am going to read several sentences. Listen to the context, or the text surrounding *state* in the sentence, for clues as to which meaning is being used. When you think a sentence is an example of Meaning 1, hold up one finger. When you think a sentence is an example of Meaning 2, hold up two fingers. When you think a sentence is an example of Meaning 3, hold up three fingers.

1. My family travels to the state of Tennessee to visit my grandparents.
    » 2
2. The ice cream left out on the kitchen counter quickly turned to a liquid state in the heat.
    » 1
3. My brother stated that he had fed the dogs.
    » 3
4. I am learning the names of all 50 states in the country.
    » 2
5. The weather reporter always states the day's high and low temperatures.
    » 3
6. The pond water changes to a solid state when it freezes.
    » 1

Lesson 10: Weathering and Erosion

Writing

30M

Primary Focus: Students will revise and edit their writing using a writing rubric and editing checklist as guides. **[W.4.4, W.4.5]**

REVISE AND EDIT A WIKI ENTRY (25 MIN.)

Activity Page 8.4

- As needed, allow students time to finish drafting their wiki entry on Activity Page 8.4.
    - **Support** You may choose to work with a small group of students who could benefit from extra support in order to guide them in using their notes to draft their wiki entry.
- Ask students to raise their hands if they recall what a *rubric* is. Review that a *rubric* is a list of behaviors or characteristics that can help writers evaluate their work.

Activity Page 7.4

- Have students turn to the Wiki Entry Rubric on Activity Page 7.4.
- Model reviewing the Volcano Wiki Entry with the Wiki Entry Rubric as a guide, just as you did in Lesson 7, by doing the following:
    - Read the first criterion listed in the Exemplary column.
    - Ask students if the Volcano Wiki Entry matches the criterion. If it doesn't, think aloud to revise the sentence(s) to better match the criterion.
    - Continue to model this process for each row of the rubric.
- Give students time to use the Wiki Entry Rubric to revise their writing.
    - **Support** You may wish to have students work in pairs to help one another revise their wiki entry. Consider having students read one another's entries and suggest ways to make adjustments based on the rubric. You may wish to do this step with students in the small group.

Activity Page 7.5

- Have students turn to Activity Page 7.5 and complete the Wiki Entry Editing Checklist. Students should add to and/or edit their wiki entry as necessary based on the Wiki Entry Editing Checklist.
    - **Support** You may wish to work with students in the small group to complete the Wiki Entry Editing Checklist.

Check for Understanding

Check that students have included the volcano name as a title and that each section of the wiki has its own header. If students have not done this, point out the first two criteria under Format on the Wiki Entry Editing Checklist.

LESSON WRAP-UP (5 MIN.)

- As time allows, have students share sentences from their wiki entry.
- Collect the drafted wiki entries to assess using the Wiki Entry Rubric provided in Teacher Resources.

End Lesson

Lesson 10: Weathering and Erosion

Take-Home Material

READING

- Have students take home Activity Page 10.3 to complete for homework.

Writing Ideas

Entering/Emerging
Help students identify/underline key words in the rubric, such as *more*, *some*, and *little to no*.

Transitioning/Expanding
Have students work with a partner to identify/underline key words in the rubric, such as those listed above. Discuss the meanings.

Bridging
Have students identify/underline the key words above on their own. Have them discuss the meanings with a partner.

Challenge

Students who have finished revising and editing their draft using the Wiki Entry Rubric and the Wiki Entry Editing Checklist can prepare their draft for publication either by rewriting it or typing it, if computer access is available.

Activity Page 10.3

SPELLING ASSESSMENT ANALYSIS

Spelling Analysis Chart

Student	1. archrival	2. paragraph	3. rupture	4. hierarchy	5. biographer	6. abrupt	7. matriarch	8. uninterrupted	9. anarchy	10. autograph	11. eruption	12. calligraphy

- It may be helpful to refer back to the Pronunciation/Syllabication Chart from Lesson 6.

Word	CK Code	Syllable Type
hierarchy	/hie*er*ar*kee/	open*r-controlled*r-controlled*open
matriarch	/mae*tree*ark/	open*open*r-controlled
archrival	/arch*rie*vəl/	r-controlled*open*ə
anarchy	/an*ar*kee/	closed*r-controlled*open
autograph	/aw*toe*graf/	digraph*open*closed
biographer	/bie*o*grə*fer/	open*open*ə*r-controlled
calligraphy	/kəl*li*grə*fee/	ə*open*ə*open
paragraph	/paer*ə*graf/	r-controlled*ə*closed
eruption	/ee*rup*shən/	open*closed*ə
uninterrupted	/un*in*ter*rupt*ed/	closed*closed*r-controlled*closed*closed
rupture	/rup*cher/	closed*r-controlled
abrupt	/ə*brupt/	ə*closed

- Students might make the following errors:
    - arch words: using 'k' instead of 'ch' for /ark/ or /arch/
    - graph words: using 'f' instead of 'ph' for /graf/
    - words ending in 'y': using 'ee' instead of 'y' for /ee/
    - words with /ə/: using 'a,' 'e,' or 'u' instead of the proper letter for /ə/
    - hierarchy: using 'i' or 'ire' instead of 'ier' for /hie*er/
    - eruption: using 'shun' instead of 'tion' for /shən/
    - rupture: using 'ch' instead of 't' for /ch/

- Although any of the above student-error scenarios may occur, misspellings may be due to many other factors. You may find it helpful to use the analysis chart to record any student errors. For example:
    - Is the student consistently making errors on specific vowels? Which ones?
    - Is the student consistently making errors at the ends of the words?
    - Is the student consistently making errors in multisyllable words, but not single-syllable words?
- Also, examine the dictated sentence for errors in capitalization and punctuation.

LESSON

11

Weathering and Erosion, Part 2

PRIMARY FOCUS OF LESSON

Reading

Students will describe the processes of weathering and erosion and identify geologic features that provide evidence of these forces. **[RI.4.1, RI.4.2, RI.4.4]**

Grammar

Students will identify and use multiple adjectives in the correct sequence. **[L.4.1]**

Morphology

Students will review the meanings and uses of the suffixes –*ly* and –*y* and the roots *graph* and *rupt*. **[L.4.4]**

Spelling

Students will practice spelling targeted words. **[L.4.2]**

FORMATIVE ASSESSMENT

Activity Page 1.3	**Evidence Collector's Chart** Students look in the text for evidence supporting geological events. **[RI.4.1]**
Activity Page 1.4	**Evidence of Changes on Earth** Students look in the text for evidence supporting geological events. **[RI.4.1]**
Activity Page 10.3	**Earth's Powerful Forces of Change** Students choose vocabulary activities to practice vocabulary terms from the lesson. **[RI.4.4]**
Activity Page 11.1	**Sequencing Multiple Adjectives** Students put adjectives in sentences in the proper order. **[L.4.1]**
Activity Page 11.2	**Review Suffixes –ly and –y and Roots graph and rupt** Students identify the correct word to complete sentences. **[L.4.4]**
Activity Page 11.4	**Practice Spelling Words** Students write spelling words and associate them with their definitions. **[L.4.2]**

LESSON AT A GLANCE

	Grouping	Time	Materials
Reading (45 min.)			
Review	Whole Group	5 min.	❑ Activity Pages 1.3, 1.4, 10.3 ❑ *The Changing Earth* ❑ Evidence Collector's Chart ❑ Scissors ❑ Glue
Close Reading	Whole Group	25 min.	
Chapter Discussion, Lesson Wrap-Up	Whole Group	10 min.	
Word Work: *Deposit*	Whole Group	5 min.	
Language (45 min.)			
Grammar: Sequencing Adjectives	Whole Group	15 min.	❑ Adjectives Chart ❑ Activity Page 11.1
Morphology: Suffixes and Roots	Whole Group	15 min.	❑ Activity Page 11.2
Spelling: Introduce Spelling Words	Whole Group	15 min.	❑ Activity Pages 11.3, 11.4, SR.1
Take-Home Material			
Grammar; Morphology; Spelling			❑ Activity Pages 11.1–11.4 ❑ Fluency Supplement selection (optional)

ADVANCE PREPARATION

Reading

- Access a digital version of The Big Question in the digital components for this unit.
- Display the Evidence Collector's Chart from Lesson 1.

Language

Grammar

- Display the Adjectives Chart on the board/chart paper, or access a digital version in the digital components for this unit.

Article	Adjective(s)					Noun
	General	→			Specific	
	Opinion/ Observation	Physical Description (size, shape, age, color)	Material	Origin	Purpose	

- Prepare the following examples on the board/chart paper.
    - The big, old, yellow dog loves to play fetch.
    - read old I a Russian folktale scary

Fluency (optional)

- Choose and make sufficient copies of a text selection from the online Fluency Supplement to distribute and review with students for additional fluency practice. If you choose to do a fluency assessment, you will assess students in Lesson 15. See the Unit 1 Teacher Guide introduction for more information on using the Fluency Supplement.

Start Lesson

Lesson 11: Weathering and Erosion, Part 2

Reading

45M

Primary Focus: Students will describe details of the processes of weathering and erosion and identify geologic features that provide evidence of these forces. **[RI.4.1, RI.4.2, RI.4.4]**

REVIEW (5 MIN.)

- Review student responses to Activity Page 10.3, which was assigned for homework.
- Tell students they will reread Chapter 7, "Earth's Powerful Forces of Change."
- Have students turn to the table of contents, locate the chapter, and turn to the first page of the chapter.
- Have one student read The Big Question at the beginning of the chapter. Ensure students understand the meaning of The Big Question before reading the chapter.
  - How do weathering and erosion continually reshape Earth's surface?

CLOSE READING (25 MIN.)

Note: Close reading lessons present excellent opportunities to ensure that English learners and other students who need additional support fully comprehend a reading selection.

The practice of close reading involves students' directing their attention to specific aspects of a text. The guided reading supports in this close reading of Chapter 7, "Earth's Powerful Forces of Change," are intended to encourage this direction.

- Read the title of the chapter as a class: "Earth's Powerful Forces of Change." As you read portions of the chapter, pause to explain or clarify the text at each point indicated.

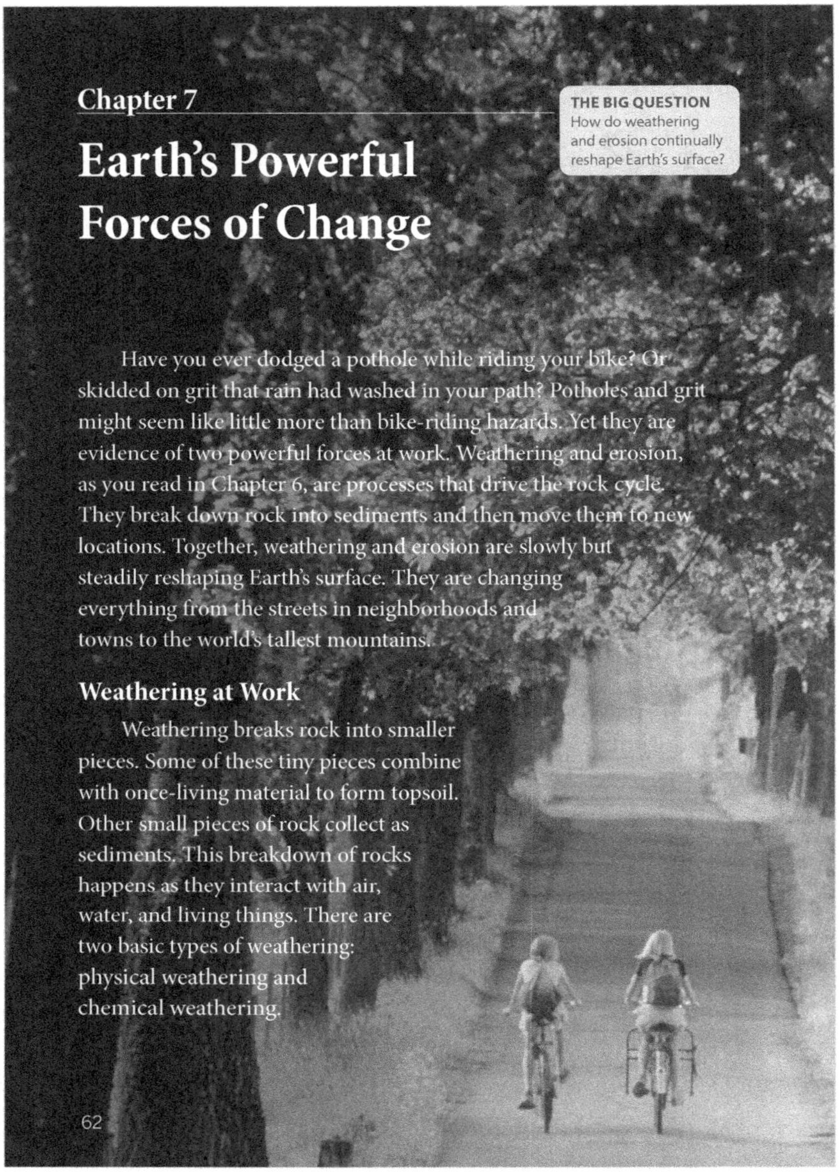

Chapter 7

Earth's Powerful Forces of Change

THE BIG QUESTION
How do weathering and erosion continually reshape Earth's surface?

Have you ever dodged a pothole while riding your bike? Or skidded on grit that rain had washed in your path? Potholes and grit might seem like little more than bike-riding hazards. Yet they are evidence of two powerful forces at work. Weathering and erosion, as you read in Chapter 6, are processes that drive the rock cycle. They break down rock into sediments and then move them to new locations. Together, weathering and erosion are slowly but steadily reshaping Earth's surface. They are changing everything from the streets in neighborhoods and towns to the world's tallest mountains.

Weathering at Work

Weathering breaks rock into smaller pieces. Some of these tiny pieces combine with once-living material to form topsoil. Other small pieces of rock collect as sediments. This breakdown of rocks happens as they interact with air, water, and living things. There are two basic types of weathering: physical weathering and chemical weathering.

62

- Have students read the first paragraph on page 62 silently.

  Inferential. A familiar meaning of the word *drive* is "to operate a vehicle and direct the movement of it" or "to take someone or something to a place in a vehicle." *Drive* can also mean "to serve as the basis for something." The author uses the word *drive* when stating, "Weathering and erosion, as you read in Chapter 6, are processes that drive the rock cycle." What does this statement mean?

  » Weathering and erosion serve as the basis for the rock cycle's happening; the rock cycle occurs due to weathering and erosion.

Physical weathering breaks big rocks into smaller ones without changing the minerals they contain. Widely swinging temperatures cause physical weathering. For example, rocks in a desert bake during the day beneath the sun's scorching heat. As rocks get hot, they **expand**. At night, temperatures in the desert fall. As rocks cool down, they **contract**, or shrink slightly. Expand, contract, expand, contract—this endless cycle gradually causes the rocks' outer layer to crumble or flake off.

Water also causes physical weathering. Water seeps into tiny cracks in rocks. If temperatures drop below freezing, the water turns to ice. Water expands as it freezes, pushing outward and enlarging the cracks. Geologists call this process ice wedging. Each time the water freezes, it opens cracks a little wider. Eventually, the rocks split apart. Ice wedging is what makes potholes in streets, too.

Plants and animals also cause rocks to weather. Tree roots squeeze into the cracks in rocks. As the roots grow, they act like wedges, forcing the cracks wider and wider. Eventually the rocks break apart. Badgers, chipmunks, and other animals burrow into cliffs and hillsides like tiny bulldozers. As they dig or tunnel into the ground, they push buried rocks to the surface where most weathering takes place.

Examples of physical weathering

63

- Have students read the first paragraph on page 63 silently.

  Inferential. *Swinging* means "shifting from one condition to another." The author states that "widely swinging temperatures cause physical weathering." What is meant by the phrase *widely swinging temperatures*?

  » *Widely swinging temperatures* means "temperatures that change drastically from one extreme to another."

Check for Understanding

Is a change in temperature from 65 degrees Fahrenheit to 63 degrees Fahrenheit and back an example of "wildly swinging temperatures"?

» No; the change in temperature, while it exists, is very small.

Inferential. How do widely swinging temperatures cause physical weathering? Have students write a sentence of explanation and share their ideas with a partner before they share with the class.

» The scorching heat during the day causes rocks to expand; as temperatures cool at night, rocks contract. Over time this cycle of expanding and contracting causes rocks' outer layers to crumble or flake off, which is a form of physical weathering.

Chemical weathering breaks down rocks by changing the minerals they contain. Rain is a powerful chemical weathering force. As rain falls, it mixes with the gas carbon dioxide in the air. The result is acid rain. Acid rain is strong enough to dissolve some minerals in rocks. Once dissolved, the minerals easily wash away, weakening the rock. Acid rain very slowly carves some rocks into different shapes. It gradually erases the lettering on old gravestones, and blurs the faces of stone statues. It eats away at the outside of ancient and even modern buildings. Where rain seeps into the ground, carbonic acid causes weathering of buried rocks as well. Over long periods of time, this often unobserved weathering creates caves deep underground.

Pronunciation Chart	
Word(s)	**CK Code**
Yunnan	/yoo*nan/
Shilin	/shee*leen/

- Have students read page 64 silently.

  What does the idiom *eats away at* mean?

  » *Eats away at* means "erodes." In this paragraph the author is saying that acid rain erodes the outsides of buildings.

- Have students work in pairs to come up with sentences that use the idiom *eats away at*. If time permits, have students briefly illustrate their sentences.

Inferential. How do geologists know there is unobserved weathering?

» Caves that form underground are evidence of unobserved weathering. Rain seeps into the ground, causing carbonic acid to weather buried rocks. When geologists find underground caves, they find evidence of unobserved weathering.

Support

Remind students that an idiom is a phrase that does not make sense through the meanings of the individual words, but that has a meaning of its own.

Reading for Information
Prefixes

Entering/Emerging
Tell students that the prefix *un–* (as in *observed/unobserved*) means "not." Write *happy*, *clean*, and *finished* on the board. Add *un–* in front of each. Read the words and explain their meanings with words and gestures.

Transitioning/Expanding
Model changing *happy*, *clean*, and *finished* to *unhappy*, *unclean*, and *unfinished* as above. Have students use these words in sentences.

Bridging
Have students use the words above in sentences and brainstorm other words with the prefix *un–*.

Another gas in the air—oxygen—causes chemical weathering in rocks. With a little help from water, oxygen reacts with iron-containing minerals. The reaction changes the minerals, making the rocks brittle and crumbly, and turning them a rusty red color.

Some plants release rock-weathering substances. Take a peek under a patch of moss growing on a rock and you'll see little pits in the rock's surface. Acid from the moss plant caused the damage.

As a result of all weathering, rocks are broken down into smaller pieces and **ultimately** into sediments. Erosion is what gets those sediments moving.

Towering rock formations created by chemical weathering rise straight up out of the ground near Kunming, the capital of China's Yunnan Province. Some formations are as tall as a 10-story building. The Chinese call this place Shilin, or the Stone Forest.

65

- Have students read the first paragraph on page 65 silently.

  Inferential. What does the author mean by the phrase *with a little help from water*?

  » Oxygen reacts with iron-containing minerals only when water is also present. Oxygen and water work together to react to iron-containing minerals, making rocks brittle and crumbly and turning them a rusty red color.

- Have students use the phrase *with a little help from* in a sentence.

Check for Understanding

Judging from the text, what might be a good clue that a rock or mineral contains iron?

» If the material crumbles and turns red when exposed to oxygen and water, it might very well contain iron.

- If students cannot answer the question, review with them the answer to the previous question.

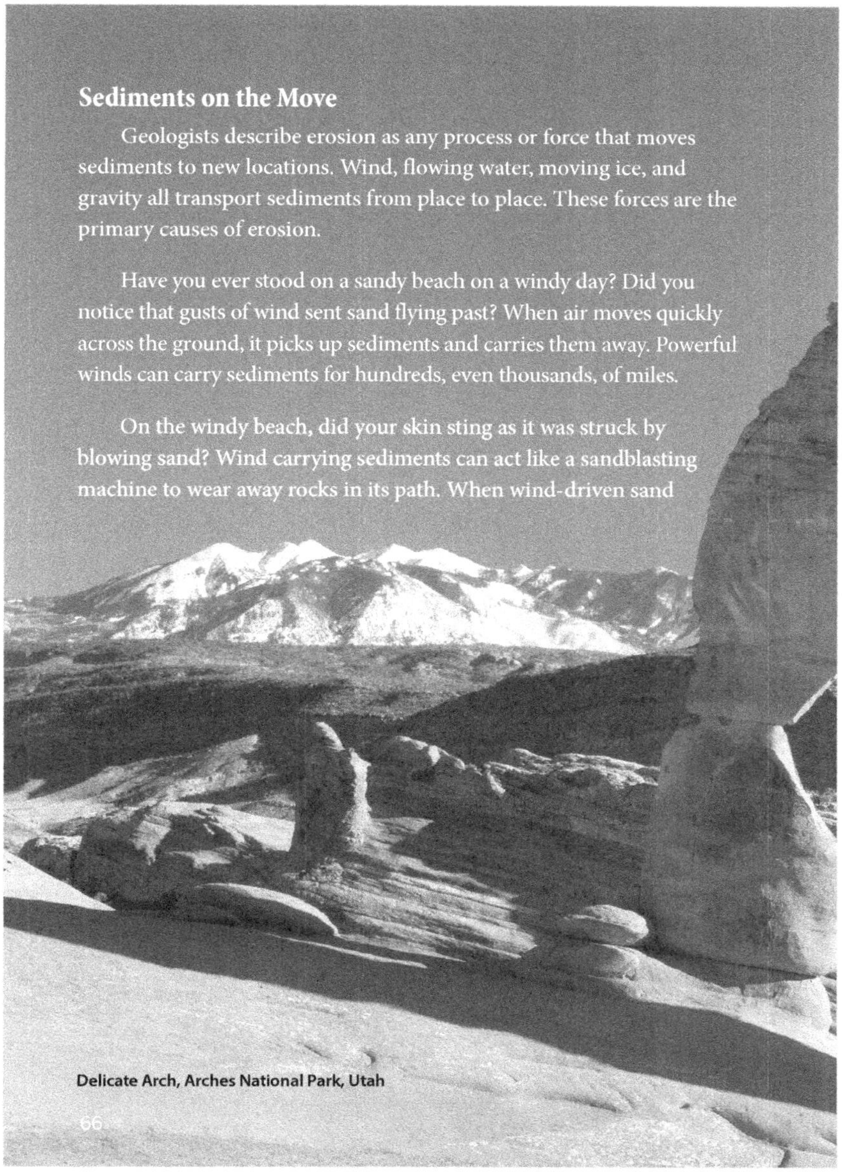

Sediments on the Move

Geologists describe erosion as any process or force that moves sediments to new locations. Wind, flowing water, moving ice, and gravity all transport sediments from place to place. These forces are the primary causes of erosion.

Have you ever stood on a sandy beach on a windy day? Did you notice that gusts of wind sent sand flying past? When air moves quickly across the ground, it picks up sediments and carries them away. Powerful winds can carry sediments for hundreds, even thousands, of miles.

On the windy beach, did your skin sting as it was struck by blowing sand? Wind carrying sediments can act like a sandblasting machine to wear away rocks in its path. When wind-driven sand

Delicate Arch, Arches National Park, Utah

66

- Have students read the third paragraph on page 66 (ending on page 67) silently.

  Inferential. Again, the author uses a form of the word *drive*. In this paragraph the author states, "When wind-driven sand hits rock, it chips off tiny pieces." What does *wind-driven* mean? Have students use Think-Pair-Share to discuss the answer to this question.

  » moved and guided by wind

Ask students what they think a sandblasting machine might be. Guide them to use contextual clues and the information in the chapter to make a reasonable guess. Have them indicate how sure they are that their answer is correct using a scale of 1 (certain) to 5 (not at all certain).

» A sandblasting machine is a powerful machine that uses air to shoot sand out at a high speed. A sandblasting machine is used to clean, polish, or decorate a surface with sand.

How does the image of the sandblasting machine help you understand how this process works?

» Sometimes wind carrying sediments blows very hard, throwing or blasting the sediments at rocks as if a sandblasting machine were being used to change them.

hits rock, it chips off tiny pieces. The wind then whisks the pieces away. Over time, this form of weathering can polish rock surfaces or **pepper** them with tiny holes. It can shape huge blocks of rock into delicate stone arches and lofty towers. Weathering and wind erosion can also leave massive boulders balanced on slim supports. Have you seen wind-carved rocks like this?

As wind slows down, the sediments it carries fall back to Earth. They are **deposited** on land or in water. Where winds deposit sediments regularly, layers of sediment slowly build up. Over time, those layers may be transformed into sedimentary rock.

67

- In this paragraph, *pepper* is a verb that means "to sprinkle or cover." *Pepper* can also be a noun that means "a food seasoning made by grinding the dried berries of an Indian plant and their black hard covers"; it can also be a noun meaning "a hollow vegetable that is usually green, yellow, or red and can be eaten raw or cooked." Students may enjoy saying—and making sense of—the sentence *I pepper my peppers with pepper and salt*.

Glaciers, like this one in Alaska, are powerful forces that can cause erosion.

Heading Downstream

Like wind, water also causes erosion. The tug of gravity pulls sediments out of wind and water. Flowing water picks up sediments and carries them downhill to new locations. A summer rain can wash fine sediments onto sidewalks and into gutters. A rushing mountain stream can sweep small stones into a valley. A flooded river can surge along with enough force to move large rocks many miles downstream.

As moving water slows, sediments sink to the bottom of the river or stream. The heaviest sediments are the first to be deposited. The finest sediments are the last. Layers of sediment accumulate at the mouths of rivers and on the bottoms of lakes. Vast layers of sediment are also deposited on the ocean floor over long periods of time. Like wind-deposited sediments, those laid down by water may someday be transformed into sedimentary rock.

Water doesn't have to be in its liquid **state** to erode sediments. Glaciers are enormous masses of ice found in polar regions and near the tops of tall mountains. Although ice is solid, glaciers do move. They flow—very, very slowly—downhill. As countless tons of ice creep over land or down mountainsides, they push, drag, and carry eroded sediments along. Moving glaciers also create sediments as they grind against rocks beside or below them. Glaciers are such powerful forces that they can carve huge U-shaped valleys through mountain ranges.

When glaciers melt, they deposit the sediments they have been carrying. About 20,000 years ago, glaciers covered large parts of North America, Europe, and Asia. As the climate warmed, the glaciers melted and retreated northward. They left behind massive deposits of sand, gravel, and **silt**, along with collections of rocks and boulders. You can still see these deposits as hills, mounds, and ridges on the landscape.

69

- Have students read the first two paragraphs on page 69 silently.
- Gravity is the natural force that causes things to fall to Earth. The author uses *tug of gravity* to emphasize that sediments are naturally pulled out of moving wind and water due to the force of gravity.

  Inferential. Why are the finest sediments deposited last? Have you ever seen this process in action? When?

  » If something is fine, it is very small, meaning it doesn't weigh much. Heavy sediments usually weigh more and sink faster. Fine sediments take longer to reach the bottom because their weight doesn't pull them down as quickly. Students may have seen this process when watching particles of dirt settle to the bottom of a pond or while watching water with some impurities being poured into a glass.

Support

Remind students that the word *fine* in this context means "small and light"; it does not indicate that something is good, as in *I am feeling fine*.

Weathering, Erosion, and Time

Weathering and erosion work slowly. It takes a long time to see their effects. Given time, these processes reshape Earth's surface on a scale so large it's almost impossible to grasp. For example, the Grand **Canyon** in the southwestern United States did not exist when dinosaurs roamed North America. Wind, rain, and the Colorado River slowly created it. These forces cut and shaped the landscape into what it is today—one of the world's largest canyons.

The Grand Canyon

70

- Have students read page 70 silently.
- The phrase *on a scale so large it's almost impossible to grasp* means that these processes shape Earth's surface in such a big way over time that it is extremely hard to understand just how much of an impact these processes actually have on Earth's surface.

Check for Understanding

Which is "almost impossible to grasp": that ice cream comes in several different flavors or that there are probably more than one million different kinds of insects?

» That there are probably more than one million different kinds of insects

- If students make the wrong choice, review with them that the phrase refers to a fact that is very surprising, especially because the numbers or the time spans involved are extremely large.

Millions of years ago, the Appalachian Mountains in eastern North America were a towering mountain range. The highest peaks may have been more than 20,000 feet above sea level. Weathering and erosion gradually wore the Appalachians down. Their highest point today is just 6,684 feet high. As permanent as mountains seem, weathering and erosion inevitably change them. Even Earth's tallest peaks—Everest in Asia, Aconcagua in South America, Africa's Kilimanjaro, and Europe's Mont Blanc—won't last. They will eventually be worn down by these endless geological processes. But don't worry. Other geological processes are creating new mountains to take their place.

71

- Have students read page 71 silently.

Challenge

What math expression could you write to find out the approximate difference between the highest peaks of the Appalachian Mountains millions of years ago and their highest point today? What is the approximate difference?

» Twenty thousand feet minus 6,684 feet; the difference is approximately 13,316 feet.

CHAPTER DISCUSSION AND LESSON WRAP-UP (10 MIN.)

Note: Activity Page 1.3 relates to The Big Question of the chapter.

Activity Pages 1.3 and 1.4

- Have students turn to Activity Pages 1.3 and 1.4 and refer to the displayed Evidence Collector's Chart.
- Remind students that this chart is being used throughout the unit to collect evidence of changes to the earth related to specific causes of geologic change.

1. What does the evidence on the chart represent?

    » The evidence represents what geologists examine to determine how powerful forces above and below Earth's surface work to change the earth.

- Have a student read aloud the information under "What is the cause?" in the sixth row. Explain that students must determine what evidence is in the chapter about weathering's breaking rocks into smaller pieces and erosion's moving these pieces, both over time. (pages 63–71)
- Have students refer to the remaining images on Activity Page 1.4. Engage students in a discussion about the images, talking about which image represents evidence of weathering's breaking down rocks and erosion's moving the pieces, both over time. (image showing the Grand Canyon)

2. Why is the image showing the Grand Canyon the correct image?

    » The image of the Grand Canyon shows the effects of weathering, erosion, and time working together to shape the landscape.

- Have students cut out the correct image, glue it to the chart in the "What evidence is there?" column, and write the following information for chapter number, key words, and letter in the chart:

Chapter #	What is the cause?	What evidence is there?	Letter
7	*Over time, weathering breaks rocks into smaller pieces and erosion moves these pieces to new locations.*	*(image: the Grand Canyon)* *key words:* processes reshape Earth's surface	C

WORD WORK: *DEPOSIT* (5 MIN.)

1. In the chapter you read, "Where winds deposit sediments regularly, layers of sediment slowly build up."
2. Say the word *deposit* with me.
3. *Deposit* means "to put or leave in a particular place."
4. During fierce storms, strong wind gusts deposit leaves all over the roads.
5. What are some other examples of ways you can use *deposit*? Be sure to use the word *deposit* in your response.
   » Answers will vary. Be sure students use complete sentences and phrases such as "____ was deposited when ____."
6. What part of speech is the word *deposit*?
   » verb

- Use a Synonyms activity for follow-up.

3. What does the word *deposit* mean? What are some synonyms, or words that have a similar meaning, of *deposit*?
   » possible synonyms: *put*, *leave*, *place*

- Have each pair create a sentence for each of the synonyms of *deposit* it thinks of.

Lesson 11: Weathering and Erosion, Part 2

Language

45M

GRAMMAR: SEQUENCING ADJECTIVES (15 MIN.)

Primary Focus: Students will identify and use multiple adjectives in the correct sequence. **[L.4.1]**

- Remind students that adjectives are words that describe nouns. Adjectives provide details about nouns, such as by specifying size, color, shape, and material.
- Have students think of adjectives to describe objects in the classroom and share them aloud, using a phrase that includes both the noun (the object) and

the adjective. Examples might include *full bookshelf*, *large board*, *sharp pencil*, *green folder*, and so on. Point out that adjectives can come before the noun (*this is a sharp pencil*) or after it. (*the pencil is sharp*)

- Remind students that the words *a*, *an*, and *the* are a special kinds of adjective called *articles*. Articles provide additional detail about the nouns with which they are used. Articles tell us whether a specific noun is being described (*the rock*; *the aftershock*) or a general noun is being described. (*a rock*; *an aftershock*)
- Tell students that when more than one adjective is being used to describe a noun, there is a common convention, or rule, for their order.
- The convention states that the order should begin with the most general adjectives and end with the most specific adjectives; the convention also refers to the specific order in which multiple adjectives are sequenced. Adjectives are classified and sequenced by type.
- Tell students that according to the conventional order, the article is first and the noun comes last. (*an earthquake*, *a big earthquake*)

4. Which would we say: *the volcano* or *volcano the*? *The fiery volcano* or *the volcano fiery*?

   » *the volcano*; *the fiery volcano*

- Refer to the chart you prepared in advance to explain the correct sequence of multiple adjectives. Read aloud the different types listed in the chart. (opinion/observation, physical description, material, origin, and purpose)

  Note: Many native English speakers will sequence multiple adjectives correctly based on their oral language experience. English learners in particular may find this chart helpful.

- Point out that "opinion/observation" refers to adjectives that describe a noun based on a particular point of view.

5. What do you think "physical description" refers to? Give some examples of adjectives that fit this category. Have students make a written list of such adjectives before sharing their answers with others.

   » Adjectives that describe the size, shape, age, or color of a noun; examples might include *big*, *small*, *round*, *square*, *old*, *new*, *blue*, *black*.

- Point out that physical description adjectives appear in a specific order: size, then shape, then age, and finally color.

6. Would we say *a big red balloon* or *a red big balloon*? Why?

   » *a big red balloon*; size comes before color

Language
Adjectives

Entering/Emerging
Help students use the adjectives *red*, *big*, and *soft* in phrases to describe classroom objects, as in *red book* or *big chair*.

Transitioning/Expanding
Help students use the adjectives above to form simple sentences, such as *I see a red book* or *The chair is big*.

Bridging
Help students use the adjectives above to form complex sentences, such as *I see a big book with a red cover*.

- Point out that *material* refers to adjectives that describe how, or with what, a noun is made; that *origin* refers to adjectives that describe a noun based on where it comes from; and that *purpose* refers to adjectives that describe a noun based on its use. You may wish to have students repeat or rephrase each of these definitions as you touch the category descriptor on the chart.
- Ask students to think of adjectives that would fall under each category. List the adjectives under each type's heading in the chart as demonstrated in the following example.

Article	**Adjective(s)**							**Noun**
	General → **Specific**							
	Opinion/ Observation	**Physical Description (size, shape, age, color)**				**Material**	**Origin**	**Purpose**	
	good	big	round	young	blue	silver	American	cooking	
	bad	small	triangular	old	red	wooden	Italian	writing	
	fun	tiny	square	new	yellow	plastic	German	sleeping	
	exciting	giant	flat	ancient	green	metal	Russian	running	

- Explain that the adjective types are rarely used all at once in a sentence. It is common, however, for two or three adjectives to be used in a sentence at one time. Whether a sentence contains two adjectives or five, the adjectives are sequenced in the conventional order as presented in the chart. For example, if there are adjectives of three different types in one sentence, such as color, size, and material, then they are sequenced in the conventional order, which is size first, then color, then material.
- Refer to the first example you prepared in advance and read it with students.
    - The big, old, yellow dog loves to play fetch.

7. What is the noun in the sentence?
    » *dog*

8. What is the article in the sentence?
    » *the*

9. What are the three adjectives in the sentence?
    » *big*, *old*, and *yellow*

- Explain that the types of adjectives used in this first sentence refer to size (*big*), age (*old*), and color (*yellow*). Note that the adjectives are listed in the proper order, with the article coming first, the adjectives describing the size, age, and color coming in that order next, and the noun coming last. Also note that when more than one adjective is used in a series, or in a row, then the adjectives are usually separated by commas.
- Ask a student to read the words in the next example.
    - read old I a Russian folktale scary
- Ask students to identify the part of speech for each word. (*read*: verb; *old*, *an*, *Russian*: adjectives; *I*, *folktale*: nouns) For each adjective, ask students to identify its type. (*old*: physical description/age; *an*: article; *Russian*: origin)
- Ask students to reorder the words to create a sentence with the adjectives ordered correctly according to the chart. Reinforce the correct order of the adjectives.
    - I read a scary, old, Russian folktale.
- Have students turn to Activity Page 11.1 and read the directions. Review the example and then ask students to complete the first item.

Activity Page 11.1

Check for Understanding

Check that all students complete the first item using the adjective order *little round underwater* to describe the vessel.

If students cannot answer the question correctly, review the chart with them and help them categorize each of the adjectives by type.

- Have students complete Activity Page 11.1 for homework, or if you feel they need more assistance, complete the activity page as a teacher-guided activity.

MORPHOLOGY: SUFFIXES AND ROOTS (15 MIN.)

Primary Focus: Students will review the meanings and uses of the suffixes *–ly* and *–y* and the roots *graph* and *rupt*. **[L.4.4]**

- Remind students that a suffix is a syllable or syllables placed at the end of a root word to change the word's meaning.

- Remind students that a root is a main element of a word that forms the base of its meaning. A prefix or suffix added to the root can change the meaning. It can also change the part of speech of a root.
- Tell students today they will review suffixes and roots that have been covered in previous lessons.
- Remind students that the suffix –*ly* is of Latin origin and means "in a ____ way" with the blank being the word to which –*ly* is added. Point out that it is pronounced /lee/.
- Remind students that when –*ly* is added to the end of an adjective, the word becomes an adverb. Remind students that adverbs describe verbs. The adverbs created with the suffix –*ly* describe how a verb happens.
- Write "busy" on the board/chart paper. Briefly discuss the meaning of the word and then use it in a sentence. (*Busy* means "having a lot to do" or "being full of activity." The department store was very busy and crowded, so I had to wait in line for a long time.)
- Remind students that when you add the suffix –*ly* to an adjective ending in –*y*, you must first change the –*y* to –*i*, and then add –*ly*.
- Change the –*y* in busy to an –*i* and add the suffix –*ly*. Have students read the new word; then discuss the meaning of the word, and use it in a sentence. (*Busily* means "in a busy way" or "in a way that relates to having a lot to do." The adults busily worked in the kitchen preparing Thanksgiving dinner.)

Check for Understanding

How would you change the word *happy* into *happily*? Explain the process.

» Change the –*y* in happy to an –*i* and then add –*ly*.

- If students cannot follow the correct procedure, review the instructions you just gave, using *happy/happily* instead of *busy/busily*.

- Remind students that the suffix –*y* is of English origin and means "full of." Point out that it is pronounced /ee/.
- Write "taste" on the board/chart paper. Briefly discuss the part of speech and meaning of the word. Then use it in a sentence. (*Taste* is a verb meaning "to test the flavor of something." When my sister tasted a lemon, she made a funny face because it was so sour.) Note that *taste* can also be a noun meaning the flavor of something.

- Remind students that when you add the suffix *–y* to a word ending in *–e*, you must remove the *–e* before adding *–y*.
- Change the *–e* in taste to *–y*. Have students read the new word; then discuss the part of speech and the meaning of the word, and use it in a sentence. (*Tasty* is an adjective meaning "full of flavor" or "delicious." The chicken we had for dinner last night was very tasty.)
- Remind students that *graph* is a Greek root that means "write" and is pronounced /graf/.
- Write "biography" on the board/chart paper. Briefly discuss the part of speech and meaning of the word. Then use it in a sentence. (*Biography* is a noun meaning "a written history of someone's life." I read an interesting biography about Theodore Roosevelt.)
- Remind students that *rupt* is a Latin root that means "to break or burst" and is pronounced /rupt/.
- Write "abruptly" on the board. Briefly discuss the part of speech and the meaning of the word. Then use it in a sentence. (*Abruptly* is an adverb meaning "in a sudden and unexpected way." We had to leave the beach abruptly when an unexpected storm rolled in.)
- Continue in this manner for the remaining words, using the following chart as a guide.

  Note: You will not write the information in the shaded columns on the board/chart paper, as that information is intended for use during oral instruction. Complete as many examples as time permits.

Root	Meaning	Affixed Word	Meaning	Sentence
kind	(adjective) doing good for others	kindly	(adverb) in a kind way; in a way that is doing good for others	My sister kindly made soup for me when I was sick.
mess	(noun) a state of disorder	messy	(adjective) full of disorder	Her dad told her she couldn't play until she cleaned her messy room.
graph	write (Greek)	photograph	(noun) a picture taken with a camera	We saw a photograph of the damage caused by an earthquake.
rupt	to break or burst (Latin)	interrupt	(verb) to stop by breaking through	My parents say that it is rude to interrupt people when they are having a conversation.

Language
Interpreting

Entering/Emerging
Make brief sketches of vocabulary words such as *photograph* and *autograph*. Have students point to each sketch and say the appropriate word.

Transitioning/Expanding
Use the activity above, but have students say a phrase or a simple sentence that uses the word, such as a *big photograph* or *I see a photograph of ____*.

Bridging
Have students make sketches of their own using the vocabulary words above and say full sentences that use the words.

Activity Page 11.2

- Have students turn to Activity Page 11.2. Briefly review the directions.

Check for Understanding

Have students complete the first sentence on Activity Page 11.2. Check that they have used the word *kind* in the blank. If students choose the wrong word, review the vocabulary words and their meanings.

- Have students solve the next two sentences together as a class.
- Have students complete the rest of Activity Page 11.2 for homework, or if you feel they need more assistance, complete the entire activity page as a teacher-guided activity.

SPELLING: INTRODUCE SPELLING WORDS (15 MIN.)

Primary Focus: Students will practice spelling targeted words. **[L.4.2]**

- Explain that students will practice 10 words related to the content of the Reader, *The Changing Earth*. Point out that these words do not follow one single spelling pattern. Tell students they will be assessed on these words and will write a dictated sentence related to one or more of these words in Lesson 15.
- Introduce the words by writing them on the board/chart paper. First say the word aloud, and then sound out each syllable, naming each letter aloud as you write it. Continue syllable by syllable until the word is spelled correctly. You may wish to use the pronunciation chart to guide students in saying the words.

  Note: Remember to point out specific spelling patterns in each word and their relationship to the sounds and spellings on the Individual Code Chart.

1. fault	6. tectonic
2. tsunami	7. molten
3. geyser	8. seismograph
4. erosion	9. epicenter
5. glacier	10. conclusion

Language
Producing

Entering/Emerging
Check to make sure students know the name and the most common sound(s) of each letter in English.

Transitioning/Expanding
Have students work with a partner to identify the name of each letter and the most common sound(s) it represents.

Bridging
Have students tell you the name of each letter along with the sound(s) it represents.

Pronunciation/Syllabication Chart

- The following chart includes pronunciation and syllabication information for the spelling words. As you introduce and write each word, it may be helpful if you point out particular spelling patterns within each word and show students where these spellings are reflected on the Individual Code Chart. For example, you might note that the final sound in the word seismograph is /f/ and then point out the *ph* spelling for /f/ that is included on the Individual Code Chart.

Check for Understanding

Have students spell the word *fault* from memory. If they cannot spell the word correctly, have them study the spelling for a few seconds and then try again. Repeat with *erosion*.

Word	CK Code	Syllable Type
fault	/fawlt/	digraph
tsunami	/soo*no*mee/	open*open*open
geyser	/gie*zer/	digraph*r-controlled
erosion	/i*roe*zshən/	open*open*ə
glacier	/glae*sher/	open*r-controlled
tectonic	/tek*ton*ik/	closed*closed*closed
molten	/moel*ten/	closed*closed
seismograph	/siez*mə*graf/	digraph*ə*closed
epicenter	/ep*i*sen*ter/	closed*open*closed*r-controlled
conclusion	/kun*kloo*zshən/	closed*open*ə

- After writing and pronouncing the words, use the following chart to define each word and provide an example of how to use it in a sentence.

Spelling Word	Definition	Example Sentence
fault	(noun) a crack in Earth's crust	Huge blocks of rock moving along a fault can trigger an earthquake.
tsunami	(noun) a gigantic wave caused by an earthquake in oceanic crust	A tsunami can travel as fast as 500 miles per hour and can grow to become a wall of water as tall as a four-story building.
geyser	(noun) an underground hot spring that periodically erupts, shooting hot water and steam into the air	Old Faithful is a geyser in Yellowstone National Park that erupts multiple times a day.
erosion	(noun) any process or force that moves sediments to new locations	Erosion can be a slow process caused by wind, flowing water, moving ice, or gravity.
glacier	(noun) an enormous, slow-moving mass of ice found in polar regions and near tops of tall mountains	As the climate gets warmer, a glacier that was once very large can melt and eventually disappear.
tectonic	(adjective) relating to the process of plate movement on Earth's surface	Tectonic plates move slowly, but their movements have dramatically changed Earth's surface over millions of years.
molten	(adjective) melted	Molten rock moves slowly, like syrup being stirred.
seismograph	(noun) an instrument used to track seismic waves traveling through the earth	If a major earthquake happens, a seismograph records the seismic waves as big zigzags.
epicenter	(noun) the point on Earth's surface directly above an earthquake's focus	Scientists compare multiple seismograms in order to pinpoint an earthquake's epicenter.
conclusion	(noun) a decision or opinion formed based on information you have	Alfred Wegener reached the conclusion that all the continents were once joined together as one landmass, based on evidence.

Activity Page 11.3

Activity Page 11.4

- Tell students the word list will remain on display until the assessment so they can refer to it until then.
- Have students turn to Activity Pages 11.3 and 11.4. Explain that they will take home Activity Page 11.3 to practice spelling the words for homework and will complete Activity Page 11.4 for homework.

End Lesson

Lesson 11: Weathering and Erosion, Part 2

Take-Home Material

GRAMMAR; MORPHOLOGY; SPELLING

Activity Pages 11.1, 11.2, and 11.4

Activity Pages 11.3

- Have students take home Activity Pages 11.1, 11.2, and 11.4 to complete for homework and Activity Page 11.3 to practice spelling the words.
- Have students take home a text selection from the Fluency Supplement if you are choosing to provide additional fluency practice.

LESSON

12 Mountains

PRIMARY FOCUS OF LESSON

Reading

Students will describe how mountains are formed, identify different types of mountains, and locate major mountain ranges on a map. **[RI.4.1, RI.4.2, RI.4.3]**

Writing

Students will plan for writing a descriptive paragraph about a rock or other item in the rock cycle. **[W.4.2, W.4.3, W.4.4, W.4.5]**

FORMATIVE ASSESSMENT

Activity Page 1.3	**Evidence Collector's Chart** Students look in the text for evidence supporting geological events. **[RI.4.1]**
Activity Page 1.4	**Evidence of Changes on Earth** Students look in the text for evidence supporting geological events. **[RI.4.1]**
Activity Page 12.2	**Earth's Mighty Mountains** Students answer questions based on the Reader text, citing the page numbers where the information can be found. **[RI.4.1, RI.4.2, RI.4.3]**
Activity Page 12.3	**Planning a Descriptive Paragraph** Students use information and creativity to plan a descriptive paragraph regarding geology and geologic processes. **[W.4.2, W.4.5]**

LESSON AT A GLANCE

	Grouping	Time	Materials
Reading (45 min.)			
Introduce the Chapter	Whole Group	5 min.	❑ The Changing Earth ❑ world map ❑ Activity Pages 1.3, 1.4, 12.1, 12.2 ❑ Evidence Collector's Chart ❑ scissors ❑ glue
Read "Earth's Mighty Mountains"	Small Groups	25 min.	
Discuss the Chapter and Lesson Wrap-Up	Whole Group	10 min.	
Word Work: *Sheer*	Whole Group	5 min.	
Writing (45 min.)			
Introduce a Descriptive Paragraph	Whole Group	15 min.	❑ Descriptive Paragraph Example ❑ Activity Page 12.3 ❑ The Changing Earth
Plan a Descriptive Paragraph	Individuals	30 min.	

ADVANCE PREPARATION

Reading

- Access a digital version of The Big Question in the digital components for this unit.
- Display a world map, or access a digital version in the digital components for this unit. Be prepared to locate the following during the lesson: India's Himalayas; South America's Andes Mountains; Germany's Harz Mountains; Wyoming's Grand Tetons; the Basin and Range Province of Utah, Nevada, and Arizona; and South Dakota's Black Hills.
- Display the Evidence Collector's Chart from Lesson 1.

Writing

- Create a descriptive paragraph to display or access a digital version of the following Descriptive Paragraph Example in the digital components for this unit.

  Descriptive Paragraph

  My name is Leah Lava, and I feel as hot as the sun! That's probably because I'm lava shooting down the side of an active volcano. I hear a deep rumble behind me as the rocks and debris spew out of the mountain, and I wonder if the plume is still reaching toward the blackening sky like an opening umbrella. As soon as I feel the air touch me, I begin to cool down. Thank goodness! It was getting awfully hot. As I cool, I harden, forming igneous rock. After all that hot activity, I like feeling wind blow across me and rain rinse my body. Sometimes I get uncomfortable in the scorching sun or the freezing cold, but I feel calm listening to the birds chirping around me and tasting the water that trickles over me.

Language

Grammar; Morphology; Spelling

- Collect Activity Pages 11.1, 11.2, and 11.4 to review and grade as there are no grammar, morphology, or spelling lessons today.

Start Lesson

Lesson 12: Mountains

Reading

Primary Focus: Students will describe how mountains are formed, identify different types of mountains, and locate major mountain ranges on a map.
[RI.4.1, RI.4.2, RI.4.3]

INTRODUCE THE CHAPTER (5 MIN.)

- Tell students they will read Chapter 8, "Earth's Mighty Mountains."
- Ask three or four students to share something they know about mountains. To check that classmates are listening closely, ask questions afterward of the form "Point to the person who told us that ___."
- Have students turn to the table of contents, locate the chapter, and then turn to the first page of the chapter.
- Preview the core vocabulary words before reading the chapter.
- Have students tell you the first vocabulary word they will encounter in this chapter (sea level).
- Have them find the words on page 73 of the Reader. Remind them that each vocabulary word is bolded the first time it appears in the chapter.
- Review that the glossary contains definitions of all the vocabulary words in this Reader. Ask students to guess the meaning of sea level. Ask classmates to raise one finger if they think the definition is probably correct, three fingers if they think the definition offered is probably incorrect, and two fingers if they are uncertain.
- Have students refer to the glossary at the back of the Reader, locate sea level, and then have a student read the definition.
- Explain the following:
    - The part of speech

Activity Page 12.1

- Have students reference Activity Page 12.1 while you read each word and its meaning. Note:
    - The page number (for the first occurrence of the word in the chapter) appears in bold print after the definition.
    - Words are listed in the order in which they appear in the chapter.

sea level, n. the average height of the ocean's surface (73)

sheer, adj. very steep, almost straight up and down (78)

bulge, v. to stick out or swell (80)

Vocabulary Chart for Chapter 8 "Earth's Mighty Mountains"		
Vocabulary Type	**Tier 3** **Domain-Specific Words**	**Tier 2** **General Academic Words**
Core Vocabulary	sea level	sheer bulge
Spanish Cognates for Core Vocabulary		
Multiple-Meaning Core Vocabulary Words		sheer
Sayings and Phrases	above sea level	

- Have one student read The Big Question at the beginning of the chapter. Ensure students understand the meaning of The Big Question before reading the chapter.
    - How do the movements and forces of tectonic plates build mountains?

Establish Small Groups

- Before reading the chapter, divide students into two groups using the following guidelines.
- Small Group 1: This group should include students who need extra scaffolding and support to read and comprehend the text. Use the guided reading supports to guide students through reading the text. This is an excellent time to make notes in your anecdotal records. Students may complete Activity Page 12.2 with your support during reading.
- Small Group 2: This group should include students who are capable of reading and comprehending text without guided support. These students may work as a small group, as partners, or independently to read the chapter, discuss it with others in Small Group 2, and then complete Activity Page 12.2. Make arrangements to check that students in Small Group 2 have answered the questions on Activity Page 12.2 correctly. You may choose to do one of the following to address this:
    - Collect the pages and correct them individually.
    - Provide an answer key to students to check their own or a partner's work after they have completed the activity page.
    - Confer with students individually or as a group at a later time.
- Over the course of the year, students may change groups, depending on individual students' needs.

Activity Page 12.2

READ "EARTH'S MIGHTY MOUNTAINS" (25 MIN.)

- The following guided reading supports are intended for use with Small Group 1.

Chapter 8

Earth's Mighty Mountains

THE BIG QUESTION
How do the movements and forces of tectonic plates build mountains?

The year was 1953. Mountain climbers Edmund Hillary and Tenzing Norgay stood on the hard-packed snow. They gasped for breath in the thin air. Their faces burned from the bitter cold wind. Despite this, they were grinning from ear to ear.

72

- Have students read pages 72 and 73 silently.

  Evaluative. Why do you think the two men might have been grinning even though they were obviously uncomfortable?

  » Answers will vary but should reference the notion that they had done something impressive.

Hillary and Norgay had just made it to the top of Mount Everest. They were the first people to reach Earth's highest point, 29,029 feet above **sea level**.

Mountains are some of Earth's most awe-inspiring features. In 1953, geologists were still searching for answers as to how mountains form. By the 1960s, scientific evidence pointed to plate tectonics as a driving force behind mountain building. As you read in Chapter 2, our planet's rocky exterior isn't one solid piece. It is broken up into a collection of gigantic tectonic plates.

Earth's tectonic plates move slowly, but their movements have dramatically changed Earth's features over time. Plate movements have shuffled Earth's continents into different positions. They have destroyed old oceans and created new ones. They have also built mountains and mountain ranges in several different ways.

73

Inferential. What role have tectonic plates had in changing Earth's features?

» Tectonic plates have dramatically changed Earth's features over many millions of years, so tectonic plates have had a major role in changing Earth's features.

Literal. What evidence in the text supports the idea that plate tectonics are important in the creation of mountains?

» Plate movements have shuffled Earth's continents into different positions; they have destroyed old oceans and created new ones; they have also built mountains and mountain ranges in several different ways.

Colliding Continents

Some of Earth's highest mountain ranges formed as sections of continental crust collided over millions of years. The collision that formed Mount Everest is a good example. Everest is part of the Himalayas, a vast, towering mountain range between India and China. The Himalayas formed when continents on two tectonic plates met head-on.

Can you find India on the map? It lies along the southern edge of Asia. India wasn't always where it is today. Hundreds of millions of years ago, India was an island. It sat out in the middle of the Indo-Australian Plate. It was separated from Asia, which sits on the Eurasian Plate, by an ancient ocean called the Tethys Sea.

The Indo-Australian Plate began creeping northward about 200 million years ago. Driven by moving magma in the mantle below, it slowly collided with the Eurasian Plate. Where the two plates met, subduction took place. The heavier oceanic crust of the Indo-Australian Plate slid under the lighter continental crust of the Eurasian Plate.

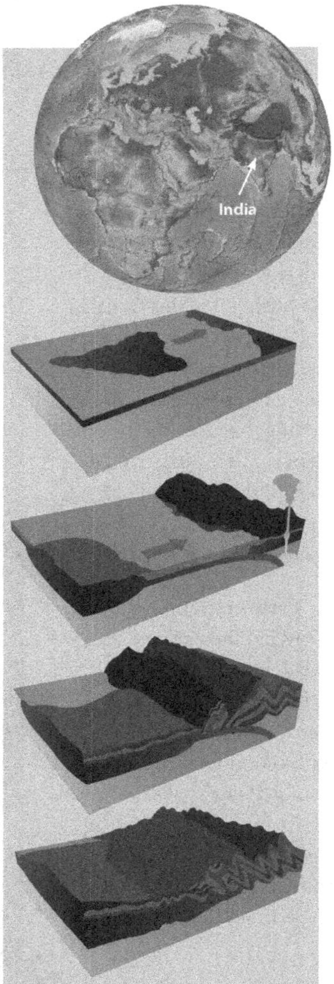

The Indo-Australian Plate moved slowly northward, carrying India along with it.

74

Pronunciation Chart	
Word(s)	**CK Code**
Tethys Sea	/teth*ees/ /see/
Eurasian	/yer*ae*zshən/
Urals	/yer*əlz/

- Have students read pages 74 and 75 silently.

- Have a student locate India on a world map. Point out the location of the Himalayas. Guide students to recognize that the Himalayas lie north of most of India.

  Literal. In which direction did the Indo-Australian plate move: north, south, east, or west?

  » north

  Evaluative. What would have happened if the plate had moved in some other direction?

  » Possible answers: the Himalayas would not have formed; Asia would not include India; the map of the world today would look very different.

As the Indo-Australian Plate kept moving northward, India was carried along. It inched closer and closer to Asia. The Tethys Sea began to disappear. India finally collided with Asia around 40 million years ago. India's rocky continental crust pressed directly against Asia's continental crust.

As the two landmasses continued to be pushed harder and harder together, the continental crust began to crumple. Enormous pressure created by the moving tectonic plate caused the rocky crust to heave upward. Great masses of rock gradually rose up into a series of enormous folds. The Himalayas were born!

More and more rocks were uplifted as the Indo-Australian Plate kept moving. The Himalayas rose higher and higher. In fact, they are still rising. They are growing taller at about the same rate that your fingernails grow!

Geologists classify the Himalayas as **fold mountains**. The name refers to the way rocks are pushed up into huge folds by moving tectonic plates. The Alps, Europe's highest mountains, are fold mountains that formed much like the Himalayas. The Appalachians in North America and the Urals in Russia also formed through collisions of continental crust.

Literal. According to the text, how are fold mountains formed?

» Tectonic plates collide, pushing continental crust together with so much pressure that the crust crumples. The rocky crust gets pushed upward, creating folds.

- Have students demonstrate movement of the tectonic plates in creating fold mountains. Show how they can use their left hands to represent the Indo-Australian Plate and their right hands to represent the Eurasian Plate. Guide students to act out how Mount Everest was created by slowly moving their left hands (Indo-Australian Plate) towards their stationary right hands (Eurasian Plate). When their fingertips touch, students should slide the fingertips of their left hands (Indo-Australian Plate) under their right hands (Eurasian Plate). Continue to have them move their hands back and forth, one over the other, gradually pushing their fingers upward to represent the rocky crust moving upward in folds.

Check for Understanding

Ask students to explain the connection between what they were just doing with their hands and the information about tectonic plates and mountains in the chapter. If they cannot explain the connection, model the hand movements and talk through what is happening at each step.

How are they formed?

» Tectonic plates collide, pressure crumples the crust, and the crust gets pushed upward, creating folds.

What are some examples and where are they located?

» Himalayas, between India and China in Asia

Like many other fold mountains, the Himalayas contain quite a bit of sedimentary rock. Why? In the case of the Himalayas, it started with the Tethys Sea. For millions of years, erosion washed sediments from Asia and the ancient island of India into the Tethys Sea. Countless layers of sediments, along with remains of ocean animals, were deposited on the seafloor. Over time, pressure and heat helped turn these sediments into sedimentary rock.

As plate movements slowly brought India and Asia together, some of these seafloor sedimentary rocks were pushed up. Heat and pressure from the colliding plates transformed some of them into metamorphic rocks. Other sedimentary rocks remained relatively unchanged. This is how fossils of ancient ocean animals ended up on top of Mount Everest.

Fossils at the Top of the World

Trilobites and crinoids are two of the most common types of fossils on Mount Everest. Trilobites were hard-shelled ocean animals related to modern-day crabs and lobsters. Trilobites lived on the bottom of Earth's ancient oceans, including the Tethys Sea. Crinoids were animals, too, but they looked more like plants. Trilobites and most crinoids became extinct about 250 million years ago. A few types of crinoids still survive far below the ocean's surface.

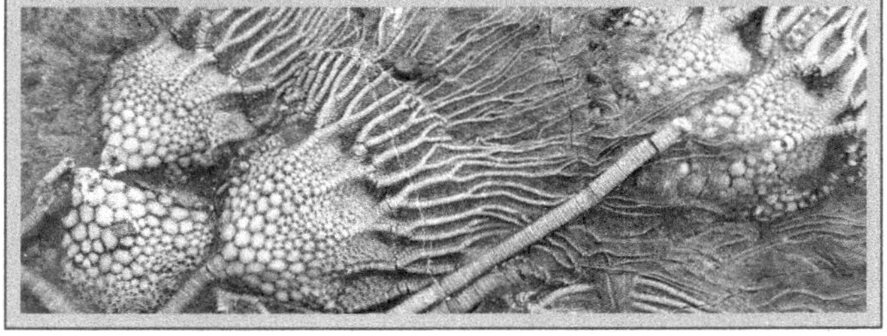

76

- Have students read pages 76 and 77 silently.

Literal. What are some common features of fold mountains?

» Answers may vary but should include: fold mountains contain quite a bit of sedimentary rock; they look like folds of rock.

Support

Help students create a simple flow chart to summarize the first two paragraphs on Reader p. 76.

Challenge

How did fossils of ocean animals end up at the top of Mount Everest?

» The movement of the tectonic plates pushed sedimentary rock that was at the bottom of the ocean upward as Mount Everest was formed. The sedimentary rock from the ocean floor includes fossils of ocean animals.

The Andes Mountains in Peru are fold mountains.

Folding at the Edges

Along South America's western coast, the oceanic Nazca Plate has been sliding under the South American Plate for millions of years. This has caused massive folds of rock to pile up along the edge of the continent. These folds are now the Andes Mountains, the longest mountain range on land.

As you read in Chapter 4, the edge of a subducting plate melts as it descends into Earth's hot mantle. The resulting magma moves up through cracks in the crust. It may erupt on the surface to form volcanoes. The edge of the Nazca Plate is melting as it slides beneath the South American Plate. Erupting magma has created many volcanoes in the Andes Mountain range.

77

Literal. What is another example of fold mountains and where are these mountains located?

» The Andes Mountains in South America are fold mountains.

- Have a student locate South America on a world map. Point out the location of the Andes Mountains.

Look closely at the map. Work with a partner. Use words such as *north*, *south*, *east*, and *west* to give your partner directions for reaching the Andes Mountains from our community. Then have the partner give directions using the same directional words for getting back home.

» Check students' work.

- Have students record the following answers about fold mountains in the appropriate places in the chart on Activity Page 12.2:

  What are common features or characteristics?

  » sedimentary rock, look like folds

  What are some examples and where are they located?

  » Andes Mountains in South America

Faults and Blocks

The longest, highest mountain ranges on land are mostly fold mountains. However, moving tectonic plates build mountains in other ways. **Fault-block mountains** form when gigantic blocks of rock move up and down along faults.

At some faults, such as the San Andreas Fault in California, blocks of rock move horizontally past each other as they slip. At other faults, slips cause blocks of rock on one side of the fault to move up. These slips also cause blocks on the other side of the fault to move down. Repeated slips gradually force these rock blocks higher—and lower—to create fault-block mountain ranges.

Fault-block mountains typically have one steep side and one sloping side. The steep side forms a high, **sheer** cliff. Germany's Harz Mountains are one example of fault-block mountains. Others include the Grand Tetons in Wyoming and the Basin and Range Province of Utah, Nevada, and Arizona.

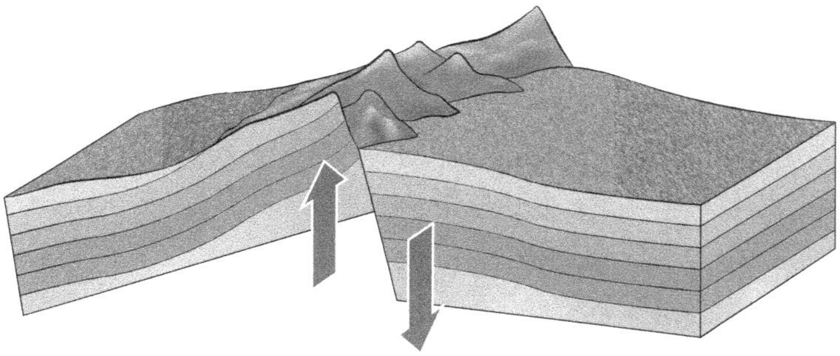

Fault-block mountains form when blocks of rock move up and down along fault lines.

78

- Have students read pages 78 and 79 silently.

  Literal. How are fault-block mountains formed?

  » Fault-block mountains form when gigantic blocks of rock move up and down along faults.

- Demonstrate the movement of tectonic plates in creating fault-block mountains by holding your hands out flat, palms down, parallel to one another, but not touching. Explain that the space between your hands represents the fault. Move one hand up and down while holding the other hand steady. Have students repeat your actions, telling a partner what they are doing and how their movements represent the forces described in the text.

Reading For Information
Interpretative

Entering/Emerging
Have students use single words and simple phrases to describe their hand movements. Rephrase their ideas in sentence form and have them repeat.

Transitioning/Expanding
Have students use phrases to describe their hand movements. Use sentence frames to guide them to rephrase their ideas into sentence form.

Bridging
Have students use simple sentences to describe their hand movements. Help students express these concepts in more complex sentences.

Check for Understanding

Literal. What is one common feature of fault-block mountains mentioned in the text?

» Possible answers: fault-block mountains typically have one steep side and one sloping side; the steep side of fault-block mountains form high cliffs.

- If students cannot answer the question, have them reread the information in the last paragraph of Reader page 78.

- Locate Germany's Harz Mountains, Wyoming's Grand Tetons, and the Basin and Range Province of Utah, Nevada, and Arizona on a world map. If the map has a symbol for mountains, you may wish to point out the symbol and relate it to the information contained in the map key, or legend.
- Have students record the following answers about fault-block mountains in the appropriate places in the chart on Activity Page 12.2:

How are they formed?

» Gigantic blocks of rock move up and down along faults.

What are common features or characteristics?

» one steep side, with a high cliff, and one sloping side

What are some examples and where are they located?

» Harz Mountains in Germany; Grand Tetons in Wyoming; Basin and Range Province in Utah, Nevada, and Arizona

Evaluative. How are fold mountains and fault-block mountains similar? How are they different?

» Answers may vary but should include: They are similar in that they both form along tectonic plate boundaries and they are both part of long mountain ranges. They are different because fold mountains form when tectonic plates collide and pressure crumples the crust, pushing the crust upward, creating folds. In contrast, fault-block mountains are formed when gigantic blocks of rock move up and down along faults, slipping past each other, leaving rocks on one side very high up and rocks on the other side lower.

Challenge

Have students discuss in pairs or in small groups whether they think fold mountains or fault-block mountains are likely to be taller. Ask them to explain their answers.

The Grand Teton Mountains in Wyoming are fault-block mountains.

Under the Dome

Most people think of sharp, jagged peaks when they hear the word *mountains*. **Dome mountains** are quite different. Dome mountains look like great humps of rock with rounded tops. They usually occur as isolated mountains on otherwise flat plains.

Some dome mountains form when magma pushes upward into Earth's crust from the mantle. The magma cools into igneous rock before reaching the surface. This huge lump of igneous rock causes the crust above it to **bulge**, like a blister on skin. Utah's Navajo Mountain is a good example of a dome mountain that formed this way.

Navajo Mountain, Utah

80

Pronunciation Chart	
Word(s)	**CK Code**
Navajo	/nov*ə*hoe/
Gutzon Borglum	/gootz*un/ /bor*glum/

- Have students read pages 80 and 81 silently.

Literal. According to the text, how are dome mountains formed?

» Some dome mountains form when magma pushes upward into Earth's crust from the mantle. The magma cools into igneous rock before reaching the surface. The igneous rock causes the crust to bulge.

- Remind students that they used their hands to model how fold mountains and fault-block mountains are formed. Ask students how they might use their hands to demonstrate how dome mountains are formed. Encourage them to think about how they could help demonstrate the process for someone who has not read the chapter and knows nothing about dome mountains.

Literal. What are some common features of dome mountains?

» Dome mountains look like great humps of rock with rounded tops; they don't have sharp, jagged peaks; they usually occur as isolated mountains on otherwise flat plains.

- Locate South Dakota on a world map and point out the location of the Black Hills. Locate Utah on a world map and point out the location of Navajo Mountain.

Check for Understanding

Evaluative. Tell students that you recently saw a picture of a mountain that was formed along a fault and included several high cliffs. Ask them to determine whether the mountain was a dome mountain, a fault-block mountain, or a fold mountain.

» a fault-block mountain

- If students give an incorrect answer, have them review what they have learned about each type of mountain and the differences between the three types.

Mountains on the Prairie

You can see the Black Hills of western South Dakota from a long way off. These dome mountains rise up from the surrounding grassy plains as dark, hunched shapes. They are the highest mountains east of the Rocky Mountains. Very ancient granite forms the core of the Black Hills. Millions of years of weathering and erosion have exposed this igneous rock in many places. The sculptor Gutzon Borglum made one tall granite formation in the Black Hills famous. He carved the faces of four presidents into the rock to create Mount Rushmore National Memorial. Another sculpture in the Black Hills has also gained attention—as the world's largest sculpture in progress. Crazy Horse Memorial honors North American Indian heritage and depicts the face of the Sioux leader Crazy Horse. Started in 1948 by sculptor Korczak Ziolkowski, work on the massive sculpture still continues today.

81

- Have students record the following answers about dome mountains in the appropriate places in the chart on Activity Page 12.2:

  How are they formed?

  » Magma pushes upward into Earth's crust, cools into igneous rock, and causes a bulge.

  What are common features or characteristics?

  » look like humps of rock with rounded tops, usually isolated on flat plains

  What are some examples and where are they located?

  » Navajo Mountain in Utah, Black Hills in South Dakota

Evaluative. How are dome mountains different from fold and fault-block mountains?

» Dome mountains have rounded tops whereas fold and fault-block mountains have steep, tall peaks. Dome mountains are usually isolated on otherwise flat plains, whereas fold and fault-block mountains are part of continuous mountain chains that are long and span vast areas.

DISCUSS THE CHAPTER AND LESSON WRAP-UP (10 MIN.)

Note: Question 1 and Activity Page 1.3 relate to The Big Question of the chapter.

- Use the following question to discuss the chapter.

1. **Literal.** How do the movements and forces of tectonic plates build mountains?

   » The different interactions of tectonic plates build different types of mountains. Fold mountains are built when tectonic plates collide at their boundaries or if a plate with oceanic crust subducts beneath a plate with continental crust. Fault-block mountains are built when blocks of rock move up and down along faults, which are usually located at plate boundaries. Dome mountains are built when the magma beneath the plates pushes up into the crust. Volcanoes, most of which form along tectonic plate boundaries, also build mountains as they erupt.

Activity Pages 1.3 and 1.4

- Have students turn to Activity Pages 1.3 and 1.4 and refer to the displayed Evidence Collector's Chart.
- Review with students that this chart is being used throughout the unit to collect evidence of changes to the earth related to specific causes of geologic change. The evidence represents what geologists examine to determine how powerful forces above and below Earth's surface work to change the earth.
- Have a student read aloud the information under "What is the cause?" in the seventh row. Explain that students must determine what evidence is in the chapter about the tectonic plates subducting and moving up against each other, and of magma pushing up into the crust. (pages 74, 75, 77, 78, 80)
- Have students refer to the remaining images on Activity Page 1.4. Engage students in a discussion about the images, talking about which image represents evidence of tectonic plates subducting or moving up against each other, or of magma pushing up into the crust.

- Ensure students understand why the image showing three types of mountains is the correct image. (The image shows an example of the three types of mountains: fold mountains, which are evidence of tectonic plates subducting underneath one another; fault-block mountains, which are evidence of tectonic plates moving up and down against each other; and dome mountains, which are evidence of magma pushing up into the crust.)
- Have students cut out the correct image, glue it to the chart in the "What evidence is there?" column, and write the following information for chapter number, key words, and letter in the chart:

Chapter number	What is the cause?	What evidence is there?	Letter
8	*Tectonic plates subduct underneath one another and move up and down against each other, and magma pushes up into the crust.*	*image: three types of mountains* *key words:* fold, fault-block, and dome mountains	E

- As needed, have students complete the chart on Activity Page 12.2. Then have students label the map on Activity Page 12.2. You may wish to display the world map found in the digital components for this unit.
- Collect Activity Page 12.2 to review at a later date.

WORD WORK: *SHEER* (5 MIN.)

1. In the chapter you read, "The steep side forms a high, sheer cliff."
2. Say the word *sheer* with me.
3. *Sheer* means very steep, almost straight up and down.
4. The sheer drop of the roller coaster as it sped down the track made me feel sick!
5. What are some other examples of things that are sheer? Be sure to use the word *sheer* in your response.
   » Answers will vary.

- If necessary, guide and/or rephrase students' responses to make complete sentences: "____ is sheer because ____."

6. What part of speech is the word *sheer*?
   » adjective

- Use a Multiple-Meaning Word activity for follow-up. Tell students the word *sheer* is a word with multiple meanings. Share the following with students.
    - Meaning 1: sheer—very steep, almost straight up and down
    - Meaning 2: sheer—very thin, almost see-through
    - Meaning 3: sheer—total, to the fullest degree
- I am going to read several sentences. Listen to the context or the text surrounding sheer in the sentence for clues as to which meaning is being used. When you think a sentence is an example of Meaning 1, hold up one finger. When you think a sentence is an example of Meaning 2, hold up two fingers. When you think a sentence is an example of Meaning 3, hold up three fingers.

1. He told us our idea was an example of sheer brilliance.

    » 3

2. The curtain was made of sheer material so that the sun could still shine through.

    » 2

3. The satin dress was covered with a lovely layer of sheer lace.

    » 2

4. I had a very difficult time hiking up the side of the sheer mountain.

    » 1

5. I couldn't make sense of the riddle; it was sheer nonsense.

    » 3

6. We were told to stay away from the edge of the island because it had sheer cliffs that were dangerous.

    » 1

Lesson 12: Mountains

Writing

45M

Primary Focus: Students will plan for writing a descriptive paragraph about a rock or other item in the rock cycle. **[W.4.2, W.4.3, W.4.4, W.4.5]**

INTRODUCE A DESCRIPTIVE PARAGRAPH (15 MIN.)

- Remind students they learned about descriptive writing in Unit 1, Personal Narratives. Remind them that they wrote a descriptive paragraph about an object.
- Tell students they will write a similar piece, but this time they will focus on a type of rock or other item in the rock cycle, such as igneous rock, lava, magma, metamorphic rock, sediments, or sedimentary rock.
- Explain that students will write one paragraph in which they personify a rock or item in the rock cycle. The assignment will showcase their knowledge of rock types and should also be fun and creative.
- Direct students' attention to the Descriptive Paragraph Example you prepared in advance:

  Descriptive Paragraph

  My name is Leah Lava, and I feel as hot as the sun! That's probably because I'm lava shooting down the side of an active volcano. I hear a deep rumble behind me as rocks and debris spew out of the mountain, and I wonder if the plume is still reaching toward the blackening sky like an opening umbrella. As soon as I feel the air touch me, I begin to cool down. Thank goodness! It was getting awfully hot. As I cool, I harden, forming igneous rock. After all that hot activity, I like feeling wind blow across me and rain rinse my body. Sometimes I get uncomfortable in the scorching sun or the freezing cold, but I feel calm listening to the birds chirping around me and tasting the water that trickles over me.

- Remind students there are specific parts in a descriptive paragraph. Ask students to take a moment to identify the topic sentence, the detail sentences, and the concluding sentence of the paragraph. Have them share their answers with a partner and talk in pairs about the purpose of each section of the paragraph.

1. Why do writers typically include a topic sentence in the paragraphs they write?
   » A topic sentence states the main idea.
2. What is the topic sentence in the Descriptive Paragraph Example? What information does it provide?
   » The topic sentence is "My name is Leah Lava, and I feel as hot as the sun!" The topic sentence tells that the paragraph will be about Leah Lava.

- Draw out from students that detail sentences support the main idea with sensory details.
- Ask students to identify a detail sentence in the Descriptive Paragraph Example and describe the details it provides. Ask listeners to make a mental picture of each detail described. Students may say any of the following about sentences two through eight:
    - Lava shooting down the side of an active volcano.
    - A deep rumble, rocks and debris spew out of the mountain, plume reaching toward the blackening sky like an opening umbrella.
    - I cool down as the air touches me.
    - Awfully hot.
    - Cool and harden to form igneous rock.
    - Hot activity followed by wind blowing across me and rain rinsing my body.
- Review with students that a descriptive paragraph should have a concluding sentence that summarizes or restates the main idea.

3. Which is the concluding sentence in the Descriptive Paragraph Example?
   » The concluding sentence is: Sometimes I get uncomfortable in the scorching sun or the freezing cold, but I feel calm listening to the birds chirping around me and tasting the water that trickles over me. This sentence describes how Leah Lava feels, as in the topic sentence. It also adds more information about Leah Lava to end the paragraph.

Check for Understanding

Look at the sentence "As I cool, I harden, forming igneous rock." Is this sentence best described as a topic sentence, a detail sentence, or a concluding sentence?

» a detail sentence

- If students do not know the answer to the question, have them make a three-column chart with the characters of each of the three types of sentences.

- Remind students that they also learned about personification in Unit 1, Personal Narratives. Personification means giving human characteristics to nonhuman things. Ask students to give brief examples of personification in literature or movies.
- Tell students they will personify, or give human characteristics to, the rock or other item they select to write about.
- Tell students that writers use personification for different effects. In the sample paragraph, the author personifies Leah Lava to create a connection between the reader and the content. Personification also captures the reader's attention because it is unusual to read about scientific information in this format.
- Tell students that when an author uses personification, it often makes the piece funny and entertaining. When the reader is entertained, he/she will understand and retain the information better.
- Tell students that the rock or other item they choose will be the focus of their descriptive paragraph.
- Explain that writers focus when they select one specific moment, object, or idea, and use precise details to write about it. A rock or other item moving through one part of the rock cycle is the focus for this paragraph.
- Redirect students' attention to the Descriptive Paragraph Example you prepared in advance.
- Tell students that several different types of literary devices are used in the Descriptive Paragraph Example. Discuss examples of personification and descriptive language in the Descriptive Paragraph Example using the following as guidelines.

4. Where does the author first use personification?

    » In the first sentence, the author personifies lava by giving it a human name, Leah Lava, and saying that she feels hot—a feeling associated with a living thing such as a human, not a nonliving object such as lava.

- Next, remind students that a simile is a comparison of two different things, usually using like or as.

5. Identify two similes in the Descriptive Paragraph Example.

    » as hot as the sun, like an opening umbrella

- Remind students that alliteration is the repetition of words with the same letter or sound.

6. Give an example of alliteration in the paragraph.

    » Leah Lava

- Remind students that good descriptive writing makes use of strong verbs.

7. Which verbs does the author use to appeal to the five senses—touch, sight, taste, smell, and hearing? Have students make a written list of at least five such verbs and share their list with a partner; then call on students to share items from their lists with the class.

    » feel/feeling, shooting down, hear, spew, reaching toward, touch, cool, harden, blow, rinse, listening, chirping, tasting, trickles

8. Point out that this paragraph shows Leah Lava changing into a kind of rock. What does Leah Lava become?

    » igneous rock

Check for Understanding

Why does Leah Lava become igneous rock?

» lava, once cooled, is igneous rock

- If students answer incorrectly or do not give an answer, review the characteristics of lava and its relationship to igneous rocks.

PLAN A DESCRIPTIVE PARAGRAPH (30 MIN.)

- Have students turn to Activity Page 12.3.
- Call on a student to read the directions for Item 1 aloud.
- Review the information in the chart as a class. Tell students that this information will help them choose a focus for their descriptive paragraph.
- Then have students complete Item 1.
- Explain that they will use the characteristics in the chart to provide details about their chosen item.
- Call on students to read aloud the remaining items on the activity page and ensure students understand what each item is about. Use the following as a guide:
    - Item 2: Point out that in the Descriptive Paragraph Example, the author used alliteration for the character name, Leah Lava.
    - Item 3: Tell students to review the information in the chart as well as information in Chapter 6, "Earth's Building Blocks," to help them think about characteristics to include.
    - Item 4: Again, tell students the information in the chart and in Chapter 6, "Earth's Building Blocks," will be helpful for choosing additional details to include.
    - Item 5: Tell students to end the paragraph memorably by using a vivid image, funny piece of dialogue, question, or statement that engages the reader.
- Tell students to complete the rest of the activity page independently.
- Circulate and check in with students, ensuring they are planning appropriately. As you circulate, ask guiding questions such as:
    - Why did you choose this name for your rock?
    - What is the most interesting fact you've learned about your rock?
    - Where would your rock most commonly be found?
    - What's the most exciting or dramatic thing that happens to the rock you've chosen?
- At the end of the period, choose several students to share the name of their main character or one of the details they have chosen to include in their paragraph.
- Collect Activity Page 12.3 to review and monitor student progress. Be prepared to give this activity page back to students in the next lesson.

End Lesson

Activity Page 12.3

Support

You may wish to allow students to work with a partner to complete the activity page.

Writing
Expressive

Entering/Emerging
Have students use pictures as well as words to fill in the blanks on Activity Page 12.3. Then guide them to expand their ideas into full sentences.

Transitioning/Expanding
Have students use words, phrases, and simple sentences to fill in the blanks on the activity page. Then guide them to create more complex sentences.

Bridging
Have students work in pairs to help each other write full sentences when filling in Activity Page 12.3.

LESSON

13

Under the Sea, Part 1

PRIMARY FOCUS OF LESSON

Reading

Students will identify mid-ocean ridges, ocean trenches, hydrothermal vents, and seamounts, and explain how they are formed and how they impact things around them. **[RI.4.1, RI.4.3, RI.4.4]**

Writing

Students will draft a descriptive paragraph based on plans from a previous lesson. **[W.4.2, W.4.4]**

FORMATIVE ASSESSMENT

Activity Page 1.3	**Evidence Collector's Chart** Students look in the text for evidence supporting geological events. **[RI.4.1]**
Activity Page 1.4	**Evidence of Changes on Earth** Students look in the text for evidence supporting geological events. **[RI.4.1]**
Activity Page 12.3	**Planning a Descriptive Paragraph** Students use information and creativity to plan a descriptive paragraph regarding geology and geologic processes. **[W.4.2, W.4.5]**
Activity Page 12.3	**Earth's Powerful Forces of Change** Students choose vocabulary activities to practice vocabulary terms from the lesson. **[RI.4.4]**
Activity Page 13.2	**Excerpt from "Earth's Undersea World"** Students answer questions based on information from the Reader text. **[RI.4.1, RI.4.3]**

LESSON AT A GLANCE

	Grouping	Time	Materials
Reading (45 min.)			
Review	Whole group	5 min.	❏ *The Changing Earth* ❏ Activity Pages 1.3, 1.4, 13.1, 13.2 ❏ Evidence Collector's Chart ❏ scissors ❏ glue ❏ Geology Riddle
Introduce the Chapter	Whole group	5 min.	
Read "Earth's Undersea World"	Whole Group	20 min.	
Lesson Wrap-Up	Whole group	10 min.	
Word Work: *Expedition*	Whole group	5 min.	
Writing (45 min.)			
Descriptive Paragraph Planning	Whole group	10 min.	❏ Descriptive Paragraph Example ❏ Activity Page 12.3 ❏ *The Changing Earth*
Draft a Descriptive Paragraph	Independent	35 min.	
Take-Home Material			
Reading			❏ Activity Page 13.2

ADVANCE PREPARATION

Reading

- Access a digital version of The Big Question in the digital components for this unit.
- Display the Evidence Collector's Chart from Lesson 1.
- Prepare and cover the following Geology Riddle or access a digital version in the digital components for this unit.

  This word is the most important tool,

  Difficult to find, challenging to rule.

  It comes in many shapes and sizes

  And is often full of surprises.

  It's the one thing scientists need to uncover.

  It's the key to what they hope to discover.

Writing

- Have feedback on Activity Page 12.3 ready to return to students.
- Display the Descriptive Paragraph Example used in Lesson 12 or access a digital version in the digital components for this unit.

Start Lesson

Lesson 13: Under the Sea

Reading

45M

Primary Focus: Students will identify mid-ocean ridges, ocean trenches, hydrothermal vents, and seamounts, and explain how they are formed and how they impact things around them. **[RI.4.1, RI.4.3, RI.4.4]**

REVIEW (5 MIN.)

- Briefly review the previous chapter with students. Ask what they remember about the chapter. Have them tell a partner one important or interesting fact they learned.

1. How do the movements and forces of tectonic plates build mountains?

   » Answers may vary but should include: some mountains were formed as the continental crust collided over millions of years; others formed when gigantic blocks of rock moved up and down along faults.

INTRODUCE THE CHAPTER (5 MIN.)

- Tell students you will read aloud Chapter 9, "Earth's Undersea World." They should follow along in their Reader.
- Have students turn to the table of contents, locate the chapter, and then turn to the first page of the chapter.
- Preview the core vocabulary words before reading the chapter.

2. What is the first vocabulary word you will encounter in this chapter?

   » *submersible*

3. Where will you find this word for the first time in the Reader?

   » page 82

- Remind students that each vocabulary word is bolded the first time it appears in the chapter.
- Explain that the glossary contains definitions of all the vocabulary words in this Reader. Have students refer to the glossary at the back of the Reader and locate *submersible*, then have a student read the definition.
- Explain the following:
  - the part of speech
  - alternate forms of the word
- Have students reference Activity Page 13.1 while you read each word and its meaning. Remind students that the words are listed in the order in which they appear in the chapter.

Activity Page 13.1

submersible, n. a small vehicle that can travel deep under water for research (submersibles) (82)

rugged, adj. having a rough, uneven surface (83)

hydrothermal vent, n. a deep-sea geyser that forms as seawater sinks down through cracks in the oceanic crust and then releases extremely hot, mineral-rich water back up through cracks in the crust (hydrothermal vents) (85)

seamount, n. an underwater volcano that forms wherever magma is erupting through oceanic crust (seamounts) (87)

underlie, v. to be located under something (underlies) (87)

firsthand, adv. coming directly from actually seeing or experiencing something (87)

school, n. a large number of ocean animals of one type swimming together (schools) (88)

Vocabulary Chart for Chapter 9, "Earth's Undersea World"		
Vocabulary Type	**Tier 3** **Domain-Specific Words**	**Tier 2** **General Academic Words**
Core Vocabulary	submersible hydrothermal vent seamount school	rugged underlie firsthand
Spanish Cognates for Core Vocabulary		
Multiple-Meaning Core Vocabulary Words	school	
Sayings and Phrases	pitch black	

- Have one student read The Big Question at the beginning of the chapter. Ensure that students understand the meaning of The Big Question before reading the chapter.
    - How does the movement of tectonic plates shape and change the seafloor?

READ "EARTH'S UNDERSEA WORLD" (20 MIN.)

- Read the chapter aloud, as students follow along in their Readers.

Chapter 9

Earth's Undersea World

THE BIG QUESTION
How does the movement of tectonic plates shape and change the seafloor?

Imagine that you are dropping down, down, down into the middle of the Atlantic Ocean. The seawater outside the **submersible** gets darker and darker. Soon the light fades completely. Outside is a watery world as black as night. Finally, the sub's lights pick up shapes below as the ocean bottom comes into view. You see lumpy hills and looming peaks of dark volcanic rock. Welcome to the Mid-Atlantic Ridge. The ridge marks the boundary between several enormous tectonic plates. Portions of these plates form the bottom of the Atlantic Ocean.

82

- Read pages 82 and 83 aloud.

Mountains and Moving Plates

In Chapter 8, you learned some of the ways Earth's slowly moving tectonic plates build mountains. Over millions of years, their movements have created many mountains and mountain ranges on land. Moving plates also build mountains underwater. In fact, there are more mountains on the seafloor than on all of Earth's continents and islands combined.

The Mid-Atlantic Ridge is a long, **rugged** underwater mountain range. It runs for thousands of miles along the boundary between tectonic plates that meet in the center of the Atlantic Ocean. The plates are very slowly moving apart at this boundary.

Remember Alfred Wegener? Wegener proposed the idea of continental drift in the early 1900s. At the time, though, no one knew of any force powerful enough to move continents around on Earth's surface. The theory of seafloor spreading was a big clue to solving the mystery.

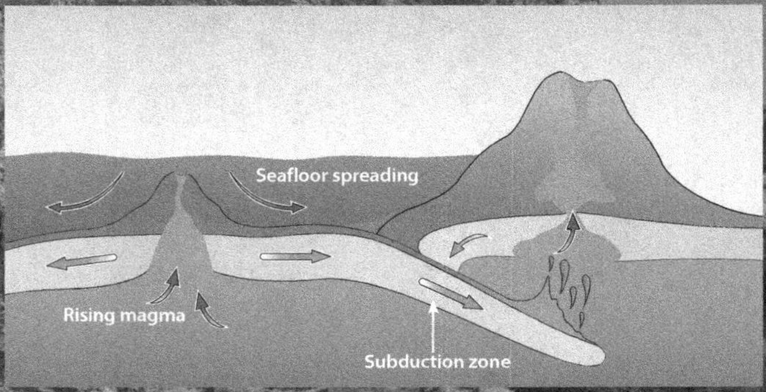

Seafloor spreading was one of several key pieces of geological evidence that led to the theory of plate tectonics. Think of the continents as riding on top of the plates. As the plates move, so do the continents.

83

Literal. What is the Mid-Atlantic Ridge?

» The Mid-Atlantic Ridge is a long, underwater mountain range. It runs for thousands of miles along the boundary between the tectonic plates that meet in the center of the Atlantic Ocean.

Inferential. What is seafloor spreading?

» Seafloor spreading is the process of oceanic plates moving apart very slowly. As the seafloor spreads, the continents on either side of the Atlantic are pushed farther apart.

Evaluative. Why is the concept of seafloor spreading important to geology?

» Seafloor spreading helps explain Alfred Wegener's theory of continental drift. For many years, scientists struggled to understand how a force would be strong enough to rip apart the continents. Now scientists know that as the seafloor spreads a few inches each year, the continents are pushed apart very, very slowly. This suggests that Wegener's theory of continental drift is correct and that the continents did not break apart in a sudden, cataclysmic event, but in a slow process that took thousands of years.

It was the study of the Mid-Atlantic Ridge that first made scientists consider the possibility of seafloor spreading. They concluded that, as the seafloor spreads, the continents on either side of the Atlantic are pushed farther apart.

Scientists soon discovered that the Mid-Atlantic Ridge is just one of many mid-ocean ridges. These ridges are found in all the world's oceans, wherever tectonic plates are slowly moving apart. Altogether, mid-ocean ridges form a near-continuous chain of mountains that wraps around the earth like the stitching on a baseball. Spanning 40,389 miles, the chain of mid-ocean ridges is by far the world's longest mountain range. It is also the most volcanically active.

The Mid-Atlantic Ridge is just a part of this gigantic underwater mountain chain. Erupting lava has built up high walls of basalt on either side of the rift. The rift itself is nearly as deep as the Grand Canyon! If you travel along the ridge, you'll soon see more than just high walls of dark rock.

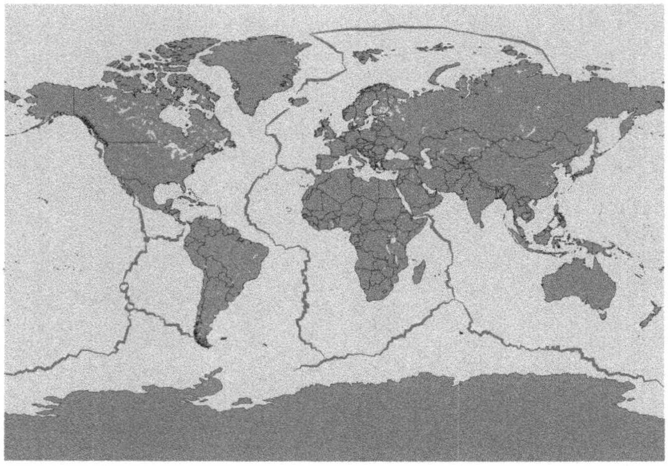

Mid-ocean ridges form a near-continuous chain of underwater mountains.

84

- Read pages 84 and 85 aloud.

Inferential. Why is the chain of mid-ocean ridges the most volcanically active mountain range in the world?

» Volcanoes form where there are cracks and weak spots in Earth's crust, which is mostly along tectonic plate boundaries. Mid-ocean ridges are found wherever tectonic plates are slowly moving apart. Because the chain of mid-ocean ridges makes up the world's longest mountain range, this also means it has the most cracks or weak spots in Earth's crust of any mountain range, making it the most volcanically active mountain range in the world.

Check for Understanding

Look at the map on Reader page 8. What do the red lines represent?

» mid-ocean ridges or underwater mountain ranges

- Students who answer incorrectly should be directed to read or reread the caption that accompanies the map.

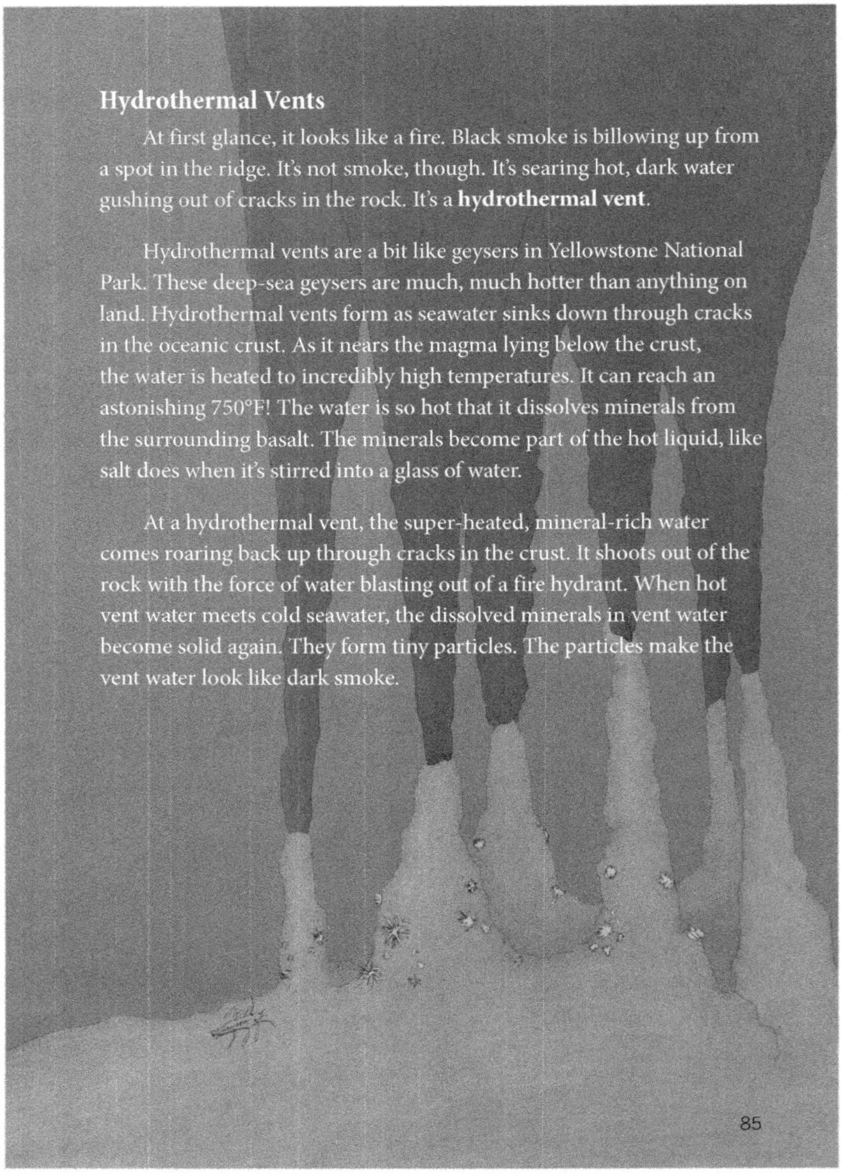

Hydrothermal Vents

At first glance, it looks like a fire. Black smoke is billowing up from a spot in the ridge. It's not smoke, though. It's searing hot, dark water gushing out of cracks in the rock. It's a **hydrothermal vent**.

Hydrothermal vents are a bit like geysers in Yellowstone National Park. These deep-sea geysers are much, much hotter than anything on land. Hydrothermal vents form as seawater sinks down through cracks in the oceanic crust. As it nears the magma lying below the crust, the water is heated to incredibly high temperatures. It can reach an astonishing 750°F! The water is so hot that it dissolves minerals from the surrounding basalt. The minerals become part of the hot liquid, like salt does when it's stirred into a glass of water.

At a hydrothermal vent, the super-heated, mineral-rich water comes roaring back up through cracks in the crust. It shoots out of the rock with the force of water blasting out of a fire hydrant. When hot vent water meets cold seawater, the dissolved minerals in vent water become solid again. They form tiny particles. The particles make the vent water look like dark smoke.

85

Literal. What are hydrothermal vents?

» Hydrothermal vents are deep-sea geysers that release extremely hot water and minerals into the ocean.

Literal. How are hydrothermal vents formed?

» They form when water seeps through cracks in the oceanic crust and is heated by the hot magma below. The very high temperatures heat the water and force it back up through the cracks in an explosion of water and minerals.

Hunting for Hydrothermal Vents

Hydrothermal vents

How do scientists find hydrothermal vents? They hunt for them from ships at sea. Hot, mineral-rich vent water moves slowly away from hydrothermal vents. It forms a plume, or cloud, of mineral particles that drifts away from the vent, like smoke from a chimney. If the scientists locate a plume, they send down a robot vehicle. When it locates the vent, the robot sends pictures back to the scientists.

There is more to hydrothermal vents than clouds of hot, black water. Communities of amazing and unusual animals live around many of these deep-sea geysers. Red-topped giant tube worms are the largest animals near vents. Some types of giant tube worms can grow as tall as a person. The vents are also home to ghostly white crabs, football-sized clams, and pale, blind shrimp.

Scientists believe there are tens of thousands of hydrothermal vents along the world's mid-ocean ridges. Scientists, however, have explored only a handful of them. Finding a new one is always exciting. Scientists often discover new types of animals as well.

Giant tube worms near a hydrothermal vent in the Pacific Ocean

86

- Read pages 86 and 87 aloud.

Evaluative. Why are scientists interested in hydrothermal vents?

» Scientists may discover new types of animals; they have discovered that communities of amazing and unique animals live around many hydrothermal vents but because scientists have only explored a handful of hydrothermal vents, there could be many more animals they have not yet discovered. In addition, hydrothermal vents occur where there are cracks in the oceanic crust, which helps scientists understand plate tectonics.

Evaluative. Which animal mentioned on this page of the Reader would you be most interested in learning more about? Tell a partner why you chose this animal.

» Answers will vary.

Evaluative. Why do you think the animals of the deep sea hydrothermal vents are so different from the animals that live elsewhere on the planet?

» Answers will vary but may mention the differences in environment caused by the heat from the vents, the pressure of the water, and the lack of sunlight.

Seamounts and Subduction Zones

Seamounts are another type of underwater mountain. Seamounts are underwater volcanoes that come in many shapes and sizes. Some are just a few hundred feet high. Others tower thousands of feet above the seafloor, although their tops are still far beneath the ocean's surface. If a seamount grows high enough to rise above the ocean's surface, it becomes an island.

Seamounts can form wherever magma is erupting through the oceanic crust. Many seamounts form alongside mid-ocean ridges or along subduction zones.

Seamount that grew into an island

Finally, seamounts can also form over hotspots far from plate boundaries. The islands that make up the Hawaiian Island chain began as seamounts. As you read in Chapter 4, each island formed over a hotspot that **underlies** the center of the Pacific Plate. As a result of repeated volcanic eruptions, each island began as a small seamount that grew over time. Eventually, its top broke the water's surface, making it an island.

Scientists estimate that there are at least 100,000 seamounts over 3,000 feet tall in the world's oceans. Since most seamounts are far below the ocean's surface, studying them is a challenge. Scientists have explored a few **firsthand**, traveling down in submersibles. More often, they send robot vehicles down to do the investigating.

87

Literal. Why are seamounts challenging for scientists to study?

» Most seamounts are far below the ocean's surface and the only way to explore them is by submersibles or by sending robot vehicles down to do the investigating.

Support

Review with students that a seamount is an underwater volcano that forms wherever magma is erupting through the oceanic crust.

Check for Understanding

What is the relationship between a seamount and an island?

» A very tall seamount might extend past sea level and become an island; some islands are the tips of very tall seamounts.

- If students cannot answer this question, have them review the material on this page with a partner.

No two seamounts are exactly alike. Many are teeming with life, even those that are very deep. Water flowing around these deep-sea volcanoes brings up nutrients from the ocean bottom. Nutrients fuel the growth of tiny, single-celled organisms in the water. These, in turn, become food for larger organisms, including animals that live on and around seamounts. Seamounts are often home to deep-sea corals, sponges, brittle stars, crabs, and anemones. Great **schools** of fish live around seamounts, too.

Deep-sea coral

Brittle star

Into the Trenches

Seamounts aren't the only undersea features that form along subduction zones. Where one plate slides under another, the seafloor dips down to create narrow, extremely deep valleys. These ocean trenches are the deepest places on the planet.

The Mariana Trench in the Pacific Ocean is the deepest ocean trench. It lies just off the Mariana Islands, east of the Philippines. The Mariana Trench is hundreds of miles long, but just 43 miles wide. It is like a deep slash in the ocean bottom. The trench's deepest known point is an area called the Challenger Deep. It is 36,070 feet beneath the ocean's surface, which is almost 7 miles down. By comparison, the average depth of the ocean is about 14,000 feet.

88

Pronunciation Chart	
Word(s)	**CK Code**
anemones	/ə*nem*o*nees/
Jacques Piccard	/jok/ /pee*kar/
Trieste	/treest/

Reading for Information
Vocabulary

Entering/Emerging
Have students use single words, simple phrases, and gestures to describe ocean trenches, mid-ocean ridges, seamounts, and hydrothermal vents and distinguish these features from one another.

Transitioning/Expanding
Have students use phrases, simple sentences, and gestures to describe the features above and distinguish them from one another.

Bridging
Have students use sentences, ranging from the simple to the more complex, to describe the features above and distinguish them from one another.

- Read pages 88 and 89 aloud.

  Literal. What is an ocean trench?

  » An ocean trench is a narrow, extremely deep valley where the seafloor dips down as one plate slides under another along a subduction zone.

- Ask students to imagine what your community, city, or state would look like if there were a trench the size of an ocean trench running through it. If time permits, you may have students draw quick pictures to show what this might look like.

What is it like in the ocean's deepest spot? It is pitch black. The temperature of the water is only a few degrees above freezing. The water pressure is very high—equivalent to having three big SUVs pressing down on every inch of your body!

Only three people have traveled to the bottom of the Mariana Trench. (More people have landed on the moon!) Several robot vehicles have also made the trip. These visits have provided only brief glimpses of this remote and extreme environment.

The Lucky Three

As of 2014, people have traveled to the bottom of the Mariana Trench only twice. The first expedition took place in 1960. The explorers were U.S. Navy Lieutenant Don Walsh and Swiss scientist Jacques Piccard. Their underwater vehicle was *Trieste*. It took *Trieste* almost five hours to descend from the ocean's surface to the bottom of Challenger Deep. Piccard and Walsh peered out a small window onto a part of the planet that humans had not seen before.

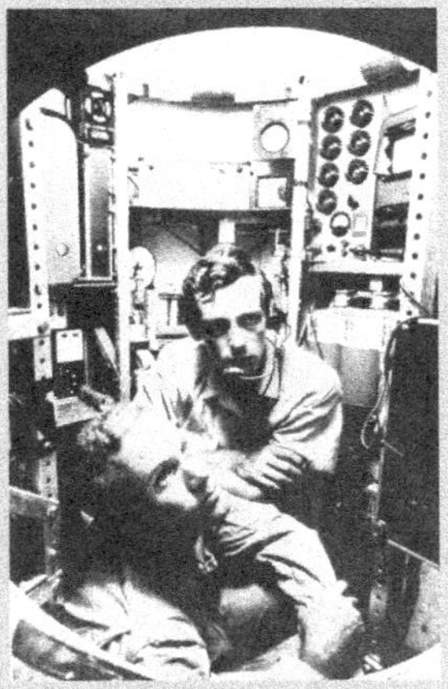

Piccard and Walsh in *Trieste*

In 2012, Canadian filmmaker and ocean explorer James Cameron also made the trip. His vessel, *Deepsea Challenger*, was a slim, one-person, underwater vehicle. Cameron's descent took just over two and a half hours. He did something Walsh and Piccard weren't able to do. He filmed the descent and the view he had of the ocean floor at 35,756 feet.

89

Inferential. Why have only three people traveled to the bottom of the Mariana Trench?

» It is the deepest ocean trench, which means it takes a very long time to reach the bottom. In addition, it is pitch black, the water temperature is around freezing, and the water pressure is very high, all of which create a challenging environment to send submersibles or robot vehicles into.

- Ask students to use the information in the text to explain why they would or would not want to visit the bottom of the Mariana Trench. If time permits, encourage them to debate the topic briefly with a partner or in a small group.

Check for Understanding

Where are you most likely to find an ocean trench: in a subduction zone, a few hundred miles away from a subduction zone, or more than a thousand miles from a subduction zone?

» in a subduction zone

- If students are not able to answer the question correctly, review the information on ocean trenches in the text.

LESSON WRAP-UP (10 MIN.)

Note: Question 4 and Activity Page 1.3 relate to The Big Question of the chapter.

- Use the following question to discuss the chapter:

4. **Inferential.** How does the movement of tectonic plates shape and change the seafloor?

    » The seafloor is covered with interesting geological features, most of which occur near the edges of tectonic plates. Tectonic plates on the seafloor are slowly spreading apart. This confirms Wegener's theory of continental drift. When plates collide or slip beneath each other under water, mountains and volcanoes are formed. As volcanoes erupt over and over again, lava builds up and hardens into mountains called seamounts. If these seamounts get tall enough, they emerge from the ocean's surface to create islands. Sometimes when plates slip under each other, deep trenches, or valleys, are formed. Studying plate tectonics helps us understand why the seafloor is not just a smooth surface, but one filled with valleys, ridges, and volcanoes.

Activity Pages 1.3 and 1.4

- Have students turn to Activity Pages 1.3 and 1.4 and refer to the displayed Evidence Collector's Chart.
- Remind students that they have collected evidence of changes to the earth related to specific causes of geologic change throughout the unit. The evidence represents what geologists examine to determine how powerful forces above and below the earth's surface work to change the earth.
- Have a student read aloud the information under "What is the cause?" in the last row. Explain that students must determine what evidence is in the chapter about seafloor spreading and underwater subduction zones. (pages 83, 84, 88)
- Have students refer to the one remaining image on Activity Page 1.4. Engage students in a discussion about why the image showing a diagram of seafloor spreading and underwater subduction zones represents evidence of the cause statement. (The image shows a diagram that illustrates how seafloor spreading and subduction impact Earth's surface under water.)
- Have students cut out the image, glue it to the chart in the "What evidence is there?" column, and write the following information for chapter number, key words, and letter in the chart:

Chapter #	What is the cause?	What evidence is there?	Letter
9	*tectonic plates interact to create seafloor spreading and underwater subduction zones*	*image: diagram showing seafloor spreading and underwater subduction zones* *key words:* deep ocean trenches, mid-ocean ridges, hydrothermal vents	V

- Note for students that they have now collected all the evidence from *The Changing Earth* in their chart. Also note they have collected eight letters along with the evidence.
- Remind students you told them at the beginning of the unit they would use the letters they collected to create a word to answer a geology riddle.
- Uncover the geology riddle you prepared in advance. Have a student read the riddle aloud. If time permits, have students write the riddle on Activity Page 1.3 in the appropriate place.
- Have students briefly work with a partner to unscramble the collected letters to answer the riddle. Caution students not to shout out the answer until all students have had the opportunity to try unscrambling the word for themselves. Students should write the answer in the appropriate place on Activity Page 1.3.
- When students have solved the riddle, call on one student to share and explain the answer. (EVIDENCE. Evidence helps geologists understand how and why the earth changes. Evidence comes in many forms, such as rock formations, volcanoes, faults, and seafloor spreading.)
- Tell students they will take home Activity Page 13.2 to read and complete for homework.

WORD WORK: *EXPEDITION* (5 MIN.)

1. In the chapter you read, "The first expedition took place in 1960."
2. Say the word *expedition* with me.
3. *Expedition* means a journey taken to explore a place no one has been before.
4. Only three people have ever made an expedition to the Mariana Trench.
5. What are some other examples of an expedition? Be sure to use the word *expedition* in your response.
   » Answers will vary.
6. What part of speech is the word *expedition*?
   » noun

• Use a Synonyms activity for follow-up.

7. What does the word *expedition* mean? What are some words that are synonyms of, or have a similar meaning to, *expedition*?
   » possible answers: *journey*, *trip*, and *voyage*

• Have students work in pairs to create a sentence for each synonym.

Lesson 13: Under the Sea

Writing

45M

Primary Focus: Students will draft a descriptive paragraph based on plans from a previous lesson. **[W.4.2, W.4.4]**

DESCRIPTIVE PARAGRAPH PLANNING (10 MIN.)

• Direct students' attention to the Descriptive Paragraph Example you prepared in advance. Remind them of the features of this paragraph and the use of personification. Challenge students to recall the three types of sentences in a descriptive paragraph before you formally go over them.
   ◦ features: topic sentence, detail sentences, concluding sentence, focus, literary devices

Descriptive Paragraph Example

My name is Leah Lava, and I feel as hot as the sun! That's probably because I'm lava shooting down the side of an active volcano. I hear a deep rumble behind me as rocks and debris spew out of the mountain, and I wonder if the plume is still reaching toward the blackening sky like an opening umbrella. As soon as I feel the air touch me, I begin to cool down. Thank goodness! It was getting awfully hot. As I cool, I harden, forming igneous rock. After all that hot activity, I like feeling wind blow across me and rain rinse my body. Sometimes I get uncomfortable in the scorching sun or the freezing cold, but I feel calm listening to the birds chirping around me and tasting the water that trickles over me.

Check for Understanding

Ask students to identify the topic sentence in the paragraph.

» "My name is Leah Lava, and I feel as hot as the sun!"

- Review the definition of a topic sentence with students if they do not answer the question correctly.

Activity Page 12.3

- Pass out students' copies of Activity Page 12.3 that you reviewed from the previous lesson.
- Remind students they planned for writing their own descriptive paragraph using Activity Page 12.3. Briefly discuss the activity page, calling on students to share information about what they are planning to write. Remind students that everyone will have different item names and descriptive details.

DRAFT A DESCRIPTIVE PARAGRAPH (35 MIN.)

- Tell students they will now draft their descriptive paragraph using planning information from Activity Page 12.3. Students may also reference Chapter 6, "Earth's Building Blocks," in *The Changing Earth* if needed.
- Review the parts of a descriptive paragraph with students as follows. Have students describe the function of each part when possible.
    - Remind them that a topic sentence states the main idea.
    - Remind them that detail sentences support the main idea with sensory details.
    - Remind them that a concluding sentence summarizes or restates the main idea.
- Explain that students should write as many clear, well-planned sentences as possible for the descriptive paragraph.
- Remind students to use literary devices like personification, alliteration, and simile.

1. What is personification?
    » descriptive language that assigns human characteristics to nonhuman things
2. What is alliteration?
    » the use of words with the same letter or sound
3. What is a simile?
    » a comparison of two different things, usually using like or as

- Read aloud one of the three definitions above. Call on a student at random to respond with the name of the device (personification, alliteration, or simile). Repeat several times until you are sure that the class can identify all three.
- Tell students to end with something memorable—a vivid image, a funny piece of dialogue, a question, or a statement that engages the audience.
- Remind students to use details to create a clear picture for readers.

Check for Understanding

Have students identify at least one detail sentence in their work.

- If students cannot identify a detail sentence, review with them what a detail sentence does (supports the main idea) and where it usually belongs (after the topic sentence and before the conclusion).

Writing
Producing

Entering/Emerging
Give students sentence starters such as *I am a(n)*___ and *I have a(n)*___ to help them create complete sentences.

Transitioning/Expanding
Have students write sentence starters of their own and share them with a partner. Then have students use the sentence starters they like best to create complete sentences.

Bridging
Have students work independently to write complete sentences, then check with a partner to make sure their sentences are complete.

Challenge

Encourage students to write more than one paragraph. They might include details about the formation of their item or how their item might change in the next stage.

- Circulate and check in with students to ensure that they are writing at least six sentences.
- When students are finished, ask them to share their favorite sentence in their paragraph with a partner. Then invite students to share their partner's sentence with the class.
- Model responses by commenting on the first two student examples. Feedback should show students how to offer constructive criticism by being specific. "I like that you chose the word ____. I like how the name uses alliteration. I like the image your sentence created in my mind because it reminds me of ____."
- Collect student narratives to review and monitor student progress. Written feedback may include comments such as:
    - "I like the creative name you chose. Nice use of alliteration."
    - "You've written a clear beginning, middle, and end. For future writing, I would like to see you consider using literary devices like personification and alliteration."

End Lesson

Lesson 13: Under the Sea

Take-Home Material

READING

Activity Page 13.2

- Have students take home Activity Page 13.2 to read and complete for homework.

LESSON

14 Under the Sea, Part 2

PRIMARY FOCUS OF LESSON

Reading

Students will explain the unique characteristics of geological features on the seafloor and the impact of those characteristics. **[RI.4.2, RI.4.3, RI.4.4]**

Grammar

Students will identify and use multiple adjectives in the correct sequence. **[L.4.1]**

Morphology

Students will use words with the suffixes –*ly* and –*y* and words with the roots *graph* and *rupt* in sentences. **[L.4.4]**

Spelling

Students will practice spelling targeted words. **[L.4.2]**

FORMATIVE ASSESSMENT

Activity Page 13.2	**Excerpt from "Earth's Undersea World"** Students answer questions based on information from the Reader text. **[RI.4.2, RI.4.3]**
Activity Page 14.1	**"Earth's Undersea World"** Students answer questions based on the reading for the day. **[RI.4.2, RI.4.3]**
Activity Page 14.2	**Sequencing Multiple Adjectives** Students choose the correct order of adjectives within a sentence. **[L.4.1]**
Activity Page 14.3	**Practice Suffixes –*ly* and –*y* and Roots *graph* and *rupt*** Students write sentences containing words with these suffixes and roots. **[L.4.4]**
Activity Page 14.4	**Practice Spelling Words** Students write sentences that include assigned spelling words. **[L.4.2]**

LESSON AT A GLANCE

	Grouping	Time	Materials
Reading (45 min.)			
Review	Whole Group	10 min.	❑ Answer Key for Activity Page 13.2 ❑ Activity Pages 13.2, 14.1 ❑ *The Changing Earth*
Read "Earth's Undersea World"	Pairs	20 min.	
Discuss Chapter and Lesson Wrap-Up	Whole Group	10 min.	
Word Work: *Firsthand*	Whole Group	5 min.	
Language (45 min.)			
Grammar: Practice Sequencing Adjectives	Whole Group	15 min.	❑ Adjectives Chart ❑ Activity Page 14.2
Morphology: Suffixes and Roots	Whole Group	15 min.	❑ Activity Page 14.3
Spelling	Whole Group	15 min.	❑ Activity Pages 14.4, SR.1

ADVANCE PREPARATION

Reading

- Access a digital version of The Big Question in the digital components for this unit.

Language

Grammar

- Display the Adjectives Chart from Lesson 11 or access a digital version in the digital components for this unit.
- Gather several different classroom objects for the ELD activity, such as colored pencils, an eraser, and a pair of scissors.

Morphology

- Determine student pairs for completing Activity Page 14.3.

Spelling

- Determine student pairs for completing Activity Page 14.4.

Start Lesson

Lesson 14: Under the Sea, Part 2

Reading

45M

Primary Focus: Students will explain the unique characteristics of geological features on the seafloor and the impact of those characteristics.
[RI.4.2, RI.4.3, RI.4.4]

REVIEW (10 MIN.)

- Using the Answer Key at the back of this Teacher Guide, review student responses to Activity Page 13.2, which was assigned for homework in the previous reading lesson.
- Tell students they will reread Chapter 9, "Earth's Undersea World."
- Have students turn to the table of contents, locate the chapter, and then turn to the first page of the chapter. Have a student read the title aloud.
- You may wish to review the following vocabulary words before you reread the chapter:

submersible, n. a small vehicle that can travel deep underwater for research (submersibles) (82)

rugged, adj. having a rough, uneven surface (83)

hydrothermal vent, n. a deep-sea geyser that forms as seawater sinks down through cracks in the oceanic crust and then releases extremely hot, mineral-rich water back up through cracks in the crust (hydrothermal vents) (85)

seamount, n. an underwater volcano that forms wherever magma is erupting through oceanic crust (seamounts) (87)

underlie, v. to be located under something (underlies) (87)

firsthand, adv. coming directly from actually seeing or experiencing something (87)

school, n. a large number of ocean animals of one type swimming together (schools) (88)

1. Where can you look up a word if you forget or are unfamiliar with its meaning?
   » in the glossary

- Have one student read The Big Question at the beginning of the chapter. Ensure students understand the meaning of The Big Question before reading the chapter.
  - How does the movement of tectonic plates shape and change the seafloor?

READ "EARTH'S UNDERSEA WORLD" (20 MIN.)

- Pair students to read and discuss the chapter. You may wish to use any or all of the following pairings:
  - strong readers with readers who need more support
  - readers of similar skill levels
  - English language learners with native speakers

  Note: Student pairings should change throughout the year. As students read, circulate among the class, monitoring students' focus and progress.

Activity Page 14.1

Reading for Information
Cause and Effect

Entering/Emerging
To help students explore cause-and-effect relationships, recite simple sentences with *because* and have students repeat. Connect the word *because* to the word *cause*.

Transitioning/Expanding
To help students explore cause-and-effect relationships, have them complete sentences using the frame *I like because* ____. Connect the word *because* to the word *cause*.

Bridging
To help students explore cause-and-effect relationships, have them create original sentences with *because*. Connect the word *because* to the word *cause*.

Support

If students cannot select the phrase that describes the Mid-Atlantic Ridge, have them reread the description of the ridge from their text.

- Using established procedures, have students read the chapter in pairs. Students may ask their partner for help sounding out or defining words, as necessary. Have students make a note of vocabulary, phrases, or concepts they do not understand, writing down the page number, so they may seek clarification.
- While they read, have students complete Activity Page 14.1 with their partners.
- Review the following pronunciations with students:

Pronunciation Chart	
Word(s)	**CK Code**
anemones	/ə*nem*o*nees/
Jacques Piccard	/jok/ /pee*kar/
Trieste	/treest/

DISCUSS CHAPTER AND LESSON WRAP-UP (10 MIN.)

- Review the correct answers to Activity Page 14.1 with the whole class. You may wish to select different students to read each question and share their responses, including the page numbers where the answer was located.

2. Inferential—Seafloor spreading explains which of the following?
   » E. A and B only

Check for Understanding

Literal. Which phrase describes the Mid-Atlantic Ridge?
» B. a long, rugged underwater mountain range

3. **Literal.** Part A. Fill in the following chart to indicate which seafloor feature the animals live around—hydrothermal vents or seamounts.

    » See accompanying table.

Animals	Where They Live
white crabs	hydrothermal vents
brittle stars	seamounts
schools of fish	seamounts
pale, blind shrimp	hydrothermal vents
sponges	seamounts
deep-sea corals	seamounts
giant tube worms	hydrothermal vents
anemones	seamounts
football-sized clams	hydrothermal vents

4. **Inferential.** Part B. Why might these animals live near these particular seafloor features?

    » Answers may vary, but could include: animals may live near these features because of the tiny, single-celled organisms that grow there as a result of the nutrients brought up by seamounts.

5. **Inferential.** Match each cause to its effect by writing the correct letter for the effect next to the correct cause.

- Seamount emerges from the ocean's surface.

    » C. islands are formed

- One tectonic plate slides under another.

    » D. a trench is formed

- Tectonic plates move apart very slowly.

    » B. seafloor spreading

- Seafloor spreading.

    » A. continental drift

- Water seeps into the earth's crust and is heated by magma.
    - » F. hydrothermal vents are formed
- Tectonic plates collide.
    - » E. mountains are formed

Challenge

Ask students to develop another simile to describe something they have learned about the Earth in this unit.

6. **Evaluative.** On page 84, the author uses a simile when describing the mountain chain formed by mid-ocean ridges, saying it is like stitching on a baseball. Explain what this simile means.
    - » Answers may vary, but should include that stitching on a baseball goes all around the baseball with no starting point or stopping point, meaning it is continuous. By comparing the mountain chain formed by mid-ocean ridges to stitching on a baseball, the author is saying that the mountain chain goes all over the earth without a starting point or stopping point, meaning it is continuous.

WORD WORK: *FIRSTHAND* (5 MIN.)

1. In the chapter you read, "Scientists have explored a few (seamounts) firsthand, traveling down in submersibles."
2. Say the word *firsthand* with me.
3. *Firsthand* means "coming directly from actually seeing or experiencing something."
4. Only a few astronauts have had the opportunity to explore the surface of the moon firsthand.
5. What are some other examples of *firsthand*? Be sure to use the word *firsthand* in your response.
    - » Answers will vary.

- If necessary, guide and/or rephrase students' responses to make complete sentences: "Something I have experienced firsthand is ____."

6. What part of speech is the word *firsthand*?
    - » adverb

- Use a Making Choices activity for follow-up. I am going to describe several situations. If the situation I describe is something that is actually seen or experienced at that moment, say, "firsthand." If the situation I describe is not actually seen or experienced at that moment, say, "not firsthand."

7. Discovering a new ocean animal while traveling underwater in a submersible.
    - » firsthand

8. Looking at a photo of a newly discovered ocean animal.
   » not firsthand
9. Reading about a car accident in the newspaper.
   » not firsthand
10. Seeing a car hit another car at a traffic light.
   » firsthand

Check for Understanding

Traveling on a plane to visit another country.

» firsthand

- If students do not answer this question correctly, review the definition of *firsthand* again and point out that the situation involves experiencing something rather than simply hearing about it.

11. Watching a movie about another country.
   » not firsthand

Lesson 14: Under the Sea, Part 2

Language

45M

GRAMMAR: PRACTICE SEQUENCING ADJECTIVES (15 MIN.)

Primary Focus: Students will identify and use multiple adjectives in the correct sequence. **[L.4.1]**

- Remind students that articles are special kinds of adjectives that indicate whether a specific noun is being described (the mountain, the island) or whether a general noun is being described (a mountain, an island). Articles are *a*, *an*, and *the*.
- Review the Adjectives Chart from Lesson 11. Remind students of the conventional order to follow when more than one adjective is used.

Language Vocabulary

Entering/Emerging
Explore adjectives with students. Display a classroom object from the items you gathered. Help students identify adjectives that fit the object, such as *sharp* for scissors or *blue* for a blue pencil.

Transitioning/Expanding
Display classroom objects as above. Have students use the sentence starter *This is a(n)* ____ and complete it with an adjective/noun combination, like *pink eraser*.

Bridging
Have students create original sentences to describe classroom objects using at least one adjective and a noun.

Activity Page 14.2

- Have students turn to Activity Page 14.2 and review the completed example. Tell students to complete the rest of the page independently.

Check for Understanding

Check that students choose the correct answer for item 1 on Activity Book page 130 (the tall, rocky mountain). If students give an incorrect answer, have them review the Adjectives Chart from Lesson 11.

- Once students have completed the activity page, review the correct answers by calling on different students to share their answers, as time permits.

Language
Roots and Endings

Entering/Emerging
Instead of working in pairs, have students work in a group with you. Guide them to create a simple sentence using each of the words in turn.

Transitioning/Expanding
Have student pairs begin by creating phrases using these words. Work with them to turn the phrases into sentences.

Bridging
Have student pairs create simple sentences using these words. Work with them to add complexity to their sentences, such as by adding extra clauses or adjectives.

MORPHOLOGY: SUFFIXES AND ROOTS (15 MIN.)

Primary Focus: Students will use words with the suffixes –*ly* and –*y* and words with the roots *graph* and *rupt* in sentences. **[L.4.4]**

Activity Page 14.3

- Have students turn to Activity Page 14.3. Select a student to read the directions aloud.
- Complete the first sentence together as a whole group. Ask students for ideas and then write an example sentence on the board/chart paper.

Check for Understanding

Have students create a sentence for item 2. Check that they have used the word *messy* correctly. If students do not use the word in an accurate way, ask them how the word *messy* is different from *messily*.

- Tell students to work in pairs to complete the remainder of the activity page.
- As time allows, ask different partner pairs to share their sentences aloud.
- If students do not complete the activity page in class, have them complete it for homework.
- Collect completed Activity Page 14.3 to review and grade at a later time.

SPELLING: PRACTICE SPELLING WORDS (15 MIN.)

Primary Focus: Students will practice spelling targeted words. **[L.4.2]**

- Tell students they will practice writing the spelling words. Remind them to use the Individual Code Chart on Activity Page SR.1 as they practice.
- Have students turn to Activity Page 14.4. Explain that they will work with a partner to create sentences for each of these words.
- If time allows, have students share some of the sentences aloud.

Check for Understanding

Write the letters *e*, *e*, *g*, *r*, *s*, and *y* on the board. Ask students to put the letters together to spell the word *geyser* correctly.

- If students cannot spell the word correctly, have them look briefly at the correct spelling and try again.

- Collect completed Activity Page 14.4 to review and grade at a later time.
- Remind students that they will complete their spelling assessment during the next lesson.

End Lesson

Activity Page SR.1

Activity Page 14.4

Language
Spelling

Entering/Emerging
Have students work in a small group with you. Help them create simple sentences for each word.

Transitioning/Expanding
Have student pairs create simple sentences using these words. Work with them to make the sentences more complex.

Bridging
Have students check their work with a partner to make sure the sentence sounds right and makes sense.

LESSON

15 Unit Assessment

PRIMARY FOCUS OF LESSON

Spelling

Students will be assessed on their ability to spell an assigned list of words. **[L.4.2]**

Unit Assessment

Students will be assessed on their understanding of the concepts and facts taught in the unit. **[RI.4.1, RI.4.2, RI.4.3, RI.4.4, RL.4.1, RL.4.2, RL.4.3, RL.4.4, L.4.1, L.4.2, L.4.3, L.4.4, L.4.5, W.4.2, W.4.4]**

LESSON AT A GLANCE

	Grouping	Time	Materials
Spelling (15 min.)			
Spelling Assessment	Independent	15 min.	❑ Activity Page 15.1
Unit Assessment (75 min.)			
Unit Assessment	Independent	75 min.	❑ Activity Page 15.2
Optional Fluency Assessment			❑ Student Copy of Fluency Assessment text ❑ Recording Copy of Fluency Assessment text, one for each student ❑ Fluency Scoring Sheet, one for each student

ADVANCE PREPARATION

Spelling

- Erase or cover the list of spelling words prior to the assessment.

Unit Assessment

- Determine how many students will be assessed for fluency, and make that number of copies of the Recording Copy of "Our Home, Earth" and the Fluency Scoring Sheet.

Fluency (optional)

- If students were assigned a selection from the Fluency Supplement, determine which students will read the selection aloud and when. See the Unit 1 Teacher Guide introduction for more information on using the Fluency Supplement.

Start Lesson

Lesson 15: Unit Assessment

Spelling

15M

Primary Focus: Students will be assessed on their ability to spell an assigned list of words. **[L.4.2]**

SPELLING ASSESSMENT

- Have students turn to Activity Page 15.1 for the spelling assessment.
- Using the following list, read the words one at a time in the following manner: Say the word, use it in a sentence, and then repeat the word.
- Tell students that at the end, you will review the list once more.
- Remind students to pronounce and spell each word syllable by syllable.

Spelling Word	Example Sentence
1. molten	Molten rock moves slowly beneath Earth's surface.
2. fault	The San Andreas Fault is one of the most famous faults in the U.S.
3. geyser	When a geyser erupts, it releases a fountain of steam and hot water.
4. epicenter	Surface waves are first detectable at an earthquake's epicenter.
5. seismograph	The first known seismograph was invented by a Chinese scientist.
6. glacier	At Glacier National Park in Montana, you can see the impact glaciers have in shaping the earth.
7. tsunami	A tsunami can do significant damage when it crashes on land.
8. erosion	Over a very long period of time, erosion can reshape Earth's surface.
9. conclusion	Inge Lehmann came to the conclusion that Earth's core has two parts.
10. tectonic	Earth's tectonic plates have been slowly moving and interacting for billions of years.

- After reading all of the words, review the list slowly, reading each word once more.
- Have students write the following sentence as dictated:
    - Scientists use records from a seismograph to determine the location of an earthquake's epicenter.
- Repeat the sentence slowly several times, reminding students to check their work for appropriate capitalization and punctuation.
- Collect all spelling assessments to grade later. Use of the template provided at the end of this lesson is highly recommended to identify and analyze students' errors.

Unit Assessment

75M

UNIT ASSESSMENT

- Make sure each student has a copy of Activity Page 15.2. You may have collected this activity page from students at the beginning of the unit.
- Tell students they will read two selections, answer questions about each, and respond to a writing prompt. In the next sections, they will answer grammar and morphology questions evaluating the skills they have practiced in this unit.
- Encourage students to do their best.
- Once students have finished the assessment, encourage them to review their papers quietly, rereading and checking their answers carefully.
- Circle around the room as students complete the assessment to ensure everyone is working individually. Assist students as needed, but do not provide them with answers.

Reading Comprehension

The reading comprehension section of the Unit Assessment contains two selections and accompanying questions. The first selection is an informational text that describes Japan's prevalence of earthquakes based on its geographic position near the intersection of several tectonic plates. The second selection is a literary text with two short earthquake myths from different Native American tribes.

These texts were created using guidance from the Common Core State Standards (CCSS) and recommendations from Student Achievement Partners (AchievetheCore.org). These texts are considered worthy of students' time to read, as they meet the Grade 4 expectations for text complexity. The texts feature core content and domain vocabulary from the Geology unit that students can draw on in service of comprehending the text.

The questions pertaining to these texts are aligned to the CCSS and are worthy of students' time to answer. Questions have been designed so they do not focus on minor points in the text, but rather require deep analysis. Thus, each item might address multiple standards. In general, the selected-response items address Reading standards and the constructed-response item addresses Writing standards. To prepare students for CCSS-aligned assessments, such as those developed by the Partnership for Assessment of Readiness for College and Careers (PARCC) and Smarter Balanced, some items replicate how technology may be incorporated in those assessments, using a paper and pencil format.

OPTIONAL FLUENCY ASSESSMENT

Materials

- Student Copy of Fluency Assessment text
- Recording Copy of Fluency Assessment text, one for each student
- Fluency Scoring Sheet, one for each student

- You may wish to assess students' fluency in reading, using the selection "Our Home, Earth." Assessing fluency requires that you work one-on-one with individual students to administer the assessment. Because this assessment requires you to work with one student at a time, you may wish to administer it either while other students complete the unit assessment or at a different time while students read enrichment selections and complete accompanying activity pages. Alternatively, you may have other time during the school day when you can administer this assessment as well.

Administration Instructions

- Turn to the student copy of "Our Home, Earth" that follows the Unit Assessment Analysis section. This is the text students will read aloud. Turn to this copy each time you administer this assessment.
- Using one Recording Copy of "Our Home, Earth" for each student, create a running record as you listen to each student read orally.
- Call the student you will assess to come sit near you.
- Explain that you are going to ask him or her to read a selection aloud and you are going to take some notes as he or she reads. Also, explain that he or she should not rush but rather read at his or her regular pace.
- Read the title of the selection aloud for the student, as the title is not part of the assessment.

- Begin timing when the student reads the first word of the selection. As the student reads aloud, make a running record on the Recording Copy using the following guidelines:

Words read correctly	No mark is required.
Omissions	Draw a long dash above the word omitted.
Insertions	Write a caret (^) at the point where the insertion was made. If you have time, write down the word that was inserted.
Words read incorrectly	Write an "X" above the word.
Substitutions	Write the substitution above the word.
Self-corrected errors	Replace original error mark with an "SC."
Teacher-supplied words	Write a "T" above the word (counts as an error).

- When one minute has elapsed, draw a vertical line on the Recording Copy to mark where the student was in the text at that point. Allow the student to finish reading the selection aloud.
- Assess the student's comprehension of the selection by asking him or her to respond orally to the following questions:

1. **Literal.** What three words are important when thinking about geology?
    » heat, pressure, and time
2. **Inferential.** Why do people have to think about time in terms of years instead of minutes, hours, and days when thinking about geology?
    » Heat and pressure take a long time to change the earth in ways that geologists can find evidence of. If you think about time in minutes, hours, and days, it is unlikely that evidence of change will be detected because geological changes happen so very slowly.
3. **Inferential.** Which rock layers in the Grand Canyon are half as old as the earth is believed to be?
    » the rock layers at the very bottom of the canyon

4. **Inferential.** Why is the Grand Canyon such an amazing thing for geologists to study?

    » There are many rock layers in the Grand Canyon and each layer provides clues about the earth's formation and history, giving geologists a lot to study and a lot of information to help shape people's understanding of how the earth formed and how it changes.

- Repeat this process for additional students as needed. Scoring can be done later, provided you have kept running records and marked the last word students read after one minute elapsed.

SPELLING ASSESSMENT ANALYSIS

Spelling Analysis Chart

Student	1. molten	2. fault	3. geyser	4. epicenter	5. seismograph	6. glacier	7. tsunami	8. erosion	9. conclusion	10. tectonic

- It may be helpful to refer back to the Pronunciation/Syllabication Chart from Lesson 11.

Word	CK Code	Syllable Type
fault	/fawlt/	Digraph
tsunami	/soo*no*mee/	open*open*open
geyser	/gie*zer/	digraph*r-controlled
erosion	/i*roe*zshən/	open*open*ə
glacier	/glae*sher/	open*r-controlled
tectonic	/tek*ton*ik/	closed*closed*closed
molten	/moel*ten/	closed*closed
seismograph	/siez*mə*graf/	digraph*ə*closed
epicenter	/ep*i*sen*ter/	closed*open*closed*r-controlled
conclusion	/kun*kloo*zshən/	closed*open*ə

- Students might make the following errors:
    - fault: using 'aw' instead of 'au' for /aw/
    - tsunami: using 's' instead of 'ts' for /s/; using 'oo' instead of 'u' for /oo/; using 'y' or 'e' instead of 'i' for /ee/
    - geyser: using 'ie' instead of 'ey' for /ie/
    - erosion: using 'zhun' instead of 'sion' for /zshən/
    - glacier: using 'sh' instead of 'c' for /sh/; using 'er' instead of 'ier' for /er/
    - tectonic: using 'k' instead of 'c' for /k/
    - seismograph: using 'ie' instead of 'ei' for /ie/; using 'f' instead of 'ph' for /graf/
    - epicenter: using 'e' instead of 'i' for /i/; using 's' instead of 'c' for /s/
    - conclusion: using 'oo' instead of 'u' for /oo/; using 'zhun' instead of 'sion' for /zshən/

- Although any of the above student-error scenarios may occur, misspellings may be due to many other factors. You may find it helpful to use the analysis chart to record any student errors. For example:
    - Is the student consistently making errors on specific vowels? Which ones?
    - Is the student consistently making errors at the ends of the words?
    - Is the student consistently making errors in multisyllable words, but not single-syllable words?
- Also, examine the dictated sentence for errors in capitalization and punctuation.

Lesson 15: Unit Assessment

Unit Assessment Analysis

QUANTITATIVE AND QUALITATIVE ANALYSIS OF THE TEXT

The texts used in the reading comprehension assessment, "Earth's Forces at Work in Japan" (informational text) and "Earthquake Myths" (literary text), have been profiled for text complexity using the quantitative measures described in the Common Core State Standards for English Language Arts, Supplement to Appendix A, "New Research on Text Complexity," (CoreStandards.org/resources). Both selections fall within the Common Core 4th–5th Grade Band.

Reading Comprehension Item Annotations and Correct Answer and Distractor Rationales

Note: To receive a point for a two-part question, students must correctly answer both parts of the question.

Item	Correct Answer(s)	Standards
1 Literal	D	RI.4.1, RI.4.2
****2 Part A Inferential***	2 – 1923 earthquake 1 – 2011 Great Tohoku earthquake 3 – 1995 earthquake	RI.4.1, RI.4.5
****2 Part B Inferential***	It was one of the strongest earthquakes known to hit Japan in recorded history, causing violent shaking and much destruction and because it triggered an enormous tsunami that caused the worst damage, with towering waves crashing ashore and surging far inland.	RI.4.1, RI.4.3, W.4.2d, W.4.4
3 Inferential	C	RI.4.1, RI 4.4, L.4.4a
4 Literal	B	RI.4.1, RI.4.3, RI.4.4
5 Evaluative	Earthquakes almost always strike suddenly and happen very quickly. This makes it very difficult to warn people about an earthquake far in advance. Even though Sendai was close to the epicenter, the earthquake early warning system was only able to give people 15 seconds of warning that an earthquake was coming because earthquakes strike so suddenly and happen so quickly.	RI.4.1, RI.4.3. W.4.2d, W.4.4
6 Inferential	B	RI.4.1, RI.4.3, RI.4.4, L.4.4a

7 Inferential	C	RI.4.1, RI.4.3, RI.4.4, RI.4.8, L.4.4a
8 Inferential	C	RL.4.1, RL.4.4, L.4.4a
****9 Part A Inferential***	B	RL.4.1, RL.4.4, L.4.5b
****9 Part B Literal***	He was true to his word by bringing several other turtles to the Great Spirit, which is what he said he would do.	RL.4.1, RL.4.4, W.4.4
10 Inferential	A	RL.4.1
****11 Part A Inferential***	D	RL.4.1
****11 Part B Literal***	Some swam in one direction and the rest in another, causing the land on their backs to rumble and shake and make big cracks appear in the soil.	RL.4.1, W.4.4
12 Evaluative	B	RL.4.1
13 Inferential	C	RL.4.1
14 Evaluative	D	RL.4.1, RL.4.2

Writing Prompt Scoring

- The writing prompt addresses **W.4.2, W.4.2a-e, W.4.4, L.4.2, and L.4.6.**

Score	**4**	**3**	**2**	**1**
Criteria	One or more clear similarities are identified across at least two of the texts and one or more clear differences is identified across at least two of the texts. Examples from the text to support the similarity and difference are provided. The similarity and difference both relate to causes and/or effects of earthquakes.	One clear similarity is identified across at least two of the texts or one clear difference is identified across at least two of the texts. An example from the text is provided. The similarity or difference relates to causes or effects of earthquakes.	A similarity or difference is identified but it is not clear which texts it references. An unrelated example is provided from the text.	A similarity or difference is not identified across texts. No example is provided in the answer.

Grammar Answer Key

1. The first expedition to the bottom of the Mariana Trench took place on January 23, 1960.
2. The text states, "Earth's tectonic plates have been slowly moving and interacting for billions of years."
3. Mount Rushmore National Memorial 13000 S Dakota 244 Keystone, SD 57751.
4. "What if," wondered Wegener, "continents were like enormous pieces of ice?"
5. Geologists found fossils of an ancient fern in similar rock layers in Africa, India, Australia, and South America.
6. A large, old, Hawaiian volcano.
7. The smooth, shiny, obsidian rock.
8. A powerful, giant tsunami.

Morphology Answer Key

1. abruptly
2. eruption
3. speedy
4. biography
5. rupture
6. carefully

Optional Fluency Assessment

- The following is the text for the Optional Fluency Assessment, titled "Our Home, Earth." Turn to this copy of the selection each time you administer this assessment.
- You will also find a Recording Copy of the text for doing a running record of oral reading for each student you assess. There is also a Fluency Scoring Sheet. Make as many copies of the Recording Copy and the Fluency Scoring Sheet as you need, having one for each student you assess.

Our Home, Earth

There are three important words to keep in mind whenever you are thinking about geology. Heat is the first. You can feel heat from a flame or from the sun on a sunny day. Heat causes many changes to the earth.

The second word is pressure, like the force you use when you push on something. Pressure also causes many changes to the earth.

Time is the third important geology word to remember. To understand geology, you need to think about time in a whole new way. Forget about minutes, hours, and days. These amounts of time don't mean much in geology. Geologists think in terms of many, many years. It takes a long time for pressure and heat to do what they do.

The Grand Canyon, located in Arizona, provides a lot of clues about the earth's formation and history. It took millions of years for rushing water in the river to carve through the rocks to make this canyon. No other place on earth allows geologists to see and study so many different layers of rock at the same time. The rock on the upper rim of the Grand Canyon is estimated by some scientists to be about 230 million years old, whereas the rock layers at the very bottom of the canyon are estimated to have formed over 2 billion years ago. That bottom rock is half as old as the earth is believed to be itself!

Student Name________________________________Date___________

Recording Copy
Our Home, Earth

There are three important words to keep in mind whenever you 11
are thinking about geology. Heat is the first. You can feel heat from a 14
flame or from the sun on a sunny day. Heat causes many changes to 14
the earth. 2

The second word is pressure, like the force you use when you push 13
on something. Pressure also causes many changes to the earth. 10

Time is the third important geology word to remember. To 10
understand geology, you need to think about time in a whole new way. 13
Forget about minutes, hours, and days. These amounts of time don't 11
mean much in geology. Geologists think in terms of many, many years. 12
It takes a long time for pressure and heat to do what they do. 14

The Grand Canyon, located in Arizona, provides a lot of clues 11
about the earth's formation and history. It took millions of years for 12
rushing water in the river to carve through the rocks to make this 13
canyon. No other place on earth allows geologists to see and study so 13
many different layers of rock at the same time. The rock on the upper 14
rim of the Grand Canyon is estimated by some scientists to be about 13

Student Name________________________________Date____________

230 million years old, whereas the rock layers at the very bottom of 13

the canyon are estimated to have formed over 2 billion years ago. 12

That bottom rock is half as old as the earth is believed to be itself! 15

Word Count: 240

Student Name__________________________________Date____________

Fluency Scoring Sheet

	Words Read in One Minute
—	Uncorrected Mistake in One Minutes
	W.C.P.M.

W.C.P.M.	National Percentiles for Fall, Grade 5
166	90th
139	75th
110	50th
85	25th
61	10th

Comprehension Total __________/4

Guidelines for Fluency Assessment Scoring

- To calculate a student's W.C.P.M. (Words Correct Per Minute) score, use the information you wrote on the Recording Copy and follow these steps. You may wish to have a calculator available.

1. Count Words Read in One Minute. This is the total number of words the student read or attempted to read in one minute. It includes words the student read correctly as well as words the student read incorrectly. Write the total in the box labeled Words Read in One Minute.

2. Count the Uncorrected Mistakes in One Minute. You noted these on the Recording Copy. They include words read incorrectly, omissions, substitutions, and words you had to supply. Write the total in the box labeled Uncorrected Mistakes in One Minute on the Fluency Scoring Sheet. (A mistake that the student self-corrects is not counted as a mistake.)

3. Subtract Uncorrected Mistakes in One Minute from Words Read in One Minute to get Words Correct. Write the number in the box labeled W.C.P.M. Although the analysis does not include any words the student read correctly (or incorrectly) after one minute, you may use this information from your Recording Copy for anecdotal purposes.

- As you evaluate W.C.P.M. scores, here are some factors to consider:

It is normal for students to show a wide range in fluency and in W.C.P.M. scores. However, a major goal of Grade 4 is to read with sufficient fluency to ensure comprehension and independent reading of school assignments in this and subsequent grade levels. A student's W.C.P.M. score can be compared with the score of other students in the class (or grade level) and also with the national fluency norms obtained by Hasbrouck and Tindal (2006). Hasbrouck and Tindal suggest that a score falling within 10 words above or below the 50th percentile should be interpreted as within the normal, expected, and appropriate range for a student at that grade level at that time of year. For example, if you administered the assessment during the fall of Grade 4, and a student scored 84 W.C.P.M., you should interpret this as within the normal, expected, and appropriate range for that student.

- Oral Reading Fluency Norms for Grade 4 from Hasbrouck and Tindal (2006)

Percentile	Fall W.C.P.M.	Winter W.C.P.M.	Spring W.C.P.M.
90	145	166	180
75	119	139	152
50	94	112	123
25	68	87	98
10	45	61	72

Reference

Hasbrouck, Jan and Gerald A. Tindal. "Oral reading fluency norms: A valuable assessment tool for reading teachers." *The Reading Teacher* 59 (2006): 636–644.

Middle-of-Year Assessment

Assessment Day 1

LESSON AT A GLANCE

	Time	Materials
Middle-of-Year Assessment		
Reading Comprehension Assessment	90 min.	❏ Activity Pages A.1, A.2
Fluency Assessment	Ongoing	❏ Activity Pages A.2, A.6 ❏ stopwatch

ADVANCE PREPARATION

- Prepare to distribute Activity Page A.1 that you may have collected from students at the beginning of the unit.
- Plan to have reading material available for students to select from and read independently as they finish the MOY Assessment.

MIDDLE-OF-YEAR ASSESSMENT

During the first day of the two-day assessment, all students will complete the Reading Comprehension Assessment (Activity Page A.1) independently. It includes four passages and corresponding comprehension questions. After students complete this portion of the assessment, use the MOY Assessment Summary (Activity Page A.2), which you will have collected from students, to analyze each student's performance. Please score the Reading Comprehension Assessment prior to Day 2 of the MOY Assessment, as you will use the scores to determine which students should complete the Word Reading in Isolation Assessment.

Beginning on Day 2 of the MOY Assessment, all students will work independently on the Grammar Assessment (Activity Page A.3) and the Morphology Assessment (Activity Page A.4).

In addition you will pull students aside, one at a time, and administer the Word Reading in Isolation Assessment to students who scored 10 or fewer on the Reading Comprehension Assessment (and, as time allows, to students who scored 11–13). Administer the Fluency Assessment to all students.

The Word Reading in Isolation Assessment uses Activity Page A.5 (Word Reading in Isolation Assessment Scoring Sheet), which you will have collected from students, as well as the Word Reading in Isolation Assessment located under MOY Assessment Day 2 in this Teacher Guide. A Word Reading in Isolation Analysis and a Word Reading in Isolation Remediation Guide have also been included under MOY Assessment Day 2 in the Teacher Guide.

The Fluency Assessment uses Activity Pages A.2 and A.6 (which you may have collected from students), as well as the student copy of the Fluency Assessment text "Scout's Honor" located under MOY Assessment Day 2 in this Teacher Guide. of this Teacher Guide. You will use Activity Page A.6 (MOY Fluency Assessment Recording Copy) to create a running record while students read the fluency passage. Activity Page A.2 (MOY Assessment Summary) includes a Fluency Assessment Scoring Sheet.

READING COMPREHENSION ASSESSMENT (90 MIN.)

- Ensure each student has a copy of Activity Page A.1. You may have collected this activity page from students at the beginning of the unit.
- Have students work independently to complete the Reading Comprehension Assessment on Activity Page A.1. Answers are provided on the next page. After you have scored the assessment, record individual scores on each student's MOY Assessment Summary (Activity Page A.2).

The reading comprehension questions pertaining to these texts are aligned to the CCSS and are worthy of students' time to answer. Questions have been designed so they do not focus on minor points in the text, but rather, they require deep analysis. Thus, each item might thus address multiple standards. In general the selected-response items address Reading standards and the constructed-response items address Writing standards. To prepare students for CCSS-aligned assessments, such as those developed by the Partnership for Assessment of Readiness for College and Careers (PARCC) and the Smarter Balanced, some items replicate how technology may be incorporated in those assessments, using a paper and pencil format.

Item Annotations and Correct Answers

Note: To receive a point for a two-part question, students must correctly answer both parts of the question.

"All-Ball"

Item	Correct Answer(s)	Standards
1. **Literal**	B	RI.4.1, RI.4.10
2. **Inferential**	C	RI.4.2, RI.4.1, RI.4.10
3. **Evaluative**	C	RI.4.7, RI.4.1, RI.4.10
4. **Inferential**	Part A=D, Part B=D	RI.4.4, RI.4.1, RI.4.10
5 **Evaluative**	B	RI.4.6, RI.4.1, RI.4.10
6. **Evaluative**	*In the beginning of the story, the narrator feels sad that her father is leaving. Then her father purchases a ball that becomes her companion, and she begins to think of the ball as a friend. One day a dog pops her ball, and she is devastated. Over time she begins ordinary activities again, and her loss of All-Ball seems to get easier as time passes.*	RI.4.3, RI.4.1, RI.4.10, W.4.4

"Marshfield Dreams"

Item	Correct Answer(s)	Standards
7. **Inferential**	D	RI.4.2, RI.4.1, RI.4.10
8. **Inferential**	A	RI.4.1, RI.4.10
9. **Literal**	A	RI.4.1, RI.4.10
10. **Evaluative**	C	RI.4.5, RI.4.1, RI.4.10
11 **Inferential**	D	RI.4.6, RI.4.1, RI.4.10
12 **Inferential**	A	RI.4.3, RI.4.1, RI.4.10
13 **Evaluative**	B	RI.4.7, RI.4.1, RI.4.10
14 **Inferential**	A	RI.4.2, RI.4.1, RI.4.10
15. **Inferential**	A	RI.4.1, RI.4.10

Reading Comprehension Assessment Analysis

Students who answered 10 or fewer questions correctly out of 15 total questions may have significant skill deficits. Administer the Word Reading in Isolation Assessment and the Fluency Assessment to these students to gain further insight as to possible weaknesses. Carefully analyze their performance on the Reading Comprehension Assessment, the Word Reading in Isolation Assessment, and the Fluency Assessment to determine whether students may need to be regrouped to an earlier point of instruction in the CKLA grade-level materials.

Administer the Fluency Assessment and, as time permits, the Word Reading in Isolation Assessment to students who answered 11–13 questions correctly out of 15 total questions. Use results from the Word Reading in Isolation Assessment to identify gaps in the mastery of specific letter-sound spellings.

You do not need to administer the Word Reading in Isolation Assessment to students who answered 14–15 questions correctly out of 15 total questions. However, please administer the Fluency Assessment to determine whether practice and progress monitoring in the area of fluency are warranted.

The following chart provides an overview of how to interpret students' scores

Reading Comprehension Assessment Analysis	
Number of Questions Answered Correctly	**Remediation**
10 or fewer	Administer Word Reading in Isolation Assessment and Fluency Assessment.
11–13	Administer Word Reading in Isolation Assessment as time permits; administer Fluency Assessment.
14–15	Do not administer Word Reading in Isolation Assessment; administer Fluency Assessment.

Middle-of-Year Assessment

Assessment Day 2

LESSON AT A GLANCE

	Time	Materials
Middle-of-Year Assessment		
Grammar Assessment	50 min.	❏ Activity Page A.3
Morphology Assessment	40 min.	❏ Activity Page A.4
Fluency Assessment; Word Reading in Isolation Assessment	Ongoing	❏ Activity Pages A.2, A.5, A.6 ❏ stopwatch

ADVANCE PREPARATION

Middle-of-Year (EOY) Assessment

During the second day of the two-day assessment, all students will independently complete the Grammar Assessment and Morphology Assessment. Together these assessments include 25 items. After students complete these portions of the assessment, enter their scores on the Grammar Assessment Scoring Sheet and Morphology Assessment Scoring Sheet in the Teacher Guide pages that follow, making additional copies if needed. Answers for the Grammar and Morphology Assessments are provided in the Activity Page Answer Key in the Teacher Resources section of this Teacher Guide.

Administer the Word Reading in Isolation Assessment based on students' performance on the Reading Comprehension Assessment. Continue to administer the Fluency Assessment to all students.

GRAMMAR ASSESSMENT (50 MIN.)

- Ensure each student has a copy of Activity Page A.3 . You may have collected this activity page from students at the beginning of the unit.
- Have students work independently to complete the Grammar Assessment on Activity Page A.3. Enter all student scores onto the Grammar Assessment Scoring Sheet on the next page.

Grammar Assessment Scoring Sheet

Skill	Nouns and Adjectives	Proper nouns and Adjectives	Adjectives and Adverbs	Adjectives and Adverbs	Subjects and Predicates	Sentence Fragments	Run-on Sentences	Sentence Types	Sentence Types	Commas	Commas	Commas and Quotation Marks	Commas and Quotation Marks	Sequencing Adjectives	Sequencing Adjectives
Question	1	2	3	4	5	6	7	8	9	10	11	12	13	14	15
Student															

Morphology Assessment Scoring Sheet

Skill	The prefix *un-*	The prefix *non-*	The prefix *en-*	The root *arch*	The root *graph*	The suffix *-y*	The suffix *-y*	The suffix *-ly*	The suffix *-ly*	The root *rupt*
Question	1	2	3	4	5	6	7	8	9	10
Student										

MORPHOLOGY ASSESSMENT (50 MIN.)

- Make sure each student has a copy of Activity Page A.4. You may have collected this activity page from students at the beginning of the unit.
- Have students work independently to complete the Morphology Assessment on Activity Page A.4. Record all student scores into the Morphology Assessment Scoring Sheet. To receive a point for multiple-part questions, students must correctly answer all parts of the question.

WORD READING IN ISOLATION ASSESSMENT (ONGOING)

Begin to administer the Word Reading in Isolation Assessment individually to all students who scored 10 or fewer on the Reading Comprehension Assessment and, as time permits, to students who scored 11–13, in order to gain further insight as to possible weaknesses.

This section of the MOY Assessment assesses single-word reading to identify the specific letter-sound correspondences a student may have not yet mastered.

Administration Instructions

- Locate the Word Reading in Isolation Assessment on the next page. Students will read from this copy.
- Cover all of the words with a sheet of paper before calling a student to complete the assessment.
- Tell the student he or she will read words aloud to you and that it is important to do his or her best reading.
- Uncover the first row of words by moving the paper down.
- As the student reads a word, mark any incorrect letter-sound correspondences above the word on the Word Reading in Isolation Assessment Scoring Sheet (Activity Page A.5 that you collected from students). Also, note whether the student incorrectly chunks letters into syllables, leading to mispronunciation. If the student reads the word correctly, place a check mark above the word.
- If, after 10 seconds, the student is unable to read the word at all, simply tell the student the word and move on. Mark an 'X' above the word on the scoring sheet.

Middle-of-Year Assessment Materials

Word Reading in Isolation Assessment					
1.	steady	asphalt	oxygen	dovetail	birthplace
2.	bravo	washtub	consume	delight	council
3.	accuse	riddle	trolley	scoreboard	cruise
4.	marvelous	betrayal	freighter	floored	guarantee
5.	blizzard	prairie	concrete	crescent	bowlful
6.	breakwater	peachy	spiffier	gherkin	qualify
7.	yearning	exercise	loathe	ivory	disprove
8.	audit	baboon	continue	taught	overdue
9.	chasm	human	pulled	warning	worthless
10.	scowl	avoidance	paperboy	courses	woodchuck
11.	switch	crumb	whopper	sprinkle	knitting
12.	calculate	mustache	partridge	singe	assign
13.	wriggle	bizarre	recommit	youthful	mistletoe

WORD READING IN ISOLATION ANALYSIS

The more words a student is able to read and the farther the student is able to progress in the assessment, the stronger his or her preparation is for further CKLA instruction. A Word Reading in Isolation Analysis chart and a Word Reading in Isolation Remediation Guide are located in this lesson.

The number of words read correctly indicates the following:

- Students who correctly score 43 or fewer words out of 63 appear to have significant deficits in decoding and word recognition.
- Students who correctly score 44–51 out of 65 words appear to have adequate decoding and word recognition skills.
- Students who correctly score 52–65 out of 65 words appear to have outstanding decoding and word recognition skills.

After scoring the assessment, you might find it helpful to determine which letter-sound correspondences students missed that caused them to score below the benchmark for word recognition. Note that one-syllable words are not included in the Syllabication Analysis.

Score required to meet benchmark of 80%						
Phonemes						
Consonants						Totals
/b/	/d/	/f/	/g/	/h/		
/j/	/k/	/l/	/m/	/n/		
/p/	/r/	/s/	/t/	/v/		166/208
/w/	/x/	/y/	/z/	/ch/		
/sh/	/th/	/th/	/ng/	/qu/		
Vowels						108/136
/a/	/e/	/i/	/o/	/u/		39/49
/ae/	/ee/	/ie/	/oe/	/ue/		25/31
/ə/	/oo/	/oo/	/aw/	/ou/		19/23
/oi/	/ar/	/er/	/or/	/aer/		27/33
Syllabication (words with 2 or more syllables)						
Closed Syllable/short						39/49
Open Syllable/long						13/17
Magic E and Digraph Syllable						21/26
R-Controlled Syllable						16/20
ə Syllable						7/9
–le Syllable						4/4

WORD READING IN ISOLATION REMEDIATION GUIDE

Write the names of students who missed questions under each header in the following chart. Refer to the Table of Contents in the *Decoding and Encoding Remediation Supplement* to locate information about specific phonemes and syllabication for remediation purposes.

Phonemes—Consonants (Item numbers in parentheses)

/b/ (1e, 2a, 2b, 3d, 4b, 5a, 5e, 6a, 8b, 10c, 13b)	/d/ (1a, 1d, 2d, 3b, 3d, 4d, 5a, 7e, 8a, 8e, 9c, 10b, 10e)	/f/ (1b, 4c, 4d, 5e, 6c, 6e, 13d)
/g/ (4e, 6d, 13a)	/h/ (9b)	/j/ (1c, 12c, 12d)
/k/ (2c, 2e, 3a, 3d, 3e, 5c, 5d, 6a, 6d, 8c, 9a, 10a, 10d, 10e, 11b, 11d, 12a, 13c)	/l/ (1b, 1d, 1e, 2d, 3c, 4d, 5a, 5e, 6e, 7c, 9c, 9e, 10a, 12a)	/m/ (2c, 4a, 9a, 9b, 11b, 12b, 13c, 13e)
/n/ (1c, 2c, 2e, 4e, 5c, 5d, 6d, 7a, 8b, 8c, 9b, 9d, 10b, 11e, 12d, 12e)	/p/ (1e, 5b, 6b, 6c, 7e, 9c, 10c, 11c, 11d, 12c)	/r/ (2a, 3b, 3c, 3e, 4b, 4c, 5b, 5c, 5d, 6a, 7d, 7e, 11b, 11d, 12c, 13a, 13c)
/s/ (1a, 1b, 1e, 2c, 2e, 3d, 4a, 5d, 6c, 7b, 7e, 9e, 10a, 10b, 10d, 11a, 11d, 12b, 12d, 12e, 13e)	/t/ (1a, 1b, 1d, 2b, 2d, 3c, 4b, 4c, 4e, 5c, 5d, 6a, 8a, 8c, 8d, 11e, 12a, 12b, 12c, 13c, 13e)	/v/ (1d, 2a, 4a, 7d, 7e, 8e, 10b)
/w/ (2b, 6a, 9d, 9e, 10e, 11a, 11c)	/x/ (1c, 7b)	/y/ (7a, 13d)
/z/ (3a, 3e, 5a, 7b, 9a, 10d, 13b)	/ch/ (6b, 10e, 11a)	/sh/ (2b, 12b)
/th/ (1e, 9e, 13d)	/th/ (7c)	/ng/ (7a, 9d, 11d, 11e)
/qu/ (6e)		

Phonemes—Vowels (Item numbers in parentheses)		
/a/ (1b, 8b, 9a, 12a, 12b)	/e/ (1a, 5d, 7b, 9e, 10d)	/i/ (1c, 3b, 5a, 6c, 6d, 6e, 7a, 7e, 8a, 8c, 9d, 11a, 11d, 11e, 12c, 12d, 13a, 13b, 13c, 13e)
/o/ (1c, 2a, 2b, 3c, 5c, 6a, 6e, 11c)	/u/ (1d, 2b, 2c, 4a, 8c, 10e, 11b, 12b, 13c)	/ae/ (1d, 1e, 4b, 4c, 6a, 10c, 12a)
/ee/ (1a, 3c, 4e, 5b, 5c, 6b, 6c, 7d, 13c)	/ie/ (2d, 6e, 7b, 7d, 12e)	/oe/ (2a, 5e, 7c, 8e, 13e)
/ue/ (3a, 8c, 9b, 12a)	/ə/ (1c, 2d, 3a, 4b, 4e, 9a, 9b, 10b, 12e)	/oo/ (2c, 3e, 7e, 8b, 8e, 13d)
/oo/ (9c, 10e)	/aw/ (1b, 8a, 8d)	/ou/ (2e, 10a)
/oi/ (10b, 10c)	/ar/ (4a, 12c, 13b)	/er/ (1e, 4c, 5a, 6a, 6c, 6d, 7a, 7b, 8e, 9e, 10c, 11c)
/or/ (3d, 4d, 9d, 10d)	/aer/ (4e, 5b)	/ə/ + /l/ (2e, 3b, 4a, 4b, 5e, 11d, 13a, 13d, 13e)

Syllabication (words with 2 or more syllables; Item numbers in parentheses)		
Closed Syllable/short (1a, 1b, 1c, 2a, 2b, 2c, 3b, 3c, 4e, 5a, 5c, 5d, 6a, 6c, 6d, 6e, 7a, 7b, 7e, 8a, 8b, 8c, 9a, 9b, 9d, 9e, 10b, 10d, 10e, 11c, 11d, 11e, 12a, 12b, 12c, 13a, 13b, 13c, 13e)	**Open Syllable/long (1a, 2a, 3c, 4e, 5b, 6b, 6c, 6e, 7d, 8c, 8e, 9b, 10c, 12a, 13c, 13e)**	**Magic E and Digraph Syllable (1b, 1d, 1e, 2c, 2d, 2e, 3a, 4a, 4b, 4c, 5c, 5e, 6a, 6b, 7b, 7e, 8a, 8b, 8e, 10b, 10c, 10e, 12a, 12e, 12d)**
R-Controlled Syllable (1e, 3d, 4a, 4c, 4e, 5a, 5b, 6a, 6c, 6d, 7a, 7b, 8e, 9d, 9e, 10c, 10d, 11c, 12c, 13b)	**ə Syllable (1c, 2d, 2e, 3a, 4a, 4b, 5e, 9a, 12e, 13d)**	**–le Syllable (3b, 11d, 13a, 13e)**

FLUENCY ASSESSMENT (ONGOING)

This section of the MOY Assessment assesses students' fluency in reading by using the selection "Scout's Honor" (literary text) located on the next page of this Teacher Guide.

Administration Instructions

- Turn to the student copy of "Scout's Honor" on the next page. Students will read from this copy.
- Using the Recording Copy of "Scout's Honor" (Activity Page A.6) for each student, you will create a running record as you listen to each student read orally.
- Explain that the student will read a selection aloud while you take some notes. Encourage the student not to rush and to read at his or her regular pace.
- Read the title of the selection aloud for the student, as the title is not part of the assessment.
- Begin timing when the student reads the first word of the selection. As the student reads aloud, make a running record on the Recording Copy of the text using the following guidelines:

Words read correctly	No mark is required.
Omissions	Draw a long dash above the word omitted.
Insertions	Write a caret (^) at the point where the insertion was made. If you have time, write down the word that was inserted.
Words read incorrectly	Write an 'X' above the word.
Substitutions	Write the substitution above the word.
Self-corrected errors	Replace original error mark with an 'SC'.
Teacher-supplied words	Write a 'T' above the word (counts as an error).

- When one minute has elapsed, draw a vertical line on the Recording Copy to mark the student's place in the text at that point. Allow the student to finish reading the selection aloud.

Middle-of-Year Fluency Assessment Student Copy

Scouts Honor
by Avi

1 Back in 1946, when I was nine, I worried that I wasn't tough enough. 14
That's why I became a Boy Scout. Scouting, I thought, would make a 27
man of me. It didn't take long to reach Tenderfoot rank. You got that for 42
joining. To move up to Second Class, however, you had to meet three 55
requirements. Scout Spirit and Scout Participation had been cinchy. The 65
third requirement, Scout Craft, meant I had to go on an overnight hike in 79
the country. In other words, I had to leave Brooklyn, on my own, for the 94
first time in my life. 99

2 Since I grew up in Brooklyn in the 1940s, the only grass I knew was in 115
Ebbets Field where the Dodgers played. Otherwise, my world was made 126
of slate pavements, streets of asphalt (or cobblestone), and skies full of tall 139
buildings. The only thing "country" was a puny pin oak tree at our curb, 153
which was noticed, mostly, by dogs. 159

3 I asked Scoutmaster Brenkman where I could find some country. Now, 170
whenever I saw Mr. Brenkman, who was a church pastor, he was dressed 183
either in church black or Scout khaki. When he wore black, he'd warn us 197
against hellfire. When he wore khaki, he'd teach us how to build fires. 210

4 "Country," Scoutmaster Brenkman said in answer to my question, "is 219
anywhere that has lots of trees and is not in the city. Many boys camp in 235
the Palisades." 237

5 "Where's that?" 239

6 "Just north of the city. It's a park in Jersey." 249

7 "Isn't that a zillion miles from here?" 256

8 "Take the subway to the George Washington Bridge, then hike across." 267

9 I thought for a moment, then asked, "How do I prove I went?" 280

10 Mr. Brenkman looked deeply shocked. "You wouldn't lie, would you? What 291
about Scout's honor?" 294

11 "Yes, sir," I replied meekly. 299

Word Count: 299

- Assess the student's comprehension of the selection by asking him or her to respond orally to the following questions:

1. **Inferential.** What does the word cinchy (paragraph 1) mean?
   » Easy.
2. **Literal.** What is the lowest rank in the author's Boy Scout troop?
   » Tenderfoot.
3. **Inferential.** Why couldn't the author meet his Scout Craft requirement close to home?
   » Because the author lived in the city and Scout Craft required hiking in the country.
4. **Inferential.** Where did the author most likely hear Mr. Brenkman warning against hellfire?
   » In church.

- Continue administering the Fluency Assessment as time permits.
- You may score the assessment later, provided you have kept running records and marked the last word students read after one minute elapsed.

Guidelines for Fluency Assessment Scoring

- Use one Fluency Assessment Scoring Sheet for each student taking the assessment. The Fluency Assessment Scoring Sheet appears on each student's MOY Assessment Summary (Activity Page A.2). To calculate a student's Words Correct Per Minute (W.C.P.M) score, use the information you recorded on the Recording Copy and follow these steps. You may wish to have a calculator available.

1. Count Words Read in One Minute. This is the total number of words that the student read or attempted to read in one minute. It includes words that the student read correctly as well as words that the student read incorrectly. Write the total in the box labeled Words Read in One Minute.
2. Count the Uncorrected Mistakes in One Minute. You noted these in the running record. They include words read incorrectly, omissions, substitutions, and words that you had to supply. Write the total in the box labeled Uncorrected Mistakes in One Minute on the scoring sheet. Note that a mistake that the student self-corrects should not be counted as a mistake.

3. Subtract Uncorrected Mistakes in One Minute from Words Read in One Minute to get Words Correct. Write the number in the box labeled W.C.P.M. Although the analysis does not include any words the student read correctly (or incorrectly) after one minute, you may use this information from the Recording Copy for anecdotal purposes.

As you evaluate W.C.P.M. scores, here are some factors to consider.

It is normal for students to show a wide range in fluency and in W.C.P.M. scores. However, a major goal of Grades 4 and 5 is to read with sufficient fluency to ensure comprehension and independent reading of school assignments in this and subsequent grade levels. A student's W.C.P.M. score can be compared with the score of other students in the class (or grade level) and also with the national fluency norms obtained by Hasbrouck and Tindal (2006). Hasbrouck and Tindal suggest that a score falling within 10 words above or below the 50th percentile should be interpreted as within the normal, expected, and appropriate range for a student at that grade level at that time of year. For example, if you administered the assessment during the spring of Grade 4, and a student scored 113 W.C.P.M., you should interpret this as within the normal, expected, and appropriate range for that student.

Oral Reading Fluency Norms from Hasbrouck and Tindal (2006)

Percentile	Spring Grade 4 W.C.P.M.	Fall Grade 5 W.C.P.M.
90	180	166
75	152	139
50	123	110
25	98	85
10	72	61

Reference

Hasbrouck, Jan and Tindal, Gerald A. "Oral reading fluency norms: A valuable assessment tool for reading teachers." The Reading Teacher 59 (2006): 636–644.

Interpreting End-of-Year Assessment Scores

To determine students' skill level for ongoing Grade 4 CKLA instruction, use the results of three assessments: the Reading Comprehension Assessment, the Word Reading in Isolation Assessment (if administered), and the Fluency Assessment. Please refer to the Grade 4 Middle-of-Year Assessment Summary (Activity Page A.2) and consider students' performance on these three assessments, in combination.

It is most challenging to analyze results for students with ambiguous or borderline scores. This might include students who answered most questions correctly on one passage of the Reading Comprehension Assessment but not other passages, or this might include students whose performance was uneven on the Word Reading in Isolation Assessment or Fluency Assessment.

In analyzing results from the Reading Comprehension Assessment, be aware that some students may not be strong test-takers. They may struggle to answer the questions even if they read the selection and understood it. You may wish to have students with borderline scores read the selection(s) aloud to you and then discuss it with you so you can better determine if their struggles are a result of comprehension difficulties or other factors.

In analyzing results from the Word Reading in Isolation Assessment, remember that not all poor scores are the same.

Students who have difficulty reading one-syllable words may have a major problem reading the words or spellings in question and need intensive remediation.

Benchmark results for individual students are not included for the Grammar Assessment or the Morphology Assessment. You should use the results of the Grammar Assessment and the Morphology Assessment to determine the extent to which students may benefit from the additional practice of certain grammar and morphology skills taught in CKLA.

Grade 4 | Unit 5

Pausing Point

END-OF-UNIT CONTENT ASSESSMENT

Use the first day of the Pausing Point to assess the content knowledge students have acquired by reading *The Changing Earth*. Make sure each student has a copy of Activity Page PP.2. You may have collected this activity page from students at the beginning of the unit.

- Allow students as much time as they need to complete the assessment during the first Pausing Point day. In most cases this assessment will take approximately 30 to 45 minutes.
- Tell students to read and answer the questions about what they have learned about geology. Encourage students to do their best and review their work once they have finished.
- Circulate around the room as students complete the assessment, to ensure that everyone is working individually.
- Use the following Remediation and Enrichment suggestions to plan activities for the remainder of the first Pausing Point day.

Content Assessment Answer Key

1. C
2. C
3. sedimentary; igneous; metamorphic
4. B
5. D
6. erosion; physical weathering; chemical weathering
7. C
8. A
9. B
10. A
11. ocean trench; mid-ocean ridge
12. B

13. extinct volcano; active volcano; dormant volcano

14. A

15. D

16. B

17. D

18. B

19. D

20. E

21. B

22. F

23. A

24. C

25. A. fold mountains; C. dome mountains; B. fault-block mountains

26. B

27. B

28. A. inner core; B. outer core; C. mantle; D. crust

29. B

30. D

PAUSING POINT FOR DIFFERENTIATION OF INSTRUCTION

Please use the final four days of this unit (or three days if you chose to pause for one day after Lesson 7) to address results of the Content Assessment, Unit Assessment (for reading comprehension; fluency, if applicable; grammar; and morphology), and Spelling Assessments.

See Program Guide for more information.

Remediation

Content

For a detailed description of remediation strategies, which address lagging skills in Reading Comprehension, Fluency, Grammar and Morphology, Spelling, and Writing, refer to the Program Guide.

Writing

Use time during the Pausing Point to return to Activity Page 8.4, the draft wiki entry that each student completed, along with the completed Wiki Entry Rubric and Wiki Entry Editing Checklist. Meet briefly with individual students to discuss areas in which improvement is needed. You may wish to allow students additional time to revise and edit their wiki entry. You may also wish to allow students to publish their wiki entry by recopying their revised and edited draft onto a clean page.

You may wish to suggest that students needing more practice write a new wiki entry on a different topic, such as the rock cycle, weathering, or erosion. Provide additional structure and guidance for students, making copies of both the Wiki Entry Rubric and the Wiki Entry Editing Checklist available (see the Teacher Resources), and circulate and check in with students as they write.

Enrichment

If students have mastered the content and skills in the Geology unit, their experience with the domain concepts may be enriched by the following activities:

- Students may read the enrichment selections contained in the Reader. One selection, "The Rock Towns of Cappadocia," describes the cave-like rock houses located in Cappadocia, Turkey, as well as rock carvings on Easter Island. Another selection, "Violent Vesuvius," provides information on Mount Vesuvius and gives an account of what it was like to witness its largest, most devastating eruption in recorded history. The final selection, "A Deep-Sea Detective Story," dives into the subject of undersea investigation, telling of important expeditions and resulting discoveries. The Activity Book contains activity pages students can complete as they read these selections.

- Students may respond to any of the following writing prompts, conducting independent research necessary to support their responses:
    - Describe the steps that would change igneous rock into sediments; sediments into sedimentary rock; sedimentary rock into metamorphic rock; metamorphic rock into igneous rock; metamorphic rock into sedimentary rock; and/or igneous rock into metamorphic rock.
    - If I witnessed a volcanic eruption, I would ____.
    - Compare and contrast what happens above and below Earth's surface to cause a specific volcanic activity (formation of a volcano, a volcanic eruption, formation of an island chain, etc.) and how that specific volcanic activity is explained in a volcano myth.
    - Write a letter from the perspective of a scientist who is going on an underwater expedition to explore hydrothermal vents.
    - Write a myth about ancient ocean fossils on Mount Everest.
- Students may share, either with a small group or with the class, the writing they generated in this unit or in response to the writing prompts in this Enrichment section.

Grade 4 | Unit 5

Teacher Resources

In this section, you will find:

- Core Connections Area of Study Cards
- Core Connections Earth Image Card
- Core Connections Geology Image Cards
- Glossary for *The Changing Earth*
- Pronunciation Guide for *The Changing Earth*
- Wiki Entry Rubric
- Wiki Entry Editing Checklist
- Resources for the Enrichment Selections in *The Changing Earth*
- Activity Book Answer Key

Geography

the study of the characteristics of the earth's surface

Ecology

the study of relationships between living things and their environment

Archaeology

the study of past human life and activities by examining bones, tools, and other objects left behind

Geology

the study of the earth's characteristics, what it is made of, and the forces and processes that change and shape it

Core Connections: Earth Image Card

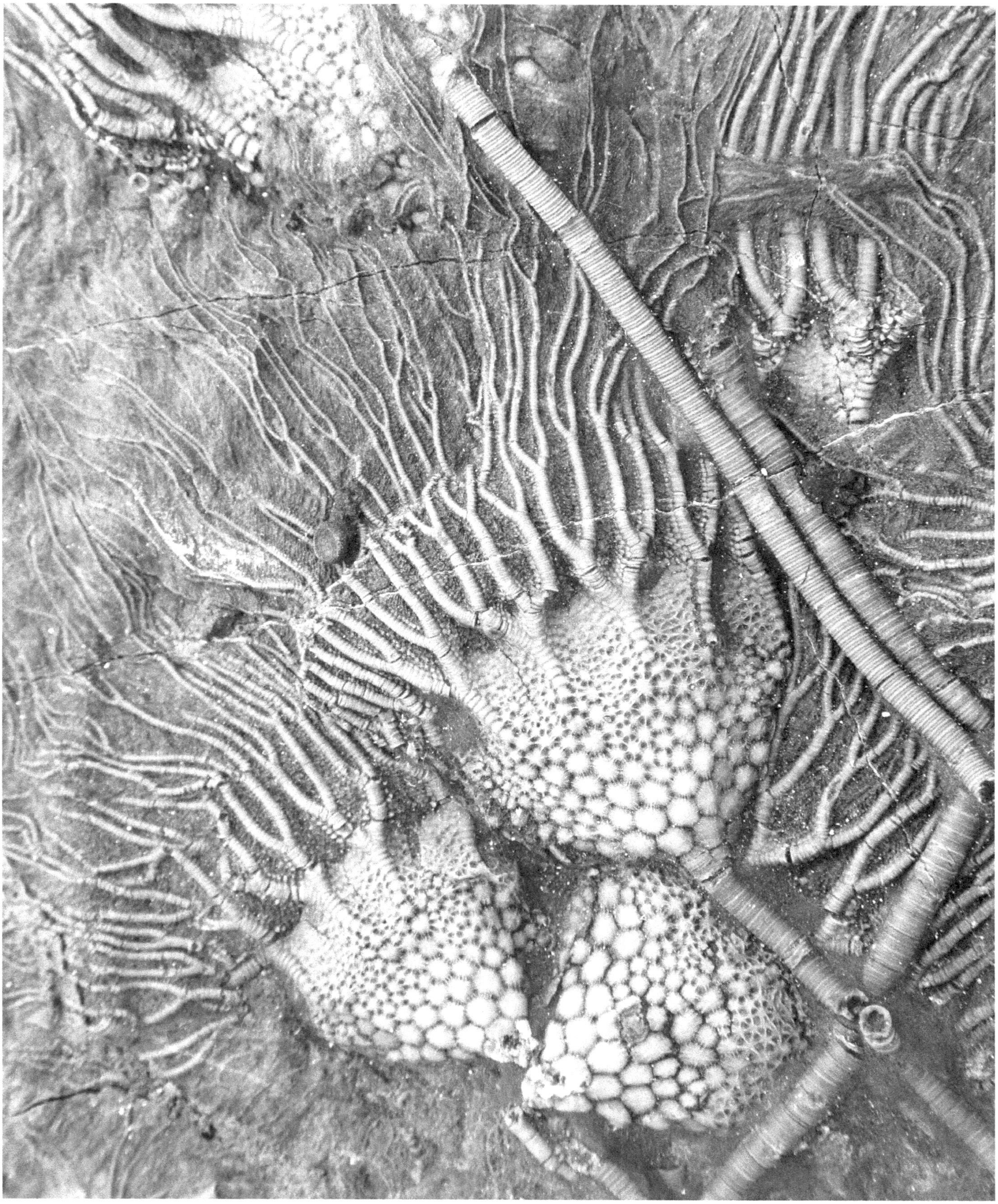

Grade 4 | Unit 5

Glossary

Words marked with an asterisk (*) are important words in this Reader that are not in the reading lessons.

A

*__active volcano, n.__ a type of volcano that has erupted in the past ten thousand years and is likely to erupt again (active volcanoes)

aftershock, n. a smaller, weaker earthquake that often follows a main earthquake event (aftershocks)

altar, n. a platform or table used as a center of worship in religious ceremonies or services (altars)

B

basalt, n. heavy, dense rock formed from cooled, hardened lava

basin, n. a large area in the earth that is lower than the area around it (basins)

bitter, adj. 1. resentful and angry because of unfair treatment; 2. very cold

bulge, v. to stick out or swell

C

caldera, n. a crater caused by the collapse of the top of a volcano

canyon, n. a deep valley with steep sides and often a stream or river flowing through it (canyons)

catastrophe, n. a terrible, sudden event (catastrophes)

*__chemical weathering, n.__ a process that breaks down rocks by changing the minerals they contain

climate, n. the average weather conditions of a particular area

clustered, adj. grouped close together

*__coal, n.__ a dark, solid substance formed in the earth from plant fossils and used as fuel

*__collide, v.__ to crash together with strong force (colliding)

compact, v. to closely pack or press together (compacts, compacting)

conclude, v. to decide something or form an opinion based on information you have (concluded, **n.** conclusion)

continental drift, n. a process in which continents slowly move over time on the surface of the earth

contract, v. to shrink slightly or get smaller

crater, n. a bowl-shaped opening at the top of a volcano or geyser

*__crust, n.__ Earth's outermost layer, featuring a rocky surface

D

dense, adj. thick or heavy (denser)

deposit, 1. **v.** to put or leave something in a particular place; 2. **n.** material laid down or left by a natural process (v. deposited, n. deposits)

descend, v. to move downward (descends)

detective, n. a person whose job is to find information about someone or something (detectives)

dissolved, adj. mixed with liquid so no solid pieces are visible anymore

distant, adj. far away in time or space

*__dome mountains, n.__ mountains generally formed when magma pushes upward into Earth's crust from the mantle and cools into igneous rock underground, causing the crust above it to bulge; usually occurring as isolated mountains on otherwise flat plains

*__dormant volcano, n.__ a type of volcano that is considered active but hasn't erupted for a very long time

*__drift, v.__ to slowly move with water, wind, or other natural processes (drifted)

durable, adj. able to last a long time in good condition

dwelling, n. a place where someone lives (dwellings)

E

elder, n. a person who is older, respected, and often in a position of authority (elders)

entomb, v. to bury (entombed)

epicenter, n. the point on Earth's surface directly above an earthquake's focus

*__erosion, n.__ any process or force that moves sediments to new locations

erupt, v. to send out rock, lava, and ash in a sudden explosion (erupted, **n.** eruption)

eruption column, n. an enormous cloud of ash, bits of rock, and toxic gas produced by a volcanic eruption that can travel hundreds of feet per second

eternal, adj. lasting forever, with no beginning and no end

evacuate, v. to remove people from a dangerous place

evidence, n. proof; information and facts that are helpful in forming a conclusion or supporting an idea

excavation, n. a hollowed-out place formed by digging or carving (excavations)

exert, v. to cause a force to be felt or have an effect (exerts)

expand, v. to get bigger

experiment, n. a scientific test to try out something in order to learn about it

*__extinct volcano, n.__ a type of volcano that has not erupted for at least ten thousand years (extinct volcanoes)

eyewitness, n. a person who has seen something happen and is able to describe it

F

fault, n. a crack in Earth's crust (faults)

*__fault-block mountains, n.__ mountains formed when gigantic blocks of rock move up and down along faults

fine, adj. very small

firsthand, adv. coming directly from actually seeing or experiencing something

*__focus, n.__ the place in Earth's crust where huge blocks of rock move along a fault, triggering an earthquake

*__fold mountains, n.__ mountains formed when rocks are pushed up into huge folds by moving tectonic plates

*__force, n.__ strength, power (forces)

fossil, n. the preserved remains of things that lived long ago (fossils)

foundation, n. the basis of something, the support upon which something else is built (foundations)

G

geologist, n. a scientist who studies the makeup of the earth and the forces and processes that shape and change it (geologists)

*__geyser, n.__ an underground hot spring that periodically erupts, shooting hot water and steam into the air (geysers)

granite, n. a common igneous rock that forms from magma that cooled within Earth's crust

H

heave, v. 1. to move up and down over and over; 2. to lift, pull, push, or throw with a lot of effort

hoodoo, n. the tallest kind of pinnacle (hoodoos)

hotspot, n. a very hot region deep within Earth's mantle where a huge magma chamber forms (hotspots)

hot spring, n. a naturally flowing source of hot water (hot springs)

hydrothermal vent, n. a deep-sea geyser that forms as seawater sinks down through cracks in the oceanic crust and then releases extremely hot, mineral-rich water back up through cracks in the crust (hydrothermal vents)

hypothesis, n. an idea that has been suggested and may be true but has not yet been proven

I

*__ice wedging, n__. a process in which water alternately freezes and thaws and so breaks rocks apart

***igneous rock, n.** rock that forms when magma cools and solidifies (igneous rocks)

***inner core, n.** Earth's deepest layer, made of very hot, solid metal

L

lava, n. red-hot melted rock that has erupted above Earth's crust from deep underground

***limestone, n.** a type of sedimentary rock, often packed with the fossilized skeletons and shells of tiny ocean creatures, that is commonly used for building

litter, v. to scatter in disorder (littered)

lofty, adj. high up

M

magma, n. melted rock in Earth's mantle

magnitude, n. measure of an earthquake's strength

***mantle, n.** Earth's largest and thickest layer, which consists of very hot, very dense rock

***metamorphic rock, n.** rock that forms when minerals in igneous, sedimentary, or older metamorphic rocks are changed by extreme heat and pressure (metamorphic rocks)

mineral, n. any of many solid, nonliving substances found in the earth that make up rocks (minerals)

moai, n. statues on Easter Island carved from tuff in the shape of partial human figures with large heads, high cheekbones, and heavy brows

O

observation, n. 1. the act of paying careful attention to gather information; 2. a statement based on paying careful attention to something (observations)

obsidian, n. a dark rock or natural glass formed from lava that cooled very quickly

ocean trench, n. a narrow, extremely deep valley formed when the seafloor dips down as one tectonic plate slides under another (ocean trenches)

offering, n. something that is presented as an act of worship (offerings)

***outer core, n.** the layer within Earth between the inner core and the mantle, which is made of very hot, liquid metal

outsmart, v. to trick or defeat someone by being clever

P

panic, v. to be fearful in a sudden and overpowering way (panicked)

pepper, v. to sprinkle or cover

***physical weathering, n.** a process that breaks big rocks into smaller rocks without changing the minerals they contain

pinnacle, n. a slender, soaring rock formation made of tuff (pinnacles)

pinpoint, v. to figure out the exact location of something

plate tectonics, n. a theory that Earth's crust and the solid top part of the mantle are broken up into sections that fit together but move against each other

plume, n. a column of magma that rises from the mantle into a chamber beneath Earth's crust

porthole, n. a small, round window on the side of a ship, submersible, or aircraft (portholes)

pressure, n. the weight or force produced when something presses or pushes against something else

pyroclastic flow, n. a sort of avalanche of intensely hot ash, rock fragments, and volcanic gas that rolls quickly down the side of a volcano (pyroclastic flows)

R

revenge, n. the act of getting even for a wrongdoing

***rock cycle, n.** the continuous cycle in which rocks are created, destroyed, and recreated

rugged, adj. having a rough, uneven surface

S

scald, v. to burn with very hot water or steam

school, n. a large number of ocean animals of one type swimming together (schools)

sea level, n. the average height of the ocean's surface

seamount, n. an underwater volcano that forms wherever magma erupts through oceanic crust (seamounts)

***sediment, n.** rock, sand, or dirt that has been carried to a place by water, wind, or other natural processes (sediments)

***sedimentary rock, n.** rock made of sediments that have been naturally compacted and cemented together (sedimentary rocks)

seismic wave, n. a surge of energy traveling out from an earthquake's source through the earth (seismic waves)

***seismogram, n.** the record a seismograph makes, showing seismic waves as jagged up-and-down lines

***seismograph, n.** an instrument used to track seismic waves traveling through the earth (seismographs)

sensor, n. an instrument that detects and measures changes, and then sends information to a controlling device (sensors)

sheer, adj. very steep, almost straight up and down

sheet, n. a broad stretch of something (sheets)

silt, n. a substance made up of very small sediments deposited by water

solidify, v. to make or become hard or solid (solidifies)

state, n. the condition of being a solid, liquid, or gas

strong-willed, adj. determined to do what you want even if other people tell you not to

***subduction, n.** a process in which a heavier oceanic plate slides under a lighter continental plate

subduction zone, n. the place where one tectonic plate is sliding beneath another tectonic plate (subduction zones)

submersible, n. a small vehicle that can travel deep under water for research (submersibles)

surge, v. to move forward quickly, suddenly, and with force (surges)

T

texture, n. the size, shape, and sorting of mineral grains in rocks

theory, n. an explanation for why something happens, based on evidence

trigger, v. to cause something to start or happen (triggered)

tsunami, n. a gigantic wave of seawater caused by an earthquake in oceanic crust (tsunamis)

tuff, n. a type of volcanic rock formed from hardened volcanic ash

U

ultimately, adv. finally; at the end of a process

underlie, v. to be located under something (underlies)

undertaking, n. something that someone takes on as a task or duty

V

volcano, n. a hill or mountain that forms over a crack in Earth's crust from which lava erupts (volcanoes)

W

***weather, v.** to break down into smaller pieces (**n.** weathering)

PRONUNCIATION GUIDE FOR THE CHANGING EARTH

The following are pronunciations for unique words in the order in which they first appear in *The Changing Earth*, translated into Core Knowledge code. Syllables are divided by asterisks (*).

Chapter 1	
Shen Kua	/shen/ /kwə/
Pangaea	/pan*jee*ə/

Chapter 2	
Inge Lehmann	/ing*gə/ /lee*mon/

Chapter 3	
Francesco Petrarch	/fran*ches*koe/ /pe*trark/
Richter	/rik*ter/
tsunami	/soo*no*mee/

Chapter 4	
Kilauea	/kee*lə*wae*ə/
Mauna Loa	/mon*ə/ /loe*ə/
Parícutin	/par*ee*koo*teen/
Krakatoa	/krak*ə*toe*ə/
Molokai	/mol*o*chee/
Maui	/mow*ee/
Kauai	/koo*wie/
Oahu	/oe*wo*hoo/
Loihi	/loo*ee*hee/

Chapter 5	
Pele	/pae*lae/
Kilauea	/kee*lə*wae*ə/
Na-maka-o-kaha'i	/no*mo*kə*oe*kə*hie/
Hi'iaka	/hee*ie*ə*kə/
Kauai	/koo*wie/
Lohiau	/loe*ee*o/
Oahu	/oe*wo*hoo/
Molokai	/mol*o*chee/
Maui	/mow*ee/
Monadalkni	/mon*ə*dok*nie/
Sahale Tyee	/so*ho*lee/ /tie*ee/

Chapter 6	
gneiss	/nies/
Agnes Nyanhongo	/ag*nes/ /nie*an*hong*goe/
Zimbabwe	/zim*bob*wae/

Chapter 7	
Yunnan	/yoo*nan/
Shilin	/shee*leen/

Chapter 8	
Tethys Sea	/teth*ees/ /see/
Eurasian	/yer*ae*zshən/
Urals	/yer*əlz/
Navajo	/nov*ə*hoe/
Gutzon Borglum	/gootz*un/ /bor*glum/

Chapter 9	
anemones	/ə*nem*o*nees/
Jacques Piccard	/jok/ /pee*kar/
Trieste	/treest/

Enrichment: The Rock Towns of Cappadocia	
Cappadocia	/kap*ə*doe*shə/
Mount Erciyes	/mount/ /er*sie*əs/
Rapa Nui	/ro*po/ /n<u>oo</u>*ee/
moai	/moe*wie/

Enrichment: Violent Vesuvius	
Pliny	/plin*ee/
Misenum	/mis*en*um/

Enrichment: A Deep-Sea Detective Story	
Galapagos	/gə*lop*ə*goes/

WIKI ENTRY RUBRIC

	Exemplary	Strong	Developing	Beginning
Introduction	Initial section(s) provide accurate, general information related to location and type of volcano.	Initial section(s) provide accurate information related to either location or type of volcano, but not both.	Initial section(s) provide information loosely related to location and/ or type of volcano.	Initial section(s) lack information related to location and type of volcano.
Body	Additional sections provide increasingly specific information about the volcano.	Additional sections provide more information about the volcano.	Additional sections provide some information about the volcano.	Additional sections provide little to no information about the volcano.
Conclusion	A final statement provides a thought-provoking summative or closing reflection about the volcano.	A final statement provides a summative or closing reflection about the volcano.	The summative or closing nature of the final statement is unclear.	No final statement is provided.
Structure of the Piece	All sentences in sections are presented logically.	Most sentences in sections are presented logically.	Some sentences in sections are presented logically.	Connections between sentences in sections are confusing.
	All information has been paraphrased.	Most information has been paraphrased.	Some information has been paraphrased.	Little information has been paraphrased.

You may correct capitalization, punctuation, and grammar errors while you are revising. However, if you create a final copy of your writing to publish, you will use an editing checklist to address those types of mistakes after you revise.

Guidance for Teacher Use of Rubrics

Rubrics are provided for evaluation of the content and structure of student writing composed within each unit. The criteria within the descriptions correspond to what is taught in the writing lessons. "Exemplary" to "Beginning" performance columns provide graduated descriptions for each criterion. The columns for "Strong," "Developing," and "Beginning" performance are shaded to help students initially attend to the description for "Exemplary" performance. The rubrics allow teachers and students to identify graduated steps for improvement when aspects of writing do not meet all the taught criteria. To do this, teachers (and students) may highlight the language from each row that best describes the student writing.

WIKI ENTRY EDITING CHECKLIST

Wiki Entry Editing Checklist	Notes
Meaning	
Is correct grammar used? • Sentences are complete with subject and predicate. • Sentences are appropriate length (no run-ons). • The student has been supported with corrections for parts of speech, verb tense, and more complex sentence structure.	
Format	
Does the student use appropriate formatting for the piece of writing? • The volcano name is the title at the top. • Each section of the entry has a heading. • Indenting is not used. • If lists are included, they are bulleted or numbered. • There is a reference list at the end in the appropriate format.	
Capitals	
Is capitalization appropriately applied? • All sentences begin with a capital letter. • All proper nouns are capitalized. • Titles and headings have appropriate capital letters.	
Spelling	
Are all words spelled correctly? • Words using Core Knowledge Code are spelled appropriately. • Words from spelling and morphology lessons are spelled accurately. • The student has been supported with the identification of misspellings of words to be looked up in reference sources as needed.	
Punctuation	
Is punctuation appropriately applied? • All sentences have appropriate ending punctuation. • Commas and quotation marks are all used as they have been taught. • The titles in the reference list are underlined or in italics.	

Guidance for Teacher Use of Editing Checklists

Editing checklists allow students and teachers to evaluate students' command of language conventions and writing mechanics within unit writing projects. They serve a different purpose from rubrics; rubrics measure the extent to which students apply specific instructional criteria they have been building toward across the unit, whereas editing checklists measure the extent to which students apply English language conventions and general writing mechanics. With regard to expectations for accountability, we recommend using the editing checklist to measure students' command of language conventions and writing mechanics only when students have received the appropriate instructional support and a specific opportunity to review their writing for that purpose.

Evaluating Student Writing

Make enough copies of the rubric and editing checklist found in this section to evaluate each student's writing piece.

RESOURCES FOR THE ENRICHMENT SELECTIONS IN *THE CHANGING EARTH*

The enrichment selections in *The Changing Earth* are intended to be used at your discretion. They are intended to be read by more advanced readers, as they are more difficult to read and include more challenging vocabulary than chapters 1–9. You may want to assign these chapters to students who need more challenging reading material. An introduction to the selections is provided here. Core vocabulary is also listed for each selection; these words are bolded in the Reader and appear in the glossary. Following the vocabulary chart, pronunciations are provided for words that may be challenging to decode.

Core Vocabulary for "The Rock Houses of Cappadocia"

"The Rock Houses of Cappadocia" describes cave-like rock houses located in Cappadocia, Turkey, as well as rock carvings on Easter Island. A brief description of how the rock dwellings came to be is included, as is information about these dwellings today. Activity Page E1.1 corresponds to this enrichment selection.

- The following core vocabulary words are bolded in the selection and appear in the glossary. Remind students they can look up a word in the glossary if needed.

clustered, adj. grouped close together (90)

foundation, n. the basis of something, the support upon which something else is built (foundations) (90)

distant, adj. far away in time or space (92)

tuff, n. a type of volcanic rock formed by hardened volcanic ash (92)

pinnacle, n. a slender, soaring rock formation made of tuff (pinnacles) (92)

hoodoo, n. the tallest kind of pinnacle (hoodoos) (92)

dwelling, n. a place where someone lives (dwellings) (94)

excavation, n. a hollowed-out place formed by digging or carving (excavations) (95)

altar, n. a platform or table used as a center of worship in religious ceremonies or services (altars) (95)

moai, n. statues on Easter Island carved from tuff in the shape of partial human figures with large heads, high cheekbones, and heavy brows (98)

Vocabulary Chart for "The Rock Towns of Cappadocia"		
Vocabulary Type	**Tier 3 Domain-Specific Words**	**Tier 2 General Academic Words**
Core Vocabulary	tuff pinnacle hoodoo excavation altar moai	clustered foundation distant dwelling
Spanish Cognates for Core Vocabulary	excavación altar	
Multiple-Meaning Core Vocabulary Words		foundation
Sayings and Phrases		

Pronunciation Guide for "The Rock Towns of Cappadocia"	
Cappadocia	/kap* *doe*sh /
Mount Erciyes	/mount/ /er*sie* s/
Rapa Nui	/ro*po/ /n<u>oo</u>*ee/
moai	/moe*wie/

Core Vocabulary for "Violent Vesuvius"

"Violent Vesuvius" provides information about Mount Vesuvius and gives an account of what it was like to witness its largest, most devastating eruption in recorded history. The selection also includes information about what scientists have learned about this eruption from excavations of towns buried by the eruption. Activity Page E2.1 corresponds to this enrichment selection.

- The following core vocabulary words are bolded in the selection and appear in the glossary. Remind students they can look up a word in the glossary if needed.

sensor, n. an instrument that detects and measures changes, and then sends information to a controlling device (sensors) (100)

evacuate, v. to remove people from a dangerous place (102)

panic, v. to be fearful in a sudden and overpowering way (panicked) (104)

sheet, n. a broad stretch of something (sheets) (104)

litter, v. to scatter in disorder (littered) (106)

entomb, v. to bury (entombed) (106)

pyroclastic flow, n. a sort of avalanche of intensely hot ash, rock fragments, and volcanic gas that rolls quickly down the side of a volcano (pyroclastic flows) (107)

eruption column, n. an enormous cloud of ash, bits of rock, and toxic gas produced by a volcanic eruption that can travel hundreds of feet per second (109)

Vocabulary Chart for "Violent Vesuvius"		
Vocabulary Type	**Tier 3 Domain-Specific Words**	**Tier 2 General Academic Words**
Core Vocabulary	sensor entomb pyroclastic flow eruption column	evacuate panic sheet litter
Spanish Cognates for Core Vocabulary	columna eruptiva	evacuar pánico
Multiple-Meaning Core Vocabulary Words	flujo piroclástico	sheet litter
Sayings and Phrases		

Pronunciation Guide for "Violent Vesuvius"	
Pliny	/plin*ee/
Misenum	/mis*en*um/

Core Vocabulary for "A Deep-Sea Detective Story"

"A Deep-Sea Detective Story" dives into the subject of undersea investigation, telling of important expeditions and resulting discoveries. Activity Page E3.1 corresponds to this enrichment selection.

- The following core vocabulary words are bolded in the selection and appear in the glossary. Remind students they can look up a word in the glossary if needed.

detective, n. a person whose job it is to find information about someone or something (detectives) (111)

scald, v. to burn with very hot water or steam (111)

undertaking, n. something that someone takes on as a task or duty (113)

porthole, n. a small, round window on the side of a ship, submersible, or aircraft (portholes) (115)

Vocabulary Chart for "A Deep-Sea Detective Story"		
Vocabulary Type	**Tier 3 Domain-Specific Words**	**Tier 2 General Academic Words**
Core Vocabulary	porthole	detective scald undertaking
Spanish Cognates for Core Vocabulary		escaldar
Multiple-Meaning Core Vocabulary Words		
Sayings and Phrases		

Pronunciation Guide for "A Deep-Sea Detective Story"	
Galapagos	/g *lop* *goes/

NAME:
DATE:

1.3 ACTIVITY PAGE

Evidence Collector's Chart

Chapter #	What is the cause?	What evidence is there?		Letter
1	At some point, Pangaea broke apart and the pieces slowly moved apart over a long period of time.		similar rocks, fossils on different continents	N
2	Tectonic plates move very slowly due to the heat and pressure in Earth's mantle.	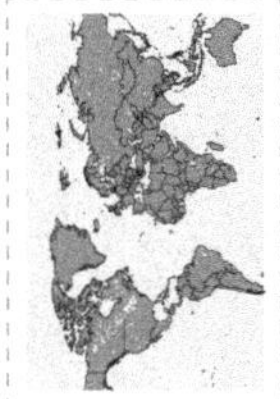	continents rearranged over time	E
3	Material in the mantle moves beneath stuck rocks at a fault, causing pressure to build over time and then suddenly release as the rocks break and slip past each other, shaking the ground.		rocks moving at a fault	E
4	Tremendous pressure and heat in the mantle force magma in a chamber below Earth's crust to move upward through a crack in Earth's surface.	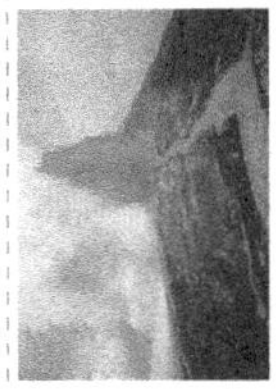	magma erupts as lava	D
6	Rocks are created, destroyed, and recreated in a continuous cycle.	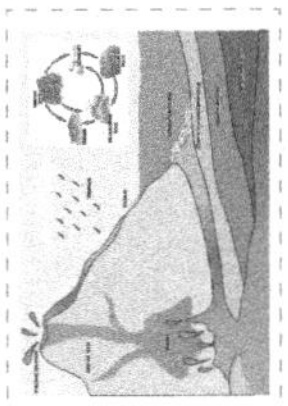	igneous, sedimentary, and metamorphic rock	I
7	Over time, weathering breaks rocks into smaller pieces and erosion moves these pieces to new locations.	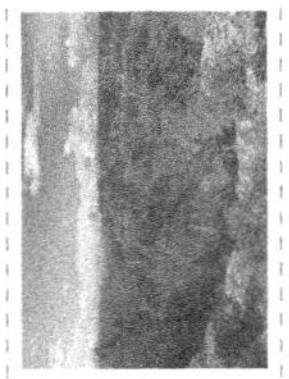	processes reshape Earth's surface	C

NAME:
DATE:

1.3 CONTINUED ACTIVITY PAGE

Chapter #	What is the cause?	What evidence is there?		Letter
8	Tectonic plates subduct underneath one another and move up and down against each other, and magma pushes up into the crust.	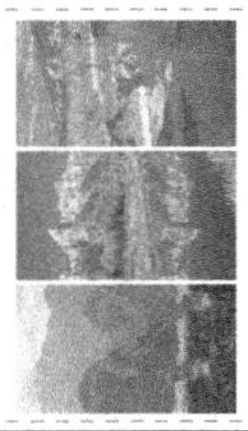	fold, fault-block, and dome mountains	E
9	Tectonic plates interact to create seafloor spreading and underwater subduction zones.	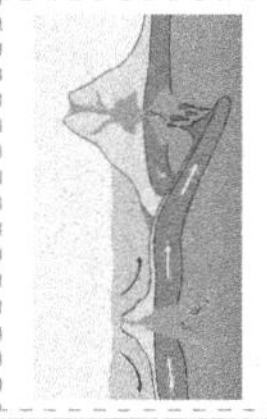	deep ocean trenches, mid-ocean ridges, hydrothermal vents	A

Riddle: ______

Answer: ______

NAME:
DATE:

1.5 CONTINUED TAKE-HOME

The following chart contains a statement about Alfred Wegener's continental drift hypothesis. Using information from the excerpt, write five pieces of evidence that support Wegener's hypothesis.

Hypothesis	Long ago, continents were joined as one supercontinent that broke apart and the pieces slowly drifted away from each other.
Evidence	1. Rock layers along the northern and eastern coasts of South America match rock layers along Africa's western coast.
	2. Deposits of coal and salt in eastern North America are similar to those in southern Europe.
	3. Fossils of the ancient fern *Glossopteris* found in similar rock layers in Africa, India, Australia, South America, and Antarctica
	4. Fossils of the ancient reptile *Lystrosaurus* found in southern Africa and India
	5. Fossils of the ancient reptile *Cynognathus* found in South America and Africa

NAME: ______________________

DATE: ______________________

2.2 TAKE-HOME

Practice Commas

For each item, insert a comma or commas in the appropriate location(s).

Examples: We went to Concord North Carolina to visit friends for spring break.
We went to Concord, North Carolina to visit friends for spring break.

I needed paper pencils erasers and a notebook for school.
I needed paper, pencils, erasers, and a notebook for school.

Seismologist Inge Lehmann was born on May 13 1888.
Seismologist Inge Lehmann was born on May 13, 1888.

1. When I was a child, my family moved from Chicago Illinois to Madison Wisconsin.
2. We have two dogs three cats a turtle and a bunny.
3. 801 East High Street
   Charlottesville VA 22902
4. President Obama was elected the 44th President of the United States on November 4 2008.
5. My dad cooked eggs bacon toast and pancakes for breakfast.
6. We traveled from Boston Massachusetts to San Diego California on our cross-country trip.
7. Earth's layers are the inner core the outer core the mantle and the crust.
8. 233 Broadway
   New York NY 10007
9. Her graduation date is scheduled for May 24 2016.

Write a sentence that includes a date or items in a series. Be sure to use correct capitalization and punctuation.

Answers may vary.

Write an address. Be sure to use correct capitalization and punctuation.

Answers may vary.

Challenge: *Write a sentence that includes at least two of the following:*

a date	a city and state	items in a series

Answers may vary.

NAME: ______________________

DATE: ______________________

2.3 TAKE-HOME

-ly: Suffix Meaning "in a ______ way"

Write the correct word to complete each sentence.

easy	easily	loud
careful	carefully	temporary
speedy	accidentally	temporarily

1. Even though his stay was only temporary, I got really attached to the neighbor's dog staying with us for a week while his owners were on vacation.
2. Amber's dad accidentally put his coffee in her thermos instead of his thermos.
3. I was careful not to wake up the baby while he was sleeping, so I listened to music quietly through headphones instead of speakers.
4. According to the continental drift hypothesis, continents move very slowly, which is definitely not a(n) speedy process.
5. The buzzer on my alarm clock is so loud that it wakes up everyone in the house.
6. The ground temporarily shakes during an earthquake, as seismic waves travel through Earth's crust and its interior.

Write a sentence using one of the words left in the box.

Answers may vary, but should include one of the following words: easy, easily, carefully

Write a sentence using one of the words left in the box.

Answers may vary, but should include one of the following words and should not include the same word as used in the previous sentence: easy, easily, carefully

NAME: ______________________________ **2.4** ACTIVITY PAGE

DATE: ______________________________

Similes about Earth's Changes

Reread the text on the page noted for each simile. Then, fill in the chart to explain what the simile is comparing and what it means.

Page	Simile from Text	What is the simile comparing?	What does the simile mean?
9	*What if continents were like enormous pieces of ice?*	Continents in oceans to pieces of ice floating in a drink.	Continents are less dense than rocks on the ocean bottom so they can float above those rocks just like ice floats in a drink, which is made with water, because ice is less dense than water.
13	*An earthquake is a bit like a rock plunking into water.*	An earthquake and a rock in water	Seismic waves travel out through the earth from the source of an earthquake just as a rock is a source of waves traveling out from the spot where it hit the water.
16	*The rift was like a seam in a pants leg, where two pieces of fabric come together.*	A rift in mid-ocean ridges and a seam in a pants leg	The seam in a pants leg dips down where the two pieces of fabric come together, so the seam lies a little bit lower than the pieces of fabric. The rift down the mid-ocean ridges dips down between the ridges; the rift lies a little bit lower than the ridges themselves.

NAME: ______________________________ **3.1** TAKE-HOME

DATE: ______________________________

Excerpt from "Earth's Layers and Moving Plates"

Read the following excerpt and use it to label Earth's layers in the diagram that follows.

Earth's deepest layer is a solid inner core of very hot metal. This metal may be nearly as hot as the sun's surface. The outer core is also made of hot metal, but it's liquid, not solid. The mantle surrounds the outer core. The mantle is Earth's largest and thickest layer and consists of very hot, very dense rock. The rock is solid in the lower and upper parts of the mantle. In between, however, is a region where the rock is neither liquid nor solid. The slow movement and behavior of this material, caused by heat and pressure, have an impact on Earth's surface. Above the mantle is Earth's outermost layer, the thin, rocky crust. There are two types of crust: oceanic crust and continental crust. Oceanic crust is covered by ocean water. Most of the continental crust is dry land, but some of the crust around the edges is covered by water. Oceanic crust is thinner but heavier than continental crust.

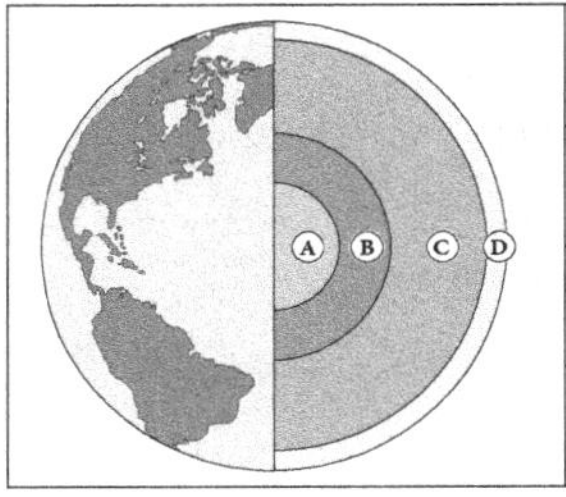

A. inner core

B. outer core

C. mantle

D. crust

Use the correct word from the word bank to fill in each blank in the following paragraphs.

trench	theory	plate	subduction
continental	tectonic	collide	

Sam is excited to tell his family what he is reading and learning about geology at school. His cousins live in the South American country of Chile, and today he learned that there is a deep ocean ____trench____ along Chile's coast. He explained, "There are two ____tectonic____ plates that meet along the western coast of South America. One is a ____continental____ plate and one is an oceanic plate. The heavier oceanic plate is sliding beneath the lighter continental ____plate____. And, this process has a big name I learned today—it's called ____subduction____!"

"I think I know how the Andes Mountains of South America are formed," exclaimed Sam's dad. "When the plates ____collide____ at plate boundaries along the Pacific Coast, I bet the continental crust crumples and gets pushed higher and higher to form the mountains. I learned about the ____theory____ of plate tectonics when I was in school, too."

Sam's dad described an earthquake that the country of Chile had recently experienced. Sam said, "Hmmm . . . I wonder if earthquakes have anything to do with moving tectonic plates?"

What do you think?

NAME: ______________________________ **4.2** TAKE-HOME

DATE: ______________________________

Excerpt from "Earth's Shakes and Quakes"

Read the first full paragraph of the following excerpt aloud to a family member and answer the questions that follow.

objects tumble from shelves, and buildings may even collapse. In 1348 CE, people had no idea what caused earthquakes. Today we know that earthquakes are the result of powerful natural forces at work in Earth's crust and mantle.

As you read in Chapter 2, scientists developed the theory of plate tectonics in the 1960s. The theory explains how Earth's surface and interior change over very long periods of time. Some plates are pulling apart at their boundaries, other plates are colliding, and still others are sliding past each other. A lot happens at plate boundaries, including most earthquakes. In fact, one of the easiest ways to locate plate boundaries is to determine where earthquakes are occurring!

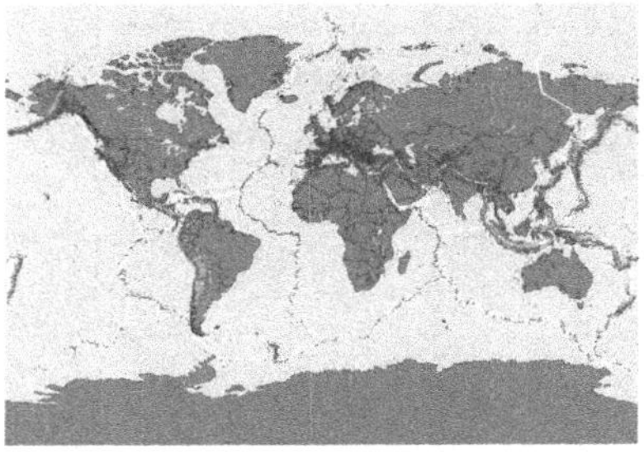

Locations of plate boundaries and past earthquake epicenters

23

1. According to the excerpt, what does the theory of plate tectonics explain?

The theory explains how Earth's surface and interior change over very long periods of time.

2. The last sentence of the excerpt states, "In fact, one of the easiest ways to locate plate boundaries is to determine where earthquakes are occurring!" How does the image on the page support this statement?

The dots marking past earthquake epicenters all sit on or near plate boundaries.

NAME: ______

DATE: ______

4.3 TAKE-HOME

Practice Commas

For each item, insert a comma or commas in the appropriate location(s).

1. My dad is from Austin, Texas and my mom is from Minneapolis, Minnesota.
2. She plays tennis, soccer, and basketball.
3. Opening night of his first play is scheduled for June 24, 2015.
4. Yellowstone National Park
   P.O. Box 168
   Yellowstone National Park, WY 82190

Write a sentence for each of the following items. Be sure to use correct capitalization and punctuation. Each sentence should include at least one comma in its appropriate location.

1. a date

   Answers may vary.

2. city and state or an address

   Answers may vary.

3. items in a series

   Answers may vary.

NAME: ______

DATE: ______

4.4 TAKE-HOME

–ly: Suffix Meaning "in a _____ way"

Write the correct word to complete each sentence.

1. Even though earthquakes are only ___temporary___ (temporary, temporarily, accidental, accidentally), they can still cause significant and sometimes permanent damage.
2. The fire engine was so ___loud___ (loud, loudly, careful, carefully) that I had to cover my ears as it drove by my house.
3. Tsunamis are ___speedy___ (loud, loudly, speedy, speedily)—they travel as fast as 500 miles per hour.
4. He ___accidentally___ (easy, easily, accidental, accidentally) dropped a glass, spilling milk all over the floor.
5. Scientist Inge Lehmann was ___careful___ (careful, carefully, temporary, temporarily) to do lots of research and analysis before concluding that Earth's core has two parts—a liquid outer core and a solid inner core.
6. It was ___easy___ (temporary, temporarily, easy, easily) to see that he loved baseball because his face lit up every time he got to play.

Write a sentence using one of the –ly words.

Answers may vary.

Write a sentence using one of your own –ly words.

Answers may vary.

Challenge: *Write a sentence using one of the root words and its –ly word.*

Answers may vary.

NAME: ______________________

DATE: ______________________

5.1 ACTIVITY PAGE

Earth's Shakes and Quakes

Answer each question thoughtfully, citing the page number(s) where you found evidence for each question. Answer in complete sentences and restate the question in your answer whenever possible.

1. Fill in the blank:

   Most earthquakes happen at plate boundaries.

   Page(s) 23

2. How much energy is released when blocks of rock that were stuck break and slip past each other?

   All the energy that accumulated in the rocks during the time they were stuck and couldn't move is released when the blocks of rock suddenly break and slip past each other.

   Page(s) 24

3. Circle the two answers that correctly complete the following statement.

   Surface waves cause ______________.

   (A.) the ground to shake, heave, sway, and lurch during an earthquake
   B. a fault to form in Earth's crust
   C. most tsunamis
   (D.) the most earthquake damage

   Page(s) 26

4. List one way in which the seismograph and the Richter scale are different. List one way in which they are similar.

   Different:

   A seismograph produces wiggly lines to show the energy of seismic waves while the Richter scale applies numbers to measure the magnitude of an earthquake based on the largest seismic wave recorded.

   Similar:

   Both a seismograph and the Richter scale are used by scientists to determine an earthquake's magnitude.

   Page(s) 27-28

5. Write two or three sentences that include one fact about a tsunami and at least two descriptive words from the text.

   Answers may vary.

   Page(s) 30

NAME: ______________________

DATE: ______________________

5.2 ACTIVITY PAGE

Take Notes on Tsunamis

Read through all the questions in the chart so you are clear about what information you should scan the Reader text for related to tsunamis. Take notes by paraphrasing the Reader text or writing information in your own words. Write key information in the shortest form possible.

Questions	Notes
What is a tsunami?	a gigantic wave of seawater
What causes a tsunami?	earthquakes that occur in the crust forming the ocean bottom
Why do tsunamis happen?	earthquakes can cause seafloor to shift, which causes seawater from the ocean bottom to its surface to suddenly start to move
How fast does a tsunami travel?	as fast as 500 miles per hour
Can we stop tsunamis from happening?	no
How can we prepare and protect ourselves?	know the tsunami warning signal where you live, quickly evacuate if tsunami approaches

NAME: ______ **5.3** ACTIVITY PAGE
DATE: ______

Tsunami Pamphlet

Draft your pamphlet by composing answers to the questions.

Question: What was THAT?

Answer: A tsunami!

Tsunamis are caused by earthquakes in the oceanic crust.

Question: What is a tsunami?
Answer: A tsunami is a giant wave of seawater.

Question: Why do tsunamis happen?
Answer: Tsunamis happen because the seafloor shifts due to an earthquake occurring in the oceanic crust.

Question: How fast does a tsunami travel?
Answer: A tsunami can travel as fast as 500 miles per hour.

Question: Can we stop tsunamis from happening?
Answer: No, we cannot stop tsunamis.

Question: How can we prepare and protect ourselves?
Answer: Scientists are able to give some warning for tsunamis. Know what the tsunami warning signal is for the area you live in. If a tsunami is approaching, you should evacuate as quickly as you can.

NAME: ______ **6.2** TAKE-HOME
DATE: ______

Commas and Quotation Marks

Rewrite each sentence, inserting a comma or commas and quotation marks in the appropriate locations. Be sure to use correct capitalization and end punctuation.

Example: The time he explained is 3:47 pm
"The time," he explained, "is 3:47 pm."

1. You don't have to look hard the teacher said to find rocks
"You don't have to look hard," the teacher said, "to find rocks."

2. Students might ask what are rocks? before reading the text
Students might ask, "What are rocks?" before reading the text.

3. Rocks are naturally occurring materials made of solid substances the author explains
"Rocks are naturally occurring materials made of solid substances," the author explains.

4. The rock cycle according to the text has been going on for several billion years
"The rock cycle," according to the text, "has been going on for several billion years."

5. Given enough time the text explains all rocks change
"Given enough time," the text explains, "all rocks change."

6. There are three types of rocks the teacher explained igneous sedimentary and metamorphic
"There are three types of rocks," the teacher explained, "igneous, sedimentary, and metamorphic."

NAME: ______ **6.3** TAKE-HOME
DATE: ______

Root *rupt*

Write the correct word to complete each sentence. You may need to add –ed, –ing, or –s to make the word correctly fit in the sentence.

uninterrupted	erupt	disrupt
rupture	abrupt	eruption

1. A volcanic ___eruption___ is usually sudden and violent.
2. When my friend lied to me, it caused a(n) ___rupture___ in our friendship.
3. My parents say it's bad for me to spend ___uninterrupted___ hours watching television, so they limit how much I can watch.
4. Old Faithful is a geyser in Yellowstone National Park that ___erupts___ several times a day.
5. Sometimes my dog ___disrupts___ my sleep when she barks in the middle of the night.
6. During an argument, my brother left the room in a(n) ___abrupt___ way instead of continuing the conversation.

Write a complete sentence for each of the following words. Be sure to use correct capitalization and punctuation.

7. *disrupt*
   Answers may vary.

8. *abrupt*
   Answers may vary.

9. *eruption*
   Answers may vary.

NAME:
DATE:

6.5 TAKE-HOME

Practice Spelling Words

Sort the spelling words into categories based on the root in each word.

uninterrupted	matriarch	hierarchy	abrupt
archrival	calligraphy	eruption	paragraph
autograph	rupture	anarchy	biographer

arch	*graph*	*rupt*
matriarch	calligraphy	uninterrupted
hierarchy	paragraph	abrupt
archrival	autograph	eruption
anarchy	biographer	rupture

List the spelling words in alphabetical order. Remember to pronounce and spell the words syllable by syllable.

1. abrupt
2. anarchy
3. archrival
4. autograph
5. biographer
6. calligraphy
7. eruption
8. hierarchy
9. matriarch
10. paragraph
11. rupture
12. uninterrupted

NAME:
DATE:

7.3 TAKE-HOME

Excerpts from *The Changing Earth*

Read the following excerpts and use them to complete the activity that follows.

Earth's Fiery Volcanoes

Using information from the excerpts, make notes on how volcanic activity is explained in the excerpts. Shaded cells indicate that no information is needed there.

Volcanic Activity	"Earth's Fiery Volcanoes"	"Mythic Volcano Spirits: Hawaii's Goddess of Fire"	"Mythic Volcano Spirits: The Origin of Crater Lake"
creation of volcanoes on an island chain	[illegible] volcano creates island, plate movement moves island and a new island starts	Pele tried to get away from her sister	
eruptions	pressure in magma causes magma to erupt as lava	Pele gets mad and sends out lava flows	Monadalkni was angry [illegible] fire
formation of a caldera		Pele's sister digs into the volcano side, eventually collapsing the top	Skell's [illegible] the upper mountain to collapse

1. What similarities do you notice across excerpts?

   Answers may vary.

2. What differences do you notice across excerpts?

   Answers may vary.

NAME:

DATE:

8.2 ACTIVITY PAGE

Earth's Building Blocks

Answer each question thoughtfully, citing the page number(s) where you found evidence for each question. Answer in complete sentences and restate the question in your answer whenever possible.

1. How might rocks differ from each other?

   Answers may vary, but should include one or more of the following: colors, textures, stripes vs. layers, hard vs. crumbly, grain size

   Page(s) 53

2. How does igneous rock form?

   Igneous rock forms when magma cools and solidifies.

   Page(s) 54

3. Which statement distinguishes between the two basic types of igneous rock?
   - A. Two igneous rocks are granite and basalt.
   - B. Different rocks have different size grains and different textures.
   - C. One type forms on Earth's surface and the other forms below Earth's surface.
   - D. The slower the rock cools and hardens, the larger its mineral grains will be.

   Page(s) 54

4. How does sedimentary rock form?

   Sedimentary rock forms when, over time, sediments collect in layers, are bound together by solid minerals, and are compacted and cemented together.

   Page(s) 56

5. How does metamorphic rock form?

   Metamorphic rock forms when igneous or sedimentary rocks (or even older metamorphic rocks) are exposed to extreme heat and pressure.

   Page(s) 58

NAME:

DATE:

8.2 CONTINUED ACTIVITY PAGE

6. What is the rock cycle?
   - A. the continuous process of volcanoes erupting
   - B. the continuous process of change in which rocks are created, destroyed, and recreated
   - C. the continuous process of sedimentary rock changing to become igneous rock
   - D. the continuous process of mineral grains making rocks smooth and shiny

   Page(s) 60

Complete the following items after you have finished reading the chapter. Match the following words with the correct definitions and examples. You may use some words more than once. Try to think of the answer to each item first from memory and then check back in the text to verify your answer before filling in the blank.

minerals	limestone	erosion
sedimentary rock	igneous rock	metamorphic rock

7. **Word:** erosion
   Definition: any process or force that moves sediments to new locations
   Page(s) 60

8. **Word:** igneous rock
   Definition: rock that forms when magma cools and solidifies; the most abundant class of rocks
   Page(s) 54

9. **Word:** minerals
   Definition: the building blocks of rocks that consist of solid, nonliving substances
   Page(s) 53

10. **Word:** limestone
Definition: a type of sedimentary rock that often has many fossils and shells of tiny ocean creatures
Page(s) 56

11. **Word:** metamorphic rock
Definition: a type of rock that forms when either igneous or sedimentary rock is changed due to extreme heat and pressure
Page(s) 58

12. **Word:** sedimentary rock
Definition: a type of rock made of tiny bits of rock and sand mixed with small pieces of things that were once alive
Page(s) 56

13. **Word:** igneous rock
Examples: basalt, granite, and obsidian are examples of this class of rock
Page(s) 54

14. **Word:** metamorphic rock
Examples: serpentine, marble, and gneiss are examples of this class of rock
Page(s) 58

15. **Word:** sedimentary rock
Examples: sandstone, limestone, and mudstone are examples of this class of rock
Page(s) 56

NAME:
DATE:

9.1 CONTINUED TAKE-HOME

Write the correct word or phrase to complete each sentence. Each of the words/phrases will be used once.

compacted	erosion	magma	igneous	metamorphic
obsidian	rock cycle	sedimentary	solidified	texture

1. Lava flowed down the volcano's side and quickly hardened to form a glassy type of igneous rock.
2. Tiny flakes of obsidian fell on the ground as an ancient tool maker worked to create a sharp blade for cutting.
3. The tiny flakes of rock were washed into a nearby stream, where they joined other sediments created by the erosion of rock from the nearby mountains.
4. The sediments formed layers on the stream bed, which compacted over time as the weight of the layers squeezed out the air and water.
5. The sediments cemented together and solidified into rock.
6. Sedimentary rock was buried by even more layers of sediments over millions of years.
7. The heat and pressure from the weight of the overlying rock changed the texture of the minerals in the rock.
8. New metamorphic rock formed and lay buried in the earth for millions of years.

9. Heat from magma below the rock melted it, turning it into igneous rock.
10. As part of its journey through the rock cycle, this piece of rock might someday be found on a beach in Maine or a mountaintop in Tennessee!

NAME:
DATE:

9.2 ACTIVITY PAGE

Commas and Quotation Marks

For each item, insert commas and quotation marks in the appropriate places.

Example: He said my favorite board game is checkers.
He said, "My favorite board game is checkers."

1. Just then, my dad asked, "What would you like to eat for dinner?"
2. I replied, "I would like to have grilled chicken."
3. "I want spaghetti and meatballs," exclaimed my sister.
4. "How about," my mom asked, "we make sandwiches?"
5. "What if we . . ." Dad paused, and then said, "order pizza?"
6. My sister and I both cried, "Yes!" in response.

Read the following passages from Chapter 5 "Mythic Volcano Spirits." Rewrite the sentences marked in bold so they include dialogue. Make sure at least one sentence is rewritten as a split quotation. Be sure to use correct capitalization and punctuation.

Example: Loha refused.
Loha said, "No."

1. *One day Monadalkni spotted the daughter of the Klamath chief, Loha. Monadalkni thought Loha was the most beautiful woman he had ever seen. Immediately he wanted her to be his wife. He came down from the mountaintop and proposed to Loha.* ***He promised her eternal life if she would agree to marry him.*** *Loha refused.*

   Answers may vary.

2. ***She ran to her father and asked for help.*** *The chief of the Klamath people called the tribal elders together. They all agreed that Loha should try to hide from Monadalkni, so she did.*

   Answers may vary.

3. *Monadalkni was very angry when he found out that Loha had refused him yet again. He raged inside his mountain, making it shake and rumble. He threw lightning bolts and spewed fireballs from his mouth. The top of the mountain exploded, which sent hot lava and choking clouds of ash raining down on the land. The Klamath people waded into streams and lakes trying to escape Monadalkni's fiery revenge.* ***They cried out to Sahale Tyee for help.***

   Answers may vary.

NAME: ______

DATE: ______

9.3 ACTIVITY PAGE

Root *rupt*

Write a complete sentence for each of the following words. Be sure to use correct capitalization and punctuation.

1. *erupt*

   Answers may vary.

2. *uninterrupted*

   Answers may vary.

3. *rupture*

   Answers may vary.

Choose the correct word to complete the sentence and write it on the line.

4. The science lesson was ____interrupted____ (erupting, uninterrupted, interrupted, erupted) when the fire alarm went off and we all had to quickly walk outside.

5. They ____disrupted____ (erupted, uninterrupted, disrupted, ruptured) a serious discussion by making jokes and acting silly, causing everyone to lose focus.

6. An ____eruption____ (interruption, interrupt, erupt, eruption) of a geyser releases hot water and steam.

Challenge: Write a complete sentence using two words with the root *rupt*. Be sure to use correct capitalization and punctuation.

Answers may vary, but should include two words with the root *rupt*.

NAME: ______

DATE: ______

9.4 ACTIVITY PAGE

Practice Spelling Words

Write the correct word to complete each sentence. Words will not be used more than once; some words will not be used.

abrupt	autograph	matriarch	paragraph
eruption	archrival	uninterrupted	hierarchy
calligraphy	biographer	rupture	anarchy

1. He left in a(n) ____abrupt____ way without even saying goodbye.

2. My grandma has a(n) ____autograph____ book that includes the signatures of noteworthy actors, sports players, and political figures.

3. A volcanic ____eruption____ can add new land to Earth's surface but can also cause a large amount of destruction.

4. A man from North Carolina won a world record for jumping rope for a(n) ____uninterrupted____ period of time—33 hours straight.

5. The ____biographer____ conducted a series of interviews to collect the information he needed to write a book about the baseball player's life.

6. The tennis player finally defeated his ____archrival____ in a heated match.

7. She wrote a(n) ____paragraph____ focusing on how earthquakes occur.

8. The queen is the ____matriarch____ of her kingdom and government.

NAME: ______________________

DATE: ______________________

11.1 TAKE-HOME

Sequencing Multiple Adjectives

Article	Adjective(s)					Noun
	General → Specific					
	Opinion/ Observation	Physical Description (size, shape, age, color)	Material	Origin	Purpose	

Reorder the words in the sentence so they are ordered correctly. Be sure to use proper capitalization and punctuation.

Example: wears she pretty a green dress
She wears a pretty, green dress

1. the underwater round data little vessel collects
The little, round, underwater vessel collects data.

2. big red a round apple fell
A big, round, red apple fell.

3. we farm old visited a small
We visited a small, old farm.

4. old the erupted Hawaiian tall volcano
The tall, old, Hawaiian volcano erupted.

Write a sentence using at least two adjectives and an article. Be sure to order the words appropriately and to use proper capitalization and punctuation.

Answers may vary, but should include at least two adjectives and an article.

NAME: ______________________

DATE: ______________________

11.2 TAKE-HOME

Review Suffixes *-ly* and *-y* and Roots *graph* and *rupt*

Write the correct word to complete each sentence. Words will not be used more than once.

messy	taste	interrupt	mess
kindly	biography	tasty	busily
abruptly	busy	kind	photograph

1. It was ___kind___ of the stranger to pick up the money I dropped and return it to me.

2. Scientists received warning of a tsunami wave far out in the ocean, so they were ___busily___ working to warn people before it reached land.

3. She didn't want to ___interrupt___ the discussion but it was time for her to leave, so she said they would talk again later.

4. Someone wanted to write a(n) ___biography___ about the geologist, but he declined because he was writing his own life story in an autobiography.

5. My dad and my sister do not like the ___taste___ of tomatoes but my mom and I love it.

6. They had to leave the soccer game ___abruptly___ and seek shelter when an announcement was made of an approaching storm.

7. She ___kindly___ agreed to take care of our dog while we went on vacation.

8. My favorite ___photograph___ from the slideshow was the one that showed the Grand Canyon.

9. The bookshelf at the library was so ___messy___ and disorganized that I couldn't find the book I wanted to check out.

10. Her dinner was very ___tasty___, so she ate it all and even asked for more.

For each word remaining in the word bank, write a sentence using the word.

1. Answers may vary, but should include the word *busy* or *mess*.

2. Answers may vary, but should include the word not used in the previous sentence: *busy* or *mess*.

NAME: ______________________ **11.4** TAKE-HOME
DATE: ______________________

Practice Spelling Words

Write each spelling word under its definition. Then identify the word's part of speech.

epicenter	tsunami	seismograph	glacier	geyser
conclusion	molten	erosion	fault	tectonic

1. an underground hot spring that periodically erupts, shooting hot water and steam into the air
   Spelling Word: geyser
   Part of Speech: noun
2. melted
   Spelling Word: molten
   Part of Speech: adjective
3. any process or force that moves sediments to new locations
   Spelling Word: erosion
   Part of Speech: noun
4. the point on Earth's surface directly above an earthquake's focus
   Spelling Word: epicenter
   Part of Speech: noun
5. relating to the process of plate movement on Earth's surface
   Spelling Word: tectonic
   Part of Speech: adjective
6. a crack in Earth's crust
   Spelling Word: fault
   Part of Speech: noun
7. an instrument used to track seismic waves traveling through the earth
   Spelling Word: seismograph
   Part of Speech: noun
8. an enormous, slow-moving mass of ice found in polar regions or near tops of tall mountains
   Spelling Word: glacier
   Part of Speech: noun
9. a decision or opinion formed based on information you have
   Spelling Word: conclusion
   Part of Speech: noun
10. a gigantic wave of seawater caused by an earthquake in oceanic crust
   Spelling Word: tsunami
   Part of Speech: noun

NAME: ______________________ **12.2** ACTIVITY PAGE
DATE: ______________________

Earth's Mighty Mountains

Answer each question thoughtfully, citing the page number(s) where you found evidence for each question. Answer in complete sentences and restate the question in your answer whenever possible.

	Fold Mountains	Fault-Block Mountains	Dome Mountains
How are they formed?	tectonic plates collide, pressure crumples the crust and the crust rocks pushed upward creating folds	gigantic blocks of rock move up and down along faults	magma pushes upward into Earth's crust, cools into igneous rock, causes a bulge
Page(s)	75	78	80
What are common features or characteristics?	sedimentary rock looks like folds	one steep side with a high cliff and one sloping side	look like bumps of rock with rounded tops, usually located on flat plains
Page(s)	76	78	80
What are some examples and where are they located?	Himalayas between India and China in Asia, Andes Mountains in South America	Harz Mountains in Germany, the Grand Tetons in Wyoming and the Basin and Range Province of Utah, Nevada, and Arizona	Navajo Mountain in Utah, the Black Hills in South Dakota
Page(s)	76, 77	78	80, 83

Use the following word bank to correctly label the map.

Himalayas	Harz Mountains	Black Hills	Andes Mountains
Grand Tetons	Navajo Mountain	Basin and Range Province	

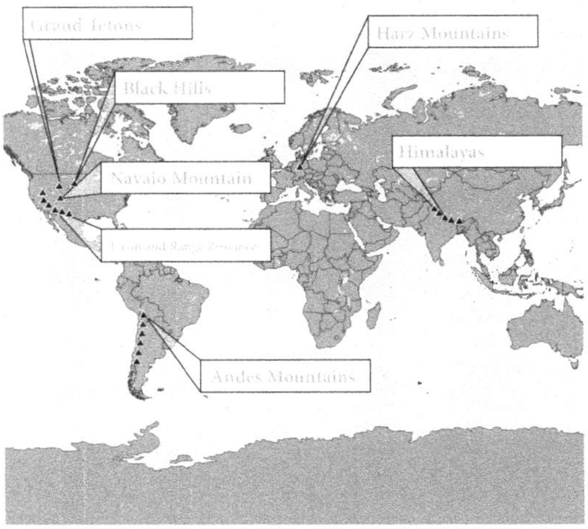

NAME:
DATE:

13.2 CONTINUED — TAKE-HOME

1. What clues tell you that you are close to a vent?

   A plume of black smoke appears.

2. How would you get close enough to observe the vent?

   A robot vehicle would get closer to the vent and take pictures to send back to scientists.

3. What would you discover on the seafloor near the vent?

   One might discover amazing and unusual sea creatures, like giant tube worms, white crabs, football-sized clams, and blind shrimp.

4. Why is it important to conduct your underwater mission?

   Hydrothermal vents are a great place to discover interesting species as well as to gain understanding of the makeup of the earth.

NAME:
DATE:

14.1 ACTIVITY PAGE

Earth's Undersea World

As you and your partner read Chapter 9, "Earth's Undersea World," answer the following questions.

1. Seafloor spreading explains which of the following?
   - A. the presence of mid-ocean ridges on the seafloor
   - B. Wegener's theory of continental drift
   - C. the formation of hydrothermal vents
   - D. All of the above
   - (E.) A and B only

   Page(s) 84–86

2. Which phrase describes the Mid-Atlantic Ridge?
   - A. a warm, dark area on the sea floor
   - (B.) a long, rugged underwater mountain range
   - C. a cluster of seamounts
   - D. a cluster of hydrothermal vents

   Page(s) 83

The following question has two parts. Answer Part A and then answer Part B.

3. **Part A**: Fill in the following chart to indicate which seafloor feature the animals live around, hydrothermal vents or seamounts.

Animals	Where they live
white crabs	hydrothermal vents
brittle stars	seamounts
schools of fish	seamounts
pale, blind shrimp	hydrothermal vents
sponges	seamounts
deep-sea corals	seamounts
giant tube worms	hydrothermal vents
anemones	seamounts
football-sized clams	hydrothermal vents

Page(s) 86, 88

Part B: Why might these animals live near these particular seafloor features?

Answers may vary, but should include: animals may live near these features because of the tiny, single-celled organisms that grow there as a result of the nutrients brought up by seamounts

NAME:
DATE:

14.1 CONTINUED — ACTIVITY PAGE

4. Match each cause to its effect by writing the correct letter for the effect next to the correct cause.

Causes	Effects
c Seamount emerges from the ocean's surface	a. continental drift
d One tectonic plate slides under another	b. seafloor spreading
b Tectonic plates move apart very slowly	c. islands are formed
a Seafloor spreading	d. a trench is formed
f Water seeps into the earth's crust and is heated by magma	e. mountains are formed
e Tectonic plates collide	f. hydrothermal vents are formed

5. On page 84, the author uses a simile when describing the mountain chain formed by mid-ocean ridges, saying it is *like the stitching on a baseball*. Explain what this simile means.

   Answers may vary, but should include that stitching on a baseball goes all around the baseball with no starting point or stopping point, meaning it is continuous. By comparing the mountain chain formed by mid-ocean ridges to stitching on a baseball, the author is saying that the mountain chain goes all over the earth without a starting or stopping point, meaning it is continuous.

NAME:

DATE:

14.2 ACTIVITY PAGE

Sequencing Multiple Adjectives

Complete each sentence by choosing two adjectives from the ones provided and writing them in the correct order in the blanks. Underline the article(s) in each sentence.

Example: **Adjectives:** strong, young, gray, Italian

A strong, gray horse galloped in the field.

1. **Adjectives**: new, Japanese, fast

   The fast, new, Japanese race car zipped around the track.

2. **Adjectives**: hardcover, good, old, science

   She looked at a good, old, hardcover science book about volcanoes.

3. **Adjectives**: canvas, blue, comfortable, walking

   He loves the comfortable blue, canvas, walking shoes he tried on.

1. Answers may vary but correct order is: fast, new, Japanese.
2. Answers may vary but correct order is: good, old, hardcover, science
3. Answer may vary but correct order is: comfortable, blue, canvas, walking

Circle the phrase with the adjectives in the correct order.

Example: a black, large, clever cat

clever, a large black cat

(a clever, large, black cat)

1. the tall, rocky mountain

   the rocky, tall mountain

   rocky, tall, the mountain

2. a sharp, wooden pencil

   wooden, a sharp pencil

   a wooden, sharp, pencil

3. old, an bicycle, orange

   an old, orange bicycle

   an orange, old bicycle

Write a sentence using at least two adjectives. Be sure to order the adjectives correctly and to use proper capitalization and punctuation.

Answers may vary.

NAME:

DATE:

15.2 CONTINUED

Questions

1. What causes earthquakes in Japan every year?
   - A. Namazu, the giant catfish
   - B. weather patterns
   - C. the Richter scale
   - (D.) plate movements

The following question has two parts. Answer Part A and then answer Part B.

2. **Part A**: Using the numbers 1–3, rank the three major earthquakes Japan has experienced in the past hundred years or so in order of strength, numbering the strongest earthquake with the number 1.
   - A. 1923, earthquake badly damaged the cities of Tokyo and Yokohama 2
   - B. 2011, the Great Tohoku earthquake 1
   - C. 1995, earthquake devastated the port city of Kobe 3

   Part B: Why was the earthquake you labeled as the strongest in Part A also the most destructive earthquake?

   It was one of the strongest earthquakes known to hit Japan in recorded history, causing violent shaking and much destruction and because it triggered an enormous tsunami that caused the worst damage, with towering waves crashing ashore and surging far inland.

3. In paragraph 5, what does the word *advanced* mean in the following sentence?

   It has one of the most advanced earthquake early warning systems in the world.

   - A. traditional
   - B. out-of-date
   - (C.) highly developed
   - D. simple

4. How does Japan's earthquake early warning system detect movements in the earth?
   - A. When people feel the earth shake, they tell others around them.
   - (B.) Seismographs across Japan send information about the slightest movements to a central location.
   - C. Scientists wait to see if a tsunami forms off the coast as a result of an earthquake.
   - D. Scientists look for earthquake epicenters on the ocean floor of the coast of Japan.

5. Why did Japan's earthquake early warning system only give 15 seconds of warning to people in the city of Sendai before the 2011 earthquake?

   Earthquakes almost always strike suddenly and happen very quickly. This makes it very difficult to warn people about an earthquake far in advance. Even though Sendai was close to the epicenter, the earthquake early warning system was only able to give people 15 seconds of warning that an earthquake was coming.

NAME: ____________ **15.2** CONTINUED ASSESSMENT

DATE: ____________

6. How is the volcano on the island of Niishima off Japan's coast acting as a creative force?
   - A. The volcano is causing terrible destruction in Japan, just like earthquakes.
   - (B.) The volcano continues to erupt, creating new rock that makes the island bigger.
   - C. The volcano creates new minerals, gases, and seafloor sediments.
   - D. The volcano has stopped erupting.

7. In paragraph 8, the author says that the world's youngest island is a volcanic work in progress. What does *volcanic work in progress* mean?
   - A. The island is getting smaller due to volcanic activity.
   - B. The island is a dangerous place to visit due to volcanic activity.
   - (C.) The island is not done growing due to volcanic activity.
   - D. The island is no longer close to Japan due to volcanic activity.

Informational Text Comprehension Score: ______ / 7 points

To receive a point for a two-part question (i.e., 2) students must correctly answer both parts of the question.

NAME: ____________ **15.2** CONTINUED ASSESSMENT

DATE: ____________

Questions

8. What does the word *tremble* mean in the following sentence from paragraph 2?

   > The myths tell of times when these animals moved or fought, making the earth tremble.

   - A. remain still
   - B. be afraid
   - (C.) shake
   - D. sink

The following question has two parts. Answer Part A and then answer Part B.

9. **Part A**: In paragraph 7, the author says the turtle was true to his word. What does this mean about the turtle?
   - A. The turtle swam away and never returned.
   - (B.) The turtle did what he said he would do.
   - C. The turtle told the truth to the Great Spirit.
   - D. The turtle didn't listen to the Great Spirit.

   Part B: How was the turtle true to his word?

   He was true to his word by bringing several other turtles to the Great Spirit, which is what he said he would do.

10. Why did the Great Spirit tell the turtles not to move?
    - (A.) If the turtles moved, they would destroy the land the Great Spirit created.
    - B. If the turtles moved, they would get angry.
    - C. If the turtles moved, their legs would get stiff and their minds would get bored.
    - D. If the turtles moved, they would help the Great Spirit create land.

The following question has two parts. Answer Part A and then answer Part B.

11. **Part A**: Why did the turtles get angry?
    - A. Their legs got stiff and their minds got bored.
    - B. The Great Spirit told them not to move.
    - C. They wanted to swim.
    - (D.) They couldn't agree on which direction to go.

    Part B: What happened when they got angry?

    Some swam in one direction and the rest in another, causing the land on their backs to rumble and shake and make big cracks appear in the soil.

12. What causes earthquakes according to this Gabrielino Indian myth?
    - A. The Great Spirit creates land on turtle shells.
    - (B.) The turtles start moving in different directions.
    - C. The Great Spirit tells the turtles not to move.
    - D. The turtles agree on which direction to swim in.

NAME: ____________ **15.2** CONTINUED ASSESSMENT

DATE: ____________

13. In the Hoh myth, why does Thunderbird grab Whale out of the water?
    - A. Whale provided food and oil for the Hoh people.
    - B. Whale got along well with the other whales in the ocean, which helped the Hoh people.
    - (C.) The Hoh people were suffering because Whale was destroying the other whales they depended on.
    - D. Thunderbird wanted Whale to live on land instead of in the ocean to help the Hoh people.

14. What caused earthquakes according to this Hoh myth?
    - A. Thunderbird grabbed Whale and yanked him out of the water.
    - B. Thunderbird stayed high in her mountaintop nest while Whale stayed in the ocean.
    - C. Whale grabbed Thunderbird and yanked her into the water.
    - (D.) Whale and Thunderbird fought as Thunderbird tried to keep her claws gripped around Whale.

Literary Text Comprehension Score: ______ /7 points

To receive a point for a two-part question (i.e., 9 and 11) students must correctly answer both parts of the question.

Reading Comprehension total______ /14 points

NAME: ______________________________

DATE: ______________________________

15.2 CONTINUED

Grammar

For each item, insert a comma or commas in the appropriate location(s). When applicable, insert quotation marks in the appropriate locations.

1. The first expedition to the bottom of the Mariana Trench took place on January 23 1960.

2. The text states Earth's tectonic plates have been slowly moving and interacting for billions of years.

3. Mount Rushmore National Memorial
   13000 S Dakota 244
   Keystone SD 57751

4. What if wondered Wegener continents were like enormous pieces of ice?

5. Geologists found fossils of an ancient fern in similar rock layers in Africa India Australia and South America.

Circle the phrase with the adjectives in the correct order.

6. old, large, Hawaiian, a volcano

   a large, old, Hawaiian volcano

   a Hawaiian, old, large volcano

7. smooth, shiny the obsidian rock

   the smooth, shiny, obsidian rock

   the smooth rock, shiny obsidian

8. a powerful, giant tsunami

   powerful, giant a tsunami

   tsunami a giant, powerful

Grammar Score: ______ /8 points

NAME: ______________________________

DATE: ______________________________

15.2 CONTINUED

Morphology

Write the correct word to complete each sentence.

1. An earthquake can seem to happen ____abruptly____ (loudly, carefully, abruptly, accidentally), but it actually happens because pressure has been building up for some time.

2. A volcanic ____eruption____ (rupture, eruption, disruption, interruption) can be calm and quiet or sudden and violent.

3. Tsunamis can be very ____speedy____ (tasty, easy, temporary, speedy), moving up to 500 miles per hour.

4. It would be interesting to read a(n) ____biography____ (photograph, biography, rupture, eruption) about Alfred Wegener.

5. A mid-ocean ridge can form along a huge ____rupture____ (photograph, biography, rupture, eruption), or crack, in Earth's crust.

6. Scientists make conclusions after ____carefully____ (careful, carefully, busily, busy) examining evidence.

Morphology Score: ______ /6 points

NAME: ______________________________

DATE: ______________________________

PP.1

Mid-Unit Content Assessment

1. The study of the makeup of the earth and the processes that change and shape it is called ______________.
   A. archaeology
   B. geology
   C. ecology
   D. geography

2. Which statement best explains the theory of plate tectonics?
   A. Earth's tectonic plates have been slowly moving and interacting for billions of years.
   B. Earth's tectonic plates are far apart and are fixed in place.
   C. Earth's tectonic plates are far apart but are slowly moving closer to one another.
   D. Earth's tectonic plates fit tightly together and are fixed in place.

3. Which of the following is the most accurate statement about myths?
   A. Myths are told to teach important life lessons.
   B. Myths help explain unpredictable natural events.
   C. Myths are told to make children laugh.
   D. Myths are historically accurate accounts of past events.

This question has two parts. Answer Part A and then answer Part B.

4. **Part A**: Place the following labels on the diagram in the appropriate locations: *inner core, outer core, mantle,* and *crust.*

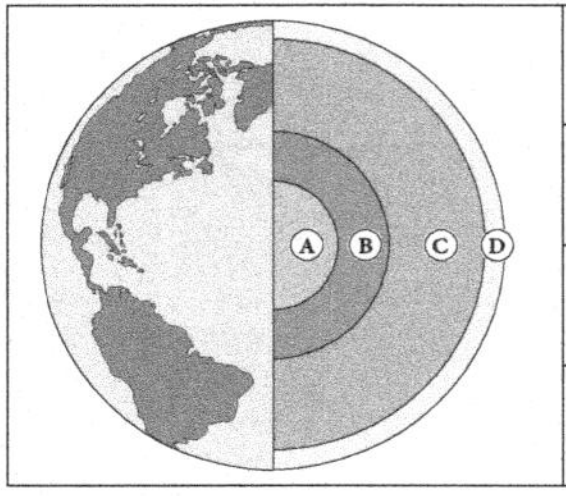

	A. inner core
	B. outer core
	C. mantle
	D. crust

Part B: Write the name of each of Earth's layers next to its characteristics in the following chart.

inner core	outer core	mantle	crust

Earth's Layer	Characteristics
mantle	Earth's largest and thickest layer; consists of very hot, very dense rock
inner core	solid; made of very hot metal; may be nearly as hot as the sun's surface; innermost layer
crust	thin; rocky; outermost layer; two types: oceanic and continental
outer core	liquid; made of very hot metal

NAME: ______________________

DATE: ______________________

PP.1 CONTINUED ASSESSMENT

5. Place a check mark next to each item in the chart that is a characteristic of tsunamis.

Characteristics of Tsunamis	Yes or No?
Tsunamis form when earthquakes occur in oceanic crust, causing the seafloor to shift.	✓
Tsunamis travel fast—as much as 500 miles per hour.	✓
Tsunamis are easy to stop as long as scientists have enough warning when they begin to form.	
Tsunamis can grow to become as tall as a three- or four-story building.	✓

6. Read the statement in the "What is the cause?" column. Choose the statement that best relates to the information in the "What is the cause?" column and write the letter of the statement in the "What evidence is there?" column.

What is the cause?	What evidence is there?
Tremendous pressure and heat in the mantle force magma in a chamber below Earth's crust to move upward through a crack in Earth's surface.	C

A. A fault-block mountain forms.
B. Glaciers deposit sediments on Earth's surface.
C. Magma erupts from a volcano's top onto Earth's surface as lava.
D. A tectonic plate subducts beneath another plate.

7. Volcano myths often explain volcanic activity by ______________.
(A.) describing how gods and goddesses cause volcano-related occurrences
B. providing scientific evidence showing how volcano-related events occur
C. telling how occurrences above Earth's surface cause volcanic activity
D. telling how occurrences below Earth's surface cause volcanic activity

8. Label each of the following volcano descriptions with the appropriate word: *active, dormant,* or *extinct.*
A. extinct a volcano that has not erupted for at least 10,000 years and is not likely to erupt again
B. active a volcano that has erupted in the past 10,000 years and is likely to erupt again
C. dormant a volcano that hasn't erupted for a long time but could erupt again

9. Which of the statements best explains the relationship between earthquakes and faults?
A. Earthquakes cause faults to form along plate boundaries.
B. Faults are cracks in Earth's crust that form when earthquakes occur.
C. *Faults* and *earthquakes* are two words to describe the same geological process.
(D.) Earthquakes begin with huge blocks of rock moving along faults.

10. Place a check mark next to each item in the chart that Alfred Wegener's continental drift hypothesis helped explain.

Continental drift hypothesis explained that…	Yes or No?
long ago, Earth had one huge landmass called Pangaea	✓
as continents moved apart, their climates changed	✓
drifting continents actually moved due to tectonic plates	
groups of plants and animals that once lived together were separated as the continents moved apart	✓

NAME: ______________________

DATE: ______________________

PP.1 CONTINUED ASSESSMENT

11. Read the statement in the "What is the cause?" column. Choose the statement that best relates to the information in the "What is the cause?" column and write the letter of the statement in the "What evidence is there?" column.

What is the cause?	What evidence is there?
Water drains down into openings in the ground above a magma chamber. Heat from the magma turns the water scalding hot. As the hot water rises back up through the openings below Earth's surface, it turns into steam, which increases the pressure, forcing the mixture of steam and hot water rushing and bubbling upward.	B

A. A tsunami forms and grows as it moves toward land.
B. A geyser explodes above Earth's surface as a hissing fountain of hot water and steam.
C. An igneous rock breaks down into sediments, later forming sedimentary rock.
D. A crater forms at the top of a volcano.

12. Which of the following word pairs completes the statements?

> Seafloor spreading is the process of oceanic plates moving apart very slowly. When the seafloor dips down as one tectonic plate slides under another, a narrow, extremely deep valley called a(n) ______________ is created. When oceanic plates move away from one another and form cracks in Earth's crust, an underwater mountain called a(n) ______________ is created.

A. geyser; hotspot
B. hotspot; geyser
(C.) ocean trench; mid-ocean ridge
D. mid-ocean ridge; ocean trench

13. Moving apart, colliding, and sliding sideways past one another are three ways in which __________________ move.
   A. continents
   B. tectonic plates
   C. faults
   D. mid-ocean ridges

14. Label the following statements with the appropriate term related to how scientists measure earthquake intensity: *seismograph* or *Richter scale*.
   A. Richter scale Numbers describe the intensity of earthquakes based on the largest seismic wave recorded.
   B. seismograph Jagged up-and-down lines show the energy of seismic waves.

15. Scientists observed that __________________, which provided evidence of changes over time on Earth's surface.
   A. land never moved or changed
   B. the same types of rocks and fossils were found in different places
   C. the climate of Antarctica was extremely cold
   D. animals that once lived on land later lived under water

16. Which of the following do geysers, volcanoes, and hot springs have in common?
   A. They form along faults.
   B. Scientists know when they will erupt.
   C. They form both along plate boundaries and above hotspots.
   D. They only form along plate boundaries.

______ */16 points*

NAME: ______________________

DATE: ______________________

PP.2 ASSESSMENT

End-of-Unit Content Assessment

1. Geysers, volcanoes, and hot springs all share which of the following?
   A. They form along faults.
   B. Scientists can predict when they will erupt.
   C. They form both along plate boundaries and above hotspots.
   D. They form only along plate boundaries.

2. In which of the following sentences is *conclusion* used correctly?
   A. Inge Lehmann suspected that Earth might have more than three layers, so she came to the conclusion that it did.
   B. In his conclusion, the scientist proposed different possibilities of how earthquakes might occur.
   C. The researcher reached a conclusion after years of collecting evidence.
   D. Once you reach a conclusion, it is set in stone and no other evidence can be examined.

3. Label each of the following rock descriptions with the appropriate word: *igneous*, *metamorphic*, or *sedimentary*.
   sedimentary a rock that is made of sediments that have been naturally compacted and cemented together
   igneous a rock that forms when magma cools and solidifies
   metamorphic a rock that forms when minerals in other types of rocks are altered due to extreme heat and pressure

4. What is geology?
   A. the study of relationships between living things and their environment
   B. the study of the makeup of the earth and the processes that change and shape it
   C. the study of the characteristics of the earth's surface
   D. the study of past human life and activities by examining bones, tools, and other objects left behind

5. The theory of plate tectonics states that __________________.
   A. Earth's continents were once all joined together as one supercontinent
   B. Earth's continents stay still and do not move
   C. Earth's crust, mantle, and core all form tectonic plates that change very slowly
   D. Earth's crust and part of the mantle are broken up into sections that slowly move

6. Label each of the following descriptions with the appropriate term: *physical weathering*, *chemical weathering*, or *erosion*.
   erosion a process that moves sediments to new locations
   physical weathering a process that breaks big rocks into smaller rocks without changing the minerals they contain
   chemical weathering a process that breaks down rocks by changing the minerals they contain

Match the item from the column on the left with the description on the right. Write the letter on the line.

7. c tsunami	a. a deep-sea geyser that forms as seawater sinks down through cracks in the oceanic crust and then releases extremely hot, mineral-rich water back up through cracks in the crust
8. a hydrothermal vent	b. an underwater volcano that forms wherever magma is erupting through oceanic crust
9. b seamount	c. a gigantic wave of seawater caused by an earthquake in oceanic crust

10. A mid-ocean ridge is ______________; an ocean trench is ______________.
   A. an underwater mountain; a narrow, extremely deep valley
   B. a deep-sea geyser; an underwater volcano
   C. a geyser; an underwater mountain
   D. a narrow, extremely deep valley; a deep-sea geyser

NAME: ______________________

DATE: ______________________

PP.2 CONTINUED ASSESSMENT

11. Seafloor spreading can cause a mid-ocean ridge and an ocean trench to form. Label each of the following causes with the appropriate effect: *mid-ocean ridge* or *ocean trench*.
   A. The seafloor dips down as one tectonic plate slides under another. ocean trench
   B. Magma erupts through huge cracks in Earth's crust as lava. mid-ocean ridge

12. Circle the answer that best supports the following statement.

   The rock cycle explains the changes that occur in rocks over very long periods of time.

   A. Rocks are created and then destroyed in a long process that occurs slowly over time.
   B. Rocks are created, destroyed, and recreated in a continuous cycle.
   C. Weathering and erosion change rocks in a long process that occurs slowly over time.
   D. Rocks are solidified from sediments in a continuous cycle.

13. Fill in the "Type of Volcano" column in the chart with the appropriate type being described: *active volcano*, *dormant volcano*, or *extinct volcano*.

Type of Volcano	Description
extinct volcano	a type of volcano that has not erupted for at least 10,000 years and is not likely to erupt again
active volcano	a type of volcano that has erupted in the past 10,000 years and is likely to erupt again
dormant volcano	a type of volcano that is considered active but hasn't erupted for a very long time

14. What evidence suggested that the continents' locations were once very different than they are today?
    A. the same types of rocks and fossils were discovered in different parts of the world
    B. maps from long ago showed that the continents were once closer together
    C. ancient records were found describing the climate of Antarctica as being warm
    D. Alfred Wegener introduced the continental drift hypothesis

15. Moving apart, colliding, and sliding sideways past one another are the three different ways in which __________ interact.
    A. faults
    B. mid-ocean ridges
    C. continents
    D. tectonic plates

16. The continental drift hypothesis explains that __________.
    A. all the continents exist on plates
    B. all of the continents were once joined as Pangaea until they broke apart and slowly moved away from each other
    C. hot water under the earth explodes on the surface
    D. climates change and animals evolve over long periods of time

NAME: __________ **PP.2** ASSESSMENT
DATE: __________ CONTINUED

17. Which of the words in the following sentence provides the best clue as to the meaning of the word *fossil*?

    Geologists found fossils of an ancient fern in similar rock layers in Africa, India, Australia, and South America.

    A. geologists found
    B. similar rock layers
    C. in Africa, India, Australia, and South America
    D. ancient fern

18. Weathering is the process in which __________; erosion is the process in which __________.
    A. rocks are mixed with liquid and completely broken down; rocks are packed together tightly
    B. rocks are broken down into smaller pieces; sediments are moved from place to place
    C. sediments are moved from place to place; rocks are broken down into smaller pieces
    D. large amounts of rocks move down the side of a mountain; rocks are broken down and the minerals they contain change

Match the item from the column on the left with the description on the right. Write the letter on the line.

19. d geyser	a. a hill or mountain that forms over a crack in Earth's crust from which lava erupts
20. e hotspot	b. a crack in Earth's crust
21. b fault	c. the violent shaking of the ground caused by huge blocks of rock moving along a fault
22. f rock	d. an underground hot spring that periodically erupts, shooting hot water and steam into the air
23. a volcano	e. a very hot region deep within Earth's mantle where a huge magma chamber forms
24. c earthquake	f. a naturally occurring nonliving solid made of minerals

NAME: __________ **PP.2** ASSESSMENT
DATE: __________ CONTINUED

25. Read the description and examples in each row and write the correct letter in the "Type of Mountain" column.
    A. fold mountains
    B. fault-block mountains
    C. dome mountains

Type of Mountain	Description	Examples
A	mountains formed when rocks are pushed up into huge folds by moving tectonic plates; often contain quite a bit of sedimentary rock	Himalayas between India and China; Alps in Europe; Appalachians of North America; Urals in Russia
C	mountains generally formed when magma pushes upward into Earth's crust from the mantle and cools into igneous rock underground, causing the crust above it to bulge; usually occur as isolated mountains on otherwise flat plains	Utah's Navajo Mountain; Black Hills of South Dakota
B	mountains formed when gigantic blocks of rock move up and down along faults	Germany's Harz Mountains; Grand Tetons in Wyoming; Basin and Range Province of Utah, Nevada, and Arizona

26. What natural occurrence does the following myth passage explain?

> The Chief of the Above World came to the aid of his people. He fought Monadalkni and the two spirits waged a violent, fiery battle. Sahale Tyee eventually gained the upper hand and forced Monadalkni back down into his mountain. Sahale Tyee caused the top of the mountain to collapse, forever shutting off this entrance to the Below World.

A. an earthquake
B. a volcanic crater being formed
C. a tsunami
D. a volcanic eruption

27. The ________________ produces lines to show the energy of seismic waves while the ________________ applies numbers to measure the magnitude of an earthquake based on the largest seismic wave recorded.

A. Modified Mercalli Intensity Scale; seismograph
B. seismograph; Richter scale
C. Modified Mercalli Intensity Scale; Richter scale
D. Richter scale; seismograph

NAME: ______________________

DATE: ______________________

PP.2 CONTINUED

28. Place the following labels on the diagram in the appropriate locations: *inner core, outer core, mantle*, and *crust*.

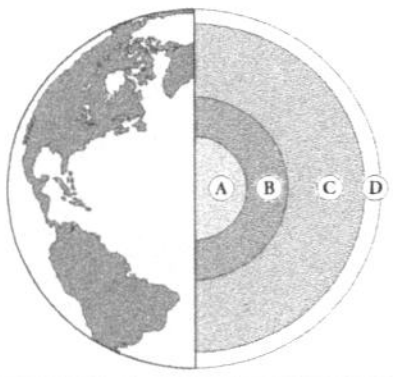

A.	inner core
B.	outer core
C.	mantle
D.	crust

29. Select the most appropriate answer to the following question.

> What do myths help explain?

A. everyday occurrences
B. unpredictable natural events
C. cultural customs
D. why people tell stories

30. Which of the following provides evidence of weathering and erosion?

A. Volcanoes like Mount Fuji
B. Geysers like Old Faithful in Yellowstone
C. Island chains like the Hawaiian Island chain
D. Large canyons like the Grand Canyon

_______ */30 points*

NAME: ______________________

DATE: ______________________

PP.3 ACTIVITY PAGE

Commas

For each item, insert a comma or commas in the appropriate location(s).

Examples: I flew to Santa Fe New Mexico on my first plane ride.
I flew to Santa Fe, New Mexico on my first plane ride.

He couldn't choose between vanilla chocolate or peach ice cream.
He couldn't choose between vanilla, chocolate, or peach ice cream.

The Olympic Games in Rio de Janeiro will begin on August 5 2016.
The Olympic Games in Rio de Janeiro will begin on August 5, 2016.

1. The three types of rocks are igneous sedimentary and metamorphic.

2. Willis Tower
233 S Wacker Drive
Chicago IL 60606

3. Edmund Hillary and Tenzing Norgay reached the top of Mount Everest on May 29 1953.

4. We visited New Orleans Louisiana on our trip.

5. My favorite fruits are apples peaches and blackberries.

6. One of the worst earthquakes in American history took place in San Francisco on April 18 1906.

7. On February 17 1977, scientists located a hydrothermal vent along a mid-ocean ridge for the first time.

8. Mount Rushmore National Memorial is located in Keystone South Dakota.

9. We learned about fold mountains fault-block mountains and dome mountains.

Write sentences for each of the following items. Be sure to use correct capitalization and punctuation. Each sentence should include at least one comma in its appropriate location.

1. a date
Answers may vary

2. a location
Answers may vary

3. items in a series
Answers may vary

NAME: ___

DATE: ___

PP.4 ACTIVITY PAGE

Commas and Quotation Marks

For each item, insert commas and quotation marks in the appropriate locations.

Example: She told me I'll be back by 5pm before she left.

She told me, "I'll be back by 5pm," before she left.

1. The text states, "The discovery of seafloor spreading at mid-ocean ridges was a turning point in geology."
2. "I wonder," he said, "if we'll get to play outside today."
3. "You're out!" shouted the umpire to the baseball player.
4. "What do you think," she asked, "about seeing a movie this weekend?"
5. "A volcano," according to the text, "is a hill or mountain that forms over a crack in Earth's crust from which lava erupts."
6. They asked, "Do you need anything from the grocery store?"
7. "Mountains," says the author, "are some of Earth's most magnificent features."
8. We both said, "Chocolate!" at the same time when asked what kind of ice cream we wanted.

Read the following passage from Chapter 5, "Mythic Volcano Spirits." Rewrite the sentences marked in bold so they include dialogue. Be sure to use correct capitalization and punctuation.

> ***Pele was pleased with her new home. She sent Hi'iaka to fetch her husband-to-be from Kauai. She told her little sister to be back in less than 40 days. She also warned Hi'iaka not to fall in love with Lohi'au herself. In turn, Hi'iaka made Pele promise to protect a grove of beautiful trees that grew on Kilauea.*** *Hi'iaka adored the trees. She was afraid that if Pele lost her temper, she would send out rivers of lava to burn them down.*

Answers may vary.

NAME: ___

DATE: ___

PP.5 ACTIVITY PAGE

Sequencing Adjectives

Complete each sentence by choosing two adjectives from the ones provided and writing them in the correct order in the blanks.

Example: Adjectives: wooden, big, play, fun

We stay in the **big**, **wooden** cabin during the summer.

1. **Adjectives:** office, brick, new, tall

   We climbed up the stairs of the tall, new, brick, office building.

2. **Adjectives:** American, long, huge, crowded

   We boarded a crowded, huge, long, American airplane.

3. **Adjectives:** enormous, Italian, attractive, ancient

   It was an attractive, enormous, ancient, Italian city.

1. Answers may vary but correct order is: tall, new, brick, office.

2. Answers may vary but correct order is: crowded, huge, long, American.

3. Answer may vary but correct order is: attractive, enormous, ancient, Italian.

Circle the phrase with the adjectives in the correct order.

Example: a purple, new, umbrella

(a new, purple umbrella)

new, a purple umbrella

1. (the fluffy, little, German dog)

   little, the German fluffy dog

   the German, little, fluffy dog

2. a blue, long fishing boat

   (a long, blue, fishing boat)

   a fishing, long, blue boat

3. an oval, ordinary desk

   ordinary, an oval desk

   (an ordinary, oval desk)

Write a sentence using at least two adjectives and an article. Be sure to order the words appropriately and to use proper capitalization and punctuation.

Answers may vary.

NAME: ______________________

DATE: ______________________

PP.6 ACTIVITY PAGE

–ly: Suffix Meaning "in a _____ way"

Write the correct word to complete each sentence.

1. She did not mean to forget her homework; it was purely ___accidental___ that she forgot.
   (accidental, accidentally, careful, carefully)
2. Mountain building is not a ___speedy___ process; it takes many years for mountains to form.
   (speedy, speedily, loud, loudly)
3. My cat only weighs 7 pounds, so I can ___easily___ pick him up and carry him around with me.
   (temporary, temporarily, easy, easily)

Write the correct word to complete each sentence.

easy	easily	careful	carefully
speedy	speedily	loud	loudly

4. In looking at a world map, it's pretty ___easy___ to see how the eastern edge of South America fits into the western edge of Africa like pieces of a puzzle.
5. He ___loudly___ walked across the room thanks to his squeaky shoes.
6. Seismic waves move more slowly through liquids and more ___speedily___ through solids.

Write a sentence using one of the words left in the box.

Answers may vary, but should include one of the following words: *easily, careful, carefully, speedy, or loud.*

Write a sentence using one of your own –ly *words.*

Answers may vary but should include a work with *–ly.*

Write a sentence using one of the root words and the same root word with –ly *added to the end.*

Answers may vary but should include a root word and that word with –ly added to it.

NAME: ______________________

DATE: ______________________

PP.7 ACTIVITY PAGE

Root *rupt*

Write the correct word to complete each sentence.

uninterrupted	erupt	disrupt
rupture	abrupt	eruption

1. If a nearby volcano begins to ___erupt___, people who live around the Bay of Naples are encouraged to evacuate.
2. It was clear my brother was studying for an assessment, so I tried not to ___disrupt___ his concentration.
3. A seamount does not become an island in a(n) ___abrupt___ way; it is a long, slow process.

Write the correct word to complete each sentence.

4. The classroom ___erupted___ in laughter as a student read a funny story.
   (erupted, disrupted)
5. Mid-ocean ridges form an almost ___uninterrupted___ chain of underwater mountains around the earth.
   (abrupt, uninterrupted)
6. My father had to go to the hospital because of a ___rupture___ in a blood vessel.
   (rupture, eruption)

Write a complete sentence for each of the following words. Make sure to use correct capitalization and punctuation.

1. *erupt*
   Answers may vary.
2. *eruption*
   Answers may vary.
3. *abrupt*
   Answers may vary.
4. *disrupt*
   Answers may vary.
5. *uninterrupted*
   Answers may vary.
6. *rupture*
   Answers may vary.

NAME: ______________________
DATE: ______________________

PP.8 ACTIVITY PAGE

Suffixes –*ly* and –*y* and Roots *graph* and *rupt*

Write the correct word to complete each sentence. Words will not be used more than once. Some words will not be used.

messy	taste	interrupt	mess
kindly	biography	tasty	busily
abruptly	busy	kind	photograph

1. The meal my grandfather prepared for us was very ___tasty___.
2. I'm sorry to ___interrupt___ you while you are writing, but I have a question.
3. It's helpful to see a(n) ___photograph___ of each of the different types of mountains to compare them.
4. Our dog is a(n) ___messy___ eater and always gets his food all over the floor.
5. We had guests coming over for dinner, so we ___busily___ cleaned our rooms that afternoon before they arrived.
6. The group members had to ___abruptly___ stop working on the project when the building started shaking due to an earthquake.
7. Would you ___kindly___ hand me the biography of Edmund Hillary?
8. It was ___kind___ of them to send me a birthday card.

Write a complete sentence for each of the following words. Be sure to use correct capitalization and punctuation.

1. *interrupt*
   Answers may vary.
2. *messy*
   Answers may vary.
3. *busily*
   Answers may vary.
4. *abruptly*
   Answers may vary.
5. *biography*
   Answers may vary.

NAME: ______________________
DATE: ______________________

E1.1 ACTIVITY PAGE

The Rock Towns of Cappadocia

Word(s) from the Chapter	Pronunciation	Page
Cappadocia	/kap*ə*doe*shə/	90
Mount Erciyes	/mount/ /er*sie*əs/	92
Rapa Nui	/ro*po/ /noo*ee/	98
moai	/moe*wie/	98

As you read the enrichment selection, "The Rock Towns of Cappadocia," answer the following questions using complete sentences.

1. How are most hoodoos formed?
   Hoodoos are formed when wind and water slowly carve tuff into ridges, mounds, and sharp pinnacles.
2. Why wasn't it difficult for people to create caves and rock houses in Cappadocia's rock formations?
   Before it is exposed to air, tuff is very soft. Once people scraped away the hard outer surface, they had only to cut away the soft tuff underneath.
3. Why did early Christians settle in Cappadocia?
   Christians were religious refugees, and wanted to settle in a place that was isolated so they could practice their religion safely and in peace.
4. What features might you find in the rock dwellings in Cappadocia?
   Answers may vary, but should include: rooms for eating and sleeping, animal stables, food storage areas, staircases, towers with windows, ventilation systems, and monasteries.
5. Why do you think people wanted to live in these rock dwellings? What were some of the advantages of these unique houses?
   Answers may vary, but should explain that these dwellings provided protection from invaders and the environment. They were easy to make and lasted a long time.

The following question has two parts. Answer Part A first and then answer Part B.

6. **Part A**: What are the moai?
   Moai are huge statues that are partial human figures with large heads, high cheekbones, and heavy brows. The Rapa Nui people carved them on Easter Island out of tuff.

   Part B: How did the Rapa Nui move them once they were finished?
   No one is sure how the Rapa Nui people moved them because many weighed over 80 tons.

NAME: ________________________ **E2.1** ACTIVITY PAGE

DATE: ________________________

Violent Vesuvius

Word(s) from the Chapter	Pronunciation	Page
Pliny	/plin*ee/	102
Misenum	/mis*en*um/	103

As you read the enrichment selection, "Violent Vesuvius," answer the following questions using complete sentences.

1. Why do scientists monitor Vesuvius so closely?

   Scientists monitor Vesuvius so closely because it has been one of Europe's most active volcanoes.

   Page(s) 100

2. What are some signs that might indicate Vesuvius is on the verge of erupting?

   The slightest movement or any unusual shaking, as well as changes in the hot gases from the crater can indicate Vesuvius is on the verge of erupting.

   Page(s) 100

3. Complete the following chart.

Geological Term	Definition
eruption column	an enormous cloud of ash, bits of rock, and toxic gas that shoots skyward from an erupting volcano at hundreds of feet per second
Plinian eruption	an eruption during which the top of the eruption column spreads outward
pyroclastic flow	a sort of avalanche of intensely hot ash, rock fragments, and volcanic gas that rolls down the side of a volcano

   Page(s) 107, 109

4. How do we know so much about the eruption of Vesuvius in 79 CE?

   We know about the 79 CE eruption of Vesuvius because a Roman named Pliny lived through the disaster and wrote about it in a letter

   Page(s) 102

NAME: ________________________ **E3.1** ACTIVITY PAGE

DATE: ________________________

A Deep-Sea Detective Story

Word(s) from the Chapter	Pronunciation	Page
Galapagos	/gə*lop*ə*goes/	113

As you read the enrichment selection, "A Deep-Sea Detective Story," answer the following questions using complete sentences.

1. Name two discoveries that changed how people thought about geology.

   The discovery of seafloor spreading and the discovery of mid-ocean ridges changed how scientists thought about continents and their movement

   Page(s) 110

2. What are some clues scientists look for when searching for hydrothermal vents?

   Heat deep in the ocean and brightly colored rocks are both clues that scientists look for, as they indicate a nearby hydrothermal vent.

   Page(s) 111

3. Why do unique animals live near hydrothermal vents but not on most other areas of the deep seafloor?

   The animals survive thanks to bacteria. Vents are home to unusual types of bacteria that use chemicals in hot vent water – instead of sunlight – to make food. Some vent animals eat the bacteria directly. Others eat the bacteria-eaters.

   Page(s) 117

4. Why do you think this chapter is titled "A Deep-Sea Detective Story?"

   Answers may vary, but should explain that a detective uses clues to solve a mystery, which is what scientists were doing; they used evidence to search for new undersea discoveries.

   Page(s) Answers may vary.

NAME:

DATE:

A.3 ASSESSMENT

Middle-of-Year Grammar Assessment

Read and answer each question. Some of the questions have two parts. You should answer Part A of the question before you answer Part B.

1. **Part A:** In the two sentences below, write *n.* above the nouns and *adj.* above the adjectives.

   Part B: Draw an arrow from each adjective to the noun it describes.

   Example: Dana imagined a faraway land where grumpy trolls lived.

   (n.: Dana; adj.: faraway → n.: land; adj.: grumpy → n.: trolls)

   Heavy rain led to a major flood in the valley.

   (adj.: Heavy → n.: rain; adj.: major → n.: flood; n.: valley)

   For the first part of the long trip, Hildy stared out the window at the spotted cows.

   (adj.: first → n.: part; adj.: long → n.: trip; n.: window; adj.: spotted → n.: cows)

2. **Part A:** In the two sentences below, write n. above the nouns and adj. above the adjectives.

   Part B: underline the letters that should be capital letters.

   In october, percy traveled to hooterville to visit his youngest daughter.

   (n.: october, percy, hooterville; adj.: youngest; n.: daughter; underlined: o, p, h)

   I know that jeremy lived on the shady side of morgan avenue.

   (n.: jeremy; adj.: shady; n.: side, morgan, avenue; underlined: j, m, a)

3. Change the adjective in parentheses into an adverb and identify the verb it describes.

   Miranda laughed (loud) at her uncle's joke.

   Adverb: loudly

   The adverb describes the verb: laughed

4. Write a sentence using the verb and adverb provided.

   verb: wrote adverb: carefully

   Answers will vary.

5. **Part A:** Write adv. above the adverbs in the sentences provided. Then draw an arrow from the adverb to the verb it describes.

   Part B: Underline the subject and and draw a squiggly line under the predicate in the sentences provided.

   Matt and his goat ran happily through the fields of Brooklyn.

   (adv.: happily → ran)

   The old miner excitedly told stories about settling in California before it was a state.

   (adv.: excitedly → told)

NAME:

DATE:

A.3 CONTINUED ASSESSMENT

6. **Part A:** Indicate whether each sentence fragment provided is a subject or predicate.

   Part B: Correct the sentence fragment by rewriting it as a complete sentence.

   Example:

   Fragment: The otter in the stream

   The fragment is a: (subject) predicate

   Corrected Sentence: The otter in the stream climbed onto our raft.

   A. Fragment: slept late on Sunday

   The fragment is a: subject (predicate)

   Corrected Sentence: Answers will vary.

   B. Fragment: Mr. Lumbly's science class

   The fragment is a: (subject) predicate

   Corrected Sentence: Answers will vary.

7. Rewrite each of the following run-on sentences as two complete sentences.

   Meredith always looked forward to math class it was her favorite subject.

   Meredith always looked forward to math class. It was her favorite subject.

   Andrew grew three inches while he was away at summer camp his school friends were surprised at how tall he was.

   Andrew grew three inches while he was away at summer camp. His school friends were surprised at how tall he was.

8. **Part A:** Punctuate the following sentences. The sentence type of each is provided.

   A. Declarative: I prefer apple juice to prune juice.

   B. Interrogative: What time does the assembly start?

   C. Imperative: Please stand closer together.

   D. Exclamatory: I got a kitten for my birthday

NAME: ______________________ **A.3** CONTINUED
DATE: ______________________

9. Circle the sentence type of each of the following sentences.
   A. The temperature today is one degree warmer than yesterday.
   (declarative) interrogative imperative exclamatory
   B. I hate getting sand in my bathing suit!
   declarative interrogative imperative (exclamatory)
   C. What is your middle name?
   declarative (interrogative) imperative exclamatory
   D. Call me first thing tomorrow morning.
   declarative interrogative (imperative) exclamatory

10. Insert a comma or commas in the correct location(s) in the following sentences.
   A. Belinda's three favorite sports are bowling, volleyball and golf.
   B. The Empire State Building
   350 5th Avenue
   New York NY 10118
   C. Neil Armstrong walked on the moon on July 24 1969.
   D. The world's largest ball of twine is located in Cawker City Kansas.

11. Write sentences for each of the following items. Be sure to use correct capitalization and punctuation. Each sentence should include at least one comma in the correct location.
   A. Write a sentence containing a date.
   Answers will vary.
   B. Write a sentence containing a city and state.
   Answers will vary.
   C. Write a sentence containing three items in a series.
   Answers will vary.

12. Which of the following shows the correct way to use a comma and quotation marks to note a quotation from a text.
   A. On page 37 of the text, the author states Abraham Lincoln was the sixteenth President of the United States
   (B.) On page 37 of the text, the author states, "Abraham Lincoln was the sixteenth President of the United States."
   C. On page 37 of the text, the author states, Abraham Lincoln was the sixteenth President of the United States
   D. On page 37 of the text, the author states "Abraham Lincoln was the sixteenth President of the United States."

NAME: ______________________ **A.3** CONTINUED
DATE: ______________________

13. Which of the following shows the correct way to use a comma and quotation marks when quoting direct speech?
   A. Luisa lost her patience and said Let's get this game started!
   B. Luisa lost her patience and said, Let's get this game started!
   C. Luisa lost her patience and said "Let's get this game started!"
   (D.) Luisa lost her patience and said, "Let's get this game started!"

14. Complete the sentences by choosing two adjectives from the ones provided and writing them in the correct order in the blanks.
   Example:
   Adjectives: big, plastic, green, new
   She brought her big , new boat into the bathtub.
   A. Adjectives: handsome, small, spotted, Mexican
   The small , spotted pony was her favorite
   B. Adjectives: long, Chinese, beautiful, old
   We traveled in a Chinese , beautiful train.

15. Choose the answer that shows the correct way to sequence multiple adjectives.
   (A.) Jenny read a fascinating, old book over the summer.
   B. Jenny read a fascinating, an old book over the summer.
   C. A fascinating, old book over the summer Jenny read.
   D. Jenny read an old fascinating book over the summer.

NAME: ______________________ **A.4** ASSESSMENT
DATE: ______________________

Middle-of-Year Morphology Assessment

Read and answer each question. Some of the questions have two parts. You should answer Part A of the question before you answer Part B.

1. If you found a rock that was unusual, what does that mean?
   A. The rock was ordinary.
   (B.) The rock was not ordinary.
   C. The rock was boring.
   D. The rock was easy to find.

2. Luis settles arguments in a nonviolent way. Describe how Luis settles arguments.
   Possible answer: Luis does not use physical force to settle arguments. He settles arguments with words.

3. Choose the word that best completes the sentences provided.

The treehouse was too small, so we bought some wooden planks to ______ it.

A. circle
B. encircle
C. large
(D.) enlarge

Lora showed great ______ by swimming across the lake.

(A.) courage
B. encourage
C. danger
D. endangers

4. Write a sentence using the word *matriarch*.

Answers will vary.

5. What is the meaning of the root *graph*?
A. something alive
(B.) something written or drawn
C. something that is seen
D. something that is not seen

6. Choose the word that best completes the sentences provided. Then identify the part of speech of the word you chose.

A. She called the plumber because the pipe was ______. (leak, (leaky))
The part of speech of the word I chose: adjective

B. A gentle ______ helped keep us cool. ((breeze), breezy)
The part of speech of the word I chose: noun

7. Turn the word gloom into a new word using the suffix -y.
A. What is the new word? gloomy
B. What part of speech is the new word? adjective

8. Circle the word that best completes the sentences provided.

A. The plane reduced its __ before it landed.
(speed) speedy speedily

B. After waking up an hour late, Bridgette __ got dressed and ate breakfast.
speed speedy (speedily)

C. The __ squirrel easily escaped from the dog.
speed (speedy) speedily

9. Identify the part of speech of the following words.

A. ease
part of speech: noun

B. easy
part of speech: adjective

C. easily
part of speech: adverb

10. What does the root *rupt* mean?
A. something written
B. very old
(C.) to break or burst
D. most powerful

Core Knowledge Language Arts

Amplify.

General Manager K-8 ELA and SVP, Product

Alexandra Clarke

Chief Academic Officer, Elementary Humanities

Susan Lambert

Editorial

Elizabeth Wade, PhD, Director, Elementary Language Arts Content
Patricia Erno, Associate Director, Elementary ELA Instruction
Baria Jennings, EdD, Senior Content Developer
Christina Cox, Managing Editor

Product and Project Management

Ayala Falk, Director, Business and Product Strategy, K-8 ELA
Amber McWilliams, Senior Product Manager
Elisabeth Hartman, Associate Product Manager
Leslie Johnson, Associate Director, K-8 ELA
Thea Aguiar, Director of Special Projects, CKLA
Zara Chaudhury, Project Manager, K-8 ELA

Design and Production

Tory Novikova, Product Design Director
Erin O'Donnell, Product Design Manager

Contributors

Amy Xu
Bill Cheng
Nicole Galuszka
Ken Harney
Molly Hensley
David Herubin
Ian Horst
Sara Hunt
Jagriti Khirwar
Kristen Kirchner
Julie Kim
James Mendez-Hodes
Christopher Miller
Jackie Pierson
Sheri Pineault
Diana Projansky
Todd Rawson
Jennifer Skelley
Nicole Stahl
Julia Sverchuk
Elizabeth Thiers
Jeanne Thornton
Amanda Tolentino
Paige Womack

Amplify CKLA

Core Knowledge Language Arts

Core Knowledge Foundation

Series Editor-in-Chief

E. D. Hirsch Jr.

President

Linda Bevilacqua

Editorial Staff

Mick Anderson
Robin Blackshire
Laura Drummond
Emma Earnst
Lucinda Ewing
Sara Hunt
Rosie McCormick
Cynthia Peng
Liz Pettit
Tonya Ronayne
Deborah Samley
Kate Stephenson
Elizabeth Wafler
James Walsh
Sarah Zelinke

Design and Graphics Staff

Kelsie Harman
Liz Loewenstein
Bridget Moriarty
Lauren Pack

Consulting Project Management Services

ScribeConcepts.com

Additional Consulting Services

Erin Kist
Carolyn Pinkerton
Scott Ritchie
Kelina Summers

Acknowledgments

These materials are the result of the work, advice, and encouragement of numerous individuals over many years. Some of those singled out here already know the depth of our gratitude; others may be surprised to find themselves thanked publicly for help they gave quietly and generously for the sake of the enterprise alone. To helpers named and unnamed we are deeply grateful.

Contributors to Earlier Versions of These Materials

Susan B. Albaugh, Kazuko Ashizawa, Kim Berrall, Ang Blanchette, Nancy Braier, Maggie Buchanan, Paula Coyner, Kathryn M. Cummings, Michelle De Groot, Michael Donegan, Diana Espinal, Mary E. Forbes, Michael L. Ford, Sue Fulton, Carolyn Gosse, Dorrit Green, Liza Greene, Ted Hirsch, Danielle Knecht, James K. Lee, Matt Leech, Diane Henry Leipzig, Robin Luecke, Martha G. Mack, Liana Mahoney, Isabel McLean, Steve Morrison, Juliane K. Munson, Elizabeth B. Rasmussen, Ellen Sadler, Rachael L. Shaw, Sivan B. Sherman, Diane Auger Smith, Laura Tortorelli, Khara Turnbull, Miriam E. Vidaver, Michelle L. Warner, Catherine S. Whittington, Jeannette A. Williams.

We would like to extend special recognition to Program Directors Matthew Davis and Souzanne Wright, who were instrumental in the early development of this program.

Schools

We are truly grateful to the teachers, students, and administrators of the following schools for their willingness to field-test these materials and for their invaluable advice: Capitol View Elementary, Challenge Foundation Academy (IN), Community Academy Public Charter School, Lake Lure Classical Academy, Lepanto Elementary School, New Holland Core Knowledge Academy, Paramount School of Excellence, Pioneer Challenge Foundation Academy, PS 26R (the Carteret School), PS 30X (Wilton School), PS 50X (Clara Barton School), PS 96Q, PS 102X (Joseph O. Loretan), PS 104Q (the Bays Water), PS 214K (Michael Friedsam), PS 223Q (Lyndon B. Johnson School), PS 308K (Clara Cardwell), PS 333Q (Goldie Maple Academy), Sequoyah Elementary School, South Shore Charter Public School, Spartanburg Charter School, Steed Elementary School, Thomas Jefferson Classical Academy, Three Oaks Elementary, West Manor Elementary.

And a special thanks to the CKLA Pilot Coordinators, Anita Henderson, Yasmin Lugo-Hernandez, and Susan Smith, whose suggestions and day-to-day support to teachers using these materials in their classrooms were critical.

Core Knowledge®

Reader Author
Rebecca L. Johnson

Expert Reviewer
Terri L. Woods

Contributor
Stephen Currie

Illustration and Photo Credits
age fotostock/age fotostock/SuperStock: 148, 249/309/333, 268; Art Archive, The/Art Archive, The/SuperStock: 24; Arthur S. Aubry/Exactostock/SuperStock: 85/105; Avi Katz : 142, 143, 144, 145, 146–147, 149, 150, 151; Biosphoto/Biosphoto/SuperStock: 168/184, 201/221, 251; Blend Images/Blend Images/SuperStock: 167/183; Brian Jannsen/age fotostock/SuperStock: 204–205/224–225; Cartesia/Exactostock/SuperStock: 244; Clover/Clover/SuperStock: 26–27/303; CnApTaK/Shutterstock: 9/311; Core Knowledge Staff: 22/333, 25, 38–39/60–61, 40–41/62–63, 42–43/64–65, 46/66, 82/102, 83/103, 122–123, 170, 172/186, 174–175/188–189/333, 244, 248, 263/333, 265, 335/352/355; Cusp/Cusp/SuperStock: 267; EastVillage Images/Shutterstock: 305; Ed Darack/Ed Darack/SuperStock: 120; Everett Collection/Everett Collection/SuperStock: 74/84/92/104/333, 84/104; First page from the Journal of *HMS Challenger*, a personal diary by Pelham Aldrich, 1872 (pen & ink and w/con paper), Aldrich, Admiral Pelham (1844–1930)/Royal Geographical Society, London, UK/Bridgeman Images: 24; Francesco Riccardo Iacomino/Moment/Getty Images: Cover; Fotosearch/Fotosearch/SuperStock: 166/182; Frank Krahmer/Exactostock/SuperStock: 168/184; FRANS LANTING, MINT IMAGES/SCIENCE PHOTO LIBRARY: 206/226; Gary Crabbe/age fotostock/SuperStock: 124–125; GERARD LODRIGUSS/SCIENCE PHOTO LIBRARY: 169/185; Gilbert, G.K./U.S. Geological Survey: 81/101; Gordon Wiltsie/Exactostock/SuperStock: 124; Hillary and Tenzing on the slopes of Mount Everest, Tacconi, Ferdinando (1922–2006)/Private Collection/Look and Learn/Bridgeman Images: 243; Iberfoto/Iberfoto/SuperStock: 18; imagebroker.net/imagebroker.net/SuperStock: 168/184, 208–209/228–229/315/333; Iñaki Caperochipi/age fotostock/SuperStock: 80/100; Ivan Vdovin/age fotostock/SuperStock: 246/317; J.W. Alker/imagebroker/imagebroker.net/SuperStock: 262–263; Jim Sugar/Jim Sugar/SuperStock: 123/137/154/313; Joel Boyer: 118–119/340, 124; Jon Arnold Images/Jon Arnold Images/SuperStock: 245; Jonathan Irish/National Geographic/SuperStock: 247/333; JTB Photo/JTB Photo/SuperStock: 202–203/222–223; Julien Capmeil/Exactostock: 64–65; khd/Shutterstock: 307; Logan S. Kline: 21, 47/67, 147; Lucas Vallecillos/age fotostock/SuperStock: 121; Micha Rosenwirth/Shutterstock: 9/311; Minden Pictures/Minden Pictures/SuperStock: 201/221, 268; Movementway/imagebroker.net/imagebroker.net/SuperStock: 168/184; Naturbild/Naturbild/SuperStock: 201/221; NOAA/SCIENCE PHOTO LIBRARY: 269; NOAA; Image courtesy of Monika Bright—University of Vienna, Austria: 266; On the top of Everest, English School (twentieth century)/Private Collection/Look and Learn/Bridgeman Images: 242; Ortahisar Rock Castle, Cappadocia, Turkey (photo)/Samuel Magal, Sites & Photos Ltd./Bridgeman Images: 319; Pacific Stock Design Pics/Pacific Stock Design Pics/SuperStock: 86–87/106–107/111/338; Pantheon/Pantheon/SuperStock: 23; Peebles/Mauritius/SuperStock: 116–117/333; Peter Eastland/age fotostock/SuperStock: 166/182; Photo by Braden Coolidge/SuperStock: 173/187; Radius/Radius/SuperStock: 171; RICHARD BIZLEY/SCIENCE PHOTO LIBRARY: 266; RUSSELL D. CURTIS/SCIENCE PHOTO LIBRARY: 83/103; Science and Society/Science and Society/SuperStock: 84/104; Siede Preis/Exactostock/SuperStock: 246; STEPHEN J. KRASEMANN/SCIENCE PHOTO LIBRARY: 169/185; Stock Connection/Stock Connection/SuperStock: 200/220; Stock Montage/Stock Montage/SuperStock: 78/98; SuperStock/SuperStock: 121; Tom Till/Tom Till/SuperStock: 250/333; Universal Images Group/Universal Images Group/SuperStock: 20, 122; Visual & Written/Visual & Written/SuperStock: 122; Westend61/Westend61/SuperStock: 121; Yoshio Tomii/Yoshio Tomii/SuperStock: 251